Charles Goodnight

COWMAN AND PLAINSMAN

-HDBugbee-

J. EVETTS HALEY

Charles Goodnight

COWMAN & PLAINSMAN

WITH ILLUSTRATIONS BY HAROLD BUGBEE

UNIVERSITY OF OKLAHOMA PRESS
NORMAN

BOOKS BY J. EVETTS HALEY
PUBLISHED BY THE UNIVERSITY OF OKLAHOMA PRESS

GEORGE W. LITTLEFIELD, TEXAN
(1943)

JEFF MILTON: A GOOD MAN WITH A GUN
(1948)

CHARLES GOODNIGHT: COWMAN AND PLAINSMAN
(Boston, 1936; Norman, 1949)

THE XIT RANCH OF TEXAS AND THE EARLY DAYS OF
THE LLANO ESTACADO
(Chicago, 1929; Norman, 1953)

ISBN: 0–8061–1453–3

18   19   20   21   22   23   24   25   26   27

CONTENTS

Contents

CUTTING FOR SIGN

THIS book is more than the biography of a man — it is the background of my own soil, a part of my own tradition. Every wind that drifts the alkali dust from the Goodnight Trail across my home range suggests a land of cattle and horses; every damp breeze carries the penetrating fragrance of grease-wood, suggestive of the bold life that rode along it. Yet the land and its life have hardly changed with the years. Today, our trails are still the trails of cattle; our problems those of aridity, of grass and water along the bitter Pecos — 'grave-yard of the cowman's hopes.'

When I was a boy learning the taste of gyp and the meaning of thirst — learning to ride the desolate range at Old Pope's Crossing — the stories of Goodnight were as much a part of the land as the trails his herds had cut through its scanty grass. He was a very old man when, fifteen years later, I hesitatingly crossed his ranch-house yard to face the flow of tobacco juice and profanity, I reverently recall, which masked his most sensitive nature, and heard him explode with a lusty vigor against those writing such 'a pack of lies about the West.'

Like many who merely came to call, I stayed to visit in the shade of the gallery, charmed by his conversation, astonished at the virility of his mind and spirit, and struck by his sturdy character. For ninety years his iron will had ridden hard upon his sturdy frame. Nor would he quit. In his tempestuous life there were no more 'hours of work' than 'days of rest.' And when, in the close shadows of a hundred years, his wide-bowed legs could no longer drive his body about the corrals from early day to late at night, he restlessly plaited rawhide ropes and bull-whips, while his mind flew faster than his hands as he outlined work, years in advance, which he felt sure there was still time to do.

The breadth of his interests indicated the broad gauge of the man. His recollections ranged from subject to subject across the face of the Western World, as striking in depth and character as the personality of the man himself. Now, a hundred and thirteen years after his birth, his massive frame still looms strong among the horsemen of the storied West.

He rode bareback from Illinois to Texas when he was nine years old. He was hunting with the Caddo Indians beyond the frontier at thirteen, launching into the cattle business at twenty, guiding Texas Rangers at twenty-four, blazing cattle trails two thousand miles in length at thirty, establishing a ranch three hundred miles beyond the frontier at forty, and at forty-five dominating nearly twenty million acres of range country in the interests of order. At sixty he was recognized as possibly the greatest scientific breeder of range cattle in the West, and at ninety he was an active international authority on the economics of the range industry.

He always rode beyond the borderlands, upon ranges of un-spoiled grass. He knew the West of Jim Bridger, Kit Carson, Dick Wootton, St. Vrain, and Lucien Maxwell. He ranged a country as vast as Bridger ranged. He rode with the boldness of Fremont, guided by the craft of Carson. The vast and chang-ing country over which he moved, the fertility of a mind that quickly grasped the significance of climate and topography, the inexhaustible energy of his mind and body, and the long period through which he constantly applied himself to the Western World, operated to produce in this man an ample nature sur-passing many of the more famous characters of frontier history.

He was filled with vigorous zest for life. His observations upon nature ranged, with remarkable freshness, from the prairie dogs of the Palo Duro Plains to the buffalo of the North-west, from the grasses of the Brazos Valley to the conifers of the

Greenhorns. He saw seven-horned sheep grazing with the Navajo flocks along the Pecos, Nature's own photograph of a giant cinnamon bear on the mineral bluffs of the Picketwire, great forests miniatured in the agate of the Rockies, and buffaloes and horses racing upside down through the mirages of the Staked Plains. He found time to turn back from the lead of two thousand Texas longhorns to see doves' nests passed over by thousands of hoofs, and left with eggs untouched. He allowed a Texas cow that escaped from his herd on the Pecos and back-trailed through four hundred miles of desert and wilderness country to die of old age upon the Keechi range she loved. He cursed the fool who cut down a lone chittam tree at the head of Dry Creek, on the JA Ranch, a fine, useful landmark in a country devoid of timber. He carried one of the little Sonoran deer fifty miles across his saddle in front of him, to add to his studies of wild life in the Panhandle.

Thus, he lived, intensely and amply. Nor is it too much to say that wherever his vibrant personality touched the life of the short-grass country, it blazed great trails, plain, straight, and long. One of these led through my boyhood range.

Twenty-three years ago I left the home ranch beside the Goodnight Trail to follow Goodnight's trail through history. It was an extended pursuit. I cut for sign from the mouth of the Rio Grande to his old range in the Rockies. I tracked his associates from the West Coast to the Gulf; from the deep South into Mexico. I confirmed my statements of fact through conventional sources in public libraries, although most of my material has been of a fresher if more difficult sort. I have backtracked tens of thousands of miles in the open country, listening to tales of Western men who knew Goodnight and his time. But still the story is incomplete.

Certain experiences in life seem to evade the written word. The faint tremors of the High Plains mirages do not dance upon my page; the 'feel' of sour-dough in a dishpan has to be felt; and the sudden loss of a horse from under the rider is not an imaginative experience. Hence I regret not the thousands of pages of unused notes in my files, and the reams of rejected though relevant material in public libraries and archives. These are tangible and still available, while the missing qualities of rugged and vibrant personality that I cannot picture in my pages have passed with the dusts of the Goodnight Trail.

I have made varied acknowledgments in my notes. Grants in aid came from the Rockefeller Foundation and other sources. Former associates at the University of Texas were of help. Besides these, my obligations were almost as wide as the West, for the Goodnight Trail always led on. At Douglas, Jim East's measured words sketched the unmeasured vitality of Old Tascosa; Charlie Siringo coughed out his estimate of the Panhandle land as we sat in his stuffy room at Venice; old Pablo Suezo, one-eyed buffalo hunter of the Taos Pueblo, told his brief tale in the crisp air of the Sangre de Cristo; Andy Adams gave his measure of the man at the head of the Fontaine qui Bouille; and on Ute Creek, old Francisco de Baca made me welcome beneath the ominous cap-rock, the *ceja* or eyebrow, of the *comancheros*. Most of the time I cut for sign on the sunny side of the one-hundredth meridian.

I used to sit on the outskirts of Amarillo and talk with old John Rumans, 'the most reckless rider' Goodnight ever had. And though his hands were as gnarled as mesquite roots, and his face was drawn with rheumatic pain, he told me tales of high-hearted living, of wild riding, and of integrity and fine devotion while driving the trail. 'There's just one more book that I want to read,' he said. 'And that's the life of the Old Man.' I am sorry to have been too late.

Walter Cochran, who contributed much to my knowledge of the range, periodically complained that I was 'going to wait until he died before finishing the book.' Upon his death-bed he loathed the soft food of the sick-room. 'Go outside, build up a fire, and broil me a steak,' he ordered. 'Build it under my window, close to the house, so I can smell it a-cooking. Then bring me the steak and some onions.' Thus died Walter Cochran, in the cow-town of Midland, as a cowman should.

The late T. D. Hobart, one of the broadest-gauged, most thoroughly civilized men I have ever known, is due my lasting gratitude. All these and many more who contributed to my story have ridden on. From among those who are still alive, I have not forgotten Clinton Henry and Jimmie Moore, and the tales they zestfully told before the fireplace at the JA Ranch; nor Harold Bugbee, the artist, honestly portraying the spirit of the times upon his sketch pad; nor for that matter any of the old hands, who, like good cowpunchers, fell in on this trail at the proper place.

Aside from my intimate associations on the range, a great, mature, and vigorous student in the gentle atmosphere of Austin has profoundly influenced my style of punching historical cows. His incisive thought, keen sensitivity, integrity, and rugged courage always reminded me of the subject of this book. Had Eugene C. Barker, professor of history at the University of Texas, lived along the Goodnight Trail, he would have ridden in the lead; he would have pointed the herds.

This book has not been an exercise in rigid academics, as the academicians will readily admit. In part it has been adventure, shared by Nita Stewart Haley, since we pitched our camps together along the Goodnight Trail.

It has been gratifying to me that this new edition has been made necessary by the continuing interest of readers of history of the American Southwest, particularly of that portion of it which has to do with cattle. The text has been occasionally slightly revised in order to bring it up to date or to include more recently discovered facts.

J. EVETTS HALEY

Canyon, Texas
March 2, 1949

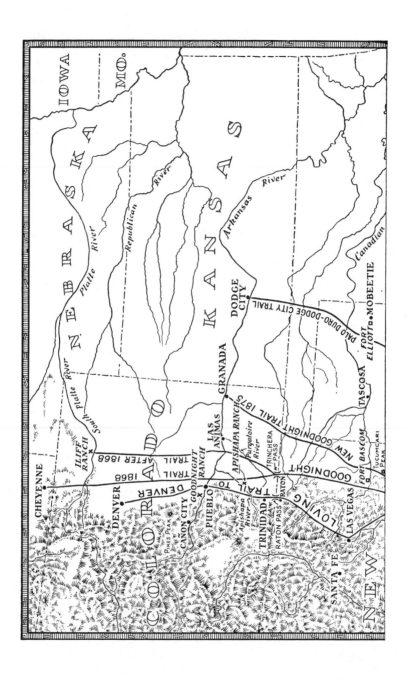

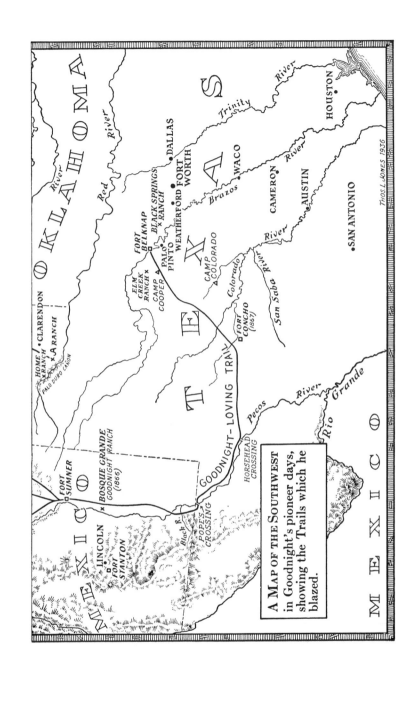

A MAP OF THE SOUTHWEST in Goodnight's pioneer days, showing the Trails which he blazed.

I. COWBOYHOOD ON THE TEXAN BORDER

ONE day in the fall of 1849, a fine old Indian warrior named
Caddo Jake was at the Goodnight home, where he regularly
came for a cup of coffee, and then invariably tanked up on but-
termilk, of which he was very fond. As he left the cabin and
crossed the mile of prairie beyond the house, the widow's thir-
teen-year-old boy trailed close in his tracks. The leaves of the
oak were tinted by frost, and many deer had already grown fat
upon abundant acorns still falling from their cups. In the edge
of the timber the Indian shot a fat, barren doe, cut her in two,
and placed the carcass upon the boy's back, a hind leg to either
side of his head. The slight youth protested at the load,
but Caddo Jake replied: 'Heap big man! You take him all
home.'

The Caddo was right. Charlie Goodnight, like so many
other lads of far-flung wilderness lands, had arrived prematurely
at the estate of a man. Upon the trail with friendly Indians,
alone in the woods, faring for himself among hard men while
yet at the age of thirteen, fighting for every advantage and for
the necessities of life, Charlie Goodnight was laying up the
physical and mental preparation that was to make him a noted
scout, a cattleman so efficient as to be termed natural born, a
trail-blazer through thousands of miles of wilderness at the
point of Texas cattle, and the foremost frontier breeder of livestock in America. Uneducated from printed sources, but closely
observant of natural phenomena, he grew up a sensitive lad

among the rough-hewn surroundings of frontier life. He was born and bound to be a pioneer.

Family tradition records the origin of the name in times of chivalry, when some man of fighting stock, who proudly lived and traveled by horse, was noted for gallantry in battle and called the 'Good Knight.' But the sober research of the gen-

ealogist disputes the claim, and apparently the Goodnights were of plebeian instead of aristocratic origin.

Michael Goodnight, who first introduced the family to America, was born in Germany, and became a part of that heavy migration away from the oppression of the Old World to the vital freedom of the New. He reached Pennsylvania in 1752, settled soon afterward in Virginia, moved to North Carolina, and late in life migrated to the 'dark and bloody ground' that beckoned men so firmly from the wilderness of Kentucky, presumably in 1777 or 1778. Through the years family tradition has built him into a virile figure of heroic proportions, often married and breeding bountifully.

In 1754, historically close on his heels, came his brother George. He, too, tarried but briefly in Pennsylvania, moved to Virginia, and from there to Mecklenburg County, North Carolina, in the 1760's, where he lived for years. He was appointed assessor there in 1778, but he probably went on with Michael and his family to become one of the early settlers of Kentucky, for in December of the same year he had three sons serving as soldiers at Ruddell's Station, thirty miles northeast of Lexington. Michael, however, located at Harlan's Station, thirty-five miles southwest of Lexington, within a mile of which, as an old man, he was killed and scalped by the Indians while travelling the Wilderness Road.

In the widespread diffusion of these families through the years, there developed much confusion about origins, and Charles Goodnight died supposing that Michael was his great-grandfather. Both were vigorous branches, and except for the satisfaction of a naturally inquisitive mind, it mattered not at all to Charlie. His world was that of adventure and accomplishment on fresh frontiers; not concern with a past beyond recall.

The record now reveals that George was the founder of his line. Both brothers came to Kentucky, as already observed, in the days of Daniel Boone, and both 'met sad misfortune' at the hands of the Indians. In June, 1780, when the Indians and the Canadians took Ruddell's Station, its three hundred people as prisoners were turned over to the Indians. Old George, as one of his descendants recorded, 'was massacreed in the most barbarous manner,' while his boys and girls 'were scattered among the Indians,' some being taken into Canada. Eventually all of them got back to Kentucky. Among these was one named Peter, grandfather of the subject of this story.

Peter acquired three hundred and ninety acres of land in Bourbon County in 1786, was commissioned a captain in the Tenth Regiment by the Governor, February 5, 1798, and, apprently in 1806, sired a son named Charles, who was to become the father of this future frontiersman of Texas.[1]

---

[1] The intriguing traditions of the Goodnight family have been preserved in manuscript, copy of which is in the files of the Panhandle-Plains Historical Society, Canyon, Texas. But the genealogy, with the factual cut away from the mythical, has been carefully prepared by Dean S. H. Goodnight, Madison, Wisconsin, in 'The Goodnight Family in America,' *Register of the Kentucky State Historical Society*, October, 1935. See pp. 2–13, his reprint in brochure, as well as S. H. Goodnight to J. E. H., March 17, 1948.

Charles grew up in Kentucky and married Charlotte Collier when he was twenty and she fifteen.[2] In 1828, three years after their marriage, they moved to southern Illinois and settled in Madison County, just across the river from St. Louis. A malaria called milk sickness, common among the early settlers of that country and often fatal, prompted the family to move north to the prairie country near the Madison and Macoupin County line. There, March 5, 1836, three days after the declaration of Texas independence, Charles, the junior, was born. A brother, Elijah, preceded him by four years, a sister, Elizabeth, by two years, and a younger sister, Cynthia, was born two years later.

Typically restless frontier energy drove the father to his farming early and kept him busy late. He gave no thought to himself and his health, and, becoming weakened from exposure, died of pneumonia in 1841. His estate was adequate, but under the administration of his wife's brother, Charles Collier, was mishandled, and the family was all but destitute at the end of a year. Those were not days of feminine economic independence, and the widow Goodnight soon married Hiram Daugherty, a farmer of the same neighborhood.

Charlie spent much time in day-dreaming, and was looked upon as a lazy boy, but the energy that was to drive him through life at furious tension did not lie dormant long. That quality of a visionary, exhibited in his day-dreams as a boy, spread to most daring but practical ventures as a man, carried him through life eager and tireless, and never left him until the end. At ninety-three he dreamed of great ranching enterprises he would yet direct.

As a child he was alert and keenly observant. The Goodnight homestead stood at the edge of hickory and oak timbered land, where he spent many rainy days watching wild animals and birds. At seven he started to school, and though able to attend only two terms, he always regretted that circumstances prevented his re-entering school. His only teacher, Jane Hager-

Charlotte Collier was born March 21, 1810.

man, inspired him with a desire to learn, and almost ninety years later he revered her memory for her 'kindness and sincerity.'

The seclusion and solitude of the timber grew upon him and was conducive to his contemplative moods. His aversion to any form of urban activity, even to living beneath a roof, lasted down the years, while this early trait of observation was heightened with every experience. He spent more and more time out-of-doors, for no other school so stimulated him.

During his early boyhood the entire nation was throbbing to the importance of Texas, the new republic to the southwest. The original colonizing schemes attracted national attention, and with the Texan War of Independence that interest grew and spread like wildfire before a prairie wind. In Washington it was fanned to new heat by intense partisan struggles over the admission of Texas to the Union. Everywhere talk of Texas flowed from the mouths of many men, and those who tore their livings from ungracious soil heard much of its fertility, its generous homestead laws, and its manifest advantages for energetic folk. Caught into the current of the migratory stream were Hiram Daugherty, his wife, and the Goodnight children.

Late in 1845, they loaded their household goods and farming tools into two covered wagons and set out for Texas. Without saddle or blanket, Charlie straddled a young white-faced mare called Blaze, and rode alongside the wagons or dropped behind as he and his mount grew tired. Saddles were then made for men, and boys early learned the sting of horse sweat in a galled crotch. The trip to Texas astride the little mare was an outstanding event in Charlie's life. A horse was carrying the boy who dreamed in the woods of southern Illinois to the land where any dreaming boy would wish to be, to young, turbulent, unsettled Texas. Early in life his spindly legs began to bow against the vibrant sides of a saddle horse, always thereafter to be more at home against the sweat leathers of a stock

saddle than moving awkwardly in cowboy walk upon the ground.

After crossing the Mississippi at St. Louis, the Daughertys moved on to Springfield, Missouri, drove to Little Rock, and ferried the Arkansas River. They crossed Red River, drove by Paris, and on to Dallas, a trading post, as Charlie recalled, consisting of a ferryboat and one log cabin belonging to some hunters and traders. The river was low, the boat reached entirely across the narrow current, and, by placing logs at either end to raise it to the level of the landings, the emigrants drove across as on a bridge, paying a toll for passage.

Along the west bank of the Trinity, Charlie saw his first buffalo. Great, powerful, shaggy-headed creatures, they must have stirred his imagination, and excited great longing to watch, perhaps to hunt, and certainly to know more about them. Hunters had rounded them up in the river bottom with a pack of curs and were leisurely shooting them down. Near Waxahachie, he again saw them rounded up and killed in the same way, thus learning that the best way of handling the buffalo was by the use of dogs, for these great, fierce, brindle dogs of the frontier resembled *lobos*, of which animal alone the buffalo had much to fear.

Across the prairie country to the south, by the extreme western road of the State, Daugherty led his family into the heart of Texas. After leaving the Trinity they passed no houses until they reached the Randall Robinson Plantation on the Little Brazos, where they crossed, and came to the main Brazos at Old Nashville. The settlers were forted up, but breathing more freely than usual as Indians had not depredated for a year or so. Pleased with the settlement and the country, Daugherty rented a farm just below the junction of the rivers, and there the family put in its first year in Texas.

The farthermost settler beyond them was an old Georgian Major — said never to have seen an army — by the name of Bryant. He had two wives whom he kept in the same house, and since he could not live around conventional folks, who disapproved of his arrangement, was forced to be the most distant settler upon the frontier — just fifteen miles up Little River from Cameron. The two wives did not live in perfect congeniality, much to the Major's disgust, who swore that it was 'damned strange, since there was no one else within fifteen miles of them.'

Settlers generally forted up and went out from a central location to work their farms or herd their cattle during the day, returning to their homes at night. In the middle forties most of them were farmers, combining stock-raising with agricultural pursuits. Their wants were ordinarily few, their needs the simple necessities of life. Corn and cotton were the principal crops; corn for home use, for bread and horse feed, and cotton for sale or exchange. Houston was the nearest point of delivery and the trade center for all the Western frontier.

Shortly after Daugherty settled in Texas, his wife quit him 'for good reason,' as Charlie explained. Again she was a widow, in a destitute, lonely, and unsettled country. Three months later a baby was born, bringing the family to five. Besides her own efforts, the only dependence was Elijah, aged fifteen, and Charlie, small for his eleven years. Elijah could find unremunerative but steady work upon neighboring farms, and fortunately Charlie found work with a merchant named Aiken at four dollars a month.

There was little stability to the tenure of their home. In 1848 they located at Port Sullivan, and again Charlie went to work, this time for an Irish farmer named Sullivan, who paid him double his first salary. Then, happily for the boy who had barely known a father, he hired to John Poole, a farmer and stock-raiser, 'a very kind and noble man,' who paid him from twelve to fifteen dollars a month besides giving him much good counsel. Eighty years later, Goodnight revered his memory, as he had admired the man at thirteen, saying: 'He was the only man who ever gave me any good advice when I was a boy.'

While Charlie was farming he was riding, for he was passionately fond of animals. Hardly had the family settled down to their new life in Texas when his brother caught a mustang colt from the herds upon the prairies. After feeding it milk by hand to keep it from starving, Charlie broke it to ride almost as soon as its body grew into proportion with its eyes. Raising it by bottle did not wean it from the fighting tendencies of mustang blood.

'That pony made me a rider, he mused. 'I guess it threw me a hundred times, and I always thought it bucked me off just for amusement.' Instead of running away and leaving him to walk, it stood and waited until he got back on.

For two years he rode much, always without a saddle, until he helped to gather a herd lost in stampede, and was presented with a rough, home-made tree without riggin' of any kind. He supplied the necessary cinch straps and sweat and stirrup leathers from rawhide, and soon was riding with the best of horsemen. For sixty-five years he was to feel the sweat of faithful horses harden and curl the saddle leathers beneath his legs. In the marvelous riding tradition of the West probably no record excels his in intensity and in time. He was as good a rider as Buffalo Bill, though abhorring the dramatic sense that

made Bill famous. He knew as much about horses as Little
Aubry, who rode the eight hundred miles from Santa Fé to
Independence in less than six days to win a bet. But he rode
of necessity, not for wager. Although a careful horseman who
favored his mounts, few riders consumed more horseflesh than he.

CHARLOTTE GOODNIGHT

At fifteen he hired to a racing outfit at Port Sullivan when
he and the saddle weighed but ninety pounds. His was the
diminutive size, and, in spite of his years, the knowledge of
horses, to make a good jockey. He trained a bad horse that
nobody else would ride, and successfully competed on the track
with men of ten times his experience. He was happy with his
horses, but extremely unhappy in the racing environment. In
spite of the high wages of fifteen dollars a month, he stayed
only long enough to draw one payment, for he could not endure
the swearing, gambling, and general roughness of the racing
camp. Becoming dissatisfied and homesick, he gave up his
job and returned to his mother.

The times were hard for the Goodnights, and it is no wonder
he remembered the story told of an emigrant Tennessee family.
One member, writing to the folks back home, was asking what
word each would like to send.

'And Grandmother,' the writer asked, 'what would you like to tell them?'

'Tell them,' she answered, 'that Texas is all right for men and dogs, but hell on women and horses!'

In the fall of 1850, the family acquired a small farm northeast of Cameron, but later located fifteen miles west of Waco, between the junction of the Bosque and the Brazos. Here Charlie worked at odd jobs. He whacked bulls, split rails, and sometimes received as much as twenty-five dollars a month for superintending slaves at various kinds of work.

He still found time to wander across the prairies, to hunt, and to fish. He saw alligators in the Brazos west of Waco, ten to twelve feet long and 'bigger-bellied' than a man; he trailed the old cows to where they had raked up great piles of leaves and twigs, and laid their eggs in the middle to be hatched by the heat of the decaying mass. They came back when the eggs had hatched, he discovered, and led the little ones into a slough away from the river to keep the old bulls from 'eating the little bulls up.'

He watched the soft-shelled turtles come from the water, dig pits in the clay banks, lay from fifteen to thirty eggs, seal the excavation over with clay dampened from their own bladders, and waddle back into the stream. The sun dried and hardened the covering; its heat hatched the eggs. Uncannily, the turtle appeared on the proper day, unfailingly picked her nest from any number of others, dampened and broke the clay covering, watched her newborn progeny swarm out, and then proudly led them into the water.

The sage grass grew high and rank in Milam County around their homestead, and once during a snowstorm an old sow disappeared. Positive of finding her somewhere with a litter of pigs, but fearing that they would be frozen to death, Charlie went to look for her. On a ridge nearly a mile away he found her in a den she had built by cutting sage grass, piling it up, and burrowing under it — the belligerent mother of nine white pigs. Succeeding in gathering the pigs into a basket, Charlie set out for the house, placed them in a pen, and went back to drive in the sow. When he got to the pen with her, he discovered that the pigs had escaped, and upon returning to their birth-place found them already back in the bed.

What remarkable sense of direction sent them scurrying back through the sage grass to their nest a mile away? What sent the turtles and the alligators to their nests to release their young upon the day of hatching; what sent the frightened Texas calf back to the spot where its mother left it; the fawn and the kid antelope to their original place of hiding; the mare to its place of foal — all with unerring instinct of direction and time? Charlie wondered, and wondering, watched more closely. He observed that nearly all animals, but the fewest of men, have this homing instinct, this unfailing sense of direction. The time was to come when the lives of many men would hinge upon the accuracy of his own sense of direction.

A love of outdoor life, a consuming interest in animals, and a combination of circumstance and place operated to launch him into the cow business. The longhorn steer had not yet become as emblematic of Texas as the lone star, but as he gently rolled a prickly-pear apple on his tongue, or slept and dreamed beneath the lacy shade of the mesquite, he was certainly on the way.

There was plenty of stock in Texas. 'She stuff,' was never sold upon the market, and old ranges were constantly over-flowing into new lands of unspoiled grass. In the decade be-ginning with 1840, the cow business was swelling to an industry of importance. Herds of longhorns, walking with the long, steady stride of the breed, were being driven north, west, and east, and from their sales much-needed money, packed in sad-dlebags or buckskin sacks in the bottoms of ox-carts, moved into Texas. Great *caballadas*, or cavvieyards, of wild ponies, some duns, blacks and *grullas*, but mainly bays with dark manes and tails, swept over the trail to the north. Wherever they passed, with long manes tossing and tails streaming al-most to the ground, they stirred the imagination of men as

surely as their hoofs stirred the dust of the trail. Steers were
worth more than hide and tallow, and many men who had been
farming and raising a few cattle were quitting farming altogether.

ADAM SHEEK

Charlie Goodnight was growing up through this period of
rapid range development. At sixteen he turned to freighting
and hauling in Waco, where he worked for two years, but in
accord with the spirit of the time he was restless to go forth
wherever fortune or fancy might dictate. In 1853, his mother
married a preacher by the name of Adam Sheek, whom Charlie
described as 'a very devout Christian man, extremely kind,
and in my estimation as nearly faultless as it is possible for a
man to be.' In 1856, Charlie formed a partnership with his
stepbrother, J. Wes Sheek, who was three years his senior.
'Between us,' he said, 'we had only three good horses, splendid
firearms, a large wagon, and six yokes of cattle.' It mattered
little, for they were ambitious, energetic, and hopeful.

Having heard of the San Saba and the fine grass country
along that be-legended stream, they took most of their holdings and 'struck south over a wild and wilderness country,'

reaching the Colorado at the mouth of the San Saba, and striking, near the river, a freshly broken road over which three settlers had just passed. The two young prospectors turned upon the trail, found the settlers located in the San Saba Valley, and camped long enough to scout around. Except for an attempt by the Indians to steal their horses, the stay was uneventful. 'After looking around for two or three days,' said Charlie, 'we decided there was no money in that neighborhood, and, as we had started out to make money, we figured we would necessarily have to go where it was before we could make it.'

Almost all their lives they had heard of California, and they had heard much of it during the last seven years. They reasoned that California must be a land of wealth, and lost no time in starting. 'We then decided to return north to the Brazos,' Charlie continued, 'which we did without road, striking it at old Fort Graham. There we found a military road leading to the upper settlements at Fort Belknap, on the Brazos. From there the immigrant road led west to California, where we had determined to seek our fortune. But small things sometimes change the whole mode of life. En route from Fort Graham to Fort Belknap we unexpectedly met my brother-in-law, Alfred Lane, who persuaded us out of our notion of going to California and into joining him in search of new land. He suggested we all buy a large valley of land on the Brazos, south of Weatherford, agreeing to carry us for our part of the investment.'

Sheek and Lane returned to Waco, but when they discovered the title to the land imperfect, the deal was not made. But late in the summer of 1856, Wes and Charlie contracted with Claiborn Varner, Sheek's brother-in-law, to take Varner's herd of four hundred and thirty head, mostly cows, and keep them on shares for ten years. They met the herd on Camp Creek, in what is now Somervell County, where Varner delivered it with the help of his negro slaves and counted it out to the young men, who were to graze it wherever they pleased, receiving every fourth calf for pay. Since there was little market for anything except beef cattle, and none whatever for calves, and since steers were not bought until they were 'four and five year olds,' the partners knew they would realize no money from the cow business inside of three or four years. But at last they were in business for themselves, and possession and responsibility settle a man's vagrant tendencies and increase his power for work.

They were both notable horsemen, had worked cattle enough to know something of methods, and had been around livestock all their lives. They chose a good winter range along the creek, and there, about fifteen miles from where Glen Rose stands and two or three miles from the Brazos, made winter camp in one side of a double log cabin, a house of two rooms separated by a dog run or open hallway. The cattle were thrown into a large bend of the Brazos and wintered in fine shape.

The country was wooded, and nearly every hollow tree was a beehive filled with wild honey. Indians often chopped into them, but no Indian ever went as straight for the brush as Sheek went for a bee tree. Charlie swore that Wes could see a bee as far as he could see a buzzard. The woods were full of game, and Wes, who dearly loved the sound of a hound's voice, was always hunting, whether he made money or not. Charlie, jealous of his hours, felt that he had neither time nor money to 'monkey with hounds.' On occasion he and Sheek hunted together, however, and always with zest. In the fall black bears grew fat upon the haws that were in great abundance, and among Sheek's pack was an ordinary hound called Lilly, a bitch with a remarkable nose, that would take a cold trail and follow it forty-eight hours before another dog could pick it up. Their little English foxhound 'was afraid of bears, and if she was following the trail of a big bear, and the trail of a smaller one crossed it, she would quit the first and take up the trail of the second.'

By spring Wes and Charlie decided to move to a better range. The general movement was up the river valleys, toward the Western Cross Timbers. They too had turned their faces toward the West; they were headed toward the open country.

II. EARLY YEARS ON THE KEECHI RANGE

WITH the rising of grass in 1857, Charlie Goodnight and Wes Sheek trailed their herd up the Brazos into Palo Pinto County, and came to permanent camp at Black Springs, in the open valley of the Keechi. This stream, named for a Texas tribe, was flanked by low wooded hills familiar to Indian raiders; a lonely place where moccasined feet had left no trails in spite of the generations of warriors that had softly passed that way. Soon it fell beneath the dread of Comanche warfare, and greasy-skinned bucks raided its ranges almost as often as the moon grew full. Fine twining mesquite grass covered the country like a saddle blanket, fresh waters flowed from the hills in springs that never dried, and timber and broken country offered protection from biting northers.

The Keechi Valley lies within the Upper or Western Cross Timbers, narrow forest belts of post oak and black jack growing in sandy soils, varying in width from a half-mile to ten miles or more, and delimiting the western margin of the Grand Prairie region of Texas. The growth extends south from Red River far into the interior, even to the south of the Colorado.

Like a great red ribbon unwound at the caprice of a drunken destiny, the Brazos twists its way through Palo Pinto County. As an indication of its violent contortions, local tradition tells of a fisherman who hooked and with a mighty pull threw a big catfish over the bank behind him, and, upon going to get it, found he had thrown it back into the river, fifteen miles upstream! Whatever the fanciful lore of its fishermen, the country was prolific of wild game — deer, turkeys, and pigeons — pigeons in flying clouds that passed with 'a roaring noise like distant thunder.'

In the middle fifties the land was scarcely rutted by rattling wagons or marred by swinging axes. In spite of Indian troubles, the frontier of 1857 was a hundred miles west of the border villages of Dallas and Waxahachie that Goodnight had seen as a boy, only a decade before. In 1853, the post at Fort Worth had been abandoned. In 1851, Fort Belknap, a good day's ride to the west, had been established on the Brazos, in Young County. A day's ride still farther west along the Clear Fork was Camp Cooper, established in January, 1856.[1] The mere existence of these posts encouraged the coming of settlers, if not frontiersmen — who came anyway.

For ten years Charlie's interests were to center about the three counties of Palo Pinto, Parker, and Young. His home county had been created the year before he came; Parker a year earlier than that. Log houses, buttressed with heavy rock chimneys at one or both ends, were being built along the Fort Belknap–Fort Worth road. In August, 1856, the village of Weatherford, a day's ride southeast of the Black Springs Ranch, was laid off near the military road, and at the outbreak of the Civil War was the most important town in that section. Deep in the hills south of the Brazos, Golconda sprang to bucolic life as the seat of Palo Pinto County, though the name was changed to that of the creek for which the county was named, Palo Pinto — 'painted wood.'

Many of the settlers came to the country with nothing, and some left or died without bettering their condition. Charlie recalls a transient who stopped at an old-timer's camp and asked to spend the night. After a frugal supper and a smoke, the cowman pulled a beef hide from a corner of the cabin, threw it upon the dirt floor, turned to the traveler, and said: 'You sleep here. I'll rough it!'

[1] Arrie Barret, 'Federal Military Posts in Texas,' Thesis, University of Texas, 172 ff.

After their arrival, Wes and Charlie watched their rangy cows graze from wide slope to wide slope along the Keechi, until they located, and then the boys began cutting logs for a cabin. The next year Charlie moved his mother and step-father Sheek to the ranch.

OX-FREIGHT

Since there was no market for calves, Charlie began freight-ing, while Wes remained with the herd. At first Goodnight handled one team of six yoke, but soon was whacking two teams — twenty-four head strung to one great wagon, for at that time trail wagons were unknown.

At first all freighting for the Cross Timbers was done from Houston, but when the Houston and Texas Central Railroad began to build, freighters loaded at the end of the line—at Hempstead, and then at Bryan. Charlie's last trip was from Bryan with thirteen thousand pounds of salt for Palo Pinto town. Off and on he whacked bulls for three years, freighting merchandise, barrels of syrup, sugar, 'and nearly always more or less barrels of whiskey on each load; in fact every commodity the human family needed.'

Then Wes married and left the heaviest work on the range, as well as on the bull trail, to his partner. Charlie quit freight-

ing to ride the Keechi range, which at that time followed the
practices developed in other wooded portions of Texas. When
they took charge of Varner's herd, in the CV brand, most
ranchmen penned their cattle each night to gentle them.
With a good-sized herd they soon discovered that this was impossible, for close penning of several hundred calves so confused their scents that by morning some of the mother cows
could not recognize their calves by smell as they habitually do.

Mess-wagons were not introduced until the cattle industry
reached the open country, after the Civil War. For short
cow hunts 'each man carried his three to six days' rations in
a wallet behind the saddle'; for longer hunts wallets gave way
to pack outfits and the Texas mule. Provisions were meager
— some good roasted coffee, a supply of light bacon, and a few
hard biscuits, though often the cowboys had no bread. Every
man made his coffee to suit himself, broiled his bacon to his
own taste, and dug his biscuits from his own wallet. Hence
there was no delay in breaking camp, no lost mess-wagon to
search for, no disaffection over the food, and no 'cussing' the
cook.

Until the Civil War there was virtually no roping on the
timbered range. Before it ended, cowmen, working short-
handed, were rounding cattle against bluffs and other protection, roping the calves out and branding in the open. During
this time dotting irons, forerunners of stamp irons, came into
use. Instead of stamping the entire brand at one application,
the character or letter was dotted on with several. There were
three dotting irons: a bar, or as it was then called a 'straight-
edge,' three or four inches long; a small half-circle and a large
half-circle. The straight-edge would be used in making the
letter *D*; the large half-circle completing the brand. Four
applications of the small half-circle would make, for example,

Straightedge   Small   Large   Dumb-bell   Ace of Clubs
   or Bar   Half-Circle   Half-Circle

a figure 8; or with the long bar, a dumbbell; or, with the short bar, an ace of clubs, or whatever the brand might be.[2]

The cattle of central Texas were different from the long-horns of the border. Many old cowboys, Goodnight among them, distinguished the dark, line-backed, mealy-nosed, round-

TEXAS CATTLE

barreled, and well-built animals by calling them Texas cattle. Seemingly a fusion of the Spanish and Southern stock, they were better cattle than the former but every bit as wild. Their horns were long and keen, set forward to kill 'like those of a buffalo.' They cared for their calves better than the Spanish cattle; their sense of smell was keener than a deer's. Like creatures domesticated from nature, they readily reverted to the wild, and ranged out beyond the settlements of central Texas. Though they were a good beef breed they were actually ferocious. A wounded bull would hunt a man by scent, like a bear, and attack a horseman as readily as a man on foot. In fact, he

[2] C. Goodnight to J. E. H., December 14, 1928; John Marlin to J. E. H., February 18, 1930.

was worse than a bear; he would tree a hunter and keep him
there until killed. In the spring they ranged the timbered bottoms by day — again like a bear — but emerged at night, and
of early morning the cowboys cut them off from the bottoms
and roped them as they fought to get away.[3]

When Goodnight and Sheek branded but four calves apiece
as their share of the first year's crop, Wes wanted to throw up
the contract, but Charlie, with his usual stubbornness to do
what he had set out to do, would not hear to it. Certainly the
growth of their business seemed slow enough to discourage, for
the next year they branded only thirty-two calves between
them. In 1858, Charlie rendered seventeen head of cattle and a
couple of horses for taxation; Wes, eighteen head. After four
years they rendered a hundred and eighty head in their own
names which indicated that the herd was beginning to grow.

Soon after moving to the Keechi, Charlie met Oliver Loving,
the most experienced cowman upon the northwest fringe, and,
since he was to exercise unusual influence upon Goodnight. his
character and work should be observed.

Loving was then running a small country store on the Belknap road. He owned a few slaves and a good-sized herd of
cattle, and, though the Cross Timbers were not yet producing
vast herds of beef, most of what were produced found a market
through him. He usually trailed them to Shreveport, Alex-
andria, or New Orleans. But he recognized no handicap of
distance, hardship, or danger. In 1858, in company with John
Durkee, he pointed a herd into the north, skirted the western
hem of American advance, weary mile upon weary mile, swam
a dozen streams, and trailed his big beef steers to the markets
of Illinois.

Then the gold rush to Colorado began, and he learned that
the Denver country was swarming with people. On the twenty-
ninth of August, 1860, he pointed a thousand steers for the
Rockies. John Dawson, besides being interested in the herd,

---

[3] C. Goodnight to J. E. H., July 10, 1928; D. W. Moore to J. E. H., February 2, 1932;
Lockhart, G. W., *Sixty Years on the Brazos*, 328.

acted as guide, and Charlie helped them beyond the Cross Timbers, and watched them swim the turbid Red to point straight into the Indian Nation. They struck the Arkansas below the Great Bend, followed the stream to Pueblo and above, and wintered the herd upon grass, where, ten years later, Charlie himself was to establish a ranch.

When spring came and melted the snows, Loving drifted into Denver and peddled his cattle out to miners and prospectors. While thus engaged, the Civil War broke and the authorities refused to let him return to Texas. He had made friends of Kit Carson, Lucien Maxwell, and other prominent mountain men, and through their intercession was allowed his freedom. He left his outfit, staged it to St. Joseph, and reached home August 9, 1861, full of plans for Southern aggression. However, the destinies of war decreed that he should feed rather than lead the men who fought, and these plans were forgotten.[4] Yet they dealt with the Indian problem — with the question of frontier defense — and were of vital interest to Goodnight.

Presumably, most of the Comanches and Kiowas were located north of Red River, but in February, 1854, the Legislature of Texas authorized the Federal Government to locate and establish not more than three Indian reserves in the state hoping thereby to simplify the problem of protection. In the summer of 1854, R. B. Marcy and Robert S. Neighbors selected eight leagues of land on the main Brazos near the mouth of the Clear Fork, in what is now Young County, for the use of the smaller tribes, which came to be known as the Lower or Brazos Reserve. Some fifty miles farther west they located a smaller reserve on the Clear Fork for the Comanches alone, and attempts at settlement were begun.

Agents looked after the Indians, and the frontier people hoped for and expected relief from their raids. There was a lull in depredations for a year or two, during which time settlements moved westward at a lively pace, though farther

[4] Major Royal S. Loving, as cited, September 15, 1930; C. Goodnight to J. E. H., September 27, 1925.

south hostile bands still struck, plundered, and fled, leaving only darkened trails through dew-hung grass — trails that grew old with the first ripple of a breath of wind.

Neighbors, hopeful and energetic, worked with conscience and zeal to make the reserves a success. A suspicion of raiding attached to the reserve Indians, but Neighbors denied the truth of the reports. Late in 1857 there was much complaint from the border people, and petitions were addressed to the Secretary of the Interior asking for the removal of Neighbors, who replied that the thievery was the work of wild Indians and renegade whites, magnified and capitalized by his enemies, and should be discounted in whole. And he had enemies, chief among whom was John R. Baylor, who made capital of every raid.[5]

Baylor, part and parcel of the frontier, was appointed agent at the Comanche Reserve in 1856, where he served until dismissed in May, 1857. He was a capable frontiersman and a fearless adventurer; a man of reckless power, of force, and of magnetism. Of commanding physical presence, he stood six feet high and as straight as a dogwood arrow. He did not forget and he did not forgive, but believed the old frontier proverb that 'good Indians are dead Indians,' and he was always wanting to make them good.

During the early months of 1858, hostility to the reserves gradually grew in intensity, and agitation for the removal of the tribes to the Territory was fanned to fever heat by the killing of the Mason and Cameron families. About the twenty-fourth of April, Indians made a clean sweep of all horses around Belknap in the first bad raid since Goodnight had settled on the Keechi. He described it in detail.

'About four miles northwest of me on the Upper Keechi lived a neighbor named Isaac Lynn. His daughter had married a man by the name of Thomas Mason, who had settled in what is known as Lost Valley, in Jack County. Mr. Lynn,

---

[5] R. N. Richardson, in *The Comanche Barrier to South Plains Settlement*, gives an excellent account of the Reserve troubles.

who was about sixty years of age, went afoot everywhere, regardless of distance. In spite of the fact that he raised and sold good horses, he never rode. It occurred to him to make a visit to Lost Valley to see his daughter. So taking his old rifle, as was his custom, he walked over there, a distance of about twenty miles from his ranch.

BLACK SPRINGS RANCH

'Upon his arrival he found that the Masons had been murdered the day before by the Indians. Mrs. Mason had got into the cow lot, where she had been shot down with a small babe in her arms. The baby had been nursing its dead mother, and was still alive when found by its grandfather. Their other child, two or three years of age, was still in the house alive.

'The Masons lived in one side of a joint or double log cabin. Mr. and Mrs. James Cameron and their very bright little boy, about ten years of age, occupied the other side of this cabin. Lynn found the bodies of Mr. and Mrs. Cameron where they had been murdered. He then took his two grandchildren to Jacksboro, where he reported the raid.

'The Indians, after leaving the scene, had roped a wild

mule, tied the little Cameron boy on it, and had driven it with their herd of horses. The horsemen of a California emigrant train, passing westward to California along what was known as the Mercer–California Trail, saw the Indians passing northwest with the band of horses and made chase after them.

'Their chase was unsuccessful, but on their return to the train they came through some high grass where the little Cameron boy was. He jumped up and said: "I'm here yet!"

'He told them that at daylight the Indians took him off the mule and put him behind a red-headed man who spoke English. When the white men made chase after the Indians, the white man, or Indian, or whoever he was, shoved the little fellow off into the grass to lighten the load. He told him to stay there until he came back. Being worn out, the little fellow fell asleep and when the horsemen rode up he awoke, and thought the red-headed man had returned for him. He was a very intelligent child and had the most beautiful blue eyes I have ever seen. He readily told them who he was and where his people had been killed, and they immediately sent him with escorts to Belknap, forty miles distant, from where he was sent back to the Keechi country and to Mr. Lynn.

'At this time there was a party of three prospectors, one red-headed, who had been exploring the country west. One of the prominent settlers, Judge Lasater, happened to meet the exploring party as it was returning to the Waco country, where it had come from, and jumped at the conclusion that this red-haired man had committed the Mason and Cameron murders.

'Since this was the first bad Indian murder that had occurred on that frontier for many years, it created an unusual excitement because those settlers were not originally frontier people. They were then not accustomed to such horrible occurrences which, a year or two later, would have attracted very little attention.

'A mass meeting of forty or fifty of the frontier people was called at Parson Maderie's ranch, on the West Keechi, not more than ten miles from my place, where amidst wild excitement they tried these explorers for two days. Sheek and I knew this prospector in question. We knew his family, we knew that he was innocent, and we had determined to prevent him being killed. We could only get four other men who were willing to stand with us, willing, if necessary, to lay down their lives for an innocent man. It was finally settled in this way. They decided to get together all the red-headed men in the crowd and see if the Cameron boy could recognize the man who had captured him. I will never forget the impression it made on me as I watched him view all the men. After every one had passed by he said the man who had him was not there. That ended the farce trial.

'Thus you can imagine my great relief when the little boy did not designate a man, for if he had, it would have ended in a tremendous battle compared with which the killing of the Cameron and Mason families would not have been a beginning.' [6]

A few weeks later the Comanches made a raid on Allen Johnson's ranch seven or eight miles west of Belknap, and, though they failed to do much damage, they fanned the Indian excitement afresh. These reserve Comanches, according to Goodnight, 'raided around and did devilment all the time they were there,' and a number of prominent frontiersmen were taking advantage of every outbreak to urge the removal of the reserves from Texas.

Along with Baylor was Old Buck Barry, another seasoned ranger, R. W. Pollard, county judge of Palo Pinto, Peter Garland, and General E. H. Tarrant. During the winter there were many Indian scares, and though parties of men came up from Bosque and Erath Counties to help with the fighting, the wild Indians were gone long before they reached the scene of

[6] See I. J. Shirley to C. E. Barnard, May 6, 1858, photostat copy, University of Texas Archives; *The Northern Standard* (Clarksville, Texas), May 5, 1858.

action. Some innocent, friendly Indians were killed: Choctaw Tom's party of seven, and Goodnight's boyhood friend, Old Caddo Jake, who was living at the Agency. A number of cowboys killed the old Indian, his wife and family. It was an outrage, according to Goodnight — 'a dirty piece of business. They just wanted to be killing some Indians. In 1859 I was by the spot on the West Fork of the Trinity, seven or eight miles north of Lost Valley, and saw where they had been killed, nearly a year before. A cowboy got down and picked up one of the arm bones of the little squaw and said he was going to make a quirt handle of it. Jack Bailey told me that all the time they were shooting at them, Caddo Jake was giving the grand hailing sign of the Masons.'

In spite of the apparent peacefulness of the Lower Reserve Indians, and the spirited fight of Neighbors in their interest, the settlers set March 20, 1859, for a drive upon them. 'The Indian Conference' at Jimmison's Peak served notice on the Government that it had just six weeks' time in which 'to remove the Indians at the Brazos Agency from the State or the citizens would remove them themselves.'[7] Neighbors was trying to hurry the officials at Washington into moving the Indians, well knowing the futility of working against the inflamed feelings of the frontier. After this demonstration he was able to announce that they would be moved in the fall or winter.

In the meantime another inoffensive Indian was killed and the attempt of an army officer to arrest the rangers who killed him so infuriated the frontier that additional ranger companies were organized, and other councils of war were held. Upon May 23, Baylor led the 'Army of Defense,' as the settlers called it — 'a mob,' the agents declared — upon the Lower Reserve and picked a fight with the Indians. Goodnight was along.

'When we reached the reservation we found the troops there to protect the Indians, and, not wishing to fight the soldiers, we passed the reservation. Shortly after we had passed, the

[7] J. H. Baker, 'Diary,' 1858–72, p. 90.

Indians commenced firing on us, a desultory fire at considerable distance, doing no harm further than annoyance.[8]

'After we had passed the reservation four or five miles, and as we were skirting a body of heavy oak timber at the right of us, McAdams, a rancher and an old Mexican War veteran, proposed to me that we flank the command up this ridge. We were riding up the steep side of the hill when the Indians, who had already reached it, opened fire on us at close range. Mc-Adams was next to the Indians, and I noticed him kicking fearfully. I asked him what was the trouble, and he said they had hit him in the foot, remarking, with some rude language: "I've got it again! Looks like I always have to get it. Had two bullets in the Mexican War."

'We ran the Indians off the ridge and returned to the rear of the command. Captain Jack Cureton, an early settler on the Keechi, was there, and he took about ten of us as a flank guard and returned to the ridge. The Indians had already passed down and commenced firing on the command at close range, killing one man and slightly wounding another. Captain Cureton threw us in line at once and ordered us to fire.

'Then the Indians came out of the timber and had to turn to the left to get by us. As they passed the flanking squad, we fired a number of shots, but I do not know whether we hit any of them. I, having a good horse, pulled out of line and intercepted their retreat as quickly as possible. As soon as I got in a straight line behind one of the Indians, I gave him a shot between the shoulders. He was just at the edge of the thick timber, which he went into like a shot, holding to the horn of his saddle with both hands, and I do not suppose he went far until he fell off.

[8] The agent at the reserve reported that the fight started after Baylor's party had induced an old Indian to join them, and then treacherously killed him. See Virginia Pink Noel, 'The United States Indian Reservations in Texas, 1854–1859,' Thesis, University of Texas, 138–42.

J. H. Baker, who took part in the fight, records in his diary that this man, a Waco chief, was captured during one of the skirmishes, attempted to shoot Captain Hamner before he could be disarmed, and was killed by the Captain in self-defense. Baker, 'Diary,' 97–98.

'About a mile farther up the valley we came to what was known as the Marlin Ranch. We stopped on the creek near the ranch-house to get something to eat,[9] as it was then about two o'clock in the afternoon. There the Indians, who had appeared in great numbers, attacked us in a body and we had to leave

A LOOKOUT

our campfires and coffee pots and fall in line of battle. Among our men was a Mr. Meyers, an old Baptist preacher, who had also put his coffee pot on the fire and set his meat to broil. After the firing had continued a while, Captain Cureton ordered me to take my horse and explore the post-oak ridge just behind us, which was quite abrupt and rocky, saying that if the Indians got in behind us they would make us trouble. I rode over the ridge and found no Indians. My return brought me across the creek where we had started to get our dinner. I ran on to Parson Meyer's coffee pot, with the contents just

[9] This ranch was owned by W. N. P. Marlin, who came to Young County in 1852 and settled about two miles west of what became reserve land. The Marlins were friendly to the Indians and Neighbors. John Marlin, son of the old ranchman, spoke of the Indian fighters as 'filibusters.' John Marlin to J. E. H., February 18, 1932.

done and warm enough to drink. The fire had gone out, but the two large slices of bacon were browned to a finish. This was too tempting. I dismounted and made a meal of the Parson's linner, then reported to my Captain that all was well.

'The Indians were in the timber. Opposite us there was a strip of prairie land along the edge of the timber. While we were firing at long range, one Indian, pretending to be much braver than the other Indians, and no doubt was, as he had a very large war-bonnet of eagle feathers, kept running his horse back and forth in front of our line. He was just out of ordinary rifle range, doing a great deal of yelling and some firing.

'Unfortunately I had a shotgun. There was a man in our neighborhood whose hobby it was to go to the saloons and get corked up and fight. But we could never get him to go on an Indian campaign, as he always had some poor excuse. When we formed this expedition, Sheek and I solicited his aid again. This time his excuse was that he had nothing but a shotgun.

'"I have the best rifle on the frontier," I said. "You take it and I'll take your shotgun."

'He could not very easily escape this proposition, so made the exchange with me, but after the first day's march toward the Indians he slipped away during the night and went home, taking my rifle with him.

'There happened to be a small bunch of brush and trees in front of us near where this Indian was riding back and forth, within shotgun range, and it occurred to me to run out, get in this brush, and shoot the Indian as he rode by.

'After seeing me take this position the same thought occurred to General Baylor, and he decided to get the Indian himself. He followed me into the brush, but I was not aware of his presence until I noticed the Indian suddenly turn and start straight east.

'Just then Baylor said: "Hold on, Charlie, let me have him. You can't get him with that shotgun."

'The Indian continued to ride east. Meanwhile, General Baylor had raised his rifle and it seemed to me he sighted a long time. When he fired a bunch of eagle feathers on the Indian's war-bonnet flew into the air. I will never forget the expression on Baylor's face. Finally, after looking at the Indian for about a minute, he said: "Damn you! If I can't kill you, I can pick you!" and was apparently satisfied with that.

'The firing continued three or four hours, but all at long range. During the battle the boys were dodging the bullets fearfully, for which Captain Cureton reproved them, saying such was not soldierly. But when he dodged from a big bullet which just missed him, he then said it was all right to dodge the big ones but never mind the little ones. The Indians slightly wounded two men. I know of only two Indians killed. No doubt others were injured and escaped, but the firing was at too distant range on either side to do much harm.

'About five o'clock, after the battle was over, we returned to the creek to finish our meal. I heard the Parson murmuring much about the loss of his coffee, but I did not have nerve enough to tell him who drank it.'

J. H. Baker, the Palo Pinto school-teacher who was along, claimed the Indians were better armed than the settlers, having government rifles, and that they were 'assisted and abetted by renegade white men.' While caring for wounded at Belknap, he observed: 'We found that we had plenty of enemies here and some friends, who were almost afraid to express themselves because of the government siding with the Indians.' [10] And in spite of Baylor's reputed boast that he would destroy both re- serves 'if it cost him the life of every man in his command,' the Army of Defense disbanded and comparative peace reigned.

Governor Runnels's commission, sent to investigate affairs at the Agency, reached Palo Pinto late in June, and Baker wrote in his diary that they had come 'to try to consummate peace between the Indians and the whites. The Government promis- ing to keep the Indians on the reservations, providing the whites will let them alone. To which we agreed, as long as the Indians

[10] Baker, 'Diary,' 98–101. He reported twenty-one Indians killed.

do not molest us.' Upon the Fourth of July the settlers met at Golconda to celebrate with a barbecue in appropriate frontier style, and though John Love, designated orator of the day, had been drunk for a week, he was still perfectly willing to make a speech. The local Templars got him off the rostrum and put Dr. S. S. Taylor up to lecture on temperance, but Love heckled him so frequently that the oratory was abandoned. Captain H. Hamner, of Jack County, proposed that they agree to let the Indians alone as long as the Government confined them to the reserves. 'The people voted the adoption of the resolutions and a company of "minute men" were organized' to see that the Government lived up to its contract.[11]

At last Washington was touched to the seriousness of the situation, on June 11 orders were issued that the Indians be moved, and by August 8 Neighbors had crossed the last of them over Red River. He returned to Belknap and was shot and killed by Edward Cornett, brother-in-law of a man whom he was said to have accused of being a horse thief. Neighbors had been in Texas since 1836 as soldier, surveyor, legislator, and Indian agent. John R. Baylor, who led the fight against him, was one of the commanders of the Confederate expedition into New Mexico, became Territorial Governor of Arizona, and returned to Texas to raise five battalions of partisan rangers. After a tempestuous career, he gradually faded from public life, to die, many years later, adventuring along the Nueces.[12]

That the attack upon the Lower Reserve was the culmination of excitement growing out of thievery and bloody forays in many sections on the one hand, continually fanned and agitated by bellicose old warriors and enemies of the Indian agents on the other, there is but little doubt. That the attack, after the order for removal of the Indians had been issued, was an ill-advised, tragic circumstance, there is none. But upon that

[11] *Graham Leader*, February 27, 1913; Baker, 'Diary,' 102–04.

[12] Richardson, as cited; James B. Barry, 'Papers,' University of Texas Archives; C. H. Walde to J. B. Barry, January 7, 1862; Thrall, *Pictorial History of Texas*, 596; *The Northern Standard*, October 8, 1859.

borderland of settlement young blood flowed fast and hot, and perhaps it was more natural to fight Indians than to reason why. One distinction at least had been made by the removal. Hereafter there might be tame Indians north of Red River, but no matter what the tribe, those who set foot on the soil of Texas were considered wild.

III. THE MAKING OF A SCOUT

MANY frontiersmen have left accounts of Indian warfare, of bloody battles with outlaws and thieves, and of desperate chances in wild and strange lands. The names of some are household words today. Perhaps none expressed the lore of the scout and guide — the technique of plainscraft — better than Charlie Goodnight, for he has given voice to those essential qualities that made Bridger, Carson, Wootton, and others live in tradition and in history.

In order to understand the lore which Goodnight himself so thoroughly embodied, it is necessary to understand the land and the life that fostered it. West of the ragged edge of the Upper Cross Timbers lies the open country. Two hundred miles or more beyond this ragged line is one more ragged still, formed by the escarpments delimiting the eastern edge of the Staked Plains. Draining from the cañons along their eastern edges are the headwaters of many of the rivers of Texas, from the three Conchos on the south, to the Colorado, the Brazos, the Wichita, and the Red, on the north. At the outbreak of the Civil War they drained an unknown country.

Only in a few places had the frontier line of Texas emerged into the open lands. Between 1858 and 1861 the outposts ebbed back for many miles, until they rested again in the shelter of the timbered zone. As Goodnight recalled, the extreme western settler in Young County, at the outbreak of the war, lived four miles west of Fort Belknap, and there was 'nothing west from there to the Rocky Mountains.'

From somewhere in that vast and unexplored prairie coun-

try came marauding Indian bands, as transient as the whirl-
winds that sucked its red dusts into the skies — almost as
elusive in the trails they left behind. Open mile after open
mile, this country stretched beyond the Cross Timbers, a
gently rolling short-grass land. In many places near the Llano
Estacado it broke into vicious stretches of choppy country, red
clay badlands, where water — when there was any — was
bitter as gall to the palate and devastating to the stomach,
where game was scarce and fuel was rare, and where, unless
the scout was the best of guides, men flung fresh horses upon a
trail to come out — God only knew where — afoot.

West of this land of gentle swells the Staked Plains reared
their high and colorful abutments, those escarpments that
broke away from the plateau in flashing reds and dull yellows,
in sober browns and subdued purples. Out of that country of
shimmering horizons, a land that has 'the vastness without the
malignancy of the sea,' gashed the rugged cañons of the Palo
Duro, with their clays and sandstones swept into turrets,
battlements, totems, and effigies by the everlasting winds of
the West. There, and in the Quitaque to the south, and on to
Las Lenguas, and Casas Amarillas, and the Double Mountain
Fork, was rough land into which Indians might sweep from
bloody forays on the Texas border. To the north were the
breaks of the Salt Fork and the North Fork, and the long valley of the Canadian, and to the east the refuge of the narrow
granitic mountains of the Wichita. Before this sheltered land
lay the open ranges of the *Tejanos*; to the west lay the markets
of New Mexico; to the northeast the traders from the Yankee
settlements. Why should the bold warriors of the Comanche
and Kiowa crave peace with the South?

Such was the country from which the Indians came, and back
into these forbidding plains to hunt them down rode the frontier rangers, adapting their methods to those of the Indians;
traveling without camp equipage, without forage, without
shelter, and almost without water; eating when the country
offered meat, but more often skimping their way out and starv-

ing their way back. Nowhere in Texas had climate and topography frowned so hardly upon the men who would master them. Nowhere were her frontiersmen compelled so completely to revolutionize their attack.

TEXAN SCOUTS

From the Rio Grande north to the southern butts of the Plains the Frontier Regiment generally ranged a well-watered country, prolific of game, excellently sheltered, provided with fuel, and often abundant with wild fruits and nuts. Upon the northwest edge only for the man who knew the land to its very grass roots was there anything but sterility. Of necessity the scout was a seasoned outdoor man, well versed in the highly technical art of plainscraft. His place was the most important and the most difficult in a frontier campaign. The company depended upon him against surprise attacks, against becoming lost in a region devoid of landmarks, against death from thirst and hunger, and even against freezing. Upon his observation and judgment depended the safety, the mobility, the usefulness, and the life of the entire command.

A scout was necessarily in camp very little, for as soon as one scouting party returned to camp another was sent out. Goodnight would have scouted continually if possible. 'Many of the men sat around playing cards. But I couldn't stand to sit in camp,' he said, 'and spent a great deal of time walking around in the woods.' The scout, along with the officers, was exempt from all fatigue duty, but rather than sit in camp and submit to a few simple formalities of discipline, Goodnight stood guard over the company's horses for many long hours.

Partly from simplicity of taste, partly from extreme isolation, and partly from the impoverishment of war, the ranger's presence was mean rather than impressive. Clothing and equipment were left largely to private initiative, but here, as elsewhere, Goodnight observed, 'there were quarter-breed men, half-breed men, and full-blooded men. Those who were up to snuff were well equipped. Some were so sorrily equipped that they were never taken on scouts or campaigns, but were left around camp to stand fatigue.' In the main, however, the regiment contained fine frontiersmen; men who really loved the smell of a campfire, the whinny of a horse, the lure of a trail — 'full-blooded' men who rode into battle with splendid abandon.

Of all the varied units of fighting men since war was history, no other has been quite the same. In their belts they carried Bowie knives often sheathed in scabbards made from the tails of buffalo calves, slipped whole from the bone and dried over a whittled stick, exactly the shape of the blade. The bushy end of the tail swung below as a tassel ornament, or was used for cleaning its owner's comb. The better equipped had six-shooters, preferably of the same caliber as their rifles, to prevent confusion of ammunition in the excitement of battle, and those without rifles were armed with double-barreled shotguns. In either case they fought at close quarters, for the rifles were of short range.

When there was scant danger of surprise, the rifle was carried on the saddle in a leather or rawhide scabbard, with the stock set forward and the barrel pointing backward. In Indian country it was carried across the fork of the saddle, swung in a short leather sling from the saddle horn. No motion was lost in case of surprise; the sling was slipped from the horn in an instant and the gun was almost in position for firing. Thus the weight of the gun was carried on the fork of the saddle, and whether at a walk or a lope was easily balanced by a touch of the hand.[1]

To facilitate speedy loading, the rangers adapted a shot pouch that swung from the left shoulder to the waistline, convenient to the right hand. Inside were buckskin scraps for bullet-patches, bullets, and a box of caps, and swinging by buckskin strings below was the powder-horn — a white horn dressed so thin that the ranger, by holding it up to the sun, could see if his powder was running low. The peg, or stopper, was usually of bois d'arc or hickory, for stoppers of soft wood might swell in rainy weather and disarm an entire command.

Attached by another string was the charger, a powder measure of horn or a small joint of cane trimmed to hold the right amount. In battle it was not used, for it was quicker to guess at a charge in the palm of the hand. In reloading at leisure the ranger might charge his gun by placing a bullet in his palm and pouring just enough powder to cover it up. Cloth bullet-patches were sometimes used, but on account of the greater resiliency of tallowed buckskin, bullets were seated tighter with it, more power was utilized from the charge, and hence longer range from the gun. In preparation for a

[1] Captain R. B. Marcy, who noticed this practice among the Texas frontiersmen, said that it was adopted, to some extent, by the army men of the West. *Prairie Traveler*, 170.

scout, each man molded fifty bullets, and on account of their ease in loading, round bullets were used exclusively.[2] Such was the equipment of the border ranger.

Out from camp regularly rode a scouting party of perhaps twenty-five men, and as they had no extra horses they took particular care of those they rode. Beneath the headstall of each bridle, encircling the nose of the horse, was a *bosal* — as we say on the border — the loop of a hair rope, the thirty-five feet of which were coiled at the left of the saddle fork, tied with a slip knot by one of the saddle strings.

Loaded with frying-pans, a little flour, bacon, and salt, two pack-mules faithfully followed behind. A pair of blankets for every two men was on the pack or behind the cantle of a saddle. Tied to each saddle was a big tin cup and usually a buffalo-horn spoon. The scout rode half a mile ahead, and conveyed his messages back to the squad by a system of signals — motions of the hat or movements of his horse.

Perhaps, as the scout reached the crest of a wave of the land, upon a creek before him was a party of Indian braves, unaware that whites were near. He dropped back from the ridge and turned his horse into the signal of a charge. Gun slings were raised from the saddle horns, slip knots jerked undone, and the coils of the stake ropes drawn under the rangers' belts. In an instant they were ready for action.

They swept over the ridge in a wild dash and bore down upon the astonished bucks with unearthly cowboy yells. The Indians scrambled for their horses and scattered like a bevy of Mexican quail, while the rangers scattered in pursuit, some using rifles, some holding fire, and some closing up to six-shooter range.

All guns were never fired at once, else in time of reloading the Indians would rush and cut the rangers down with arrows at close range. Goodnight, superbly mounted and riding in the lead with the old-timers, felt there was greater danger of being shot by raw and excited recruits from behind than by the

[2] Goodnight to J. E. H., June 15, 1929.

Indians in front. If the Indians were not rushed down, tactics changed, for a horseman with a rifle fights at disadvantage with a cool man on the ground. The captain might order his men to foot, and some swung off at a run, reins flying loose, stake ropes jerked free in their left hands.

If held by the reins most horses shy from a gun. Hence, as his feet hit the ground, the ranger flipped the free end of the rope around his hips, drew it into a slip knot, and gave his attention to the Indians. If his horse ran on the end of the rope the nose-hitch ordinarily kept him from dragging the rider, who in case of emergency could pull at the loose end of the slip knot and set the mount free. If his company retreated, the ranger gathered up the rope as he ran to his horse, swung into the saddle and tucked the coils back under his belt as he rode.

After Goodnight's first shot, the butt of his gun swung to the ground, the barrel in the crook of his arm. His right hand grabbed the powder-horn, he jerked the stopper out with his teeth, and poured a charge into the palm of his left hand. As he poured it into his gun, he slipped out the rod with his right, then caught up the leather loader with his left, pressed a ready-patched bullet into the barrel, and rammed it home with the hickory rod. As he lifted his gun with his left hand, his right pulled a cap from his belt and slipped it in place, and he was ready to shoot again.

After a fight the old-timers gathered the plunder of value while the raw recruits picked up the relics. If other Indians were near — and the scout had to know — the rangers went into camp before dark, staked their horses upon grass, cooked and ate their suppers, and made all preparations for spending the night. After dark they quietly moved to a spot the scout had selected a few miles away, where they both hobbled and side-lined their horses, making stampede impossible, posted a guard, and went to sleep.

Thus were the rangers equipped and thus did they operate. But the work of the scout and guide was not only the work of the regular ranger but a great deal more.

Perhaps the guide's simplest qualification, and yet one of the rarest among civilized men, was a faculty of direction. Few men, even scientifically trained and frontier grown, have this faculty.[3] 'And yet,' Goodnight mused, 'the fellows who can-

WILD BEEF

not keep a course are always quarreling with you — afraid you are going to get them lost.

'It was the scout's business to guide the company under all conditions. Thus, above all things, the scout and plainsman had to have a sense — an instinct — for direction. He had to have the faculty of never needing a compass. With the point of destination fixed in his mind, a thorough plainsman could go to it as directly in darkness as in daylight, on a calm, cloudy day as well as in bright sunshine with the wind blowing steadily from one quarter. Few men have this instinct. Yet in the few it is to be trusted as absolutely as the homing instinct of a wild goose. A man with such an instinct relies on what is in his mind more than he does on stars or winds or the sun or landscape features. I never had a compass in my life. I was never

---

[3] After many years upon the border, Captain R. B. Marcy was impressed with this fact. In wonder he wrote of his Indian guide who could 'start from any place to which he had gone by a sinuous route, through an unknown country, and keep a direct bearing back to the place of departure; and he assured me [Marcy continued] that he has never, even during the most cloudy or foggy nights, lost the points of compass. There are very few white men who are endowed with these wonderful faculties, and those few are only rendered proficient by matured experience.' *Prairie Traveler*, 180.

lost. In all my frontier experience, I knew but one man who had keener senses than I had. He was a Tonkawa Indian and his eyesight would carry farther than mine.

'As matches were unknown, we used various methods of obtaining our fire, the most common of which was punk and steel. But in the prairie country, where there was no punk, we had to avail ourselves of other ways, the most common of which was to burn red corncobs to ashes, put them in a tin plate, and make them into a thin mush with water. Into this mush we put colored calico — white might do but colored was much preferred — and old cloth was the best. We saturated the rags thoroughly and carried a supply with us. When dry they would catch fire readily from flint and steel.

'Another method was to twist a wad of cotton into a joint of cane until it stuck out at the other end — a four-inch joint was enough — after which we set the cotton on fire. As it burned, we untwisted the wad at the other end, and the cotton crawled back into the cane and went out. When we wanted to catch fire, we twisted the cotton again until the charred end stuck through, and then used the flint and steel as usual. From the smoldering cotton we lighted a kindling rag and started our fire from it.

'If we had none of these materials, we would char a soft cottonwood root, which would catch like punk, from which we would light our kindling rag, cedar bark, rotten wood or grass.'

Like other outdoor men, the rangers were sometimes soaked from head to foot, and a fire became a matter of serious concern. As a last resort the scout rubbed a dampened calico rag through powder, held in the palm of his hand, until it was saturated with half-melted explosive. Then he placed a percussion cap upon one spoke of a rowel of his Mexican spurs, wrapped the powder-laden rag below it, and 'busted the cap' with the back of his Bowie knife. The rag caught the sparks and flashed into a blaze as the powder burned.

In an arid wilderness the problem of water was the most serious problem of all. The logs of the Western trails, the stories around mountain campfires, and the journals of pioneer folk, all attest the anxiety, the suffering, the failure, and the tragedy exacted by a land of little water.

'I think that I learned pretty thoroughly the requirements of scout and plainsman,' observed Goodnight. 'The first requirement is that by merely looking at the country the scout should be able to judge accurately in what direction water lies and the approximate distance to it. He should be familiar with every grass and shrub that indicates water. He should be able to tell by watching the animals, if animals there be, whether they are going to or coming from water.'

The scout and plainsman should know the significance of the vegetation as well as the animal life of the country he ranges. By both, but mainly by observing the plant life, he usually estimates his elevation, and certainly his approximate latitude and longitude.

'You can blindfold me, take me anywhere in the Western country,' Goodnight once said, 'then uncover my eyes so that I can look at the vegetation, and I can tell about where I am. The mesquite, for instance, has different forms for varying altitudes, latitudes, and areas of aridity. It does not grow far north of old Tascosa in the Texas Panhandle.

'When I was scouting on the Plains, I was always mighty glad to see a mesquite bush. In a dry climate — the climate natural to the mesquite — its seed seem to spring up only from the droppings of an animal. The only animal on the Plains that ate mesquite beans was the mustang. After the mesquite seed was soaked for a while in the bowels of a horse and was dropped, it germinated quickly. Now mustangs rarely grazed out from water more than three miles, that is, when they had the country to themselves. Therefore, when I saw a mesquite bush I used to know that water was within three miles. All I had to do after seeing the bush was to locate the direction of the water.

'The scout had to be familiar with the birds of the region,' continued the plainsman, 'to know those that watered each day, like the dove, and those that lived long without watering, like the Mexican quail. On the Plains, of an evening, he could take the course of the doves as they went off into the breaks to water. But the easiest of all birds to judge from was that known on the Plains as the *dirt-dauber* or swallow. He flew low, and if his mouth was empty he was going to water. He went straight too. If his mouth had mud in it, he was coming straight from water. The scout also had to be able to watch the animals, and from them learn where water was. Mustangs watered daily, at least in the summertime, while antelopes sometimes went for months without water at all. If mustangs were strung out and walking steadily along, they were going to water. If they were scattered, frequently stopping to take a bite of grass, they were coming from water.

'West of the Cross Timbers water became very scarce, and near the Plains extremely bad. Most of it was undrinkable, and the water we could drink had a bad effect on us. At times we suffered exceedingly from thirst, which suffering is the worst torture of all. At night we tossed in a semi-conscious slumber in which we unfortunately dreamed of every spring we ever knew — and such draughts as we would take from them — which invariably awakened us, leaving us, if possible, in even more distress. In my early childhood we had a fine spring near the house under some large oaks. A hollow tree had been provided for a gum, as was common in those days, and was nicely covered with green moss. Many times I have dreamed of seeing that spring and drinking out of it — it would seem so very real!

'Suffering from thirst had a strange and peculiar effect. Every ounce of moisture seemed to be sapped out of the flesh, leaving men and animals haggard and thin, so that one could not recognize them if they had been deprived long.

'Interior recruits had little knowledge of how to take care of themselves in such emergencies. In case of dire thirst, placing a small pebble in the mouth will help, a bullet is better, a piece of copper, if obtainable, is still better, and prickly pear is the best of all. Of course there were no pears on the Plains, but in the prairie country there were many. If, after cutting off the stickers and peeling, you place a piece of the pear in your mouth, it will keep your mouth moist indefinitely. If your drinking water happens to be muddy, peel and place a thin slice of pear in it. All sediment will adhere to it and it will sink to the bottom, leaving the water clear and wholesome.

INTO THE STORM

'After water came the problem of food. The country in which we served was mostly a barren wilderness, and outside of buffaloes had virtually no game. Any frontiersman knows that in a wilderness there are practically no rabbits, as the wolves devour most of them. Consequently, when we were outside the buffalo range there was nothing for us but the prairie dogs, and the only fault we could find with them was that they were too small and very hard to get. I believe that fully half of them, even after their heads were shot off, would fall back in their holes and kick themselves below the first bend, where they couldn't be reached.[4]

'Meat was our main fare. We rarely had bread, but when we did we baked it over the coals on sticks; a forked stick was our

[4] Goodnight, 'Recollections,' ii, 46-47.

skillet. We always tried to keep a little flour on hand to thicken soup, using it for this more than anything else. Prairie dogs were fat and made good soup, but it was not satisfying as one became hungry again in two or three hours. We would boil a prairie dog or two, the more dogs in the kettle the better, and with a little flour make quite a pot of soup. A command could be carried farther with a little flour soup and meat than with anything else.

'We always had plenty of bacon in camp,' Goodnight recalled, 'as the settlers were well supplied with hogs. At the start of a scout, some of the boys would throw away their bacon skins, but I would go around, gather them up and put them in the pack. Some of the men used to laugh at me, but before we got back I'd be broiling those skins and making good meals off of them. Invariably, those who had made fun of me at first would be the ones asking for some of them back.

'Suffering for food is not so intense after the first forty-eight hours. I noticed that tobacco-chewers seemed to feel the hunger less than those who did not use it — it appears that tobacco has a tendency to stay the appetite.'

Besides these qualifications — sense of direction, ability to provide fire, water, game, and shelter — there were others a scout had to have. In order to be 'a proper guide,' as Goodnight expressed it, and a true and efficient plainsman, either in the wilderness then or in a wild country now, the veteran insisted that one must have these further mental and physical qualifications: [5]

'The scout's eyesight must be perfect; he must be able to see as far as any Indian. He must have the faculty of being absolutely cool under all conditions; surprises should not flustrate him. His coolness and presence of mind not only protect himself but those under him. He must be able to decide instantly what to do in cases of emergency. He must be able to judge the

[5] These last observations are reconstructed from my notes; from an unpublished manuscript by J. Frank Dobie, 'Charles Goodnight, Observer and Man'; and primarily from the copy of a very remarkable, undated letter from Goodnight to Mrs. G. A. Brown.

nature of the country ahead of him as far as he can see, and take the way that has the least resistance to his command, keeping out of sight as much as possible — picking the routes that will expose him least to the enemy. He must have the faculty of reading men accurately, and he must have their full confidence — they must have faith in their guide.

'He must have the faculty of not only seeing the tracks and other evidence of the Indians, but a good scout or plainsman must be able to tell how old the tracks are. To do so he must be an accurate judge of temperature and the effect of the sun. If he sees a broken twig, a broken blade of grass, or a bit of weed cut off by a horse's hoof, he must be able to tell how long it has been withering. It is easy to determine whether a track has been made before or after daylight. A track made during the night will be marked over with minute insect tracks. Even on desert sands this is true. By getting down and putting his eye close to the ground, the scout can observe the insect tracks.

'A good plainsman is a good trailer. He can tell whether a horse track has been made by a loose horse, a riderless horse being led, or a horse with a man on him. Suppose I am on the hunt for a man that I know to be riding a bay horse. I find the tracks of a horse carrying a man. But is the horse a bay horse? I follow the tracks until I find where the rider has unsaddled his mount to let him graze. When the saddle is taken off, a horse that has been ridden any distance generally rolls on the ground. I find where the one I am trailing has rolled. I examine the dirt or the grass for hairs. I find a few. Their color tells me whether the horse is bay.

'His hearing must be perfect; not only perfect, but trained to the precision of the operator of the telegraph. To read sounds correctly will have much to do with his ability as a scout, as much of his experience will be in exploring wild and untrodden countries.

'The old-time plainsman, if he was a good one, could detect the most skillful imitation of any animal sound. The Indians often used those imitations to locate themselves at night. But no man's cry of bird or beast could deceive him. The wild turkey may be fooled by a quill; the doe may be deceived by a mechanical bleat; the anxious mother cow may be lured by a cowboy's counterfeit of the calf's bawling; a coon may be drawn from a tree by sounds of coon fighting imitated by some boy. But the trained ear of a plainsman cannot be so deceived. One thing to remember is that the human voice echoes more than any other; in fact, it almost alone of all voices echoes at all. The hoot of an owl will not echo in a cañon anything like an Indian's hooting. The *lobo* wolf's cry will echo more than any other wild animal sound. Of course on the Staked Plains, we do not have this advantage, as there is nothing to create an echo, but in the mountains and cañons and broken country the old Indian warriors I have talked with agree with me that no human can exactly imitate the sound of beast or bird. I realize that this will be doubted, but I will ask you how the operator reads the sounds of the key when they all sound alike to you.'

IV. MINUTE MEN OF TEXAS

BY THE time Sam Houston was called from comparative retirement by his election as governor, Indian raiding of the frontier was the worst it had ever been. Immediately Houston called for Federal troops and supplies, dispatched Texas Rangers to the upper frontier, and authorized organization of Minute Men in the border counties.

Colonel M. T. Johnson and his rangers were stationed at Belknap — from which the regular army troops had been moved about a year before — Houston leaving to his discretion the disposal of warring Indians '*wherever* they may be found and upon whatever soil.'[1] Operating under these generous instructions, Johnson scouted into the Indian Territory, where actually the Texans had no right to go, and there, instead of hunting bad Indians, his men held high carnival by chasing buffaloes, playing poker, and drinking good liquor.[2]

The frontier fretted as *The White Man* declared the project 'the most stupendous *sell* practiced on the frontier people,' and lamented 'to think that all these bright anticipations' should have resulted only in the rangers' 'eating twice their weight in beef at 11 cents per pound, . . . drinking bad water, and cursing the day they were induced to soldier for glory, in a campaign that has resulted in the killing of two citizens, and the marriage of the Col. of the Regiment.'[3]

[1] Houston to Johnson, May 7, 1860, *Executive Record*, State Library, Austin.
[2] Willis Lang, 'Diary, 1860,' University of Texas. Lang was one of Johnson's volunteers.
[3] *The White Man*, September 13, 1860.

Discovering that Johnson seemed 'to have no plan digested for future operation,' Houston removed him in September, and ordered Sul Ross, of Waco, whose father had been agent at the Brazos Reserve, to raise a company of sixty mounted men and repair to the neighborhood of Fort Belknap for service.

MINUTE MEN OF TEXAS

Late in November, 1860, a band of Comanches and Kiowas swung west of Mesquiteville, now Jacksboro, and killed several people. They passed from Lost Valley farther into the settlements, and fifteen miles northwest of Weatherford stole the horses from the ranch of John Brown, killed the owner, 'cut off his nose, and lanced him in every part of the body.'

On their way out to the open country they came to where a man by the name of Sherman had settled on Stagg Prairie, in the western edge of Parker County. Sherman was not a frontiersman, knew nothing about Indians, and did not even have a gun. It was raining heavily as five warriors dismounted, drove the family out, seized Mrs. Sherman, tied her to the ground, violated her, and shot two or three arrows into her body. She lived until next day, giving birth to a dead child.[4] After taking everything from the house, including the family Bible, the Indians proceeded into Loving's Valley and out by the Keechi, gathering horses as they went. About dark one of Goodnight's neighbors rode in to tell him of the raid and report that the Indians were headed west with a large herd of horses.

'I started immediately to warn the neighborhood,' said Goodnight, 'and get together enough men to follow them and make a fight. The rain was falling in torrents and continued to do so all night. I believe it was one of the darkest nights I ever experienced. I knew every tree of note in that neighborhood, and every hill and path, yet I had great difficulty in finding my way from ranch to ranch and back home. I rode all night, telling the men and boys, eight in number, to meet me at Isaac Lynn's at daylight and we would try to cut the Indians off. I got there first.

'The cabins were old-fashioned, double log houses, with a passageway ten or twelve feet wide between, and a gallery on each side. In going into the passageway just at daybreak, I noticed the door into the right-hand cabin was open. On entering, I found Mr. Lynn, sitting before a large log fire in the old-fashioned fireplace, with a long, forked dogwood stick, on which was an Indian scalp, thoroughly salted. The hair was tucked inside. As he turned it carefully over the fire, the grease oozed out of it, and it had drawn up until it looked as thick as a buffalo bull's scalp.

'He looked back over his shoulder, bade me good morning, and then turned to his work of roasting the scalp. I do not think I ever looked upon so sad a face. It was not my intention to annoy him or break his sad thoughts, but my curiosity got the better of me and I asked him what he was trying to do with that infernal scalp. He replied: "The weather's so damp and bad I was a-feared the damn thing would spoil."

'After the murder of the Masons, his daughter and son-in-

---

[4] *The Northern Standard*, December 22, 1860; *Dallas Herald*, December 5, 1860; G. H. Holland, *The Double Log Cabin*, 42.

law, he had a great craving to kill Indians, and asked all of us boys in the neighborhood to bring him the scalps of any Indians we killed. The day before, the boys just northwest of me had got into an Indian fight and got the scalp for him. They took the entire scalp, which must have been off of a rather prominent Indian, as I noticed three tiny silver bells tied in the hair. There were probably other bells in it, but I did not care to annoy the old gentleman for further examination.

'It was still raining, but we struck out in a westerly direction aiming to intercept the trail of the Indians, who had taken a northwest course from Loving's Valley. We followed the trail all day, passed through the Western Cross Timbers, and were some miles west, in the open country, when night overtook us. We appeared to be very close on their trail, as we had ridden faster than they could with the large herd of horses — about a hundred and fifty head.

'Just as dark overtook us, we came into the main drift of the buffaloes, making trailing more difficult. But at daybreak we took the trail again with all speed practicable, and by dark we had reached Pease River, a few miles above where Vernon now stands. The Indians continued up the river in a westerly direction. They seemed to have driven all night, as the trail at sundown was not as fresh as it was the evening before. It was their custom, in going out, especially, to scatter their herds when striking gravel or hard ground to make trailing as difficult as possible. But now, beyond where they thought white men would follow, they had quit all such precautions and were driving in a body. Still we had not got west of the buffalo herd. We reasoned we could not catch them before they would reach large bodies of their own people, which would make it folly for us to attempt an attack, which reasoning afterward proved correct.'

The trailers had nothing to eat, except what they could shoot, and of course no bedding, and, upon considering the condition of their horses, decided to return to the Keechi Valley. Their report probably led to the Ross Expedition.

A total of twenty-three persons had been reported killed in the raids, and the atrocious nature of the killings struck terror into everyone not inured to border life. A native ranchman reported that

> The most intense excitement and dire alarm pervades the whole country. Men, women, and children may be seen hurrying on horseback, on foot, and in sleighs to Camp Cooper and Weatherford; leaving behind their homes and property, unguarded and exposed to the ruthless hand of savage invasion.
>
> The entire settlement west of Weatherford have fled to the interior, and it . . . is left the extreme frontier post.

Caravans headed east. Ranchmen moved their families into the settlements, and before a month had passed one traveler reported having seen more than a hundred deserted houses and farms.

While Goodnight was scouting, his neighbors were flocking to old Jack Cureton, and organizing for a thorough campaign into the Indian country. The company moved out on the frontier and camped near Belknap, receiving recruits until it numbered seventy. On the thirteenth of December, 1860, Cureton was joined by forty-seven rangers under Ross, and twenty-three dragoons from Camp Cooper under an Irish sergeant named Spangler. At last they were ready to march, to fall in upon the old trail Goodnight and his party had abandoned nearly two weeks before.[5]

The country toward the escarpments of the Plains was practically unknown, but 'because of my slight knowledge of the western territory,' Goodnight modestly explained, 'I was designated by Cureton as scout and guide.' Behind the scouts came Ross's rangers, then Cureton's volunteers, and then the pack-mules. The cavalcade rode on through the bitter cold of the open country by day, and wrapped in blankets and buffalo robes shivered about frugal fires by night. On they marched, through thousands of buffaloes, until Goodnight cut the sign of the raiding party, which he easily did in spite of its age, as the ground had been muddy when the sign was made.

Upon the evening of the eighteenth, Cureton camped on the south side of Pease River, while Ross's rangers and the regulars crossed over and camped on the north bank. The rangers and dragoons, better trained and disciplined than Cureton's cowmen and settlers, broke camp and got off ahead of them next morning. Cureton's command then got started and continued on the Indian trail, which Ross had intercepted again about a mile up the valley.

The guide carried a man to keep course for the command while he explored ahead, for which purpose Goodnight had chosen a ranchman and lawyer by the name of William Mosely. Before they struck the trail where Ross had intercepted it, Goodnight picked up Mrs. Sherman's Bible, where it had been dropped by the Indians. It had fallen with the lids closed and was undamaged by the rain.

'The Indians knew as well as we did,' explained Goodnight, 'the resistance paper had against bullets. It offered more resistance than anything to be had upon the frontier unless it was cotton. When they robbed houses they invariably took all the books they could find, using the paper to pack their shields,

[5] According to the reminiscent account of one of Ross's men, travelers from Fort Cobb, in the Territory, reported an Indian camp on the Pease, which report reached Ross and resulted in his preparations for the scout. J. A. Rickard, MS. of interview with B. F. Gholson, Archives, University of Texas.

which were made of a circular bow of wood two or three feet across, over each side of which was drawn the toughest and thickest untanned hide of a buffalo's neck. They filled between the hide with paper.'

After picking up the Bible, Goodnight noticed some chittam trees in the sand hills south of the river, a tree bearing a berry distasteful to whites but liked by Indians. Knowing their fondness for this fruit, Goodnight told Mosely to keep the course and he would ride to the grove and see if Indians had been there. Immediately he saw fresh signs indicating they had not been gone over ten minutes, and could hardly have been more than out of sight. Their trail led west.

The waters of the Pease were salty and gyppy, but Goodnight knew that just ahead Mule Creek, a fresh-water stream, entered the river from the south. He concluded that the Indians were camped on this creek, and immediately loped out on the edge of the sand hills, in sight of Cureton's command, and signaled the Captain, without knowing that Ross had already discovered the camp.

'We went pell-mell up the river,' he recalled, 'of course following Ross's trail. I suppose we went a mile or a mile and a half before we came to where this creek entered the Pease. A short distance from the river a row of sand hills intersected the course of the creek, and just south of these the Indians were camped. They had packed and were ready to leave, but did not see Ross until he topped the hill, not over one hundred and fifty or two hundred yards away. He charged at once, ordering the Sergeant to deploy to the right to cut the Indians off from the sand hills along the river.

'From the creek to the foot of the first hills to the west was about a mile and a half of perfectly level ground, as smooth and as naked as a floor, as the buffaloes had eaten off the grass. The Indians apparently lost their heads when they saw Ross's command so close. Instead of going into the sand hills, they crossed the creek twice, where it made some short bends, then struck a bee-line for the foothills with Ross and his men after them. The rangers passed through the squaws and shot the bucks as they came to them. The Sergeant and his men fell in behind on the squaws, whose horses were loaded so heavily with buffalo meat, tent poles, and camp equipage that they could not run, and killed every one of them, almost in a pile. One proved to be Chief Nocona's second wife, a Spanish woman he had captured. She was seriously wounded and crawled off through the high grass to the bank of the creek, the only spot the buffaloes had not eaten clean.

'When we topped the sand hills, we were in plain sight of the ensuing battle. I remember looking back to see how many of our party were up. There were only six or eight of the fast horses and the Captain. The rest were strung out fully a mile down the river; a sight I shall never forget. Instead of seeming to be eighty men, they looked like a regiment. With their tin cups, pans, and guns glistening in the bright sun they made a thrilling sight which was very impressive. I regret to say that there were some good horses behind, but probably the riders' appetites were not craving lead. Seven or eight of us were on the field before the fight ended, but not in time to take part in it.

'The fight, which lasted only a few minutes, continued on the plain until all the Indians were killed. Ross had a hand-to-hand fight with the chief and killed him. One of the squaws was riding a good iron-gray horse, and in spite of the fact that she had an infant in her arms, kept up with the six or eight bucks. I understand that Ross ordered one of his rangers, Tom Kelliher,[6] to take charge of her, fearing, I suppose, that the regulars would come upon her, as they had the others, and kill her. To the credit of the old Texas rangers, not one of them shot a squaw that day. The Sergeant in charge of the military squad probably did not know them from bucks and probably did not care.

'After the fight we all returned to a cottonwood grove along the river to camp, taking with us the squaw and her infant in

[6] Willis Lang's 'Diary' gives this spelling. Ross reported the child as one year of age.

arms. We rode right over her dead companions. I thought then and still think how exceedingly cruel this was.

'When we reached the timber where the Indians had been camped, we had as captives the woman and a little Comanche boy, whom Ross picked up during the fight and set up on his horse behind him. The Indians could get more out of their

horses than anybody, and in hard runs to get away they would throw off their bridles, moccasins, and everything of any weight — even their children. Before Ross caught up with the chief, he pushed this little boy off on the ground. No doubt Ross picked him up to save his life, though by that time our squad of seven or eight men had passed the regulars and would have saved him had Ross not done so.[7]

[7] Unfortunately, there seems to be no contemporary report by Ross. Years later he wrote an account that Goodnight claimed was erroneous in many details. The supposition that he had killed Nocona was an example. Goodnight's memories, though set down long after those of Ross, clarify a few hitherto obscure points. See Rickard, 'Ben F. Gholson'; Francis M. Peveler to J. E. H., October 14, 1932; and Goodnight to J. E. H., November 13, 1926. Baker gave a detailed account of the fight, evidently elaborating his original diary from memory in later years.

'The squaw was in terrible grief. Through sympathy for her, thinking her distress would be the same as that of our women under similar circumstances, I thought I would try to console her and make her understand that she would not be hurt. When I got near her I noticed that she had blue eyes and light hair, which had been cut short.[8] It was a little difficult to distinguish her blonde features, as her face and hands were extremely dirty from handling so much meat.

'After speaking a few words to her, I turned back to the creek, where there was great excitement over the fight, came in contact with Judge R. W. Pollard, and told him we had captured a white woman. His reply was "No!"'

'"Go see for yourself," I said.

'He did, and in five minutes it had been reported among the entire crowd. I do not believe that anyone knew until then that she was white, though I never verified this statement with Governor Ross.[9] Her grief was distressing and intense, and I shall never forget the impression it made on me. I think here Ross got the impression that he had killed her husband, Nocona, as she was saying a great deal about Nocona, meaning, however, that she was in the Nocona band of Indians, a word which, as I understand, means to go, ramble, and not make friends.'

Ross seems to have always believed that he killed Nocona, and history has so recorded since. He did kill a chief whose name was No-bah, but Nocona died a long time afterwards while hunting plums on the Canadian.[10]

---

[8] 'The Comanche squaws cut their hair as a token of grief when any of their family was killed. When I came to the Palo Duro and established my ranch in 1876, I found enough of their hair to make cinches.'

[9] Ross claims that he recognized her as a white woman even before Kelliher had herded her back to camp. J. T. De Shields, *Cynthia Ann Parker*, 65.

[10] George Hunt to C. Goodnight, March 28, 1927.

The first account of the battle appeared in the *Dallas Herald*, December 23, 1860. In the issue of January 30, 1861, the captive was reported as the niece of Isaac Parker. See also the issue of February 6, 1861.

Baker's account reads: 'When the squaws attempted to get on the horses with them the bucks pushed them off and rode away. One of his men had his gun leveled at the

Ross carried his captives and some forty head of Indian ponies back to his permanent camp on Elm Creek, west of Belknap. Failing in numerous efforts to escape, the woman became sullen and morose. With the supposition that she might be the long-lost Cynthia Ann, Ross sent word for

CYNTHIA ANN

Colonel Isaac Parker to come out and attempt to identify the woman, and for Ben Kiggins, a ransomed Indian captive, to do the interpreting. Kiggins reached camp first. When Colonel Parker arrived, Kelliher accompanied him to the captive's tent.

'Colonel, it appears to me that the last thing she would remember of her home life would be the name that her family called her,' ventured Kelliher.

'I do know well that my brother and his wife called her Cynthia Ann,' replied the Colonel.

prisoner, when she cried "Don't shoot, me Mericana." Tonight Dec. 19th as we sat about the campfire, a discussion arose as to her identity, and . . . someone remarked that years ago a family by the name of Parker had been killed . . . and a child Cynthia Ann Parker had been carried off. At once the woman spoke up and said, "Me Cynthia Ann." ' Baker, 'Diary,' 209–11. Apparently Baker elaborated his original account of the incidents after time had confused their sequence. This statement seems in error.

The woman bestirred herself and Parker repeated the statement. She arose, faced him, patted herself and said: 'Me Cincee Ann.' Her answer caused considerable commotion, and after talking with her awhile, Kiggins turned to the others:

'She says that she much regrets it, but it is a fact that she had a paleface pa and a paleface ma, and they had a name for her, and that name was Cincee Ann. She says that now, though, she has a redman pa and a redman ma, and they have a name for her, and this name is Palux.'[11]

Then she described Parker's Fort, on the Navasota, where Comanches and Caddos massacred her people in 1836, and from where she and others were carried into captivity.[12]

Prairie Flower, the little girl she had carried beneath the folds of her great buffalo robe, soon died. Cynthia Ann was sent to relatives in the piney region of Texas, where she was oppressed by a strange terrain as well as crowded by strange people. No longer of the race of the hated *Tejanos*, she yearned for the treeless Plains where Nocona and her sons still hunted the buffalo, and sinking with grief and loneliness, she died, apparently of a broken heart, in 1864 — an expatriate among people of her own blood. Her tragic story is a part of the Texas tradition.[13]

Ross reported that he had killed all the Indians in the band,

[11] Other accounts give the name as 'Preloch.' De Shields, as cited, 73.

[12] Rickard, 'B. F. Gholson,' as cited.

A literature has grown up around the tragedy of Cynthia Ann Parker. For accounts of her capture see H. Yoakum, *History of Texas*, II, 170; John Henry Brown, *Indian Wars and Pioneers of Texas*, 39–42; J. T. De Shields, *Cynthia Ann Parker*; and Rachel Plummer, *Narration of the Perilous Adventures*, etc.

In 1852, Captain Marcy reported that her brother had been ransomed, and sent back after Cynthia Ann, who refused to leave the tribe. R. B. Marcy, *Exploration of the Red River of Louisiana*, U.S. Senate Ex. Doc. 32d Congress, 2d Session, No. 54, p. 103. Other sources controvert this statement, and it seems unlikely that John Parker was ever ransomed. There is a story that he was deserted by the Indians while sick with smallpox, was nursed by a Mexican captive girl, recovered, went to Mexico, married the girl, and settled to life below the Rio Grande. De Shields, as cited, 27–29, and Thrall, *Pictorial History of Texas*, 455–56.

[13] Years later her son Quanah, then a chieftain of the Comanches, removed her body to rest in Oklahoma, and the Texas Legislature appropriated money for a monument to her memory.

but Cureton, knowing the country and the Indians, was dubious. Besides, he was fretting because he had failed to get into the fight.

'I don't believe Ross got all of them,' he said to Goodnight, after Ross pulled out. 'I never jumped on a band yet but what some escaped. You take a man or two, go out and cut sign, and see if his statement is correct.'

Goodnight took William Cranmer and rode west of the battle-ground. They parted, one cutting for sign to the north, the other to the south. Goodnight had ridden but a hundred yards when he struck the trail of two ponies leisurely ridden westward. He signaled Cranmer and they followed the trail to the top of a mesa, where, according to the sign, the two riders had stopped upon hearing the shots, and watched the fight below. Then they broke their horses into a run, throwing away all extra equipment to lighten the loads. Goodnight picked up the stuff the Indians had discarded, returned to camp, and reported two scouts had escaped to the west.

'They are going directly to another band,' Cureton said. 'Take your scout and follow them up, and I'll rest the men and horses until you return.'

Goodnight took ten men and left on the trail. They carried no salt — for they had none in camp — no provisions, and no blankets. At night they camped on the prairie, hobbled and side-lined their horses, and slept on their saddle blankets. They planned to eat if the country furnished meat; they would go hungry if it did not. A bitter storm had come on, the buffaloes were to the south, and as it turned out, they fasted until they got back. The next afternoon, fifty or sixty miles from camp, they entered the head of a cañon that coursed westwardly to join the South Pease, and, as they rode down it, commenced finding exhausted ponies, by ones and twos and threes, and near its mouth fifteen or twenty in a bunch.

'"Look out, fellows," said the guide, "hell's going to be a-poppin' pretty soon. We're close to them." And a few minutes later, they came in sight of the main camp on the South Pease.

'Fortunately, the Indians had not seen us approaching. There were approximately a thousand Indians here, and it appeared they were breaking camp. I later learned that when the two guides reached the main body of Indians, they reported there were ten thousand of us, and we did look like a regiment, strung out as we were with our tin cups glistening in the sun. As soon as they could get ready, they moved back north, and wintered from the Washita to the Wichita Mountains, suffering much for want of provisions, as they were entirely north of the buffalo.'

Goodnight and his men hurried back into the cañon and took refuge in a sharp bend, where the rush of seasonal floods had undercut the bluff, forming excellent protection. Here they hid until dark, knowing full well there would be no chance in event of discovery.

'Up to that time,' Goodnight concluded the story, 'I had never believed that tale about the sun standing still for Joshua's battle. But that experience made a believer out of me. The sun certainly poked that day.'

As soon as the long dark shadows flowed out of the cañons across the slopes, they struck a lively gait for Cureton's camp. On Christmas Eve, four days after their departure, they rode in to report, and the news they brought caused concern. In the heart of Indian country, with no grass for their worn-out horses, no food for days past except that taken from the Indians, forces reduced from a hundred and sixty-five to hardly half as many, and dissension among the remnant, Cureton wisely decided to turn back.

Back from their expedition to the foot of the Plains, Cureton's and Ross's men found the settlements still seething with excitement. Buck Barry and Tom Stockton had already been commissioned to raise companies of frontiersmen, and *The White Man* averred that 'two better rangers are not on the frontier.'[14]

'Jack' Baylor, as the frontier knew the belligerent old

[14] *Dallas Herald*, January 2, 1861. See Greer, *Buck Barry, Texas Ranger*, 125.

Colonel, was in charge of two hundred and fifty men who set out in January, 1861. With grim facetiousness, the frontier alluded to them as 'buffalo hunters.' They left in high spirits, Baylor leading them westward to strike the Pease, apparently in his search of the trail Goodnight had discovered a month before. His horses suffered severely in the alkali country, and soon were drawn 'gaunt as hounds' from crossing a hundred miles of range eaten clean by buffaloes. Tom Stockton, scout and guide, did not go to the old camp and take the trail from there, but cut southwestward toward the head of the Colorado. Most of the buffaloes were farther south, and the wily Indians farther north. The expedition, hungry and half afoot, straggled back down the Wichita and into the settlements, where the 'buffalo hunt' was reported upon by Baylor, the 'Colonel, Commanding Anti-Base Line Rangers.'[15]

There was one hero for even this story of utter failure. Upon this scout went Isaac Lynn, the breeder of good horses, but walking, as usual, and burning with lust for a terrible vengeance upon the murderers of the Masons. He carried his rifle across his shoulder, walked to the source of the Pease and scouted the butts of the Plains to the breaks of the Colorado, never mounted even to ford the icy streams. Horses played out and were left behind, and men half-starved upon scant rations of buffalo meat, but old man Lynn, spurred by consuming bitterness, hunted with a zeal born of blood and nurtured by hate, and walked back to his ranch on the Keechi, apparently none the worse for several hundred miles of starving and scouting. In that day of horses and horsemen he was deserving of scalps.

In the meantime the Union was broken. The Secession Convention met at Austin on January 28, and almost at once General Twiggs surrendered Federal posts, arms, and munitions in Texas.

Upon his surrender the military situation immediately

---

[15] *Dallas Herald*, February 27, 1861; *The Standard*, March 23, 1861. Baker, 'Diary,' 247.

passed into the hands of three colonels designated by the Convention, 'Old Rip' Ford, Ben McCulloch, and his brother, Henry E. McCulloch. The frontier was divided into three sectors, the first of which, on the south, was assigned to Ford, the second, extending from near Fort Duncan north to Fort Chadbourne, went to Ben McCulloch, and the northern district, extending to Red River, was placed under his brother. Later, the middle and northern districts were combined under Henry McCulloch,[16] who had already taken charge of Camps Colorado and Cooper.

McCulloch placed Buck Barry and forty men at Camp Cooper, and authorized a patrol of a hundred men between there and Red River. The Secession Convention authorized each of the thirty-seven frontier counties to organize companies of not more than forty Minute Men, with patrols in constant action, while L. P. Walker, Confederate Secretary of War, commissioned Ben McCulloch to raise a regiment of mounted men. He passed the charge on to his brother, and companies of mounted volunteers were organized and sent to posts at Camp Colorado, Fort Chadbourne, and Camp Cooper.[17]

In April, Colonel Earl Van Dorn assumed command in Texas, and late in May issued an order establishing two military lines so extended as to be impossible of defense. The first, reaching from the junction of the Conchos to Red River, opposite Forts Cobb and Arbuckle, was to be under the command of Henry McCulloch and the first regiment of Texas Mounted Riflemen. The second line, under Rip Ford, extended from Fort Bliss by Forts Stockton and Lancaster to Camp Wood.[18]

Early in May, Colonel William C. Young led some two

---

[16] W. C. Holden, 'Frontier Defense in Texas During the Civil War,' *West Texas Historical Association Yearbook*, 1928, IV, 16–19; *Dallas Herald*, February 27 and March 6 and 20, 1861.

[17] Holden, as cited, 18–19; Greer, *Buck Barry, Texas Ranger*, 127–29; H. E. McCulloch to James B. Barry, March 27, 1861, Barry Papers.

[18] Caroline S. Ruckman, 'The Frontier of Texas During the Civil War,' 19–20, 34–36; *The Northern Standard*, June 16, 1861.

thousand Texans across Red River to take charge of Forts Arbuckle, Cobb, and Washita, and begin peace negotiations with the reserve Indians. The Confederacy sent Albert Pike as commissioner, and Henry McCulloch and Ed Burleson crossed the river to facilitate negotiations. Treaties were made with some of the tribes, but many of the wild Indians had already fled. McCulloch decided to strike into the Indian country to treat with them for peace with Texas and the Confederacy. He took twelve or fifteen men, and, with Goodnight as guide, rode north and west from Belknap. In the Buck Creek country of the Panhandle, north of Red River, he found the Indians in camp, following the drift of the buffalo, and met Satank and Satanta, the notorious Kiowa leaders, and Lone Wolf, Red Bear, and Eagle Chief, of the Comanches.

But according to Goodnight: 'The Comanches flatly refused to join the Confederacy, saying we Texans were heap rich in cattle and horses, and that they preferred to fight us and steal from us and trade to Mexico — which they did. We were at the Indian camp only a day and night — there was no use staying with the buggers.'

By the middle of March, some semblance of quiet was enjoyed by the frontier, and hundreds of settlers were returning to their homes, planting crops, and again tending their cattle. Yet there was grave fear of war, and the Overland Trail was crowded with caravans bound to California, getting away from the South. By June the Overland Mail had stopped, and there was agitation for private service from North Texas to Fort Smith, Arkansas.[19]

In spite of the defense lines, there were, in the fall of 1861, numerous complaints to Governor Edward Clark of the 'great number of Indian depredations.' While always joining in pursuit of those raiders striking the Belknap country, Goodnight had not yet joined the forces, but was working on

[19] *Dallas Herald*, March 13, May 27, and June 12, 1861; *The Northern Standard*, June 1, 1861.

the Keechi range. An accident delayed his entering the service. About a year before, a small farmer had sold out and left the country. Sheek and Goodnight bought his hogs, and in the fall, after the hogs had fattened on the mast, went over and killed what they needed for meat. By the fall of 1861, the

PLAINS WARRIORS

others had turned wild, but the young men took their dogs and returned to lay in another supply of pork. In the course of the hunt they jumped a large hog, and quickly, according to Goodnight:

'The dogs brought him to bay and caught him by the ears. I got up first, aiming to shoot him, but thought the bullet would go through him and kill the dog on the other side. I then stepped directly in front of him, but he made such a sudden, unexpected lunge that he jerked loose from the dogs, struck my right leg just above the ankle, and cut it to the bone for about seven inches up. The dogs caught him again and at the same time I shot him in the head, killing him instantly.'

Goodnight rode home in the ox-wagon that was brought for the meat. While he was on crutches, a call was made for volunteers, and many of his neighbors went into the Confederate army. Though much opposed to war himself, Goodnight would have gone, too, had he been able. While convalescing, 'I had much time to think,' he said, 'and I decided that if I was going to fight I had better fight to defend our homes.'

As soon as he could ride, he and Alf Lane, his brother-in-law, went to Belknap to join the Frontier Regiment, for which a call had just been made.

With the Confederacy too busy to defend the frontier, the Legislature saw that more permanent organization was needed. On December 21, 1861, a law was passed creating the famous Frontier Regiment of ten companies of rangers, to be stationed along the front from Brownsville to Red River, and discontinuing the Minute Men after the first of March.

Governor F. R. Lubbock appointed Colonel James M. Norris, of Waco, to its command. Many seasoned old Indian fighters on the outer edge, beyond the plantation and slave-holding regions, being less enthusiastic over secession than Texans to the east, decided as did Goodnight and Lane. Captain Jack Cureton immediately went into the service and settled down to fight Indians for the period of the war.

Norris placed half of Goodnight's company at Camp Cureton, on the Trinity, and the other half remained in camp near Belknap. Throughout most of the war, Goodnight was to be located at the old army post. By March, 1862, Cureton's company was well organized; in April he had one hundred and twelve men, and J. A. Hall and Joe A. Woolfork became first and second lieutenants. The 'cream of the frontier' joined, and the company was sworn in at Belknap by J. W. Trockmorton.[20]

To the south, Captain John Salmon's company occupied Camp Breckenridge, upon Gunsolus Creek, and about a day's ride below was another camp, and so the line ran into the south until it abutted against Mexico, station after station

[20] J. J. Cureton, 'Monthly Return,' April, 1862; Oath, May 10, 1862, Adjutant General's Office; Goodnight, 'Recollections,' II, 29.

for Indian fighting men. It was a line much shorter than that laid out by Van Dorn, and constituted the first chain of defense since the Federal troops had been withdrawn.

Only nine companies were enlisted, but with 1089 men the line from end to end was to be patrolled at least every other day. Along this patrol the rangers were to report any ingoing Indian trail, and arouse the forces up and down the line, while a party pursued the Indians. It was not a sure defense, for raiders sometimes came into the settlements on foot, leaving no trail for a jogging horseman to catch, and, once mounted on fresh horses inside, cut loose their hounds of war and hell and hit a high lope for the open country. Not often were they caught.[21]

Accompanying Norris upon his first survey of the line of defense were Lieutenant-Colonel A. T. Obenchain and Major J. E. McCord. Norris was not a fighting man and was a misfit in the service. McCord, located at Camp Colorado, rarely if ever came north. Though Obenchain wished an active part in handling the regiment — particularly Cureton's company — Cureton himself was the strength of the northwest fringe, being referred to as the 'Jack Hays of the frontier.' Goodnight described him as 'a splendid frontiersman who had no military training except what he had picked up. But he was a fine man, an excellent Indian fighter, and a very popular commander.'

The organization was effected, and when Cureton left the settlements and headed into Indian country, in advance of his column scouted Charlie Goodnight, straight, slim, and strong. Across the fork of his saddle swung his fine long rifle, and engraved upon its barrel was this appropriate sentiment: '*Seek ye first the kingdom of God and His righteousness, and all these things shall be added unto you.*' But at which end of the gun did the legend apply?

[21] Holden, as cited, 19–21.

V. SCOUTING UNDER OBENCHAIN

At the outbreak of the Civil War the frontier line was receding before the fierce assaults of the Indians. With abandonment of the most distant ranches, Fort Belknap was again thrown upon the extreme frontier. Notwithstanding the fact that it had been vacated by the Federal troops since 1857, it was still a strategic point in the protection of the northwest border. Its location above the muddy waters of the Brazos was admirable, and its substantial red sandstone buildings were suitable for a permanent camp. A few settlers still lived about the post when, late in March, 1862, Cureton made it the main camp for Company B of the Frontier Regiment.[1] One detachment was located on Hubbard Creek, thirty to forty miles south, and another about an equal distance to the northeast. Captain Joe Ward's Company, near Victoria Peaks, extended the line of defense to Red River.

Lieutenant-Colonel A. T. Obenchain, having some longing for actual fighting, came to Belknap and took charge of Cureton's forces, to the chagrin of the old rangers, and in spite of his good intentions, to the detriment of the service. He was a Virginian and a man of prominence, born in Buchanan County, February 11, 1824. In 1853 he came overland by ox-team and settled in Rusk County, two years later moved to Weatherford, taught the village school, and in time was elected to the Legislature. In partnership with B. L. Richey, he bought *The White Man* in October, 1860, and published it

[1] J. J. Cureton, 'Monthly Return,' Company B, Frontier Regiment, April, 1862, in Adjutant General's Office, Austin, Texas.

until December, 1861, when the office was destroyed by fire. After participation in the Secession Convention he was commissioned second in command of the far-flung Frontier Regiment.[2] He was a man of commanding presence, over six feet in height, well-proportioned, and so very dark that he was wont to boast that he bore Indian blood — that he was 'a descendant of Pocahontas.'

'He must have got the command because there was nobody else to get for an officer,' said Goodnight. 'He had no idea of frontier service and would give the scout enough work in one day to do for two. We did not pretend to obey orders. We would get out of his sight and do the best we could.

'Cureton was popular with the regiment, but Obenchain had to be military and put on all sorts of dog that we were not used to. He was tyrannical and arrogant, and straightway assumed unfitting military airs about which he merely had read, and to which the frontier men were unaccustomed. He openly and continually stated that an officer should never associate or be familiar with his men, and kept himself entirely aloof except to give us tyrannical orders.'[3]

By the very nature of the men, Cureton and Obenchain seemed destined to clash. Their trouble was more than the conflict of two personalities; it was rather the conflict of two systems of social life and conduct. Obenchain did not understand the frontier nor its men. Cureton knew the land to its very grass roots and belonged there.

Cureton moved his family to Belknap to occupy one of the large abandoned buildings at the fort. He had slaves and hence plenty of domestic help, so that a few of the rangers, when in camp, boarded at his home and enjoyed the welcome change from cooking their own food on forked sticks.

Soon a general order came that no families should live at the ranger camps, and Obenchain read it and sent it to Cureton by

[2] H. Smythe, *Historical Sketch of Parker County*, 141; Goodnight, 'Recollections,' II, 28; Francis M. Peveler to J. E. H., August 6, 1932.

[3] Goodnight, 'Recollections,' II, 36–37: Goodnight to J. E. H., August 2, 1928.

Lieutenant Woolfork. Cureton refused to move his family, and Obenchain ordered the men to stop boarding at his house, which so aroused their animosity that Rex Stockton and Tude Whatley openly quarreled with him.

Lieutenant Joseph A. Woolfork, ranking company officer under the Captain, and perhaps the only friend Obenchain had in camp, was a little, peppery, white-bearded lawyer from Kentucky, who suffered some unpopularity in his own right.

Several months after mustering of the company, he led a small scouting party into the prairie country, and when they turned back toward the settlements the men were starving badly. Upon reaching the Big Wichita a number scattered to hunt. Dick Jowell, Tom Pollard, Dr. J. P. Vollintine, physician for Cureton's company, Goodnight, and Simpson Crawford all struck out in search of game.

During the evening Vollintine came to a grove of wild china, and killed two deer browsing upon the bitter, amber berries. Elsewhere, Goodnight and Crawford saw two poor old buffaloes coming in to water. From behind a ledge within range of the trail, the scout killed one of the stragglers as he came ambling along, but let the other go. 'An old poor buffalo that could barely get out of your way,' he explained, 'was mighty hard to eat. We could eat the tenderloins, the tongue — which wasn't good — and sometimes the seeds.' After cutting out these parts the two made their way back to camp. Soon the long shadows deepened to darkness, but neither Pollard nor Jowell appeared. 'Pollard was an engineer and Jowell had been raised on the frontier, and together they got lost.'

Next morning Goodnight reported to Woolfork and asked permission to hunt them. Woolfork refused, saying that they should have kept up with the scout, and when Goodnight answered that he would go anyway, Woolfork threatened court-martial for disobedience of orders.

'Court-martial and be damned,' replied Goodnight as he set out in search of the missing men. During the day he brought them into camp, and except for slight enmity between him and Woolfork, history discloses no other results.

Feeling between Obenchain and Cureton continued to grow until, on the fifth of June, 1862, Obenchain placed the Captain under arrest for insubordination, and pending the calling of a general court-martial, prepared for an Indian expedition. He took a large scout of some fifty men and struck southwest, bent upon showing these Texans how to fight. With Goodnight as guide he headed his men up the Elm, traveling on to where its upper reaches extended out into the level plain, and where there was water only at occasional holes.

'When I came to the last one,' remarked Goodnight, 'being nearly sundown, I halted until the command reached me. I was approached by Colonel Obenchain, who was in the lead and who asked me, in an indignant manner, why I had stopped. I told him I thought perhaps he would want to camp there, as it was the last water hole we would find until we reached the Double Mountain Fork of the Brazos. He asked me the distance. I told him that it was probably fifteen or twenty miles, and said: "You see that round peak in the distance. It is about five miles this side of the Double Mountain Fork."

'With an oath he declared the distance could not be more than eight miles, and ordered me to go on and not halt until he gave me a signal, which I did.

'In coming across the plateau he threw out flank guards on each side of the command, which seemed preposterous to us old rangers, as one could see for miles on either side. An old Irish soldier, who had served many years in the United States Army, was ordered to the south of the command, and a Belknap citizen by the name of Williams to the north. As night came this Irishman fell in line, but Williams, being either afraid to come in or not knowing enough to do so, did not.

'As dark approached, I fell back to the lead of the column. I presume we reached the breaks of the Double Mountain Fork about eleven o'clock, finding, in a small dry lake, some buffalo tracks filled with water, as it had rained just before we reached the place. Colonel Obenchain dismounted and sucked up enough of the water to satisfy his thirst and ordered camp.

'After encamping I took some of the men and all the canteens and went down to the river for water, bringing back enough for the rest of the men. But Obenchain did not know this.

'At daybreak the command moved across the Double Mountain Fork to a spring on the north side, a mile or two from the river, where I knew there was water, wood, and grass. There we halted for breakfast. Williams had not appeared yet. I was then ordered to take a squad and go in search of him, which I did, bringing him into camp about noon.

'Obenchain insisted on having roll call. Williams was supposed to be the bugler, but at our last encampment he said he could not blow the horn, and handed it over to me. I blew it, all right, then threw it into the water hole, and thus ended the roll call. Next morning Williams said he had lost the horn, which was quite a relief to me, but many years afterward I found it in a valley where it had been washed out by the water, and it made me feel sorter guilty.'

Somewhere Obenchain had secured a Melish map, made,

Goodnight always suspected, 'by a Frenchman who had never seen Texas.' This map showed the North and South Canadians as the Red River and the Brazos. It did not show the Pease or the Wichita, but the Colonel seemed to place implicit faith in it, consequently discounting everyone's knowledge of the topography. Hence the map caused much confusion and no end of trouble for Goodnight.[4]

The command continued a west-southwest course for nearly a hundred miles, two to three days' march, until it struck the high blue ridge that divides the muddy waters of the Colorado from the salty stream of the Brazos. As it came up on the Staked Plains the sky was mottled with thunderheads, the plain below was freckled with their drifting shadows, and on the horizon appeared the most elusive of all drifting things, the High Plains mirages. They danced between earth and heaven in infinite heat waves, distorting everything that passed into them, and flowing, more gently than quicksilver, from one vast lake into another, always just beyond.

And there maneuvering in dangerous fashion, Obenchain discovered his first Indians. He stopped, signaled Goodnight back from his regular position and asked him what the objects were. The scout informed him that they were antelopes.

'Being dubious, as usual,' Goodnight observed, 'he declared they were Indians on horseback, as in the meantime he and some of his raw recruits, who had never seen the Plains before, who knew nothing about the service, and had joined merely to escape the Confederate conscript, had been studying them through his spyglass. They all agreed that they were Indians, horseback.

'Some of these recruits were mounted on very poor horses, in contrast with those of the old frontiersmen, or rangers proper, whose mounts were owned individually and were the very best the country could afford.

'The Colonel was quite aware of this fact, of course, and I

[4] Melish's map of 1819 figured in the Texas–United States boundary treaty. Sam Houston to Wm. H. Russell, April 29, 1860. *Executive Record Book*, 1859–61, Austin.

shall never forget the order he gave us after he had formed us in line for the charge.

' "American stock, full speed! Spanish stock, half speed! Charge!" which we did, the old-timers roaring with laughter. And furthermore we put the bunch of antelopes to flight without the loss of a man.

'We had gone only about five miles farther when the same thing happened again, and again we succeeded in routing the antelopes without loss or injury.'

After the second charge, Obenchain continued westward upon the Plains, by a course that would have kept his men without water for days. Men had died of thirst in that shimmering land, and in the sand hills beyond, and yet others were to feel the terrible agonies of its thirst and the mockeries of its mirages.[5] Obenchain consulted his map, which indicated a well-watered country ahead, and abruptly ordered Goodnight to take his position in the lead and not come back unless he was called. Good plainscraft dictated that the scout should never be so far in advance of the column that he could not be signaled back, but Goodnight knew there was a vast, waterless land before them, and some ruse must be managed to escape the Colonel's stubbornness. Gradually he increased his lead until he was out of calling distance, and then little by little he bore to the north, slowly drawing toward the Yellow Houses, or *Casas Amarillas*,[6] a high bluff in which were some caves, so called because of their color, and their resemblance to a city

[5] The outstanding example of a mismanaged expedition in the South Plains country was that of Captain Nicholas Nolan, in 1878. He followed an Indian trail into the sands southwest of where Lubbock now stands, and, in spite of the fact that he had a number of buffalo hunters with him, came near losing his negro troopers. See John R. Cook, *The Border and the Buffalo*, 259–85. In 1879, Captain G. W. Arrington, of the Texas Rangers, led a party into the same country in mid-winter, but, seasoned frontiersmen that they were, they experienced great difficulty in getting out. *Panhandle-Plains Historical Review*, 1928, pp. 61–65; 1934, pp. 56–62.

[6] The Yellow Houses were a noted landmark of the Llano Estacado. Near a large basin of the Plains, in which were two salt lakes, rose a high bluff, at the foot of which was a small hole of brackish water. In 1875, Colonel W. B. Shafter reported two dug springs at the foot of the bluff. Thrall, *Pictorial History of Texas*, 44–45; Goodnight, 'Recollections,' I, 1; L. F. Sheffy, 'The Arrington Papers,' *Panhandle-Plains Historical Review*, 1928.

when seen through a mirage. Beneath the yellowish bluffs was plenty of water.

And there Goodnight led the party into camp. When the command came up, the Colonel seemed out of humor, claiming the scout had not kept a good course. He thoughtfully replied that he had never been more careful in his life.

THE BUFFALO CHASE

'Sah, you've been circling all day,' complained the Colonel.

'He had been watching me, all right,' smiled the scout, nearly seventy years later, 'but by trying to deceive him I saved the command a useless march and the horrors of two days without water.'

The next day the command turned east to the cap-rock of the Plains and scouted northward along the breaks to Blanco Cañon. Below the Plains, at the point where Catfish River leaves the cañon and enters the undulating country, were two small lakes, where the rangers camped.

According to the scout, 'The old Colonel was too dignified ever to camp with us, but always had us put up his little tent some distance to one side. You can imagine the disgust of this tent to the Texas ranger. Some of us scarcely had shirts.

'We expected to lay over to rest up our horses on account of good water and grass. At daybreak he called me over to his tent and asked me which way I intended scouting. I told him I expected to go up Blanco Cañon. He then became curious and questioned me further. I said:

'"Well, there is good fresh water up there; and at this season there will be fresh fruits such as grapes and plums; and if there are any buffaloes in the country, they will be there; and if any Indians, they will be there."

'He then said he understood there was a tributary of the Brazos to the northwest called Duck Creek, which he ordered me to explore, and report to camp that night, saying that he would go up the cañon himself. On such occasions, when the entire command was not to go along, it was necessary to call for volunteers, but no one volunteered to accompany him except a few of the raw recruits and Tom Pollard, a frontiersman, but void of the faculty of making his way in a wild country. Thus Obenchain had no guide, as Lieutenant Woolfork went with me to take charge of my squad.'

Obenchain rode up Blanco Cañon early that summer morning with half a dozen raw recruits and one experienced ranger. To rest his regular saddle horse he rode a pack-mule that the boys called 'Old Rebecca,' an animal that perhaps could not, and, mule-like, certainly would not, be induced to run. Up past the junction of the Crawfish, past Mount Blanco, where Hank Smith was to locate as the first South Plains settler some fifteen years later, and on up into the cañon where the wild plums grew and the Indians came to eat them, the Colonel proudly led the scout on Old Rebecca — proudly, as befitted a descendant of Pocahontas.

About ten miles above camp he suddenly found his squad encompassed by a party of from ten to fifteen Indians, and realized that he had only one man seasoned enough to fight. His squad wanted to run, but Old Rebecca could not keep up, and the Colonel called a halt to the flight of his recruits, fortunately being able to take refuge beneath the projecting ledges of a bluff.

'And, by God, sah,' Obenchain later ejaculated to Goodnight, 'I had to hold them there with my gun.'

Under the bluff he got his men slightly composed, but the
Colonel declared he could have cut their heads off and they
would not have bled a drop, they were so white with fright. He
called for a volunteer to go for Woolfork, who he supposed was
still in camp. A young man named Sid Davidson, who was
mounted upon a beautiful blue horse, the third fastest in the
regiment, immediately volunteered.

The Indians gave chase until they saw they could not catch
him, and knowing that he had gone for aid they left the siege
and passed over the north rim of the cañon, where they killed a
buffalo and stopped to butcher it.

In the meantime Davidson fogged into camp ahead of a
streak of dust and reported the sad plight of the Colonel, and
the command of about twenty-five men saddled and rode for
the place. After finding him safe, they all took the trail over
the rim of the Staked Plains, saw the Indians finishing up the
buffalo, and charged upon them. Being cut off from the shelter
of the Blanco, the Indians fled to the northeastward, hoping to
reach the breaks of the Quitaque, some forty miles away.
From high noon until sundown the rangers were hot upon their
trail, and soon the Indians were throwing away everything they
carried, except their weapons, to lighten their loads. By night
some of their horses were quitting, forcing them to ride double
on the others. And then they reached the welcome breaks of
the Quitaque and were lost in the rough country.

Instead of going into the breaks, where he could have found
water and wood, Obenchain 'turned his command back toward
the Brazos, and, strange to say, did not know enough to keep
his own trail.' During the night he stopped to rest his horses
and men and then resumed his traveling. But on the unbroken
Plains he had no man who could keep a course, and gradually
they bore into the west, where there was no water nearer than
the Pecos, about a hundred and fifty miles away.

Goodnight had followed orders, scouted down Blanco to

Duck Creek, turned up the stream to explore its course, and found some interesting country that might well have harbored Indians. Though his squad found none, it was late in the night when they reached the camp at Twin Lakes. There they found one of their men, the old Irish soldier, who had been left at camp, alone. He had all the mules packed, and was nervously pacing around them with rifle in hand. Goodnight greeted him:

'Billy, what's up?'

'The Comanches have the Colonel and gone to hell over the Plains,' he answered in his excitement, 'with orders to march at once.'

'Billy, we can't march now.'

'But, be God, sir, its orders.'

'It doesn't make a damn,' answered the scout. 'We've got to follow that trail, and we can't follow it at night. Unpack those mules.'

'As he was an old soldier,' Goodnight said, 'he thought we had to pull right out.'

They unpacked. At daylight Woolfork and Goodnight took the squad and pack-mules and rode to the bluff where the Indians had besieged the Colonel.

'From there,' Goodnight continued, 'we followed the trail with all possible speed. In passing over the Plains I noticed some gulls, which appeared in the mirage, about two or three miles east of us. I knew this meant water, although it was August, and the Plains were dry. Not being in need of water we kept the trail.

'The mirages were numerous and I finally sighted the Colonel's squad in one of them about ten miles away, so far west of their own trail that they were beyond the oval of the Plains and completely out of sight. The mirage had lifted them so high into the air that it was possible for us to see them. I called one of the men who had a good horse and said: "You scoot across there and keep them from heading off in another direction."

'When we reached them they were indeed a pitiful sight to

behold. The Colonel's tongue was very thick and he could not speak plain. His first words were:

'"Can you get us to water?"'

'"I can."'

'"How far is it, sah?"'

'I told him, and we started. In addition to being raw recruits, this squad was composed mostly of interior men, not accustomed to riding in an arid country without water, and had suffered more than we would have. Striking straight across the Plains to where I had seen the gulls rise, we found the lake and plenty of water, though it was shallow and tasted fearfully of the gulls. Otherwise it was good. We strung out Woolfork's ten men to see that the Colonel's men did not drink too much, as it is dangerous for a person to drink too much water after a long drought. Tom Pollard bellied down like an old coon and did not stop when I cautioned him, so I had a man pull him out. It enraged him so that he wanted to get his gun and fight. Under such circumstances it is better to wash the face freely, and still better to take a vessel and pour water over the entire body. The system, which has been drained of all its moisture, seems to take it up like a sponge, and one soon feels as good as ever.

'Not having enough men to watch the horses, they of course

filled up with all that they could hold and lay down, apparently in great misery. I thought they would die, but finally they got up and commenced grazing. In the evening a dozen or so antelopes came in to drink.

'"You and Parker Johnson slip down and see if you can't get some fresh meat," Obenchain said.

'We bellied down across the country and got two bucks. We camped at the lake, and there I saw a fight over a pile of buffalo chips. One man had gathered them up, and another came by and tried to steal them. The horses, after being run the forty miles from Blanco to the Quitaque, and doing without water, were in terrible shape. After a two days' rest we went east about fifteen miles, until we got off the Plains, and thence back to Belknap, as the horses were in no condition to go farther.[7]

'This incident proves that everything in nature is useful if we only know its use. The mirage, no doubt, was the means of saving the lives of those lost, water-starving men, as when found they were circling, and it is questionable whether they would ever have got off the Plains, as they had already been without water about thirty-six hours, and the horses could not have held up much longer. Had the horses given out and compelled the men to go on foot, they would have scattered; the Colonel would have lost control, and likely none of them would ever have reached water.

'And had I not seen them in the mirage I should have trailed them on to where their chase ended, and by that time would have been forced into the breaks for water myself, which would have consumed most of that evening. I would then have taken their back-trail until dark, when I would have been forced to camp, and it is hardly reasonable to suppose that I could have got up with them next day in time to get them to water if they had been living, which would have been doubtful, as the weather was so extremely hot and dry. Besides, if their horses

---

[7] Goodnight, 'Recollections,' II, 37–43; Goodnight to J. E. H., August 2, 1928, and June 15, 1929. Tom Pollard wrote his memoirs, giving portions of this story with slight variations.

had perished and they had gone on foot, the trailing would have necessarily been more slow and tedious.'

Obenchain was glad to get back to the settlements, and the old rangers maintain that he boasted no more of his descent from Pocahontas.

Late in June, he had transmitted to Colonel Norris four formal charges against Captain Cureton. Soon after his return he prepared for the court-martial. In view of the generally recognized usages of war, it seems that he was in the right. It is evident that the rangers were held together, not by provocative precepts of formal discipline, but by a leader in whose judgment, skill, and bravery each had confidence. Hence Cureton had the sympathy and the support of his men, even though he might break all the rules of war when applied by an impractical superior.

On the sixteenth of August, Obenchain started south to Camp Colorado, regimental headquarters, on a tributary of the Colorado River, near present Coleman. Though Goodnight was suffering with whooping cough and measles, and was in no condition to ride, Obenchain took him along too. The first day out they stopped for dinner on Fish Creek.

After dinner Obenchain said he wanted to go by Camp Breckenridge, but, instead of asking for the guide, he told Woolfork to designate Whatley and Stockton as escorts, a surprising request, since the Colonel had quarreled with them over the arrest of Cureton. Woolfork was to proceed upon the direct course, while Obenchain turned to the west to visit Camp Breckenridge, planning to rejoin the squad on Big Creek, about thirty miles to the south, at noon next day.

'But when we reached the place designated,' said Goodnight, 'the Colonel was not there. We waited until noon next day and he did not appear. Just at this time it happened that Woolfork and I were not very friendly, but I noticed he was getting uneasy, and about noon condescended to ask my advice. I feared Obenchain had been killed, as I believed that he would again raise a quarrel with the two men, and that Stockton might kill him. I believed Whatley was a murderer at heart, but a coward. I told him I would report to Camp Colorado as quickly as possible, and if the Colonel was alive and should not overtake us, he would surely be there next morning.'

Major James E. McCord ordered two men back up the line, but they rode to Belknap without finding a trace of him. There the Lieutenant sent out a posse in charge of Alfred Lane to continue the hunt. Lane took the usual route to Breckenridge, cutting straight through the woods without bothering with roads, and above a lonely mesquite prairie, some ten miles from the latter camp, saw a flock of buzzards, some wheeling high in the air on steady wings while others were gyrating in wide spirals toward the ground. They rode for the spot and found all that was left of Obenchain. Though it was four days since his murder, and the buzzards had left little to bury, Lane and his men dug a grave, scraped the remains into it, and rode back to report. The spot is unmarked and unknown. Thus passed Obenchain when only thirty-eight years of age — a man of capacity, but not for the borderlands. One of his escorts followed the Goodnight Trail to Colorado after the war, and the other died in the penitentiary.[8]

On the twenty-seventh of August, 1862, a general court-martial convened above the pleasant waters of the Jim Ned, by order of Governor F. R. Lubbock and Adjutant-General J. Y. Dashiell. Only six officers were detailed to hold the court, as more men could not be spared without impairing the service. Cureton was found guilty of a majority of the charges and sentenced to dismissal. The Reviewing Officer, however, recommended to the Governor that in view of his protracted solitary imprisonment, which was harsh and 'apparently unwarranted,' the sentence be mitigated 'to suspension from rank and all pay for the period of three months,' and that he be 'reprimanded in published regimental orders by the officer commanding the Regiment.' [9]

[8] Goodnight, 'Recollections,' ii, 48–49; Goodnight to J. E. H., August 2, 1928; Mrs. Ed East to J. E. H., October, 1928; Smythe, *Historical Sketch of Parker County*, 141.
[9] MS., 'Review of Proceedings of Court-Martial in the Case of Capt. J. J. Cureton, Co. I, Frontier Regiment,' Adjutant-General's Office, Austin.

And thus ended, in the death of Obenchain and the court-martial of Cureton, one of those unpleasant jealousies that touched the life of Goodnight and detracted from the efficiency of the Frontier Regiment, of which he was so proud.

VI. RANGING THE OPEN COUNTRY

Soon after Obenchain's death, Major McCord was promoted to the rank of Lieutenant-Colonel, and James Buckner Barry to that of Major.[1] Reorganization of the rangers early the following year into 'The Mounted Regiment of the Texas State Troops' resulted in McCord's promotion to the command, following Colonel Norris's resignation. The colorful Buck Barry — fighting Texan, hater of Indians, lover of outdoor life, and unique wilderness character — assumed command of the upper border. He was a natural leader and served the regiment faithfully and well until the break-up came.

Life for the rangers resolved itself into a succession of scouting expeditions, as detachments ranged the prairie country almost continually. At best, equipment and provisions were meager, and as the war advanced Texas suffered the effects of blockade, while the isolation of the border country hastened its own destitution. Life on the frontier was early reduced to the most simple forms.

When physical misfortune befell the rangers, they administered whatever remedy they had at hand, and trusted to luck and God and natural resistance to do the rest. When Jim Tackett was shot with a metal spike that embedded itself in his skull between an eye and the brain pan, his companions broke the shaft away and left the problem to time. Dr. J. J. Inge, surgeon for the Frontier Regiment, told Tackett to leave it alone

[1] F. R. Lubbock to J. Y. Dashiell, September 22, 1862. Adjutant-General's Office, Austin.

until it began to hurt like a boil. After a week the symptoms were right; festering had loosened the spike and it was easily removed. Upon every raid Indians gathered all the hoop-iron they could find, even breaking up barrels and buckets to get the hoops, which they easily fashioned into arrowheads. Some men carried steel spikes in their bodies for years without suffering serious effects, but hoop-iron spikes were poisonous, and resulted in death if not soon extracted.

In cases of rattlesnake bite the rangers scarified the wounds with deep incisions and packed them full of salt. If a favorite dog got strychnine, they gave an antidote of salt; if a horse became stricken with fistula, they crammed the orifice full of salt; and if a ranger was suffering with piles, Goodnight prescribed a suppository of pure salt and applications of buffalo tallow as 'a sure cure.' Salt water was the usual antiseptic for wounds, and cold mud or wet clay poultices were used in reducing fever and relieving pain. Lacking mud, they pounded and applied prickly pear.

It followed as a natural result of the bodily chemistry that while ranging for weeks in a country of bad water — a country that gave such names as Bitter, Alkali, Gyp, and Croton to its streams — and living on meat alone, the rangers suffered much from diarrhea. More water and more meat accentuated the trouble, and they resorted to indigenous remedies. They found that bachelor's button or snakeroot was an astringent, and a strong brew of it proved an effective remedy, though nothing was better, so far as they discovered, than a batter of flour and water as salty as the patient could drink. Usually they had no flour, and, when snakeroot was hard to find, they could always resort to the cottonwood that grew along the streams. Goodnight recalled that they 'would get the inside bark, boil it to a strong tea, and drink liberally. It is a hell of a drink, a wonderful astringent, and a bitter dose. But it is a sure shot.'

And thus, out of the soil itself they treated their ailments, simply and fiercely, until they were well. After all, there was little sickness. They were a hearty, vigorous breed — they had to be.

With Cureton back in the service, the old rangers of Company B, or Company I, as it was later called, went happily about their job of hunting Indians, and Goodnight's most vivid recollections of the service were in association with 'Captain Jack.'

THE BIGGEST BUFFALO

In the winter of 1862, Cureton led an expedition up the Brazos, across to the Wichita, and struck due west to the edge of the Plains. South and west of Roaring Springs a snowstorm struck and forced his command into the breaks, and by the second day they were out of provisions. The tablelands nearby were alive with buffaloes, and Cureton ordered Goodnight and Parker Johnson, the 'second scout,' to get some meat and to bring back plenty of hide, as some of the men were practically barefoot.

As the two prepared to leave, Jerry Williams volunteered to go along and help pack the meat. They rode up on a flat where buffaloes like to graze, and estimated the herd before them at fifteen hundred animals. Towering above them all was the largest bull, with the biggest and finest head, that

Goodnight ever saw. Parker proposed that they kill him, and they rode into the herd to get within range. The bull broke into a run with the rangers in hot pursuit, and his strength was so great that he charged through the excited herd with remarkable speed, knocking aside the animals that happened to be in his way. At last the rangers brought him to the ground, but the wild charge of the packed herd carried them on, endangering them and their horses. By staying close together, firing an occasional shot to make the animals give way, and working out sidewise, they finally reached the edge of the herd without mishap, and turned back to get their meat.

When they reached the bull, they looked around for Jerry. He was nowhere in sight. Thinking that he might have grown tired of waiting and returned to camp, the two fell to skinning the buffalo. They packed what meat their horses could carry and took the skin from the neck, the heaviest of rawhide, back to camp for making moccasins. There they found that Jerry had not returned, and, fearing he had entered the herd and been killed, they immediately back-tracked to hunt for him.

Soon they met him coming in afoot. He had followed them into the herd, his horse had either stepped into a dog hole and fallen, or had been knocked down by the buffaloes — they were so thick about him that Jerry never knew which — and had in terror stampeded off with the herd, carrying his rider's gun and six-shooter on the saddle. How Jerry got out alive was a miracle.

He grieved over the loss of a mighty good mount, nearly three hundred miles from home. Yet the horse turned back toward the settlements, and made his way to his old range forty miles east of Belknap, where later he was found. He had lost the bridle and guns; the saddle was still on him, intact.

Again a party of fourteen scoured the foot of the Plains from the Quitaque to the Brazos, and, having had nothing to eat for two days, turned homeward, following Bitter Creek, a tributary of the Brazos, extremely bitter with salt and gypsum. Upon the third day without food, Goodnight found a large catfish, about two feet long, which had lodged in the creek, probably washed down from some fresh-water stream in the hills, as he had not been in the water long enough to die from the salt and alkali. The rangers relished him at any rate.

'As we were passing along the creek,' continued Goodnight, 'in what is now probably a part of the Matador Ranch, a small fawn jumped out of the grass. I killed it before it got out of range. The fawn and the catfish were all we had for three days. Next day we passed through the country where Seymour now stands. I was ahead, as usual, and came on to a very large rattler. I dismounted to kill him, and being under orders not to shoot unless necessary, I had some trouble in getting this old fellow. While doing so the command came up.

'The Captain told me to hand the snake up to him, and after questioning, he said he intended to eat it. Toward evening we approached the Upper Round Timbers on the Brazos.[2] Knowing there would be deer in the timber, I told the Captain if he would keep the men back I would go into it and try to get some game. Strange to say, most starving men shoot wildly.

'A school-teacher who had volunteered to go with us on this trip for an outing asked me if he might go into the timber with me to help carry the game. On reaching the undergrowth I got a young panther, which is not very bad eating. I tied it behind my saddle, and had not gone far when I came on to four or five old bucks. I killed one the first shot, loaded, and killed another, and then told the school-teacher he could shoot. Knowing he could not shoot accurately, I held him off until I had got enough. But when he fired he actually hit one of the bucks in the back of the head.

'I had told the second scout, who was left behind to guide

[2] The Upper Round Timbers were a narrow fringe of post oaks along the Brazos, east of Seymour. Below them is another narrow fringe known as the Lower Round Timbers. To the east of them returning expeditions struck the Upper Cross Timbers. John Marlin to J. E. H., February 18, 1930.

the party, to go to the spring north of the Timbers where we would camp for the night. It happened that we reached the spring with the deer before the command came up. I noticed the Captain halt just before he got into camp and untie the old rattler from his saddle, and I said:

'"Captain, I thought you were going to eat him."

'"If you had not got the deer I should have done so," he said, "but I've no hankering for snake when there is plenty of venison." He said he had eaten snakes on former occasions when forced to, and they were very good eating.

'After men have starved for some time they get hungry every two or three hours, and during the night those fourteen men actually ate up most of the three deer. This sounds preposterous, but it is astonishing how much men can eat when they have nothing but meat, especially after a long starve. One naturally thinks they would prefer lean meat, but the reverse is true. Lean meat does not satisfy hunger as well as fat.'

About a year after his enlistment, Goodnight guided a party of twenty-five rangers out of Belknap, striking northwest to the Quitaque country, from where they turned south, scouting out the country as they rode. Just south of the Pease, and opposite the head of the Big Wichita, Goodnight spied out the camp of six or eight Kiowa warriors engaged in drying buffalo meat at a little spring at the foot of the cap-rock. Behind them rose the broken cliffs of the cap. For half a mile before them stretched a little plateau, making surprise impossible. A few hundred yards to their north the breaks of the Plains were quite rough, the arroyos covered with brush and scrub timber; their horses were staked nearby grazing with *bosals*, or half-hitches, around their noses.

Goodnight sneaked back and circled the command to the south for the best approach. They still had the plateau to cross and they raised it at a run. The Indians broke, pell-mell, for their horses, and, jumping on them bareback, struck for the breaks to the north. Goodnight and Jim Tackett, splendidly mounted, led in the charge across the flat, and Goodnight drew within range of two of the bucks as they approached the roughs. They turned on the sides of their horses away from him, as was their custom, and prepared to shoot their arrows back from under their horses' necks. Just then they reached the breaks, and, taking his last chance, Goodnight cut loose with his six-shooter. While scarcely more than the leg and thigh of each were showing, and the angle was difficult from a running horse, he hit one so badly that he dropped his shield, and Goodnight thought he had given both fatal wounds.

After the fight he took the shield to camp, and out of curiosity opened its double fold of buffalo hide, hardened in fire, to see what had been used for padding, and found a torn-up book, a history of Rome almost complete. Literature of any kind was rare in a ranger camp, and even a history of Rome was a matter of news. Its various fragments were passed around like a continued story, and, according to Goodnight, they 'had a hell of a time reading it.'

For fifty years the scout believed he had killed these two Indians, but while he was ranching at Goodnight, Texas, a party of Kiowas came to his home.

'You shot at me and ran me into the brush one time,' an old warrior said describing the fight.

'I wished I had killed you at the time,' replied Goodnight, 'but I'm damned glad I didn't now,' and to prove that he meant it, he prepared them a feast.

This Indian had retained his shield, and when he died he left it to the 'Leopard Coat Man,' as they called Goodnight, because of a vest of spotted wildcat hide he had worn in the war. In presenting it to the American Bison Society, years later, Goodnight wrote Secretary M. S. Garretson its history and significance.

'Under the Indian laws and customs they pledge themselves to protect it and to die with it, and if they desert it in battle or allow it to be captured under any circumstances without ... life going with it, they are banished from the tribe. Hence few ever take the pledge and shield. The history of this shield is as follows: There was a noted Kiwah warrior whose name in English would be Long Horn. He talked good Spanish and I have had much conversation with him. Accord-

SYMBOLS OF THE FRONTIER

ing to his memory and mine, we had met in combat. Now this old warrior had made and pledged himself to this shield I have. He, regarding me as his best American friend, on his death ... willed it or sent it to me. The aged widow brought it and was here several days. On parting she cried bitterly, telling me we would never meet again. Whether this was caused by her affection for me or the shield, I know not. In any event, it is a sacred emblem of war and must be kept by you as such.' [3]

But to return to the foot of the Plains and the scene of the

[3] Goodnight to M. S. Garretson, December 31, 1917, and June 5, 1918. The story of the fight is told in 'Recollections,' II, 32–35, and Goodnight to J. E. H., November 13, 1926.

fight: The sudden attack forced the Indians to abandon all their camp equipment, and next day, Goodnight explained, 'Old Captain Cureton suggested that we auction off the trophies, and that the amounts bid for same by each of us would be taken out of our wages, when the State paid us — which it never did — and be placed in a camp fund for charitable purposes.'

None of the old rangers would have picked up the stuff had it been free, but a number of raw recruits from the interior were along, some of whom had never before seen Indians or their traps. As soon as the old-timers found that they were interested in the stuff, they too heartily favored an auction. Out of pure cussedness they bid the articles up to ridiculous prices, but always let the recruits buy in the end. One mess of five or six raw recruits bid in four Indian saddles and a number of lariats. It was their luck, too, to have the wildest and the meanest pack-mule in the company. The new men generally had the worst mules, as when the order was issued for the heads of messes to draw mules for an expedition, the old rangers invariably roped out the best mules and left the mean, outlaw, and unbroken ones for the greenhorns. This caused no particular trouble until the day following the auction, but it is a notable fact that nothing so scattered the wits of a frontier mule as the smell of an Indian.

'On the march this day,' the scout continued, 'I had agreed with the second guide to go to the mouth of a certain arroyo, on the waters of the Pease, where I would meet him that night. The Captain had ordered me to take my squad and explore quite a scope of country to the west. This took me into the night, the country being very rough and choppy. I came into the head of this cañon some miles away from the command, and in order to make speed, continued down it. It happened that the moon was shining brightly. After traveling down the cañon a mile or so we heard a fearful racket, coming up, and we all thought it was the Comanches charging us. I threw the men into a short bend of the creek, under an overhanging rock wall, to receive the charge. A moment later this bad mule appeared, dragging the four Indian saddles and ropes, which made a tremendous noise. When the men at camp had started to unpack him, he broke away from them, losing every pound of their rations — everything but the pack-saddle, the Indian saddles, and the ropes. As soon as we saw him, I threw the men across the cañon and took the mule back — minus the rations. And I am ashamed to say we left the Indian saddles.' [4]

As a party of Cureton's rangers returned from a scout into what is now the Matador country in the winter of 1862-63, they crossed an Indian trail northwest of the Upper Round Timbers. After noting the sign, Goodnight concluded that it was made by the friendly Tonkawas, and at Belknap so reported to Major Barry. 'Old Buck' reprimanded him for not following the trail. He said in defense that his party had been out for forty days, their horses were leg-weary, their provisions were gone, and game was scarce.

Barry ordered A. M. Dyer — Goodnight's future brother-in-law — a man who knew the Tonks and spoke signs fluently enough to converse with them, to command a small squad and take the trail. He followed the scout's directions, cut for sign above the Round Timbers, picked up the trail, and followed it south to where a little band of Tonkawas had camped at the mouth of Miller's Creek, on the Brazos. He had no trouble in bringing them in, and for their own protection against the wild tribes they were allowed to camp near Belknap.[5]

Almost from the beginning the Tonkawas had been friends to the Texans. They had moved westward with the frontier until they were settled on the Brazos Reserve. There Goodnight came to know them as 'a harmless, inoffensive, rather lazy, dirty bunch of Indians. Being hated by all other tribes, they stayed along the frontier and mixed with the frontier

---

[4] Goodnight. 'Recollections,' II, 35-36.
[5] See Greer, *Buck Barry, Texas Ranger*, 159.

people. Game was plentiful and they hunted for a living, and had a habit of begging roasting ears and all the dead cattle they could find. But they were always ready and anxious to help us trail and fight other Indians, and when mixed with the white people they were splendid trailers and excellent fighters.'[6]

When the settlers rose in arms against the reserves, the Tonkawas were moved to the Nation along with the wilder tribes that despised and hated them, not only because they were traditionally ill-natured, thieving vagabonds, and friends of the whites, but on account of their resort to cannibalism. At the outbreak of the war, Henry McCulloch conferred with them while attempting to treat with the various wild tribes for peace with the South. Then, using their friendship for the Confederacy as an excuse, a body of Delaware, Shawnee, and Caddo warriors fell upon their camp at the Anadarko Agency on the night of October 25, 1862, and massacred one hundred and thirty-seven of their men, women, and children.[7] A pitiful remnant escaped in the darkness, fled from the reserve, crossed

[6] Goodnight to J. E. H., November 26, 1928.
[7] F. W. Hodge, *The Handbook of American Indians*, II, 778–83.

Red River into Texas, and headed toward their ancestral home.

Old Placido, long-tried friend of the Texans and the tribe's last great chief, was killed in the massacre. He was fighting in the Texans' ranks before their land was a republic, and he fought for them a quarter of a century after it became one. In 1860, twelve wounds upon his body — lance, arrow, and gunshot — attested the valor of a real warrior, and the fame of those fighting Texans, Caldwell, Burleson, Hays, and Mc-Culloch, owed much to this wary old man who had scouted for their companies.[8]

His son, Charlie, knew how to run, and escaped with the remnant to Texas, where he assumed their leadership. He was so infernally sorry that Barry 'dethroned him,' as Goodnight put it, and made Castile, veteran of the Mexican War and a fighter of distinction, chief in his stead. In Texas all went well until Castile's little daughter took sick and died. The medicine man had worked his charms and invoked his gods to no avail, and Castile, in rage and grief, shot the old conjurer dead.

Whereupon Charlie, the pretender to leadership, had Castile tried by Tonkawa custom in hope of getting him killed. Instead of death he got the peculiar verdict that henceforth Castile must lead in all battles against the Comanches, and if he ever flinched or wavered he was to be shot immediately, by his own people. Then Charlie left the disposition of Castile to fate and the Comanches, gathered his followers about him, and wisely moved to the interior away from danger, while Castile's friends and their squaws continued to live at Belknap.[9] As months passed and no papooses came to brighten or share the squalor of their camps, the rangers were mystified. They finally learned that the squaws wanted no children for their red enemies to butcher and kill, and were controverting

[8] Willis Lang, 'Diary,' 1860, pp. 25–26.

[9] Goodnight to J. E. H., November 26, 1928; Greer, *Buck Barry, Texas Ranger*, 163, tells that one little band under Campo stopped near Waco.

the course of nature by using a native herb to bring on the menses.

The Tonks appealed for a permanent home in Texas, but in spite of their value as scouts and spies, the Governor, without special legislative action, declined to authorize their subsistence at Belknap. Yet the decimated tribe settled down to twenty more miserable, tragic years in the land of its birth.[10]

Because Texas had not the resources to support an elaborate scheme of frontier defense, Governor F. R. Lubbock, on the first day of October, 1862, directed Adjutant-General J. Y. Dashiell to tender the Frontier Regiment to the Confederacy. It was accepted by the commander of the Military Department of Texas and Arizona upon condition that it be reorganized and tendered without restrictions as to service and command. In February, 1863, it was reorganized as The Mounted Regiment of Texas State Troops, and in March the Legislature authorized the Governor to tender it to the South upon one condition of service — that it 'remain upon the Indian frontier of the State of Texas.'

Major-General Bankhead Magruder, in charge of the military district embracing Texas, accepted the regiment, but President Jefferson Davis refused to sanction his action. An act of May 28, 1864, passed under Governor Pendleton Murrah's administration, authorized unconditional transfer of the troops, and the offer was accepted.[11] But the hoped-for relief in money and supplies did not materialize, for the South was too poor to help. Throughout the course of the war the cry for ammunition re-echoed from every portion of the border. That which was available was inferior, for unreliable pewter percussion caps and non-explosive powder disheartened the bravest of men.

Foodstuffs became prohibitive in price, and to add to the

---

[10] It was soon moved to Fort Griffin, and thence back to the Territory in 1884. Hodge, as cited, ɪɪ, 783; Quayle to Murrah, September 8, 1864, Adjutant-General's Office.

[11] Gammel, *Laws of Texas*, v, 607–08 and 770; see also Caroline S. Ruckman, 'The Frontier of Texas During the Civil War,' 81–91, Archives, University of Texas.

suffering, a bad drought fell over the country in 1863, and continued until 1864. The Brazos quit running, and it was said a man might ride the three hundred miles of its course through the Palo Pinto country and hardly wet his horse's hoofs. Large bodies of post oak died between Camp Cooper and Breckenridge, crops withered and failed, and corn for the rangers was hauled from East Texas.[12]

In the cattle country, where there were few slaves, the ordeal was particularly severe for the war widows, those women whose husbands were away with the army. In May, 1863, the Commissioners' Court of Young County levied a war tax of twenty cents on the hundred dollars for the support of them and their families, and accepted the offer by the War Board of eleven pairs of cotton cards at ten dollars a pair for distribution among the frontier women. Each did her own spinning and weaving, while the men at the front were singing, 'Hurrah for the Homespun Dress the Southern Ladies Wear.' But in spite of all efforts to bolster the frontier, the line was yielding before the combined onslaughts of a seemingly unkind nature, of dire poverty, and of Indians, and on April 10, 1863, Young County abandoned her organization and closed her records.[13]

There is little wonder that two rangers, Tom Pollard and Alec McClosky, composed a bit of doggerel, and sang out the words in camps. Soon it was roared from many lusty if unmusical throats all up and down the line.

> Come listen to us rangers, you kind-hearted strangers,
> Our song, though a sad one, you are welcome to hear.
> We have kept the Comanches away from your ranches,
> And followed them far over the Texas frontier.
>
> So look to your ranches and mind the Comanches,
> For sure they will scalp you in less than a year.

---

[12] *Mineral Wells Index*, clipping, n.d.; Jep Brown, 'Reminiscences,' Panhandle-Plains Historical Society, Canyon.

[13] *Graham Leader*, March 13, 1913.

We're weary of routin' and scoutin' the bloodthirsty brutes
Over prairie and wood; no beets no tomatoes — jerked beef as dry
      as the sole of a shoe.
All day without drinking, all night without winking,
I say, kind stranger, this will never do.

These great alligators, our state legislators,
Loafing two-thirds of the time, never put in our pockets a tenth
      of a dime.
They do not regard us, they will not reward us,
Though election is coming and there will be drumming
And praising our valor to purchase our votes.

So it's glory for payment, without provision or raiment —
No longer we'll fight on the Texas frontier.
So look to your ranches and mind the Comanches,
For sure they will scalp you in less than a year.

Sure it may grieve you for us rangers to leave you
Thus exposed to the knife of the foe.
But guard your own cattle and fight your own battles,
For back to the States we are determined to go,

Where the states have more people, and churches have steeples,
Where the laws are more equal and the ladies more kind,
Worth is rewarded, work is regarded, and pockets are lined,
Where pumpkins and vegetables are plenty of every kind.

    So look to your ranches and mind the Comanches,
    For sure they will scalp you in less than a year.

In the midst of this destitution arose the most dreaded of war-time contingencies — internal dissension! In the beginning many farmers and cowmen, beyond the plantation zone and the region of profitable slavery, were opposed to war. 'I thoroughly believe,' Goodnight once said, 'that fully half of Jack Cureton's rangers were in fact Union sympathizers. I know positively that Captain Cureton, while a slave-holder in a way and a Southern man all his life, as were his ancestors, believed the war to be cruel, wrong, and uncalled for.'

With the 'peace party' scare, wholesale hangings, and organized desertions, the war dragged on to a sorry end.

After the end of the war many deserters remained on the frontier, helping to swell to unhealthy proportions the indigenous criminal element. Lee's surrender did not bring peace to the borderlands, and the experiences of Reconstruction proved almost as unhappy as the horrors of war.

FOR five years, during the Civil War, practically no beef had been sold, and not a hoof of she-stuff had ever left the Western Cross Timbers. Prolific seasons had overrun the ranches of Texas without the usual expansion upon ungrazed grass to balance the ratio between cattle and range. Vast herds of wild, unbranded cattle filled the country when the cowmen returned from the war to find more than Indians to fight. Cow thieves were riding in the dust of mavericks, gathering, branding, and driving from the State these hitherto unbranded cattle, the rightful property of men long absent from the roundups. In discussing the range ethics of the pre-war period, Goodnight said:

'There had been no stealing upon the northwest frontier so far as was known, and I think it was the general custom —an unwritten law — to mark and brand every calf in your range to its owner, if you knew him. If the mother cows were strays, or unknown, you branded the calves in the same brand that the cows wore. In all roundups and gatherings it was our custom to send the stray cattle as far toward their own ranges as possible. I would take them to the end of my journey, my neighbor to the end of his, and so on until they generally reached home.

'Now, when the war got in good swing, taking all the available men from the ranges to the army, and all the border men had to go into the ranger service, virtually no one was left to take care of the cattle. At least the help was entirely inadequate for the work, with the result that the ranges were soon covered with unmarked cattle, probably two or three unmarked for every one that was branded. At first this condition did not seem to have a decidedly bad effect, but certain scattered men over the country could not withstand the temptation and went to branding these cattle for themselves.

AFTER A MAVERICK

'For the first year or so this was not tolerated by the masses, as one incident will show. When in the ranger service I used to carry dispatches from the frontier into Weatherford and Decatur, sometimes to State and sometimes to Confederate authorities. Once I was sent from Belknap to Weatherford. The straight route brought me by my ranch. I had asked for and got permission to spend one day at home, which happened to be Sunday. I took my half-sister and rode across country due north, three or four miles, to where we had established the log church for the neighborhood.

'At church there was an old gentleman who was conspicuous in taking yearlings, and at that time the only one for miles around who was so acting. After hitching my horses I happened to pass by three or four other cattlemen who were talking to him, and I stopped, purposely, to listen to the conversation. They were telling him plainly that he was a thief, taking the property of men who were either in the army or protecting the frontier from the Indians, that his conduct was intolerable, and that neither they nor their children would ever recognize him if he did not stop it!

'During the war the cattlemen of the Keechi neighborhood formed a protective association with Jim Loving as leader, a loose association in effect until law and order were established. And yet,' said Goodnight, 'in a year or two's time this stealing or so-called mavericking became public. You could count the honest ones on your fingers and still have one hand left. In all my knowledge of my immediate surroundings, I know of about four men who held aloof and did not steal. It was the custom for neighbors to go in together and brand up the war widows' cattle, even cleaner than they did their own. When the stealing got into full swing, this noble custom was dropped, and the thieves took everything these poor women had. During the war there was no one available to hire, at any price, to look after our affairs and property at home. So when we did get back home, the stay-at-home fellows had the cattle, and we poor devils had the experience.'

Early in 1864, Goodnight's term of ranger service expired, and he rode back to Black Springs to devote his time to his cattle. After seven years he estimated that the CV stock had increased to some five thousand head; yet he had hopes of gathering no more than a thousand. As he viewed the sorry plight of the country and his own affairs, he decided to consult his old friend, Major George B. Erath, a German frontiersman, who exercised partial control of the border. Thoroughly discouraged, he rode two hundred miles to find the old warrior at his home near Cameron. He told him that while he had been away carrying a gun for his country, thieves were marking his yearlings and stealing his cattle, so that now most of his stock was in the hands of his immediate neighbors. He was disgusted with the country and the people, he explained, and wanted permission to leave Texas.

He might have headed into Old Mexico with the remnant of his herd; he might have pushed out into sparsely settled New Mexico. The main thing, he thought, was to go. Since he must have permission to leave, on account of the restrictions of war, or else travel as a fugitive, he sought his old friend as a likely person to secure him official leave.

'All right, Charlie,' Erath said in his broken English, 'I first gives you permission to go away, and then gives you some advice. Your mother lives here, your sisters live here, and you ought to stay. I loses all my money, you loses all your money.[1] But I makes more money, you makes more money, and if I be you, I stay.'

'He was a fine old character,' praised Goodnight, 'and the advice was good. Better lose your fortune than your honor.'

And yet after the war prospects in Texas were gloomy, and in his disappointment Goodnight declared that 'it looked like everything worth living for was gone. The entire country was depressed — there was no hope. We could not see what the Reconstructionists would do, nor how long they would hold out.'

He joined a half-dozen other Cross Timber cowmen upon an exploring trip in search of a new and suitable cattle range, one less exposed to Indian raiders and carpetbag jurisdiction. They met at Palo Pinto village, provided themselves with a good pack-mule, and took a southwest course away from the settlements. They crossed the San Saba at the old Spanish fort, where they found a good range for six to eight thousand cattle, but wanting a bigger country, they kept on.

Goodnight made up his mind that 'after all it would be better

[1] For reference to Erath's losses **see** *The Southwestern Historical Quarterly*, xxvii, 1923, p. 161.

to hunt a market for his cattle than a home for them.' He discussed the matter with Alfred Lane, his brother-in-law, who agreed with him, and next morning they cut the pack and turned their horses back toward Palo Pinto, while the others pushed on with plans to enter Old Mexico.[2]

Back on the range Goodnight set himself to the task of gathering his remaining cattle. Outside the gentle Keechi Valley much of the country was rough and wild. Southeast was a heavily timbered mesa country that dipped off into rocky gulches. On the south, where the breakoff came, were two considerable waterings called Turkey Springs. To the west, Turkey Creek ran only during rainy seasons, and cattle came to these springs for water. A wild bunch formed around each, a hundred and fifty to two hundred in all.

In the spring of 1865, Goodnight and Wes Sheek took Alfred Lane and a cow-hand, 'One-Armed' Bill Wilson, and slipped down into the mesa country quiet and easy, lay out in the timber until the cattle came into the springs, swung in around them, and with Goodnight working in the lead, succeeded in getting them into the open.

North of the mesa, and eight miles east of Black Springs, lived an 'Arkansawer' named R. C. Betty. 'He pretended to be,' said Goodnight, 'and I think was, in his way, a pretty religious old Methodist,' at least halfway true to the Arkansas breed which was 'always ready to drink whiskey and fight.' He did not drink.

In this, as in all wild herds of that day, were a few of everybody's cattle. As they approached Betty's place, Goodnight sent word for him to come out in the valley and cut his stock. Simp Crawford [3] and Parson Burns, who lived out toward the

[2] Goodnight to J. E. H., February 27, 1929; *Prose and Poetry of the Live Stock Industry,* I, 61.

[3] Simpson Crawford was born in Estill County, Kentucky, October 13, 1824. He was a veteran of the Mexican War, emigrated to Titus County, Texas, in 1852, and three years later to Palo Pinto County. In 1859 he branded 1000 calves; in 1864 he had 4000 cattle, but lost nearly half of them to the Indians. He continued ranching in the Keechi Valley until his death, April 17, 1908. S. O. Crawford to J. E. H., December 21, 1931.

Salt Works, seven or eight miles west of Goodnight's ranch, joined them in working the roundup. Parson Burns, who was in the cattle business too, would, according to Goodnight, 'drink awhile, fight awhile, preach awhile, and swear awhile. But he was a very good man in spite of these faults.' And it

WORKING THE RANGE

happened that he and Crawford were great practical jokers, always ready to stir up trouble for fun. According to their latest joke, Betty had killed a big stray beef, and these two were guying him about a man of his apparent intelligence 'killing a sixteen-hundred-pound beef to feed five men.' By the time he had cut his yearlings and twos they had him boiling mad.

A few days later he joined a number of settlers at the Works in making salt. Parson Burns, poking around the country, dropped by for a brotherly call. Betty was still mad, and, feeling that he had failed to get as many of the unmarked yearlings as he deserved, accused Goodnight of stealing some of his cattle. Considering Goodnight's views and temper, probably Betty cut none whose ownership was subject to question, and in an attempt to be scrupulously honest, Goodnight consistently refused to take his just portion of the mavericks, even when Sheek truly urged that the animals were 'as much theirs as anybody's,' because by so doing, he said, he would be classing himself with the rustlers.

Goodnight and Charlie Wilson — 'One-Armed' Bill's brother — still hunting cattle, stopped at the Parson's to spend the night, and were told of Betty's remark. Ranchmen hid out their horses at night to keep the Indians from getting them, and after supper Goodnight took Wilson and rode toward the Salt Works, probably a mile away. After the horses were hobbled in a thicket, he said he would go to the Works and see Betty.

'I didn't tell Wilson what I was going to do,' he recalled, 'and didn't let on to Burns, but I went intending to kill him.'

He found Betty and four or five of his neighbors tending the fires under a row of immense pots. Close by was a large pile of cordwood; the fires lighted the clearing almost as day. He went straight to Betty, informed him of what Parson Burns had said, and added that he had come to see him retract.

Betty, who had built quite a reputation as a fighter, replied: 'Yes, I said that, and have nothing to take back.'

'You know it is a damned lie,' Goodnight replied, and again asked him to take it back.

He refused, saying: 'I'm not afraid of you, sir!' and reaching down, caught up a large stone and threw at Goodnight, who dodged the missile.

'I don't know why I didn't shoot him then,' said Goodnight. 'He was launched forward in throwing the stone, and I hit him as he came up, knocking him back fully six feet. Before I had time to get on him, he was back on his feet again, quick as a cat, a-coming at me. I knocked him down four more times as fast as he got up, but he kept coming. The fifth time he was a little weak, and called to the grangers: "Men, don't let him hurt me!"

'They commenced fogging around me like the devil, and I yelled to Wilson: "Charlie, clean those sons-o'-bitches out," and Wilson jerked his gun and yelled: "Get up on that cordwood or I'll kill you all."

'The sixth time I knocked Betty down, he was weak and a little slower in getting up. I recovered from my swing and made a run at him. He kicked at me like a bay steer. I had just been breaking a mule that kicked like the devil, and I thought, as I dodged, "If I can dodge that mule I surely can dodge you." I was on top of him, beating him in the sides and stomach, when Charlie finally called that I had beaten him up enough. When I looked around, he had those grangers perched up on the cordwood like so many owls, and was walking back and forth in front of them with his gun out.

'As we walked back toward the Parson's ranch, I said: "Charlie, why did you put all those fellows up on the cordwood?"

'"Damn them," he replied, "I wanted them where I could watch them all at once."

'We spent the night with Parson Burns — who thought it had taken us a long time to hobble our horses — but didn't tell him a word because it would have given him too much pleasure.

'I didn't want my mother to know about the fight, as she disapproved of such things, and was sometimes worried about me. But she found it out in two or three weeks and asked me about it.

'"Yes, I did it," I replied.

'"What did you do it for?" she said.

'"I whipped him because he accused me of being a thief."

'"You did just right," she answered. "If you hadn't, I'd have whipped you when I heard of it."'

Goodnight did not meet Betty again until the summer following, after he and Loving had laid out their trail to Fort Sumner and he had returned to the Texas frontier for the second herd. When ready to start, he rode into Weatherford to hurry delivery of his flour.[4] As he left the mill, Betty hailed him from across the street, saying he wanted to talk with him.

'I want to apologize,' Betty began; 'I was wrong in that matter and you did me right. I want you to be as friendly as you used to be.'

'We agreed to be so,' said the cowman. 'I told him I would visit him, but before I got the opportunity the old gentleman passed away. He was a gritty old son-of-a-gun, and I found out later that he had licked everybody in the country except me.'

Demoralization continued, thieves were as thick as could be, and few men trusted their neighbors even if they were honest. During the war, Simp Crawford and Alfred Lane had gone into the sheep business. Later, Crawford traded his share to Fuller Millsap, an old-timer who lived southeast of them on the edge of Millsap Prairie, and in exchange received between three and four hundred cows branded in Millsap's brand ᴍ (a rounded M). Crawford rebranded them with an *O*, turned them loose on his ranch, and quite naturally, a few drifted back to their old range on Millsap Prairie, fifteen miles away.

Goodnight and Sheek were still engaged in their cow-hunts, gathering the CV cattle, a great many of which had scattered to Millsap Prairie and beyond. 'One-Armed' Bill Wilson worked with them, and, as often as they gathered more than one man could hold in day herd, they quit hunting and carried the strays back home. As was the general custom, too, they gathered those belonging to their immediate neighbors and took them along. They passed through the valley where Mineral Wells now stands with their first herd, and there came upon another ᴍO cow. Goodnight dropped her and her calf into the herd.

Sometime before, but unknown to Goodnight or Sheek, Crawford had sold the cow to a farmer named Herrington, who, upon leaving the country, sold her back to Millsap.

[4] The mill in Weatherford was built in 1860 by John H. Prince and J. H. Phelps. Smythe, *Historical Sketch of Parker County*, 137.

Neither had counter-branded her, and of course Goodnight brought her along thinking she still belonged to Crawford.

On the way they passed a settler who bore a hard name. He saw the stray cow as he rode by, and then trotted down the valley to tell Millsap that Goodnight had stolen her. Goodnight had sent word to Crawford to come out to the forks of the roads and get his cattle. As soon as he rode up, he sighted the 𝓜𝐎 cow and calf, and said: 'Charlie, you've played the devil. You have old Fuller Millsap's cow,' explaining, then, how she had gone back to her original owner. As soon as their calves were branded, Goodnight again set out for Millsap Prairie to continue the hunts, drifting the cow and calf along, and dropping them at the spot where he had picked them up.

Down in the edge of the timber old Fuller Millsap was foaming at the mouth. He, too, was a man jealous of his rights, disagreeable and dangerous when crossed, and extremely moral at a time when fighting was a virtue. Already he was reputed to have two dead men to his credit. Soon after he heard the report he sent a man fifteen miles to deliver a note to Goodnight, accusing him of stealing his cow. Goodnight rarely mentioned the incident in after life, but once he did, observing: 'A man will do some foolish things.'

'I wrote on the note and returned it by the courier, saying: "You are a liar and a coward! No gentleman would use such language without just cause!" But I did not tell him that the cow had been returned.

'Millsap, outraged at the reply, sent his courier back with a challenge to firearms. Instead of writing back and telling him to go to hell and take care of himself when we met, I accepted, choosing shotguns for his convenience, naming October 10, twelve o'clock, as the time, and a big dry hole near the forks of the road, about two miles from his house, as the place. I was considered the best pistol shot in the country, but I was afraid he might back out, and, though I rather expected to be killed, I figured on cutting him in two.

'I chose Sheek and Lieutenant George Waugh, late of the Confederate Army, as my seconds. Waugh was a small, heady fellow, a perfect hyena and hellion. We met at the dry hole, promptly, on time. There we found Judge R. W. Pollard, Millsap's father-in-law, and Pollard's two sons. We dismounted and waited until about two o'clock, when Judge Pollard said that he knew Millsap would not come, and that we had just as well adjourn. They had the privilege of offering a second, but he said they had none to offer.

'It appeared that Old Millsap's appetite for lead had entirely soaked up. It was six or eight months before I met him, and if there ever was a man overloaded with friendship, it was Millsap. In about a year he ended his own life.'[4a]

Fortunately for both, Millsap realized the mistake in time. Had Goodnight been less fiery, he might have overlooked the initial insult and advised Millsap that he had returned the cow. But to the end of his long life he hated the very tracks a cow thief made. In some rare cases he may have forgiven theft; in none did he ever forget. As extended interests brought and kept him in closer contact with the world, he abhorred all hypocrisy, dishonesty, cant, and religious intolerance. But he was more familiar with the widespread crime of cattle rustling, saw its devastating and demoralizing effect upon the frontier of Texas, and hated it with all the vigor and the intensity of his soul. As a personal affront the greatest insult of all was a reflection upon his honesty, and his anger knew no bounds when his integrity was impugned. And yet in age he mellowed somewhat: 'I often think that only the weak steal; the strong do not.'

Soon after the war the custom of swapping brands grew up, whereby a ranchman might gather, drive, and sell his neighbor's beeves, with the understanding that the neighbor was to take in payment strays found upon his own range. Once a year they met and balanced tallies. This practice gave free

[4a] W. W. Millsap protests this account, saying that his father was 'coming over the hill . . waving his hat . . . all ready for the duel.' W. W. Millsap to J. E. H., February 13, 1939.

rein to thieves and legalized a method which enabled them to take possession of stray cattle, sell them where they pleased and move on to the next county for another herd. Since some of them had no herd of their own, the swapping was entirely one-sided. The custom spread throughout the state, not only encouraging promiscuous theft, but dishonesty among those who had cattle upon the range.

'As soon as the war ended,' Goodnight continued, 'leaving us all disfranchised, carpetbagger courts came in and took possession of our affairs. These fellows at once saw their opportunity and passed through the Legislature what they termed the "tallying law."[5] This law seemed to assume, first, that you were a cattleman, and second, that you were an honest man. It will be remembered that cattle emigrated many miles from home for want of attention. This law permitted anybody who wanted to put up a herd of cattle to go out on the ranges and gather anything he came to, and have the herd tallied by an inspector appointed by a carpetbagger court. As a rule these inspectors were the most unreliable men who could be picked, and if you would make it to their interest you could tally, by miscalling the marks and brands, in any manner you wanted. All the individual had to do was to take this tally and record it in the county courthouse, then move the cattle wherever he pleased, pretending that he would pay for them whenever he returned. This was rarely done because *the driver could never find the owner*, and after this had continued for a few years, nearly every courthouse in the cattle-raising sections of the State was burned. This obliterated the tallies on record and settled the "count."

'While this lawless condition existed, it became a custom to kill everybody's beef but your own. Every fellow killed the other fellow's beef, believing it did not cost him anything, when in fact that fellow was killing his. There was no attempt to save the meat, and the waste from this habit was appalling. Within a mile of my ranch lived a widow who got to be a cattle

[5] Gammel, *Laws of Texas*, v, 1141–42; passed November 13, 1866.

lady by virtue of her boys' picking up yearlings. When it happened that they got out of beef, she told the boys they must find some, but not to get one of hers, because, she said, she "would as leave eat one of her little children as one of her own beeves."'

Old-timers laugh and joke about this obsolete practice to-day, and for the person who will sit and listen in the shade of ranch corrals, these old stories will be told again. He will hear how Burk Burnett pressed the vigorous Dan Waggoner to stay for dinner by promising him something he never before had eaten. Upon staying and seeing nothing unusual, Waggoner reminded the host that he was to furnish something he had never tasted before: 'I am,' said Burnett, picking up a platter, 'taste a piece of your own beef.'

And in pleasant rejoinder one could, until recently, hear Tom Waggoner, who raised the famous Three D race horses, chide the genteel Will Ikard, who had read the *Baptist Standard* since its founding, of the time that he dropped into the Ikard Ranch for dinner and ate a mess of his own beef, which made him deathly sick. And if he listens well he may hear the tale of the man who moved into the Cross Timbers with a yoke of steers, which increased to a mighty nice herd. Now he may safely doubt, but there was a time when the old settlers silenced the biologically wise by pointing out the man and his herd in proof.

Despite the uncertain future Sheek and Goodnight had, in 1864, traded for Claiborn Varner's entire stock of CV cattle, agreeing to pay for them 'at the rate of seven dollars per head in gold.' Within three years the debt was paid with money Goodnight earned upon the trail, and with land that Sheek received from his father-in-law's estate. The land, however, was not transferred until 1867, because of a contractual provision that land would be accepted only in case it was not confiscated by the Federal Government, as was at one time feared.[6]

[6] Deposition of John W. Sheek in Indian Claim, 9133, pp. 4–5, September 30, 1899; Deposition of Charles Goodnight in same claim, September 4, 1899, pp. 3, 64–65, 71–72, Court of Indian Claims, Washington, D.C.

At the time of purchase neither the cowmen nor Varner knew how many cattle they had, but the two had been enlarging their holdings, and by the end of the war estimated that they owned at least eight thousand head, running in a half-dozen brands. Seeing that some must be moved to grass, Goodnight secured a furlough in the spring of 1864, drove a thousand head up the Brazos, and located them upon Elm Creek west of Belknap, twelve miles beyond the nearest settlement. He threw in with an old German named Charlie Neuhous, and built some large corrals which came to be called the Neuhous Pens.

In July of the same year he gathered another herd of twelve to fifteen hundred head, and set out on the trail to the new ranch, short-handed. Alfred Lane, a splendid scout and frontiersman, overtook the herd, saying he had come to help it through. After a three days' drive through the timber, they reached Fort Belknap and camped for the night about a mile west of the old post. In spite of advice that he delay a couple of days, until Goodnight could accompany him home, Lane left in the evening, saying that since they had reached the open country he was not needed. He spent the night at a friend's house nearby, and next morning, July 15, 1864, set out, not knowing that during the night Indians had stolen all of Goodnight's cow-horses except those ridden by the night guard.

Lane rode a big iron-gray horse named Drive, which had been stolen by Indians two or three times, each time to escape and come back home. The road led past Lookout Mountain, a peak in the western edge of Jack County, used by the Indians for reconnoitering. Indians, hidden at its base, gave him a death shot with an arrow as he rode by.

His horse broke into a run, quit the trail and turned into the timber, though Lane clung to the saddle for three hundred yards, until a limb knocked him off. The horse circled to the right and the Indians, thinking the rider still on him, gave chase for some distance. They failed to find the body, for it was not scalped when picked up next day. That night the big iron-gray reached home with an empty saddle, and the family, knowing Lane had been killed, sent word by courier to Goodnight's ranch, twenty-five miles beyond Belknap, and went out and found the body. In looking over the ground where the Indians had chased Lane through the timber, Goodnight discovered this tragic irony; the tracks that led in pursuit were made by his own fine mount, stolen from his herd near Belknap the night before.[7]

In the fall Goodnight returned to the Keechi to move another herd to the Elm. He had about two thousand head under herd, and was making his last roundup in Loving Valley before starting west. The valley bounded on the east by heavy timber and on the west by a ledge of naked hills, was open except for two groves of timber. As his hands dismounted on the north side of the timber to get dinner, they saw a band of loose horses to the east. Wilson, a neighbor, was supposed to have joined them on the drive, and though his son was present he had not appeared. When the cowboys remounted to continue their work, the loose horses ran up to them, one carrying an arrow that had just been shot into its side.

Thinking the Indians were immediately down the valley, all broke away in that direction to engage them. The main band of about thirteen warriors had sighted them and had whipped south into the timber. 'About a quarter of a mile below,' said Goodnight, 'we sighted two Indians holding a herd of stolen horses. We were going full speed and would have got right on to them before they knew it, had not young Wilson hollered. As soon as we saw the arrow in the horse, he conceived the idea that the Indians had killed his father, as he had not met us per agreement, and I suspected the same thing.

'When Wilson gave the war-whoop the two herders looked around, saw us, lost their heads and started across the valley towards the hills. I went to the right of one of the mottes to cut them off, but when they saw their mistake they abruptly

[7] Goodnight, 'Recollections,' II, 59–60; H. W. Taylor to J. E. H., January 24, 1930.

turned back into the nearby timber. This caused me to have to ride much farther than the men coming straight across the valley, who intercepted the Indians, just as they struck the timber, and fired several shots. There I saw a very amusing sight. Sam Ham, a Mississippian about twenty-five years of age, heading the party, got within ten or fifteen feet of the Indians, fired several shots, and missed them. When his old Spanish horse got wind of the Indians, he did some fearful bucking. Ham was a poor rider and when I passed him he was not touching the horse anywhere. He looked like a great spider up in the air, but the horse must have circled around in time for him to 'light in the saddle, as Ham stayed on him. My horse was also afraid of the Indians and threw down his head to buck. I spurred and pulled on him so viciously that when he threw his head up he hit me in the face, causing my nose to bleed profusely.

'Just ahead the country pitched off six or eight feet down a rocky bluff. The hindmost Indian — the one I was after — was riding a big bay mare stolen from Parker County. One of the boys, coming up at an angle from behind, fired with a dragoon pistol, breaking the old mare's neck, and she fell over the bluff dead, with the Indian still on her. At this instant I was right above him and saw him 'light on his feet fair and square.

'Not wanting to jump my horse over, I jumped off and down the cliff, by which time the Indian had gone some little distance. When out on horse-stealing expeditions they always carried one or more ropes, which they drew up through their belts with the loops hanging down. This Indian's rope hung low enough to catch in his feet, which caused him to fall twice and gave me the advantage in the run.

'I had determined not to fire until I was close enough to get him, and as I was getting close he whirled and let an arrow at me. I fired at him instantly, without good aim, but the ball passed through his arm in two places. Fortunately, it was the arm in which he held his bow, which no doubt saved my life, as it caused him to miss his next shot. I have never seen an Indian that could stand powder at close range, and in all my frontier life, I have known but few men who would not flinch when powder was burned close.

ON THE WARPATH

'An instant after he shot, I again fired, hitting him right between the shoulders, and as he went down I gave him another shot in the back of the head, which made a good Indian of him right now.'

The country seemed alive with raiding parties, and as they were already depredating along the Elm, Sheek and Goodnight decided to move no more cattle at that time. They turned the day herd loose, and about dark that evening Goodnight set out to ride the forty miles to Belknap, on his way back to the outside ranch. At sunup he rode in to find the little village 'in great turmoil and excitement.' The day before, October 13, 1864, several hundred Indians had made a raid upon the Elm Creek settlers, had killed about a dozen people, and carried seven into captivity.

They came in from the north and struck near newly formed Fort Murrah, about twelve miles up the Brazos, killed Jowell Meyers, at least two other settlers, and five rangers in sight of the fort, passed down the river to the mouth of Elm, and swept back toward its head, intending to clean up everything in their path. Everyone was seeking sanctuary and help when Goodnight rode in, and against the advice of all, and heedless of the fear and excitement, rode on alone for the Neuhous Pens, twenty-five miles farther into hostile territory.[8]

Goodnight crossed the Brazos, started up the Elm, and came to the ranch of Mrs. Elizabeth Fitzpatrick. Her house had been destroyed by fire, her daughter had been killed, and she and her two grandchildren, Millie and Lottie Durgan carried into captivity. Since Old Nigger Brit, who lived at the same place, was away at mill, they had taken his wife and two of his children as captives. Unable to catch his little boy, they shot him down and left him unscalped, for, as Goodnight explained, 'Indians rarely scalp a negro.' The bodies lay as they had fallen.

The Indians had ripped open Mrs. Fitzpatrick's feather beds and pillows, and emptied the feathers out on the ground. 'A strong north wind blew them southward into the timber and foliage,' Goodnight said, 'where they seemed to cover an acre or more, resembled snow in the midst of the green, and would have been very attractive had it not been for the sad sight at the house and the thought of the unfortunate inmates. The same thing had happened at Mr. Hamby's, about half a mile farther up the creek.'

Hamby met Goodnight at the bottom of the hill upon which

[8] Francis M. Peveler to J. E. H., August 6, 1932; Greer, *Buck Barry, Texas Ranger; Frontier Times*, September, 1925, and April, 1926; Goodnight, 'Recollections,' II. 60–63: Goodnight to J. E. H., April 8, 1927.

his home was built, and told him the Indians had taken everything except what the family wore. As he lamented the loss
of his bedding, Goodnight gave him a good Spanish blanket
taken from the Indian he had killed the day before. Still he
bemoaned the loss of his plum preserves, of which he was very
fond, saying: 'Those dirty devils took every jar of them out
into the yard, ate what they could, and then stirred sand
in the rest.'

As the Indians advanced, Hamby had hidden his wife and
children in a cliff nearby, and with his son rushed up the
creek to Harry Williams's home. Williams being away, his
family hid in a briar thicket, and the men hurried on to where
George Bragg lived — the last settlement upon the creek
except Goodnight's ranch, twelve miles farther west.

'At the Bragg Ranch they made a fight,' said Goodnight,
'and I don't think such a fight was ever made before or since.
The Bragg house was an *jacal* — the timbers being set on end,
daubed with mud between and covered with dirt — probably
sixteen by twenty feet. Bragg had two married sons besides his
own family. Doc Wilson and wife were also there; in all four
women and some children who lay under the beds on the dirt
floor.

'Old man Hamby took the only window in the house, and
the others took care of the door. In front of the house was a
small stockade of post-oak logs, and in front of the door, close
to the stiles over the stockade, stood an oak tree. An Indian
got behind it early in the fight, killed Wilson and severely
wounded old man Bragg.

'Hamby told me he tried to get a shot at the Indian for some
time. Finally some Indians went down to the barn and got a
pick and mattock, and commenced to dig out the pickets which
formed the house. Knowing they could not protect themselves
if the Indians got another opening, young Hamby told old man
Bragg to get on the bed, punch the mud out of the cracks in the
side wall and fire down at random among them. Bragg had
been shot in the breast and replied that he was dying, but

luckily the arrow had struck a rib and followed it around to his back, where it was taken out next morning. Hamby bully-ragged Bragg until he made the effort, and when he fired he hit an Indian right in the eye.

'It seemed to have created quite a commotion among the diggers, and the Indian behind the tree leaned out to see around the corner. Hamby, who had been watching him closely, shot him with a double-barrel gun. He fell across the stile, and from appearances the shot had almost cut him in two, as the steps were a mass of blood when I got there, though the Indian had been dragged away.

'Old man Hamby received several wounds in his arms and a slight cut on his breast, as it was necessary to expose himself a little in order to get good aim at the Indians. He must have done some splendid shooting, as the ground in a semicircle around the window was smeared with blood. Of course the Indians took away all their dead except the one on the stile, which they could not get, and it will never be known how many were killed, but their loss must have been considerable. A day or two later some of us followed the trail about forty miles, and we found several who had died of wounds.' [9]

Goodnight made his way on to the Neuhous Pens, and to his surprise found that the ranch had escaped the raid. It was newly settled and the Indians probably had not discovered it, as from Bragg's they had headed toward Red River. After seeing that his cattle were safe, Goodnight turned back and joined a company of volunteers in taking the trail, followed it two days, but being hopelessly outnumbered, gave up the pursuit. Great numbers of cattle had been driven off — Goodnight and the volunteers estimating at least ten thousand head.

In the spring of 1865, Goodnight, again deciding to move, began gathering a beef herd to drive to New Mexico and Colorado. He and Sheek rounded up their cattle in Young, Palo Pinto, and Jack Counties, threw them west upon the Elm Creek range, and loose-herded them near the Neuhous Pens.

[9] Goodnight, 'Recollections,' i, 63–67; H. C. Williams to J. E. H., February 14, 1930.

By the first of September they had about two thousand big steers and dry cows ready to drive.

At the same time 'One-Armed' Bill Wilson was preparing to drive a small herd to Old Mexico. He had worked for Sheek and Goodnight off and on for five years, and with three years' time due him, had taken his pay in cattle. He, too, was gathering and holding in Young County, and was about ready to take the trail.

Early in September the Indians stampeded Goodnight's herd, fought off the hands and drove the cattle away. Goodnight was not in camp, but was informed of the loss next morning. Fourteen outside men immediately took the trail. Bill Wilson heard of the steal and joined Goodnight and his men, who got started later. After trailing them for twenty-five miles, Goodnight knew, by the unshod horse tracks and the number of moccasin prints where the herd crossed the Brazos, that the Indians were so numerous that it was useless to follow farther, and so turned back to protect what he 'could in case there were other Indians in the country.' [10]

With his beef herd gone and fall coming on, Goodnight gave up the idea of driving to market that year. George Reynolds left old Fort Davis, in Stephens County, that winter and drove a small herd into New Mexico, and late in the year Neuhous trailed a little bunch to market at New Orleans. Goodnight picked up about a dozen big steers, averaging around twelve hundred pounds, and threw them into the Neuhous herd. Fortunately, they came in on a good market and he received nearly forty dollars a head in gold.

He continued to ride the range, but his mind was busy with other matters. Resolved for over a year to take the trail with his cattle, he planned to move with the coming of spring's fresh grass. Disastrous Indian troubles, the uncertainties of Reconstruction, and thieving neighbors sped his plans and strengthened his resolution to leave the country for good.

[10] Depositions in Indian Depredation Case, No. 9133; Charles Goodnight, March 2, 1893, pp. 2–8, and September 4, 1899, p. 6; Frank P. Mayes, July 6, 1893, p. 2; Martin V. Scoggins, July 6, 1893, pp. 3–5; Wm. J. Wilson, June 26, 1893, pp. 2–3; 'Claimant's Brief,' 1–5; Goodnight to J. E. H., December 3, 1928.

VIII. BLAZING THE GOODNIGHT TRAIL

GOODNIGHT'S experience and training had been of an elemental nature. Mentally and physically he was equipped for the wilderness. He was lithe, tireless, and young — only thirty years of age — yet seasoned in the ways of the frontier and eager to venture where others were afraid to follow. Using the money from the Neuhous sale, he began outfitting for his first drive in the spring of 1866, and from the Elm Creek range gathered his cattle with the growth of the season. He began shaping up his herd in the spring, but because of white and Indian thieves, he could muster hardly a thousand head of beeves and dry cows fit for driving.

While he knew that the Southern States were destitute of cattle, he knew, too, in spite of Neuhous's good fortune, that they were bankrupt besides. He conceived the idea that 'the whole of Texas would start north for market' along the old trails fairly beaten before the war, 'and thought it safer to go west for two reasons. First, the mining region would have more or less money,' he said, 'and, second, in that region there was a good cattle country, so if I could not sell I could hold.' He wanted money, he wanted range, and he wanted to escape the turbulent Texas border.

He bought the gear of a government wagon, pulled it over to a wood-worker in Parker County, and had it entirely rebuilt with the toughest wood available, seasoned bois d'arc. Its axles were of iron instead of the usual wood, and in the place of a tar bucket he put in a can of tallow to use in greasing. He prepared to take twelve yoke of oxen, six to be used at a time.

For the back end of the wagon he built the first chuck-box he had ever seen, and recalled that 'it has been altered little to this day.' Its hinged lid let down on a swinging leg to form the cook's work-table, and inside was probably the first sour-dough

CHARLES GOODNIGHT

jar that ever went up the trail. Since that time, among outfits in the open country, the keg of sour-dough has become a favorite institution, even as the biscuits it has produced have become a fragrant memory. Goodnight learned its use from his efficient mother, who kept a jar brewing at home.

Next to good hands, horses were the most important part of a trail outfit. As the Indians had stolen him out, Goodnight went to the interior to buy his mounts, making his way to Gary's ranch, on Mary's Creek, near Fort Worth. When he reached the place, he found the owner engaged in breaking broncs by tying the head of the wild horse close up to the tail of his own gentle saddle horse, placing his little boy on the wild animal, and chousing or worrying the bronc until he was used to the saddle. As it is impossible for a horse to pitch with his head up, the most the bronc could do was to jerk and scramble about. Goodnight selected a number of horses, but turned back a good blue pony because he was too chunky. Gary saddled the cut-back as he prepared to leave, and the boy, afraid of the horse, began to cry at the prospect of having to ride him.

'Never mind, son,' said Goodnight, as he stopped to throw his own saddle upon the powerful blue, 'I'll ride him.' He cheeked the horse and stepped into the saddle. Immediately the blue fell in two and chinned the moon, but Goodnight sat above him with ease. He stopped pitching, broke into a run, headed for a ten-foot bluff along the creek, and went full drive over the top. Goodnight started to quit him as he left the ground, but, seeing he might 'light on his feet, stayed in the saddle.

'He hit in the mud and bogged to the saddle skirts,' said the rider, 'but didn't turn over. He was so strong that he scrambled right out and ran back toward the house. I got off and told Gary I would take him; he was good enough for me.'[1]

After his horses came his hands, and the men he chose were to the border born. 'One-Armed' Bill Wilson came first. It is not of record under what ill stars the Wilsons were born, but it is a matter of tradition that they were born for trouble, and they never belied their birthright. In 1857 the family came from Arkansas to settle on the Keechi, where they kept the Carruthers stock until after the war, and when the country went to hell the boys went to punching cattle. Bill, the best cowman of the bunch, worked for the CV outfit for several years, but continually went up on his wages until Sheek and Goodnight could not pay him.

Bill was an adventurer, and failing to fare well at one thing, he always dared to fare at something else. He went into the saloon business, much against the advice of his former employer. With a little money and a little credit, he went to Weatherford, got a few barrels of whiskey, and set out for Jacksboro, which of all places after the war was one of the worst for a rank rebel to be. A garrison of Federals was stationed there and the

[1] Goodnight to J. E. H., June 15, 1929.

Unionists, who had migrated to Kansas during the war, returned and began to intimidate the country. Yet 'One-Armed' Bill had a perfect genius for finding trouble, and hence to Jacksboro he was bound to go.

Living between Black Springs and Jacksboro was 'an old red-headed fellow named Fox,' Goodnight said, 'who had a head on him that looked like an owl's. One night he and another fellow went up to Jacksboro and robbed Bill, cleaning him out, after which Bill came back to the Keechi. I told him to go to Weatherford, tell his creditors that I would pay them, and come back and go to work for me — but to let the robbers alone.' But Bill met Simpson Crawford, a fighting Irish-American, who gave him some typical Irish advice:

'I'd kill those fellows if it was me,' said Simp laconically.

'Now that was bad advice,' reflected Goodnight. But it was as good as gospel to 'One-Armed' Bill, and more pleasant to ruminate upon than peaceful words.

Among the outlaw bands at the time — and anyone who ran counter to the carpetbag courts was outlawed — was one of about thirteen members headed by a man named Brooks. In order to get his revenge, Bill joined Brooks's band. One pitch-dark night they rode up to Fox's house and yelled:

'Hello!'

'Hello,' answered Fox, 'who's that?'

'Godfrey and Milligan,' answered the band, giving the names of two old scapegoats with whom Fox consorted, and Fox came pottering out. Brooks shot him dead, the band dispersed for the tall timbers, and Bill headed for his father's place at Weatherford. Fox's wife suspected Bill, and though it was too dark to recognize anyone, went to Jacksboro, and swore that he was the man who shot her husband. A detachment of soldiers arrested him, took him back to Fort Richardson, at Jacksboro, and put him in the guard-house pending his removal to Decatur for court-martial. Goodnight felt he would be shot as surely as the court-martial convened.

From among his neighbors he gathered up all the silver

money he could find — 'six or seven dollars in all' — took a good fast horse from his own *remuda*, gave the horse, the money, and his big Spanish spurs to a special messenger, and sent him to Jacksboro to get in touch with Bill. He was to exchange horses, give him the spurs, the money, and a message:

'Tell him,' Goodnight instructed, 'to buy all the whiskey this money will get when the escort starts with him to Decatur, pretend to drink but keep sober, get his escort as drunk as he can, and when he hits the Trinity Bottom, swing these spurs into his horse, trust to his luck, and leave them behind.'

'He made the break,' the cowman said, 'and they shot up the woods, but never touched him. I left instructions for him to stay away from my place and away from my herd until after I had started on the trail, and then he could come to me.' This time Bill followed good advice.

Goodnight arranged for other hands, and was almost ready to start when the news of his plans filtered through the Timbers, and threatened to bring on a clash with the Jacksboro Unionists. Sometime before, he had been on the verge of trouble with them.

These Unionists had fled to sanctuary in southern Kansas during the war. After the war they stole horses from the friendly Jayhawkers and rode back to Texas, where, in favor with Federal authorities, they began wreaking their vengeance on the Texans who had run them out. Goodnight referred to them as 'alleged Unionists,' who were neither loyal nor honest, for they began the promiscuous gathering of cattle, and threw a herd together on Bean's Prairie, east of Jacksboro.

'In so doing,' he explained, 'they got several of mine and Sheek's CV cattle, as well as a number of my neighbors'. I proposed to Sheek and Crawford that we go up and cut these cattle out. They contended that it would be dangerous, that we would be killed if we went, and that besides we would not get them. I took a different view. I hadn't stolen anybody's; nobody should steal mine if I could help it; and I was going to get these cattle. Unfortunately, when I got to Jacksboro a man from Kansas had purchased the herd, about a thousand head, and had given the money in advance. When he saw the people who had gathered the herd — the Unionists who had been in his neighborhood in Kansas and were now there on his neighbors' horses — he was much alarmed for fear he would never get the cattle and get away.

'I assured him that I thought he would get the cattle; that if he didn't I would raise a little crowd of men and come up and see that he did — that they should not rob a man in a civilized country. I had no difficulty whatever in cutting mine and my neighbors' cattle and the old gentleman left with his herd in good shape. I mention this circumstance to show that these were not honest Union people, but were "Union" for the protection it would give them in their thievery.

'As I prepared for the trail, they sent a man with a note to tell me they would take my cattle if I tried to leave. I told him to go back and tell them to send some sons-of-guns they never wanted to see again, as I'd guarantee they would never get back. These fellows were against everybody that had anything, and remind me of the story of the Dutchman who lived in Missouri during the war. Sometimes his country was held by the Confederates and again by the Federals. The first time he met a band they asked him what he was: "I'm Confederate," he said, and they took everything he had. The next time he was challenged he said: "I'm Federal," and they took everything he had. Upon the third challenge he answered: "Py God, I'm nodding!"'

From his experience with the rangers, Goodnight had gained sufficient knowledge of the terrain to blaze a direct, northwest trail to Colorado. But the Comanches and Kiowas still held the country, and would have taken his herd had he so ventured. Nine years of residence in uncomfortable proximity had taught him as much. It had taught him more — that he could get to Colorado by taking roundance, by swinging down the old Butterfield Trail to the southwest, turning up the Pecos to the Rockies, and paralleling them northward. By such a course, almost twice as long as the direct one, he might escape the Indians and eventually reach Denver.

Two other cowmen whom he expected to go with him backed out as the time for starting approached. Undaunted, Goodnight went ahead with his plans. When his outfit was ready, he hurried for Weatherford to buy flour and other necessary supplies, on the way passing Oliver Loving's camp, where the older man was gathering his cattle. Loving motioned him by and asked about his proposed drive, particularly the trail he was going to take. Then he enumerated the hazards and uncertainties of such an undertaking and commented upon the desert, of many miles without water, which the herd would have to cross.

Upon finding the younger man was still determined to go, he said: 'If you will let me, I will go with you.'

'I will not only let you,' came the eager answer, 'but it is the most desirable thing of my life. I not only need the assistance of your force, but I need your advice.'

It was agreed and settled. They joined herds twenty-five miles southwest of Belknap, two thousand head in all, with an outfit of eighteen men, fairly well armed.

And thus, upon the sixth day of June, 1866, the most momentous day in young Goodnight's life, he left the frontier of Texas to blaze a new trail for longhorned cattle. The thousands of flinty hoofs that cut its grass to dust traced his name as well as his trail across the face of the Western World. Upon the dusts of that trail rose the tradition of the man, no longer a man only of Texas, but now a man of the West.

Oliver Loving, fifty-four years of age, mature in years yet sturdy as a liveoak tree, took charge of the drive at Goodnight's insistence, and the cattle were pointed westward.

For many miles their course was plain as they followed the trace of the Southern Overland Mail, with which the name of Butterfield is synonymous. Captain R. B. Marcy, the army explorer, Boundary Commissioner John R. Bartlett, Captain John Pope, and others had explored portions of the course in the late forties and fifties. Travel by the Emigrant Trail to California had removed some doubts concerning the country they faced, but none of its difficulties and dangers. They trailed out into a tried, but still an uncertain, land.[2]

POINTING THE HERD

On either point rode two experienced cowboys — the best hands in the outfit — who directed the herd along the course indicated by the owners. Behind these rode the other trail hands, holding the herd to the proper form and size, and shifting their positions daily to relieve those driving on the leeward and dusty side. Far in the lead, often twelve to fifteen miles ahead, scouted the observant Goodnight, exploring to either side for water holes, range and suitable bed grounds, and doubling back, at intervals, to signal to the pointers the way the herd should come.

It was pretty work and they marched on smoothly and happily into the wilderness, past Camp Cooper, and on west by the gaunt and haunted chimneys of old Fort Phantom Hill.[3]

[2] For something of the development of the trail across Texas through the explorations of Lieutenant F. T. Bryan, Rip Ford, Major R. S. Neighbors, Bartlett, Pope, and the others, see: *Reconnaissances of Routes from San Antonio to El Paso*, Senate Ex. Doc. No. 64, 31st Cong., 1st Sess.; Pope, *Report of Exploration of a Route for the Pacific Railroad*, 1854, pp. 66–73; Bartlett, *Personal Narrative*, i; Ford, MS., 'Memoirs,' The University of Texas; R. N. Richardson, 'Some Details of the Southern Overland Mail,' *Southwestern Historical Quarterly*, xxix, pp. 1–18.

[3] There is a tradition to the effect that in this region the early Western travelers and soldiers first saw, in their perfection, the mirages of the Plains; hence the name of Fort Phantom Hill

The outfit turned south and passed in the neighborhood of present Abilene, still following the trace of the old Southern Mail, and thence through be-legended Buffalo Gap. They marched past Fort Chadbourne, on south and west to cross the North Concho about twenty miles above where San Angelo was later to be built, plodded across the divide to the Middle Concho, and followed its course westward to where it headed in the Staked Plains.

They stopped on the headwaters of the Middle Concho to recruit and let the herd get a good fill, and made preparations for the most severe drive on all the Texas trails. Stretching for miles beyond the headwaters, on into the west and the Staked Plains, was Centralia Draw. Along its course the Butterfield stages of six years past had cut their ruts and pointed the way to Horsehead Crossing, on the Pecos. At the western extremity of the Plains were the Castle Mountains, through which the old stage road passed by way of Castle Gap, a cañon about a mile in length.

Twelve miles beyond Castle Gap was Horsehead Crossing, the most noted ford along six hundred miles of the sinuous Pecos; a river less than a hundred feet wide and always swimming; a treacherous stream that squirmed and fought its way through a vast arid world loath to let it flow. Rising clear and cold in the mountains of northern New Mexico, its pure waters cut through rough country that changed its flood to turbid red. Then it emerged into the alkali plains of southern New Mexico, and dropping some of its sand, lifted up bitter alkaline salts. After it twisted in violent contortions through a desolate greasewood country to the cañons of its lower reaches in Texas, its waters were briny and its effect disastrous to those who drank from its channels, though, in time, one became sufficiently inured to its laxative properties to drink in comparative safety, and Chisum's cowboys carried salt in their saddle-pockets and seasoned to taste such fresh-water holes as they found in riding the range — so the story goes.

In its tortuous meanderings it is often cursed by the natives as 'the crookedest river in the world.' Goodnight used to tell how Pete Narbo, a Palo Pinto ranchman, shot a steer that someone had dropped from a herd. He swam over to get the beef, but had to swim back again, discovering that he and the animal had been on the same bank. And though that was a long time ago, the Pecos has not improved with age.[4]

Horsehead Crossing was on the main Indian trail from the Plains to Chihuahua, and when the Comanche was in his prime the settlements of northern Mexico were no more exempt from his knife than those of the Texas border. He stole great *caballadas* from the *haciendas* to the south, and trailed them back to the Plains by the way of Horsehead. The origin of the name is befogged in legend, but according to old Rip Ford, returning Comanches drove so hard from the last water hole, sixty miles beyond the Pecos, that their thirsty horses sometimes drank their death of the Pecos brine. From the great number of skulls lying about, and others once stuck in mesquites to mark the crossing, the place derived its name.[5]

Loving and Goodnight paused and planned the drive across from the Concho, nearly eighty miles without water, though they thought the distance nearer a hundred. They held their herd on water during the heat of the day until the old steers would lazily suck up no more; they filled their canteens and water barrels to overflowing; and in the afternoon they pointed their herd into the setting sun. They trailed until late, camped for the night, and early next day pushed on. Twelve to fifteen miles is a good day's drive with a mixed herd, and in summer cattle ordinarily water daily. Driving increases thirst, and when they camped the herd that night the cattle were too dry and restless to bed down. All night they walked and milled between the night herders, and most of the crew of eighteen men were called out to hold them.

[4] W. S. Mabry to J. E. H., April 15, 1929; I. H. Bell to J. E. H., March 18, 1927. Narbo was a pioneer of the Cross Timbers. After the outbreak of the Civil War he drove a herd of 225 big steers to the east, selling a few at Memphis and the rest to the Confederacy.

[5] John S. Ford, MS., 'Memoirs,' III, 515–16, Archives, The University of Texas; *The Northern Standard*, July, 30, 1861; Bartlett, as cited, I, 96.

Next morning Goodnight said to his partner: 'Mr. Loving, this will never do. Those cattle walked enough last night to have got to the Pecos. This camping won't work; we've got to let them travel.'

'I guess you're right, Charlie,' said the older man. 'You take charge of them and see what you can do.'

So they toiled on that day, the cattle growing wearier with each mile, but still urged on by the sleepy cowboys. The hot summer sun beat down from a merciless sky, the canteens were sucked dry, and by night the barrels had been drawn to the final dregs. The white, bitter dust rose in clouds further to torture the bleary-eyed riders, their lips cracked open from heat and brine, and their throats burned with the fires of thirst and alkali. Ahead the pointers were holding the leaders back, behind the drag hands were fighting the weak stuff forward, and with their shouts and curses arose the mighty din of a herd of cattle bawling and moaning for water. Their ribs stood out like the bars of a grill, their flanks were drawn and gaunt, their tongues lolled far from their mouths, sometimes sweeping in the alkali dust, and their eyes sunk in their sockets with approaching death. Often a wild-eyed animal stopped, turned, and attempted to fight. There was no worrying with it; already it was as good as dead. They dropped it out and struggled on.

Such suffering of cattle alone places an almost unbearable strain upon the men who handle them; nerves grow taut and keen, and the best of friends have been known to fall out, fight and kill. All through that drive rode the energetic and domi-nant Goodnight, here and there where he needed to be — riding without rest a chunky black horse as durable as he — not batting an eye in sleep for three days and nights. And with the drags was the patient Loving, toiling to save from the ruthless desert what little the vicissitudes of war had left them.

Upon the third evening, Goodnight took an ox-bell from the wagon, put it on one of the horses in the lead, and told the hands with the drags that when the herd got too long for safe driving — they to judge by the sound of the bell — to send word up to him by one of the line riders and he would hold the leaders until it was again the proper length. And so as the evening shadows brought relief from the heat, if none from thirst, and the stars came out and bathed the Plains in a ghostly light, the herd moved on. The wagon advanced to the lead and the cook served strong, black coffee as each hand rode by, while from out of the cool darkness ahead came the clear, sharp clatter of an ox-bell, indicating to those behind when the herd should be closed up.

About two o'clock in the morning they came to Castle Cañon, from which a gentle, damp breeze was blowing. Thinking they smelled water, the cattle stampeded down it. Goodnight, riding wildly in the darkness ahead, succeeded in holding the leaders until the rest of the herd came up. Then leaving the boys on guard, he changed horses at daylight, took all the canteens and loped down to the river, twelve miles away, to fill them.

'This was the third day the cattle had had no water,' he said, 'and they became crazed and almost unmanageable.' I took four of the best men, the horses, and all the strong cattle — about two thirds of the herd — and let them go as fast as possible to the water. There was an alkali pond near the river which would have meant death to them, but by pulling a few hairs from my horse's neck and letting them float to the ground, I detected the exact course of the breeze and took advantage of it, so that when the cattle smelled the water, they would strike for the ford of the river instead of the pond.

'As soon as they smelled the cool air, they became wild for water, and when they reached the river those behind pushed the ones in the lead right on across before they had time to stop and drink. I was in the lead and as soon as they all cleared the river, I turned them back and they readily went in again, drinking as they swam back. They crossed in such volume and force that they impeded the current, and the water was halfway up the bank in a perfect flood. As soon as I got them watered, I put them to grass and placed one of the best men, Charlie

Wilson, in charge of them, telling him to hold them while they grazed, but not to let them go back to the river for a while. None of us had had any sleep, and all were dead for want of it. I gave him my watch — I happened to have one then — and said: "Charlie, take this watch and let the men sleep ten or fifteen minutes at a time, one and then the other, but for your life don't go to sleep yourself."'

SWIMMING THE PECOS

Goodnight then set out to help with the drags, but glancing back, saw six cows on their way to water again — Wilson and the boys had already gone to sleep. The cows stopped at one of the detached, strongly alkaline pools found in the Pecos Valley, and though he loped hurriedly back, three finished drinking before he reached them. As they turned away from the water, one after another dropped in her tracks and died — the others were dead in a few minutes — so poisonous was the concentrated Pecos water.[6]

'I returned as quickly as possible to meet Mr. Loving,' continued Goodnight, 'who held the remainder of the herd — about five hundred head. In the meantime the wind had

---

[6] Today these alkali holes are fenced. In recent years a peculiar malady developed in the Pecos country through livestock's eating salt grass and other native herbage and drinking the impregnated Pecos water. Cattle suffering from it — they did not always die — were said to be 'alkalied.'

shifted, and as soon as they smelled the water they became unmanageable. They were virtually crazy and would go either to the water or not at all; all hands on one side could not turn them. The point of the river for which they were headed was like a ditch, with banks from six to ten feet high. When they reached the river they never halted, but poured right over the bank and the remainder of the horses went with them.'

Many of the cattle drowned, while some found precarious footing along the sharply cut banks, where they stood in the water, and others drifted into a short bend of the river which was bad with quicksand. The cowboys piled into the river in an attempt to save some portion of the heaving, struggling mass, and for two full days fought the shifty current, the cut banks, and the tenacious quicksands. The owners concluded that if they stayed in the water longer, exposed, short of rest, and worked to a frazzle, they would save but few of their cattle and would probably lose some of their hands. They rode off and left over a hundred head in the river, alive, bogged in the quicksands and stranded beneath unscalable bluffs. Along the desert trail for miles behind them were more than three hundred others, dead, grim markers of the course, proof of how dearly this early trail was blazed.[7]

In looking back, not only on his own but on the losses of practically every other cowman who followed their lead, Goodnight humanized the Pecos and its bleak terrain, and hated it as a man hates an implacable, imperturbable foe. 'The Pecos — the graveyard of the cowman's hopes,' he would say with savage feeling. 'I hated it! It was as treacherous as the Indians themselves.'[8]

After three days for recruiting their herd and horses, they started up the east side of the Pecos through the most uninviting country Goodnight had ever seen. In fact, he observed:

[7] Goodnight, 'Recollections,' ii, 68–71; Goodnight to J. E. H., June 15, 1929; Goodnight, 'Starting the Longhorn Westward,' *The Fort Worth Star Telegram*, September 15, 1929; E. B. Bronson, 'Loving's Bend,' *McClure's*, November, 1908, p. 86; J. Frank Dobie, 'Charles Goodnight, Trail Blazer,' *Country Gentleman*, March, 1927.

[8] Max Bentley to J. E. H., October 15, 1932.

'At that time the Pecos was the most desolate country that I had ever explored. The river was full of fish, but besides the fish there was scarcely a living thing, not even wolves or birds. I never saw or heard a wolf until my second trip. The first one seemed to be unconscious of the advent of man; the only animal of this kind I ever saw that was not afraid. He probably scented our provisions which we were carrying on our pack-mule. I saw nothing on earth for him to live on except mesquite beans, unless it was the rattlesnakes, of which there was an abundance. He looked so lonely and so desolate that I thought it would be an act of charity to kill him, and did.'[9]

But rattlesnakes? They were there by the hundreds, and still are. One of the hands, Nath Brauner, a cross-eyed cowboy, killed all the snakes he saw, and his sight was really defective. After the war ammunition was hard for the rebels to get, and on the trail Goodnight ordered his men to shoot no more than necessary. Brauner had his own ammunition, and plenty of it, and blazed away to his heart's content. He kept the rattles to send to his home in Kentucky, and upon reaching Fort Sumner had seventy-two in all. Really his affliction was a wonderful advantage, he said, for he could watch the cattle with one eye while hunting rattlers with the other.

Jack Potter, trail driver and range veteran of eastern New Mexico, declares this trail up the river the worst driven by Texas cowmen. During a decade of ranching at Fort Sumner, he never saw a herd come up the Goodnight Trail but that its men were afoot. Steep, narrow trails led to the water, down which cattle slid and drank while standing on their heads. If they stepped in a little too far, the quicksands pulled them under, and after drinking they often had to back up the trail. But as the herd slowly trudged toward Pope's Crossing, near the New Mexico line, the drivers had other troubles than those imposed by the severity of the soil.[10]

[9] Goodnight, MS., 'My Remembrance of and What I Know About Buffalo,' 6–7. Sixteen years before Bartlett reported 'scarcely a living object' on the river. As cited, I, 103.

[10] Goodnight to J. E. H., September 29, 1929; Jack Potter to J. E. H., August 26, 1932. Bartlett was particularly impressed with the difficulty of watering stock.

All cowmen know that a mixed herd on the trail is awkward to handle. The stride of a steer is stronger than that of a cow, and a calf must frequently break pace to keep up with either. Trailing of cows seems to hasten the dropping of calves, and each morning the last guard found new ones on the bed ground. They could not keep up with the herd; there was no way to haul them; the owners could not delay.

'We killed hundreds of newborn calves on the bed grounds,' said Goodnight. 'I always hated to kill the innocent things, but as they were never counted in on the sale of cattle the loss of them was nothing financially. In our outfit we had a nigger named Jim Fowler, but who called himself Jim Goodnight. Every morning I'd give Jim a six-shooter and tell him to kill the calves dropped during the night. One morning he said he wished I'd get somebody else to do the killing.

'"I just don't like to kill them little calfies," he said.

'"Well, Jim, I don't either, but it has to be done." And Jim kept at the job.

'After a cow is driven away from her calf, whether dead or alive, she naturally tries to go back. Often we had to put on a double guard at night to hold them, and they would bawl all night long, and then all day, until their voices became mere ghosts of voices. Sometimes if the calves were coming too thick, we'd neck a cow to a steer, or we'd hobble them. If we drove a cow away the instant she was delivered of her calf, before she had a chance to smell it or give it suck, she would not make any trouble.

'We had so much worry with the cows and calves that I determined never to drive another mixed herd the Pecos route, and I never did, though I afterward trailed lots of cows over other routes.'

Just below the Texas–New Mexico line was Pope's Crossing, one of the few fords along several hundred miles of the river. Captain John Pope crossed there while making one of the preliminary surveys for the first Pacific railway in the early fifties, and later drilled a well nearby in search of artesian

water. It too had become a noted ford. Loving and Goodnight
crossed to the west side of the river. They trailed on north
across the Delaware and Black River, and above the site of
Carlsbad, crossed back to the east in order to place the stream

APACHE

between themselves and the Mescalero Apaches, who rendez-
voused in the Guadalupe Mountains to the west. And thus
they drove without serious incident by Comanche Springs,
by Bosque Grande — the big timbers — and on to Bosque Redondo, or Fort Sumner.

Three years before, Fort Sumner had been established as a
reservation for the Navajo and Mescalero Indians. Largely
through the aggressive campaigns of Kit Carson, there had

been concentrated upon it, by the end of 1865, about eighty-five hundred Indians. But as a reservation it was totally lacking in merit. In spite of attempted irrigation, the soil was poor and unproductive, fuel was scarce, and provisions inadequate.

Besides the troublous limitations of the soil and the unhappiness of the Navajos upon having to leave their mountains and live in a sterile plain, the tribal combination was unfortunate. The Navajos and Mescaleros were old enemies, culturally diverse. The Mescaleros were bolder warriors, but greatly outnumbered, and in 1866, after ceaseless quarreling and bickering, they ran away from the reserve 'after their agent had been driven off on a charge of irregular dealings in cattle.' When the trail drivers reached Fort Sumner, the Indians were still on the verge of starvation, and they found a ready market for their beeves.[11]

The Government could not supply the need, though it had been paying as much as sixteen cents a pound for beef. Loving and Goodnight sold their steers — 'twos, threes, and up' — for the high price of eight cents a pound on foot. The general contractor, an ex-captain of the California Volunteers named Roberts, and the sub-contractors, Jim and Tom Patterson, would not take their stock cattle. Thus seven to eight hundred head of cows and calves were left unsold. But never had Goodnight known so much money to be made on cattle, and he and Loving were elated as they turned to the disposal of the cutbacks.

They drove up the Pecos to a creek called Las Carretas, where they rested for a few days on good water and grass, and celebrated the Fourth of July with the best dinner the cook could prepare, which was bad enough for any day. Putting their heads together they decided that Loving should carry the stock cattle on into Colorado, in accord with their original plan, while Goodnight returned to Texas to trail another herd before

[11] For discussion of the reservation see *The New Mexican* (Santa Fé), October 27 and November 24, 1866; House Ex. Doc. 248, 40th Cong., 2d Sess., pp. 2–8; Twitchell, *Leading Facts in New Mexican History*, II, 358–59; Bancroft, *History of Arizona and New Mexico*, 730–33.

the coming of winter. They parted full of plans, ambitions fired by this undreamed initial success. Goodnight eagerly set out on the seven-hundred-mile saddle trip back to Texas, down the trail that was to bear his name.

LOVING took the outfit and the stock cattle, drove by Las Vegas, and kept a northerly course until he crossed the Ratón Range. From there he skirted the base of the Rockies, crossing the Arkansas near Pueblo, and in the vicinity of Denver sold the cattle to that great Western ranchman, John W. Iliff. Thus was laid out the Loving Trail from Fort Sumner north, though Goodnight later extended it beyond the Platte and into Wyoming, after which it came to be known as the Goodnight and Loving Trail. Loving turned back to join Goodnight and the second herd at Sumner.

When they parted, Goodnight packed a mule with provisions and some twelve thousand dollars in gold, the money received for the beeves, and as there was not a habitation between Bosque Redondo and Fort Belknap, he carried provisions for the trip. With three cowboy companions, he took the trail and pushed on the reins toward Texas, so that they might have time to return before winter set in. They rode saddle mules, because of their staying qualities, but each led his fastest horse behind. In case of Indian attack they planned, if necessary, to mount their horses, abandon their mules, and shoot their way out.

They rode down the Pecos at night, lay up in out-of-the-way places by day, and each evening as dusk fell took the trail again. Goodnight led the way, followed by the pack-mule, and in turn by the cowboys. As they came to the most dangerous point on the trail, where the Guadalupes jut out near the river, a bad storm struck, with lightning, thunder, rain, and heavy wind. They pushed on.

At the height of the storm something scared the pack-animal, whether a waylay of Apaches or something else Goodnight never knew, but the mule went by him like a bat out of a brush pile. He thought of the money in the pack, and spurring his saddle mule to the limit, took the lead within a quarter of a mile, and at the risk of his neck, flung himself off and grabbed at the runaway as he went by. In spite of the darkness he luckily caught the pack-rope, one end of which was tied around the animal's neck. The mule bucked, ran, 'bellered,' and did his best to get away, but Goodnight, thinking of the money, hung on like a badger and worried him to a standstill, declaring, however, that between them they 'tore up enough ground for a circus.'

'When the fuss was over, I found the money intact,' he said, 'as it had been bound tight, next to the saddle, with the provisions on top. But the provisions were all gone. We could not find them in the dark, so there was nothing to do but camp in the most dangerous place on the whole road.

'When daylight came, we found one little piece of bacon about six inches square and not very thick. Close to the mountains the coyotes were numerous and had got all the food, even the tobacco, which they probably carried away in the sacks. It is a question yet as to which the boys missed the most. This left us with only a little piece of bacon, fully five hundred miles from anywhere. We hid until dark, then started our march.'[1]

While in the ranger service a severe spell of measles had impaired Goodnight's hearing. The sense never returned in its original keenness, and when he was sick or suffering with a cold, his hearing became quite dull. The exposure and grueling work of the recent drive had so depleted his strength as to bring on this dullness, which was particularly unfortunate as the lower Pecos was lined with rattlesnakes.

'I could not see in the dark,' he said, 'and could not hear the

---

[1] Goodnight, 'Recollections,' II, 72–74.

rattlers. Every little while the boys behind would yell: "Look out, Charlie, there's another rattler." To say the least, it created a mighty uncomfortable feeling. Not being able to see or hear them, I didn't know which way to jump. They kept yelling at me until finally I stopped and said: "I'm going to read the riot act to you fellows. Take your damned rattlers and go straight to hell or any other place you want to, and leave me alone."'

With no provisions, and no game within two hundred miles, they hurried on toward Horsehead. They shot a catfish or two, but usually they dreaded to shoot for fear of attracting the Indians, and long before they reached the Crossing, the bacon had given out, though they 'ate it very sparingly, rind and all.'

They filled their canteens and left the Pecos for the long stretch of plain, and when daylight came they kept going, as on the desert they were not likely to meet Indians, and besides there was no place to hide from them. When yet twenty-five miles from the Concho, they saw something in the distance which all took to be a party of Indians.

'It was useless to turn back,' said Goodnight; 'it was useless to stop; we had to go on. The mass looked like about twenty Indians and the boys were frightened in the extreme. I had splendid sight and after watching the object intently told the boys I did not think it was Indians.

'Yet in spite of the fact that the boys were pale as death, and felt their time had come, and I was ill with a high fever, for some reason I had full confidence that I would escape, and I can't tell you why. I learned a lesson that I never forgot as I looked at the boys and thought to myself: "Here you are with more gold than you ever had in your life, and it won't buy you a drink of water, and it won't get you food. For this gold you may have led three men to their death — for a thing that is utterly useless to you!" I never got over the impression it made on me, and I believe it is one reason why I have never worshiped money since.

'We quit our mules and saddled our horses for the fray. I

instructed the boys as best I could, telling them especially to hang together — but not too close; to keep the saddle and pack-mules up with me if they could, and if not to leave them and follow me; that with my pistols I would open a lane through the Indians, and for them not to shoot unless an Indian forced them to.

'When we had gone a mile farther, I again told the boys that I felt sure it was not Indians, as the line was still unbroken and there were no stragglers on either side. When we did meet the object, it was old Rich Coffee — who lived at the upper settlements on the Colorado below the mouth of the Concho — with a six-yoke ox-team and a wagonload of the biggest watermelons you 'most ever saw. I knew him well and asked him where he was going. He said he was going over to the Pecos, to the great Salt Lake to load back with salt, and expected to sell the watermelons to the Mexicans, who came there about twice a year from the El Paso country with great numbers of carts.

'I told him it was the wrong time of year to meet the caravans; that they always came over in the early spring and late in the fall, between the rainy seasons, when the salt was more abundant. But I assured him that he had a market right there for some of the melons.[2] We sat in the shade of his wagon, as he was kind enough to stop for two or three hours, and ate those cold melons, and let me say that watermelons never tasted as good to me as they did that day. They cooled my fever and I soon felt good. Mr. Coffee gave us enough provisions to do us until we reached the settlements at Fort Belknap, which we made without further mishap, and when I saw him again he told me he buried the remaining watermelons in the sand.'[3]

On the seventeenth day after leaving Sumner, Goodnight

---

[2] 'Sometimes the Mexicans came with seventy-five to a hundred carts, the tongues of which were made of tree trunks, the felloes of the wheels tied in with rawhide — there was no metal whatever about them. The Mexicans did not fear the Indians as they had been at peace and had traded with them for many years.' Goodnight to J. E. H., April 8, 1927.

[3] Goodnight, 'Recollections,' II, 75–77.

was in Weatherford to engage supplies for his return trip, having averaged forty miles a night — very good traveling for that distance on grass stock. He contracted his supplies to be delivered at Belknap, rushed back to the range, hired his hands, gathered what beeves he could from his and Sheek's herds, and bought others here and there, receiving most of them on the Brazos, near Belknap.

Cattle were abundant and cowmen of the surrounding country helped him to gather, receive, and road-brand about nine hundred head. He wanted four hundred more, and decided to go about ten miles inland where he could round out the herd with ease. In the first drive on Locke Williams Prairie, the outfit threw together some two thousand head. Late in the day they penned the roundup, planning to cut it next morning, and the crew of thirty to forty men camped nearby. Goodnight had five or six of his own outfit to help in receiving the remainder of his herd.

Then, as later, he had great confidence in intuitive warnings of danger, in the promptings, perhaps, of the subconscious mind, declaring that they saved his life several times. When he had a 'feeling' that things were not right, he would always beware.

'During the night,' he recalled, 'I was awakened from a sound sleep with a subconscious warning that the Indians were there and would endeavor to get our horses. I awoke the men and told them to help me get the horses and get away, as Indians were somewhere around. But they just laughed at me, saying: "When did you get Indian bit? We thought you were an Indian fighter!" They ignored my advice and warning, but I took my men and horses and went about two miles away, to a briar thicket — a mean place to get into — with an open glade in the middle, in which I turned my horses loose and slept soundly until daylight.

'When I returned to the camp, there was not a horse left. The cowmen commenced to shout:

'"Give us your horses and we will follow and get them."

'"Not much," I said, "you've never caught them yet," which made them quite indignant. I also told them that I had followed many an Indian trail in pursuit of stolen horses and rarely caught them, and never unless I followed them a great distance. I reached my camp on the Brazos that night, and by daylight next morning I was on the move out of the settlements.' [4]

Within ten or twelve days Goodnight had hired his hands, organized and equipped another outfit, received and branded twelve hundred big steers, and again 'put to sea' across the rolling plains. One peculiar circumstance enlivened the trip.

The steers had been stampeding, running enough to be nervous and difficult to handle. Fall had come and the buffalo migration was on. Already the sexes had separated and the trail outfit intersected the course of the buffalo bull herd, which was headed southeast while the steers were pointing southwest. This column of migratory flesh reached for miles to the northwest, urged on by that strange wild lust that irresistibly sent it southward in the fall and back in the spring. Yet its leaders hesitated at the sight of this curious caravan

[4] Goodnight, 'Recollections,' ii, 53–54; Goodnight to J. E. H., July 10, 1928, and September 29, 1929.

that intersected its trail, and Goodnight thought he had room and time to pass. He was about halfway by when the buffaloes stampeded and came south on the run.

He and two of his men tried to turn them, but they might as well have attempted to turn the wind, for they cut the herd of cattle in two near the middle, and those snuffy old steers went crazy as these black apparitions burst among them. About half the herd tore back toward the Brazos bottoms; the others curled their tails toward Horsehead Crossing, while every cowboy rode hard on their heels. Goodnight quit the buffaloes and swung to the lead, sent the other hands racing with the drags, and by fast work kept the herd from scattering far and wide. For three quarters of an hour the buffalo herd poured between them, the ground seeming to tremble and quake with their rush; a sensation accentuated by the illusory vibrations of the sound waves.

After the buffaloes had passed, the cowboys brought their longhorns together and Goodnight was relieved to find that none had been lost. Yet they were forced to ride line on scattered buffaloes to keep them out of their herd until they reached the Middle Concho.

They trailed up the stream and prepared for the drive across the desert, this time having no difficulty in crossing, as they had learned their lesson before.

'We left the Concho about noon, having first allowed the cattle to drink all they would,' explained Goodnight. 'We put to the trail and kept them moving until just before sundown. Then we gave them all the grass they could eat — cattle will not drive well if hungry. We then drove them all night, next morning again grazed them until they were full, then trailed. After that they did not want to eat much, as they commenced to get dry. We moved them all that day and the following night. Naturally they were difficult to handle, but we never lost a head after learning this system of crossing the Plains.'

By the time they had crossed the Llano Estacado, the old

steers had quieted and gentled like milk-pen cattle, and trailed on without trouble. In approximately forty days, Goodnight was camped at Bosque Grande, forty miles below Sumner. There he was rejoined by Loving, and they went into winter camp, the first Texans to establish a ranch in southern New Mexico. They dug into the bluffs on the east side of the river, constructed such dugouts as suited their convenience, and lived in comfortable quarters until spring.

The Patterson brothers also established a camp there, and Frank Willburn, who followed with a little herd, from Texas, wintered nearby and shared in some of the contracts held by Loving and Goodnight.

Until this time Goodnight and Loving had handled their cattle under separate ownership, but upon Loving's return he suggested that, since they got along well together, they form an equal partnership for the purpose of buying and selling cattle. Accordingly, the accounts were adjusted and they prepared to handle the second herd under the new and oral agreement. Thus the firm of Loving and Goodnight came into being in a dugout at Bosque Grande in the wilderness. No papers were executed and no instruments drawn; yet its conditions bound its parties as strongly as the threads of life.

Once a month during the winter they cut off a hundred head of beeves, drove them to Santa Fé, and delivered them to government contractors, a little Jew called *Chiquito* and a big German whose name is forgotten. According to Goodnight, they were long on butchering and short on principle. He and Loving finally gave the contract up because the deliveries were small and troublesome, but they continued monthly deliveries at Fort Sumner.

Upon finding that some of the cattle, stolen by the Comanches in Texas, were being brought in by New Mexican traders along the Canadian, they crossed over the high undulating Plains to Fort Bascom,[5] and asked the co-operation of the

[5] Fort Bascom was established on the north bank of the Canadian, August 15, 1863. Hamersly, *Army Register*, II, 124.

officers in suppressing the illicit traffic. The officers agreed to take charge of any cattle coming over the *comanchero* trail and deliver them to Loving and Goodnight in the future, if they had powers of attorney authorizing them to receive the various brands. Pleased with this assurance, they rode back to the Bosque.[6]

With the letting of new contracts at Fort Sumner, a man named Andy Adams outbid the Pattersons by agreeing to furnish beef at two and a half cents a pound on foot. Loving and Goodnight could not afford at this low price to put in the cattle they had bought; neither could Roberts and the Pattersons buy from trail drivers and supply him. But Adams had gone to Texas and on the San Saba frontier contracted, on credit, several thousand cattle from J. D. Hoy.

Early in 1867, Hoy started two herds in charge of Lew Soyer and George Fowler, and planned to bring a third himself. Since Loving and Goodnight's first drive, the Comanches had discovered their trail, and parties had swung south to waylay it in the vicinity of Horsehead. Hoy's first herd was taken from Soyer in Castle Cañon; some of his men turned back to Texas; others went on to Sumner. The second herd was also taken by the Indians after it left the head of the Concho. Goodnight heard the particulars and related the story:

'George Fowler told me the herd was strung out some distance when the Indians made the attack in considerable numbers, and the men, being scattered, commenced to give way and retreat down the road. Nearby was a pecan grove with a great deal of underbrush, into which some of the hands escaped. An Irishman, well-mounted, had become so frightened that he would not let his horse run. Fowler went up beside him and tried to get him to turn the horse loose, and when he did not, Fowler left him and went into the thicket. In a few seconds the Indians seized the poor Irishman

[6] Goodnight to J. E. H., September 17, 1928; Goodnight, Deposition in Indian Depredation Claim, 8532, October 25, 1898, pp. 15–16.

and actually cut him to pieces alive. His cries were most pitiful.

'With the same outfit was an emigrant and his wife named Whitehead, going through with the herd. He seemed to be a merchant and had a remnant of goods with him, among which was quite a number of linen shirts. It happened that another traveler called "Honey" Allen — who had gathered pecans and wild honey on the Devil's River in 1866, and had made his way through and sold them at Fort Sumner — was caught on the Plains nearby. He had gathered a lot more pecans and honey, and had started out in a big wagon, pulled by several yoke of cattle, aiming to cross the Plains alone, as he had done before.

'After getting out ten or twelve miles, he concluded his cattle were too dry to make it across, and so unyoked, left his wagon, and started back to the Concho to water them. He ran right into the band of Indians, and of course they took his cattle. He was riding a good horse and escaped. While getting away, he passed the Whiteheads, who had thrown their bedding out, doubled their cattle back, and were standing the Indians off the best they could. Only one of the trail hands had gone to help them, and he had received a wound in the back of the neck, which temporarily disabled him.

'Allen hid out in the pecan grove the rest of the day and most all night. Just before day he went back to where he had seen the emigrants corralled. Afraid to call lest the Indians would hear him, he crawled up to where they had stopped, finding Mrs. Whitehead on guard in order to let the men rest. She saw him crawling up in the dark and immediately awakened her husband, who shot a nip out of his ear. He jumped up with a shout. Whitehead invited him in and they had a very pleasant greeting.'

When the straggling cowboys reached Fort Sumner and reported, Adams knew he must fail to meet his contracts unless he could find other cattle immediately. Otherwise, the Government would buy on the open market and Loving and Goodnight would supply the beef. The only other herd in the country was one of about sixteen hundred head recently arrived from the San Saba, belonging to Hubbard and Farrar, camped on the Hondo at the site of Roswell, nearly a hundred miles below.

Adams started two men south in a buggy to buy the herd, their course bringing them near the Bosque Ranch. They passed about night, stopped at the Patterson camp, and asked for directions. As soon as they left, the Pattersons excitedly rushed over to see the Texans and propose that they beat Adams's buyers to the Hondo and purchase the Hubbard and Farrar cattle, as well as another small herd of seven hundred head coming through the mountains from toward El Paso.

The Texans agreed, and it was decided that Goodnight should leave at once. He saddled, crossed the Pecos, and started his all-night ride down its west bank. Some miles below he had to cross Salt Creek, which was impassably boggy in places. The men in the buggy had missed the crossing and bogged in the marsh. They had left the buggy in the mud, extricated themselves and their horses, and had gone to sleep on the ground. Goodnight quietly found the crossing and passed without their knowledge, reached the Hubbard and Farrar camp a little after daylight, and did not parley long before buying the cattle at a fair price. Then he left on the trail west, toward Fort Stanton.[7]

'The upper Hondo country was entirely unsettled,' he said, 'but more or less inhabited by Apaches, making it not very desirable to go alone. But I kept the high ground and made as good time as possible.

'Fortunately, just about sundown I met Jim Burleson, the owner of the other herd, whom we all knew. He had driven out from Texas the fall before, had crossed to the Rio Grande country, and, failing to dispose of his cattle, was coming back across the mountains. He insisted on my staying all night, but I pretended to be in a hurry to go on to Fort Stanton, though I was not too hard to persuade to stay over.

'Here I found the most peculiar, the strangest, cow outfit I have ever seen from that day to this. Burleson was a gambler and a sport. He had with him a pack of hounds, two race horses, several baskets of game cocks, plenty of good whiskey, and about the poorest cattle I ever saw, handled principally by a lot of Mexicans, on foot.

'In the morning I bought his cattle with the understanding that he was to deliver them at the crossing of the Pecos, some twenty miles below the Bosque, where I was to meet him and receive them. This I did, and Burleson and his strange outfit took the Loving and Goodnight Trail home.'

Thus the Adams contract was tied up and the two partners began putting their cattle in on the Agency purchases through Captain Roberts and the Pattersons. Whether because of a

---

[7] Fort Stanton, near the head of the Bonita, one prong of the Hondo, is high in the mountains about seventy-five miles west of Roswell. It was established May 4, 1855. Hamersly, as cited, II, 154.

general order by the War Department or only a local ruling, Goodnight never knew, but at the time no contracts were let to rebels. The Texans were barred from bidding, but those who held the contracts bought where they pleased, and Goodnight and Loving sold to them. While this may have served the cause of patriotism, it did not profit the Government otherwise, for according to Goodnight's belief, the contractor was a nefarious swindler.

After delivering some five hundred head on the contract at eight cents a pound net, and expecting to return to Texas for more cattle in the spring, Goodnight and Loving rode in to the fort and called on Roberts for a settlement. In the meantime, it seemed — and they always suspected Roberts as the perpetrator — an order had been issued to prevent rebels from drawing money for cattle placed through someone else's contract. Roberts curtly informed them that under the ruling they were not entitled to pay, and he expected to abide by the rule. They were astounded. Without loss of time they forked their horses and left for Santa Fé.

They presented themselves at the general headquarters for the military district and requested an audience with Colonel Charles McClure, head of the quartermaster's department. Upon reassurance that such orders had been issued, Loving stated their case and asked McClure what he would do about it. Pointing to a box above his desk, he said:

'Such unjust rulings sometimes fall into that box. I have not officially received the order not to pay this money,' he continued, 'and have already given Captain Roberts notice that I would never pay him another cent on his contract until he gave me orders to pay you. Mr. Loving, I am going to pay you for several reasons. First, it is just and right; second, you have put in the best cattle that have ever been killed in this Agency; and you have been a gentleman and have not tried to swindle or wrong the Government in any way, which is more than I can say for the contractor.'

Again the cowmen were happy. 'McClure proved to be a

man of high standing,' praised Goodnight. 'In fact, I have found nearly all military officers to be high-class men.'

On their return to Fort Sumner, they were met by Joe Loving, the old man's son, who reported that the night before five Mexicans had stolen six big mules and all their saddle horses except the few on picket. He had followed their trail about thirty miles to the northeast and found that they were taking a diagonal course across the plain between the Pecos and the Canadian, which would not bring them to water within seventy-five to a hundred miles. He had quit the trail and turned west to the fort to report, and by good fortune his father and Goodnight rode in about the same time.

The post commander furnished Goodnight a fresh horse, a sergeant, and five soldiers, and they struck out with Joe in a northeasterly direction to intercept the rustlers' trail where he had left it. After riding for about half a day they observed, a few miles in the distance, four horsemen coming toward the Pecos. Their course caused Goodnight to think they were Navajos, and knowing the troops had orders to keep them within certain bounds, he knew they would run upon seeing the soldiers. Hoping to find out whether or not they had seen the trail of the stolen stock, as they were coming from the direction in which the stock must have passed, he requested the soldiers to let him go on alone.

'When I got within a half-mile of them,' he said, 'they turned to run. I had a splendid horse and pursued them. The first one I caught was an old Mexican riding one of our horses, which immediately proved their identity. Finding no water and having been without it a day and night, they had started back to the Pecos, hoping to reach it before their horses gave out.

'Having to hold the old man until Joe and the soldiers reached me gave the other three quite a start. But their horses were grass-wintered, were suffering for water, and could not run, so I soon caught another one, and when the soldiers caught up and relieved me of him, I went after another.

The last two seemed to be better mounted and made quite a run, but their horses soon gave out, and they dismounted and went into the high grass afoot.

'The soil being sandy, the grass was quite high, but I kept my eye on them while getting every inch out of my horse, and when I got within thirty yards both raised up out of the grass. One of them had a brass mounted yager; the other had a very large, old-fashioned six-shooter. I shoved my spurs farther into my horse and told them in Spanish to drop their guns. The man who had the yager commenced to raise it and I fired instantly, made a lucky shot and killed him dead in his tracks. The other fellow might have used his pistol had not Loving and the soldiers been in sight, coming as fast as they could with the other prisoners.'

The one Goodnight had killed proved to be a noted desperado, who, with his brother, had robbed and murdered a peddler some time before. Yet they had accounted for only four of the five rustlers. Goodnight soon learned that the brother of the dead desperado had, with more courage than the others, kept on across the plain with the stolen horses, bearing farther to the east more quickly to strike the Canadian.

The sergeant detailed two soldiers to take two of the captives back to the fort.

'We took the first old chap I had caught,' continued Goodnight, 'as guide to cross the plains, who repeatedly swore on the cross he carried that he would help me get the mules, and I really believed he would have done so if I had not lost faith in him.

'The troops had a canteen of whiskey but no water. We had gone all day without. By midnight we had crossed the plain and reached the foot of Tucumcari Mountain, where the old Mexican thought we would find water. But it was very dry and none was there. Meanwhile, the soldiers had been drinking the whiskey, had become crazed for water, and were in a terrible condition. All my efforts to prevent them from drinking it had been in vain. When we found no water at

Tucumcari, they wanted to kill the old Mexican, and actually commenced to hit him with their carbines. Thief that he was I could not stand to see a prisoner abused, so Joe and I took charge of him until daylight.

'Prior to this time I had passed from the Pecos to the Canadian, and knew where there was drinkable water about fifteen miles to the west. It was necessary to get the men and horses to it as quickly as possible, which I did. The horses were in such bad condition that it was impracticable to continue the pursuit farther.'

From this water hole they made their way back to Fort Sumner, and leaving the Mexicans in the guard-house, went on to Bosque Grande to join Loving. In the early spring they gathered the remnant of their herd, some five hundred head, placed it in charge of James Foster, a responsible young man, and started it for northern New Mexico. Foster summered it on the Capulín Vega, west of the Capulín Mountain crater, with the entire country to himself. Loving and Goodnight fitted up with saddle and work stock the best they could from purchases around Fort Sumner, and took their way back to Texas with plans to make heavier drives than before.[8]

With barely enough horses for their return, they could haul only the most needed equipment. Farrar, whom they had bought out on the Hondo, and Frank Willburn wanted to go back with their outfit, and the trail blazers rationed them through.

'Old man Farrar was too stingy to buy a good horse or mule,' said Goodnight, 'although he had more money than he had ever owned in his life. He undertook to go through on an old pony which had wintered without grain. In a few days the pony gave out and was left on the road, but the boys, of course did not let the old man walk, taking turn about letting him ride while they walked. Willburn was riding a good mule, but never asked Farrar to ride, and I think kept ahead of the outfit rather than be impolite to him.

[8] Goodnight, 'Recollections,' II, 80–82; Goodnight, Deposition in Indian Claim Case, 9133 (1899), p. 81.

'We were approaching Horsehead, just below which we knew a lot of Indians had been camped all fall and winter, taking herds of cattle — Adams's and others. At noon I told Willburn that if he did not obey orders and stay with the men, I would not sacrifice them to protect him. He gave me to understand, however, that he could protect himself.

SCOURGES OF THE TRAIL

'In our march I kept half the men behind the wagon and the other half in front — about a dozen in all. I was in the lead and just after lunch Willburn fell in by me. The soil was sandy, our teams somewhat weak, and it had been necessary to use the saddle horses a good deal to help pull the wagon. Thus we had to travel slowly. Willburn and I had unconsciously allowed our mules to walk too fast, and before I was aware of it had thoughtlessly crossed a little sharp sand ridge near the river bank, upon which we discovered fresh tracks.

'"Yes, it's Indians," I said, and just then the bullets commenced to fly. There were six of the Indians, and it seemed as if all had fired at once, as the bullets came quite thick. Willburn lost his head and started down the road, where I knew the Indians would come out and cut him off. I shouted to him, I cussed the country blue, and finally succeeded in making him hear me. But instead of coming straight back, he came in a circle through the mesquite brush, which was thick and about waist-high. He was spurring and whipping his mule all over, which made quite an amusing sight.

'After getting out of the line of the bullets, I turned my mule across the road to stop the rest of our men, who were just coming over the sand hill, as I knew they would charge. By this time the Indians had come out from under the river-bank, just missed Willburn on his circle, and struck across the valley through the mesquite.

'My boys begged pitifully to go into them and make a killing, which could easily have been done, and had I been mounted on my saddle mare, which was hitched to the wagon to help pull it, I probably would have pursued them. They were poorly mounted, and we, no doubt, could have killed every one of them, but I did not think it was best to make the fight. Just then I felt it was more important to get the money through to safety, and not have any wounded men on our hands that far from a doctor.

'When Willburn came around on his circle as fast as he could get his mule to go, he ran into mine and almost knocked him off his feet. He stammered excitedly that the Indians had shot at him, and noticing they had burned his forehead and split the crown of his hat with a bullet, I said: "From the looks of your hat, I believe they have." I had no further difficulty in keeping Willburn in rank.'

The outfit made its way to Horsehead by sundown. Knowing the Indians would probably plan to attack them at Castle Cañon next morning, and knowing that they were then being spied upon, Goodnight made all preparations for camping at the Crossing. The cook prepared supper and the cowboys staked their horses on grass. But as soon as dark came they reloaded the wagon, saddled their horses, and quietly pulled out on the trail, hurrying along to pass through the cañon and reach the Plains before day.

They traveled steadily until the sun rose in their faces, and still pushed on as their jogging shadows shortened to catch, to pass, and to lengthen before them. During the day they met a herd strung out for a mile and a half, as a large dry herd will readily do if its leaders are not held back. Goodnight, thinking of its indefensible condition, inquired of the pointers for the boss. They said he was somewhere behind. Along the 'swing' he cut through the marching herd from one side to another, inquiring of the men he met, until finally he found the boss and told him he had better 'check up,' or bulk his herd, as the Indians would give him trouble.

'How do you know?' the man inquired.

'They shot at me yesterday,' Goodnight answered, 'and I can recollect twenty-four hours pretty well.'

'Let them come,' replied the trail boss, who didn't know them. 'I'd like to sample those damned Comanches.'

'Good-day sir,' bade Goodnight, clearly out of patience with such foolishness. 'You'll find them.'

And he did. At Castle Gap they took his entire herd, burned his wagons, and left him nothing but his saddle horses and sad experience.

When the sun slid below the placid rim of the Plains, the outfit was still plodding wearily down the long slope that led to the Middle Concho. For nearly forty-eight hours they had traveled without rest for horses and men, but the pace was telling, and in the early morning, Loving, the oldest man in the outfit, grew tired and proposed they stop and rest. They were only about fifteen miles from the Concho, and while he and most of the men slept, Goodnight, Joe Loving, and a trusty negro they always had along, took the stock, which had become very dry, and started them on to water. They had gone but a little way when they observed an object in the road. Still fearing Indians, they sent the horses and mules back by the negro, telling him to awaken the men and tie the stock to the wagon, while Joe and Goodnight investigated.

'We dismounted and crawled down the road,' Goodnight related, 'trying to make out what the object was. Soon we heard a mysterious buzzing noise and questioned each other as to what in the devil it could mean. Just then we stumbled on to an ox-yoke, which cleared up the situation at once. It proved to be old "Honey" Allen's wagon, where he had left it when he went back to water his stock. In the wagon were a lot of pecans, honey, and about a dozen bee gums, which accounted for the buzzing we had heard. As there were no bees in New Mexico, "Honey" Allen had contracted to deliver some to the farmers.

'Our men had assembled by this time, filled their pockets with Allen's pecans, and started on the trail again. When we reached the Concho, we found Whitehead and his wife, the wounded cowboy, and "Honey" Allen. A few miles down the river were two herds of Texas cattle, which supplied Allen with oxen and enabled him to get across the Plains.

'Early that morning I happened to meet my old Captain, Jack Cureton, outfitted with a pack-train, and fifty or sixty men going out to prospect for gold in the country between the Pecos and the Rio Grande. I told him of the Indians camped below Horsehead Crossing. He begged me to go back with him and clean them out, but I told him I did not care to, as I had had enough of it during the war, and besides we were going in for more cattle and hoped soon to be on the return trip with them.'

Meanwhile Hoy's last herd, designed to fill the Adams contract, crept up the verdant course of the Concho. Besides a Mexican cart for hauling water, his outfit included a light spring wagon in which rode Mrs. Hoy and her four small children. At the headwaters, Hoy found the venturesome Cureton and 'Colonel Dalrymple's gold hunters,' camped for rest.

Hoy gained the pass at Castle Cañon, and his cattle caught scent of the river and stampeded away from his hands. After they had watered, he readily regained control, and threw the herd away from the river to graze. A large party of Indians charged them, took the cattle and the horses, and wounded three men and the valiant Mrs. Hoy, who tended the wounds of the others and loaded guns until she was too weak to go on. As the Indians drove the cattle across the river, Hoy placed his wounded in the wagon, and with the vehicle pushed and pulled by the men, carried them to refuge in the old adobe walls, the ruins of the Butterfield stage stand. There they were besieged for three days. On the fourth they saw dust rising in the direction of Castle Gap, and as the Indians raised the siege, crossed the river, and took the trail of the herd, Colonel Dalrymple rode up with his men. He had found where the Indians had burned Hoy's wagon and carts in the cañon, and had rushed on to discover the fate of the outfit.

Cureton said that as they rode into view, fifteen to twenty men, clad in white shirts, rode down the river, and they could not imagine how so many cowboys could be dressed in white. Then the besieged ran out, and began shouting and throwing their hats in the air, and the gold hunters learned that the mounted men were not cowboys, but Indians, dressed up in Whitehead's linen shirts, plundered from his wagon on the Plains.[9]

Thus went the last of Adams's herds, to pass along the trails of the *comanchero* trade. The Whiteheads already had enough of the wilderness, and turned back to the settlements in Texas. 'Honey' Allen whacked his bulls with his wagonload of delicacies on toward New Mexico, while Hoy took the last doleful news north to Andy Adams, the contractor. Dalrymple and Cureton rode west to hunt for gold that has never been found, while Loving and Goodnight continued their back-trail toward the Keechi range.

[9] Goodnight, 'Recollections,' ii, 83–91; Mrs. Kate Longfield, 'Three Days in 'Dobe Walls,' *The Lampasas Record*, September 3, 1931.

When they crossed the divide between the Concho and Colorado, they came into country where buffaloes had wintered in great numbers. The annual spring migration started with the growth of grass, but in 1867 rains did not come until June, and the herds had gathered here in such numbers that they had eaten the country clean. For some strange reason they had not mounted the mesa and crossed the divide to the west, to the Concho side, where there was still good grass.

'But here,' to let Goodnight continue the story, 'they had remained until the grass was gone, and had died from starvation by thousands and thousands. The dead buffaloes, which extended for a hundred miles or more, were so thick they resembled a pumpkin field, and their carcasses had hatched millions and billions of what is known as screw flies. The air was so full of them we positively could not eat during the daytime. In spite of all we could do, our cups, plates, and cooking utensils would become full of them. Thus we did not attempt to stop during the day. Fortunately, we had a little corn for the horses, and getting our breakfast and breaking camp before daylight, we made all speed possible and never stopped again until dusk.

'Our northeast course was much the same as the drift of the buffaloes, and we did not get rid of these conditions until we reached the Elm tributary of the Clear Fork of the Brazos, where grass was fairly good. I presume the buffaloes had died the full width of the herd in the same proportion as they had along the trail. From our observation the herd would average twenty-five miles wide, which meant that several million head had perished that spring for lack of food alone. This may sound unreasonable — no one would believe it who had not seen the immense numbers of flies.'

X. THE PECOS — 'GRAVEYARD OF THE COWMAN'S HOPES'

NEWS of the success of Goodnight and Loving had spread and a number of daring cowmen were planning to venture upon their trail. Loving began gathering cattle in the Palo Pinto country, while Goodnight made his way back to the extreme frontier to put up a herd. He moved the CV cattle from the Elm Creek Ranch, and, by buying from others, concentrated a herd about fifteen miles south of the Neuhous Pens, at Cribb's Station,[1] where Loving agreed to meet him. As the cattle were bought and gathered, they were placed in the circle road brand and held under herd. Best beef steers were worth around twenty dollars in gold; stock cattle about seven dollars in the same medium. For those who bought and paid in greenbacks, steers cost five and stock cattle two dollars more. Loving and Goodnight were paying in gold. They secured powers of attorney from neighboring ranchmen to gather any of their stolen cattle found in New Mexico, and Loving packed the papers in his saddlebags.

They hoped for a peaceful and profitable drive, but in 1867, 'the sign just wasn't right.' They were barely beyond the settlements, on the Clear Fork near old Camp Cooper,[2] when Indians attacked during the night and stampeded their herd.

[1] An old stand on the Butterfield Southern Mail line, once kept by a man named Cribb. The arroyo upon which it was located was tributary to the Elm.

[2] Fort Griffin, at first called Camp Wilson, was established on the Clear Fork below Camp Cooper, July 31, 1867, a short time after the herd passed by. *Frontier Times*, April, 1929, pp. 296.

The ground was soft from recent rains, and next morning
Goodnight saw where they had gone into the brush along the
Clear Fork Bottom to hide. He took this to mean another
attack that night, and so warned Loving, advising him to move
the herd into an open valley nearby, where they might have

some chance of defense. While Loving was void of fear and
caution, he moved the herd into the valley, but camped at the
lower end, near the brush, and within a few feet of a deep washout. Goodnight and another hand trailed the lost cattle north
toward their old range, recovered them about fifteen miles
away, turned back, and near midnight topped the Clear Fork
hills, and saw Loving's campfire burning brightly in the valley
below.

'If the Indians needed any notice of our whereabouts,'
Goodnight said, 'Loving had surely given it plainly. As soon
as I reached camp, I extinguished the fire, but failed to saddle
a fresh horse, which I should have done. I had had no sleep
the night before and was tired, so I told Mr. Loving to let me
sleep about an hour and wake me, because we would probably
have trouble. I did not take time to unroll my bed; just threw
my buffalo robe down, fell on it, and was asleep in an instant.
One edge of the robe caught on the high grass, which held it up
about a foot from the ground. Mr. Loving was out with the
boys to keep them encouraged and to their places, but did not

awaken me, saying next morning that he was afraid I would give out for want of rest and sleep.

'Just before day about a dozen Indians got in the gully, only a few feet away, and opened fire — a tremendous lot of gunfire besides the arrows. One of the arrows would have hit my body about midway had it not struck the lower edge of my buffalo robe, which, held up by the grass, turned the arrow beneath me and saved my life.

'My horse was still standing beside me, too tired to move, when the shooting occurred. I had carelessly dropped my pistols, and in the dark I seemed to scratch up enough hay to feed a horse before I got my hands on them. By that time the bullets had ceased, somewhat, but much yelling continued. I heard someone giving loud commands, which I believed to be orders to charge and stampede the horses, and I guessed it right, for the Indians made for the horse herd, which was close by — between the cattle and the camp for safety.

'Several of the boys were up, and I told them to come with me and we would save the horses. I went into the Indians and the horse herd, supposing the boys were with me, but they seemed to be too dazed to move. Thus I was there shooting at the Indians alone, but I think they figured there were more of us, as they skipped off into the brush and I saved the herd. They shot at me many times, but always missed.

'During the shooting they sent an arrow into Long Joe Loving's neck, a young man of the same name, but not related to Mr. Loving. The spike struck in the bone just behind his ear. It was rather long and had gone in full length — nothing of it projected except the little end, which was fastened in the wood with sinew. As it was hoop-iron and not steel, it had to be removed before it corroded. The only hope was that the point had turned downward, which proved to be the case. Pulling it out was ticklish. If it was too near the brain pan, I knew it might cause a fracture and kill him. If left in, it was certain to kill him, so nothing could be done but take a chance and extract it. The only instrument we had with us was an old-fashioned pair of shoe pinchers. Two strong men held him down and I succeeded in pulling it out with the pinchers, but lifted the three men in doing so, as it was quite crooked.

'Young Loving felt sure that he would die, as he knew of a man who had recently died from a similar wound. But I assured him he would get well. Sheek joined us about day and I told him to take the boy to the first settler's; to lay up during the day and keep the wound poulticed with cold mud, which should be changed as often as it got warm; and to move him on each night until he reached the Keechi Ranch, where my mother, who was a wonderful nurse, would care for him. This was done and he fully recovered.'

While Goodnight was saving the horses, the cattle again stampeded and scattered. The outfit put in the day rounding them up, and when tallied out over a hundred and sixty head were short. Since the Indians were so numerous and the cattle in such bad condition, Goodnight decided they should start that night. They grazed the cattle thoroughly, had supper, and threw them upon the trail, though it was raining.

'We had not moved far,' continued Goodnight, 'until about half the herd began to run. I had placed two first-class men in the rear, on what we call "the corners," and took "One-Armed" Wilson and went on the point myself. As the stampeders came up one side of the herd, Wilson and I caught them and turned them back. As they raced to the rear of the herd, the corner men caught them and turned them back up the opposite side, toward the pointers.

'The strange part of it was that over half the herd moved along quietly in the dark, while the others ran around them as described — actually ran until their tongues were out. Wilson and I were on two of the best horses we had, and it took all we could get out of them with quirts and spurs to head these cattle.

'Late in the night it commenced to storm fearfully, and became very dark. At times the lightning was intense. During such flashes we could see clearly, and it looked as though the bellies of the steers were almost touching the ground — they were going so fast. By ten or eleven o'clock they seemed to be entirely run down. By one o'clock the storm became so dense and the wind at such velocity we had to stop. We could see nothing but the electricity on our horses' ears, which I have never understood or had explained. I have often taken hold of their ears, but could feel no sensation when I did.'

One of the work oxen was belled, and Goodnight soon knew, by the clatter of the bell, that the herd had split. Yet he could see nothing but two balls of fire working back and forth in the darkness with his horse's ears. The wind was blowing a gale, and his portion of the herd drifted with it, though he attempted to hold the cattle to a slow pace. While working his horse alongside the herd, he came to Bose Ikard, an ex-slave and one of the best night riders he ever had, and a boy named William Taylor, who had been picked up at Denver by Loving the year before 'while on starvation.' They drifted on with the storm until they reached high and rocky ground, where, when the lightning faded, Goodnight could see nothing but the sparks his horse's shoes struck from the stones. Here they stopped the herd, which, greatly fatigued, soon went to sleep, and the cowboys, worn to a frazzle by three nights in the saddle, dozed on their horses as they circled around it. At daylight Goodnight awoke the boys and told them they must try to get back to camp. Shortly after mid-morning they cut the trail, only two or three miles north of their camp. They turned the cattle down it, strung them out, and Goodnight dropped back from the point and counted them, finding they had six hundred head. Within an hour they reached the wagon where Wilson was holding the remainder of the herd.

Once cattle start to stampede their nervousness spreads as by contagion, and they are not easy to stop. Night after night they have been known to run, each time to exhaustion, until fat beef steers were but ghosts of their former prime. This drive of 1867 was such an experience.

'The cattle had been so shot to pieces,' said Goodnight,

'and so badly spoiled that they continued stampeding, and after we had passed through Buffalo Gap we had a run which I shall never forget. They had been quiet all night, and at daybreak I told Bose, who was on guard with me, to watch them and I would wake the cook. I reached camp and tied my horse to the wagon wheel, giving him some rope so he could get a little grass. Then I commenced to wake the men who were asleep around the wagon on the side next the herd. Something happened, in an instant the herd stampeded right down on the camp, and it looked as though the men would be trampled to death. There certainly was some scrambling, as most of them had not got out of bed.

'I jerked a blanket off one of the beds, jumped in front of the cattle that were coming at full speed, and by waving the blanket and doing all the yelling I could, succeeded in splitting the herd around the wagon and beds. Charlie, powerful, fast, and the best-trained horse I ever rode in a stampede, was still tied to the wagon. He knew his business, of course, wanted to go, and got to the end of his rope, where the stampede knocked him down and many cattle went over him. I had my belt knife ready, and as the last steer cleared him, I cut the rope and he got up with me on him. I supposed he would be scared out of his wits and run from the cattle, but at once he struck out at full speed with the herd.

'By this time it was light enough to see. I kept going up the side of the cattle as fast as possible, wondering why Bose had not turned the front. When I had almost caught up with him, he looked back and saw me, and immediately his horse shot out like lightning and he threw the leaders around. After we got them circled, I asked him why he had not turned them sooner.

'"I'll tell you, sah," answered the cautious Bose. 'I wuzn't sartin who had dis herd 'til I saw you. I t'ought maybe de Indians had 'um."'

Since they were having so much trouble, the owners decided to push on with all speed possible, and they drove the cattle hard, fifteen to twenty miles a day. They reached the Pecos, watered, threw the herd out two hundred yards from the river, and bedded. The night was bad, Indians were in the country, and during a hard rain the cattle began to run. The hands were continually in danger of being forced over the cut banks of the river, which no one could see in the darkness, and the owners finally sent them to the wagon to wait until the storm was over, while Goodnight took after some cattle that broke away.

When morning came and they tallied, over two hundred head were missing. Leaving some of the hands to hold the herd, Goodnight took others and described a circle. As the rain had wiped out the oldest portion of the trail, they widened the arc until, four or five miles from camp, they came upon the tracks of the runaways, pointing downstream. On their way they met Jim Burleson's trail outfit, whose first herd Goodnight had bought on the Hondo the year before. His hands had lost their herd of about two thousand head, a few of which had gone over the banks into the river. Goodnight stopped to help him gather his cattle, while Yankee Bill, 'One-Armed' Bill, and John Kutch went down the river after his own missing stock. When Burleson got his herd together and started up the river, Goodnight returned to his own outfit.

The three cowboys followed the sign down the east bank of the Pecos for about twenty-five miles. Sometime in the afternoon they looked up from the tracks and saw the cattle, held by a large band of Indians at the foot of a mountain, near a bend in the river. Already they were within a few hundred yards of the camp, and Wilson saw that not only was recovery of the cattle impossible, but that they might be hard put to escape with their scalps. He was always as cool as a cucumber, and instead of whirling his horse and starting back up the Pecos, he calmly rode on south into the bend of the river where the mesquite was high and thick. The Indians raced below to cut him and his companions off, but by the time they discovered their mistake, the cowboys were fairly started back toward Horsehead Crossing.

They would have made good time had it not been for the

mule that Yankee Bill had the misfortune to be riding. Nevertheless, by plying quirt and spur, they did very well for the first fifteen miles, when Yankee Bill got stubborn, too, and swore he wouldn't run a good mule to death just because there were a few damned Comanches in the country, and they a long way behind. Wilson and Kutch rode on and left him.

Knowing their force was insufficient to recapture the cattle held by the Indians, the owners calculated the loss among the fortunes of war, and trailed on up the bitter stream, keeping to the high ground as much as possible, but coming in to the river to water each day.[3] At last the herd seemed broken to the trail and for nearly a hundred miles they drove in peace. As they saw no sign of Indians, Loving became impatient about the letting of contracts at Santa Fé. As this was late July and the contracts were to be let early in August, he decided to go ahead to be present at the bidding. He discussed the matter with Goodnight, who undertook to dissuade him from going, at least until after they had passed the dangerous spurs of the Guadalupes. Upon Loving's insistence he finally agreed to the plan.

'I assured him,' recalled the younger man, 'that it would be safe enough for him to go if he would travel only at night and hide out during the daytime, selecting his stops with a view of defense. He readily agreed to this, but knowing his fearless nature and unshaken faith and confidence in his religion, I felt uneasy, and after he had mounted to go I again went to him and tried to impress him with the importance and necessity of caution. I detailed "One-Armed" Wilson, who was by odds the coolest man in the outfit, to go with him.'

The two men jogged past the point of the herd and along the trail toward Pope's Crossing. They rode that night and two nights following, abiding by the promise Loving had made, by which time they crossed the divide to the north of the Delaware and reached Black River about daylight, stopped, rested, and

<hr />

[3] Depositions, Goodnight in Case No. 8532, October 25, 1898, pp. 11 and following; W. J. Wilson in same, June 26, 1893; Goodnight, 'Recollections,' II, 100–01.

slept until noon. Loving told Wilson that he detested night riding, that they had seen no sign of Indians, and that he favored continuing the trip by day. Wilson was hardly conservative; they saddled their horses and again set out.

From Pope's Crossing the trail took the high ground to the Delaware and Black River, after which it stretched sixteen miles across the tableland again to strike the Pecos. In crossing this plain, with the breaks of the Pecos far to their right and the high-pitched peaks of the Guadalupes farther still to their left, the riders could be seen for miles. When about two thirds of the way across, Wilson saw a large band of Indians charging them from toward the end of the Guadalupes. They quit the trail and rode for the Pecos by the nearest course. Though it was a four-mile run, they easily beat the Indians to the riverbank, and spurred their horses over the incline. A sand dune intervened between the foot of the bluff and the stream, about a hundred yards away, upon which grew a few stunted bushes. The drainage from the bluff had cut through it to form a wash a few feet wide and probably two feet deep, which described a turn near where it entered the river, thus forming a shallow retreat open to view only from across the stream, at this point about thirty steps wide.

Loving and Wilson jerked their saddle holsters free and took refuge in the crook of the ditch — a position further obscured by smartweeds and scrub oak, or shinnery, as we say in the West — as the Indians poured over the crest and took possession of the horses. Wilson carried Goodnight's revolving six-shooter rifle and saddle holsters as well as his own six-shooter. Loving was equipped with side-arms and a repeating Henry rifle, the first metallic cartridge gun Goodnight had seen. The Indians swam the river and surrounded them, and as they swarmed down the bluffs, Wilson estimated there were several hundred in all. The first that attempted to get a bead on them from across the river, through the mouth of the ditch, was shot by Loving, and no others tried the position.

Late in the evening, as Texans call the waning hours of day, someone began calling from the bluff in Spanish, proposing terms. The whites suspected a ruse; yet their situation bordered on the hopeless, and Wilson said he would try to talk with them if Loving would cover the rear. He stepped up on the dune with Loving behind him, the older man carrying his Henry in

THE LOVING FIGHT

hand, his holsters across his arm. Already Indians had reached a clump of *carrizo*, or cane, behind them, and as Wilson stepped into view to address the warriors on the bluff, a bullet tore through Loving's wrist and plowed into his side. Wilson whirled to take refuge in the ditch, and gave his attention to the charge. Loving felt sure the wound was mortal, but after checking the flow of blood, they settled back to endure the siege.

The Comanches shot their arrows high into the air to make them fall at a sharp angle into the ditch, while Wilson and Loving hugged close to the low but perpendicular wall of the washout, and the arrows either stuck in the sand above them or passed over their backs into the other bank. The Pecos hills are covered with gravel, and resorting to these the warriors showered the retreat, with no better results. Wilson scanned the dune about, saw the tops of the smartweeds shiver, part ever so slightly, and then close back. A Comanche, separating the weeds in advance with his lance, was crawling upon them. 'One-Armed' Bill shifted to greet him. When he was almost in view, he aroused a rattlesnake. There was a vibrant, *whir-r-r,* and the Comanche backed off more rapidly than he had come.

The evening wore into dusk and the quick chill of night brought relief from the hot sun and sand. Loving, grown weak from loss of blood, was racked with pain and fever. Wilson slipped to the water's edge and brought a bootful for the suffering man, but as the night dragged at a heavy stride, Loving felt he would die before day. His mind turned to his family in Texas, and he implored Wilson to leave him, to escape, if possible, and carry the story of his fate down the river to Goodnight and to his own people at home. With the burning anxiety of a suffering man, of a man close-drawn by the ties of family and home, he dreaded an unknown death in the wilderness. He assured Wilson that he would stand the Indians off the best he could, and, failing, he would not be taken and tortured to death, but would shoot himself and fall into the river. If the Indians left him and he found strength to travel, he would slip downstream a couple of miles and hide. They calculated carefully; if Wilson could hold out for a day and a half, they reasoned, he should meet the advancing Goodnight. Finally Wilson agreed to make the attempt.

He spread their five six-shooters and Goodnight's rifle by Loving's sound arm, but took the Henry and its metallic cartridges, which would be unaffected by water, for to escape by the river was his only chance. When the moon went down, he told Loving good-bye, moved to the mouth of the gully, and divesting himself of his clothing, hid his clothes in one place, and his knife, which dropped from his pocket, in another, all beneath the water. He pulled off everything but his hat, drawers, and undershirt, which he hoped would protect him from the sun, and slipped into the treacherous stream. At this point the river passed over a gravel shoal and was only three or four feet deep. To prevent his escape an Indian sat his bareback horse in the middle of the stream, scarcely a hundred feet below, and gaily patted the sole of his foot in the water. Fortunately a cloud had come up, and Wilson edged close against the bank and the overhanging polecat bushes Then he struck deep water.

And here is displayed the remarkable coolness of 'One-Armed' Bill. With a Comanche sitting nearby, and others all around, he made three attempts to swim with the gun. Each time he almost drowned, but instead of dropping the gun he clung to it with his one good arm until the current drifted him into the perpendicular bank, about seventy-five feet below. Calmly he stuck the muzzle into the sand and pushed the stock against the bank, beneath the water, so the Indians could not find it. Then he swam into the current, passed beyond the watchful warriors, and made his famous 'getaway.'

He climbed up the bank into a cane brake, and by day was well on his way. He lay up a portion of the day. That night he pushed over the gravelly hills that line the Pecos, and when day came did not tarry, but kept on across the burning table-lands. In spite of cactus, rocks, and heat, he trudged on, sure of meeting the trail herd sometime during the day.

But upon finding a pleasant place to recruit the exhausted herd, and to give time for the washing of clothes and saddle blankets, Goodnight had stopped for a day and a half below the Texas line. Instead of being forty or fifty miles away, he was close to eighty. Without food or rest, Wilson stayed on the trail, swimming the river at times to shorten the course, and on the third day, weak, feverish, and emaciated, staggered to the crest of a hill that overlooked the trail.

'Meanwhile,' to let Goodnight continue the story, 'I overtook and passed the Burleson herd, now in charge of an old man by the name of Campbell. He had sold it to Burleson and was going along to be sure to get his money. Burleson and two of his men had left some days before to go ahead and look after his contracts. On the way they got careless, let the Apaches capture their pack-mule and all provisions, and almost starved before reaching Fort Sumner. And now his outfit, mostly Mexican hands and a sorry bunch at that, was out of provisions and were making very poor progress. I told Mr. Campbell to fall in behind me and I would help him through; that my crew would force his to work, and that I could easily ration them to Fort Sumner.'

For about three hundred miles not a tributary breaks into the Pecos from the east, the broad sand-hill belt absorbing the little water that falls. Hence by following the river valley the trail was unimpeded. Near the New Mexico line there is a valley probably two miles long and a mile wide, near the upper end of which the gravel hills jut in close to the river, leaving only good trail ground between. A cave, extending back into one of these hills ten or fifteen feet, had been found on a former trip. The trail wound around the hills, as the river bent northward, which made a splendid place for the Indians to hide, surprise, and take the herds.

'I was pointing the herd opposite Wilson's brother,' said Goodnight, 'of course watching carefully for Indians, suspecting they might be behind the hill, and was confident I saw a man come out of the cave and go back into it, though Wilson contended no one was there. I told him to check the herd, bulk it for a fight, get the men together, and I would go over the hill and investigate.

'I purposely loitered along trying to make-believe that I did not suspect anything until I reached the curve in the trail. I then put the spurs to my horse, aiming to run up, look over the hill, see what was there, and get back without being cut off. When I started the run, Wilson came out of the cave, a quarter of a mile away, and gave me the old frontier signal "come here." Intuition or the subconscious mind comes in under strange conditions.

'The river water was red with sediment, and his underclothes were as red as the river itself. But when he beckoned to me, I knew positively that it was Wilson, and how I knew I will never understand. I immediately put the horse down to full speed and went to him. For a few moments he seemed unable to talk, probably overwhelmed with emotion, knowing his life was saved at last. He was the most terrible object I ever saw.

His eyes were wild and bloodshot, his feet were swollen beyond all reason, and every step he took left blood in the track. I inquired about Loving, but he could scarcely make a reply, and what he did mutter was entirely unintelligible. I put him on my horse and got him to the herd as soon as possible, which his brother had already got together for action. I tore up a blanket, wet it, wrapped his feet to remove the fever, and then made him a light gruel of meal, which I gave him at intervals for about an hour. By then he was perfectly himself. I asked him for particulars and he told me in detail of their trip and the attack by the Indians.

'When Wilson finished his story, I decided to start immediately. He could ride in the wagon and manage the herd while I was gone. I explained the matter to Mr. Campbell. He at once volunteered to go and to help me out by taking two of his men, and I took two of my picked men, making six in all. However, one of his men was a Mexican, who belonged in New Mexico.

'This occurred about five. We rode the rest of the evening and all that night. It not only rained, but it rained torrents, and was so dark at times we were forced to halt. When I reached the place where Wilson told me he had left the trail, I recognized it easily from his description, although the plains were unmarked, or would have appeared so to the untrained. Besides his description, the place was distinguished by the fact that a bunch of Comanches had again come out of the mountains and passed over the same trail they had taken when chasing the two men. Their tracks seemed as fresh as ours, and we supposed they were under the bluffs still trying to get Mr. Loving.

'Where they left the main cow-trail the Indians had taken a leaf out of Mr. Loving's daybook, and had drawn a Comanche and a white man shaking hands, and it was a splendid drawing for an Indian at that. The white man was wearing a two-story, silk hat. I have always wondered at this, as no one in the West wore them. They pinned the drawing with a mesquite thorn to a bush at the junction of the trails. I recognized the piece of paper as being from Loving's book, but it gave me no special alarm, as Wilson had told me the Indians got the horses, and Loving always carried the book in his saddlebags.

'Within two hundred yards I ascertained definitely that the trail of the Indians was that of the two horsemen also, and we put our horses on the run. When near where the plains pitched off to the river — all of us thoroughly believing the Indians were just underneath — I halted for a moment to give the men their instructions, thinking, and having a good right to believe, they were the last. In a moment the rest of the men rode up and Mr. Campbell asked what I intended to do.

'"I am going in to Mr. Loving. Will you go with me?" I will never forget how he looked. It seemed every drop of blood left his face, returning in a moment, and with a steady voice he said: "Yes, sir, I'll stay with you!"

'"Boys," I said, "put your spurs to your horses, full speed," and as we raced for the bluff, Campbell came up beside me, saying: "That Mexican is going to desert us and go in with the Indians!" I was confident of the same thing. The New Mexicans and Indians were at perfect understanding with each other, and all he would need to do would be to get among them and help kill us. He had a good horse and I could see clearly enough from the way he was handling him what he intended to do, but I said to Campbell: "Don't fear. As he passes me, I will kill him." I had my pistol ready for him, and we all went in on the full side as fast as our horses could run, aiming to take the Indians by surprise and shoot our way to the bank of the river. We had our guns and four pistols apiece, and I have no doubt we would have reached the river, even had the Indians been there — at least most of us. When we got to the top of the bluff, there was not an Indian in sight. They had just marched around a short bend in the river, and could not have been a half-mile away, as the water had scarcely stopped running down the banks where they had ridden out. In a moment I found where Mr. Loving had been in the ditch, which was now half-filled with stones, and its banks perforated with probably a hundred arrow shafts, though the Indians had gathered the arrows before leaving. I knew they had not got him, as there was ample evidence that they had been hunting for him everywhere. We searched down the river as he had requested, but the rain had been heavy and no tracks could be found. I believed he had carried out his threat; that he had shot himself and floated down the river, the torrent obliterating all traces.'

Goodnight looked under the bank for Wilson's clothes and gun, and so accurate had been the recital that he found them, even to the pocket-knife. 'It seemed to me very remarkable,' Goodnight recalled, 'that he should have had such coolness under that terrible stress and risk. Few men but would have dropped the gun in the river upon finding they could not swim with it.' After dark the party sadly made its way back to the herd, and again took the trail.

Yet Loving was not dead. For two days he waited in vain for the successful venture of Wilson's trip; for two days and nights he fought the Indians at bay while enduring the pangs of hunger and the fever of his wounds. And when help did not come, he concluded the Indians had captured the herd and killed the hands, and decided that he must follow Wilson's lead. Though the wound in his side had not proved serious, few could endure a shot-shattered wrist and three foodless days and sleepless nights without collapse, but in spite of his age, Loving was blessed with a constitution of iron. The Indians had continued to shower his position with rocks, and tunneled through the dune to within a few feet of where he lay, but lacked the courage to break upon him. On the third night he crawled into the water and started upstream, instead of down, hoping to reach the trail crossing about six miles above, where, with good fortune, some passer-by might lend him aid.

At last he gained the crossing and lay down in the shade of a clump of wild china, only about four feet above the water. He attempted to shoot some birds that came into the trees, but the river had soaked his powder and caps and his guns were useless. He tried to eat his buckskin gloves, but could not kindle a fire to parch them to a crisp, and again settled back to wait. For two days and nights he stayed there, too weak to move, but satisfying his thirst by tying his handkerchief to a stick and dipping it in the river below. On the third day his superb endurance broke and he sank into a stupor.

Three Mexicans and a German boy, in a wagon drawn by three yoke of oxen, passing through on their way to Texas, stopped at the crossing to prepare their dinner. The boy went into the motte to gather some sticks for firewood, and there found Loving, apparently asleep. When he called, Loving awoke, and thinking the Indians had discovered him, grabbed and leveled his six-shooter at the boy, but remembering that it would not shoot, immediately dropped it and fell back on the chunk of wood upon which his head had been resting.

He was taken to the wagon, where the Mexicans prepared him some *atole*, similar to our corn-meal mush, a most suitable food for a man in his condition, after which he offered them two hundred and fifty dollars to take him to Sumner, about a hundred and fifty miles away. They swung their oxen around, lifted him into the wagon, and slowly set out on the rough and tedious journey.

In the meantime, Burleson had grown anxious as he awaited the arrival of his herd at Fort Sumner, and scouted down the Pecos as far as he dared, hoping to locate his outfit. Instead he met the Mexicans with Loving, and returning to the fort as fast as horse could take him, got the government ambulance and doctors, and met the party some fifty miles down the trail. After dressing Loving's wounds, they put him in the ambulance and carried him to the post, the Mexicans following to receive their pay.

Loving's misfortune brought no comfort to the restless Burleson, and again he rode to the south hoping to hear of his cattle. The Loving and Goodnight herd, and the Burleson herd behind it, had moved up the Pecos, crossed back to the east side near the china motte, and trailed on toward Comanche

Springs, a few little seeps eastward from the site of Roswell.

'Knowing we had to pass through some broken country before camping time,' Goodnight said, 'I went ahead, as customary, to ascertain whether any Indians were present or not, and to prevent surprise. I went into these breaks two or three hours by sun, at least a mile north of the trail — it being my custom never to follow the trail on such an excursion, knowing the Indians would waylay it first. I saw a man coming into the hills probably three quarters of a mile away, carefully sneaking around from point to point. I felt sure he was an Indian, and knew there would be more not far away. I maneuvered around, aiming to cut him off from the breaks, get him, and return to the herd. I got in behind him all right, but when I got close enough I discovered he was a white man, and rode to him, finding that it was Burleson. He at once inquired about his herd, which I told him was safe and just down the river. Then he commenced to tell me what Loving had said.

'"Loving was killed by Indians, way below on the Pecos!" I said.

'"Loving is at Fort Sumner," he replied.

'"Impossible!"

'"I tell you, he is in Fort Sumner right now and is very anxious to see you,"' Burleson answered, after which Goodnight heard the complete story. Together they hurried back, met the herds, passed over the hills, and camped. Then Goodnight saddled old Jenny for his long and remarkable ride to Sumner.

Since leaving the Indian-ridden Texas frontier, Goodnight had not unrolled his bed. For thirty-two days and nights his iron will rode whip and spur over his tireless body, and the sleep he got was principally on the back of a horse, snatched in the saddle while around the herd at night and on the trail by day.

On this drive Fate rode hard beside them, and Goodnight, riding too in his prime, was determined not to be outdone. But for a few short naps on a buffalo robe or against a wagon wheel during meal-time, he was with the herd night and day. 'It wasn't so hard,' he explained, simply; 'you got to where you could sleep on a horse without any trouble.' This year marked his supreme and unsurpassable effort against all the unfriendly fortune that befell the cattle drive. He and his hands drove relentlessly, hating their own physical limitations, while loving and sparing, so far as possible, only the mounts between their knees.

Goodnight's ride up the Pecos, climaxing a restless month when man and horse were actually one, is worthy of the finest traditions of the riding West. The ride from the resting herd to Bosque Redondo was one hundred and ten weary miles. Old Jenny, the saddle mule, was, he believed, 'the second best I ever saw in my life.' She was easy-gaited, a good single-footer, and could take a canter and go all day. From experience she knew the trail better than a man, could smell an Indian as acutely as a bear, and would travel of her own free will. In the middle of the night she carried her rider up the river past the familiar Bosque Grande, where, quitting the cattle trail, Goodnight reined her to the left and took the Navajo trail directly up the river. It was a wild country, looking wilder still by night, but much of the time Goodnight was dozing in the saddle. Several times he waked, the mule steadily swinging along at a canter or a lope, and, viewing the dark country with concern, he thought to himself: 'Well, old Jenny is lost, sure as hell.' And then a familiar landmark rose from the night to meet him, and again he relaxed and dozed. By early morning the hundred-and-ten-mile ride had dropped with the dusts behind him, and stiffly he stepped to the ground to greet his old partner.

Though the wound in his side had healed, and Loving was up and about, his arm was not doing well. Nevertheless, while confined at the fort, he had learned the whereabouts of their horses and mules stolen the spring before, and after Goodnight rested a couple of days, Loving advised him to go and recover them. Still uncertain as to the wound, Goodnight demurred, saying he did not wish to leave, but Loving insisted for fear the stock would be moved.

For eighty dollars the outlaw had sold Loving's six work mules and Goodnight's fine saddle mule to a priest at San Miguel, and had sold their horses from above Las Vegas through the mountains toward Santa Fé. Goodnight went and took the scattered stock by force, but when he reached San Miguel, he said: 'I had to go by law.' By chance he met a German lawyer, a partner of Steve Elkins at Santa Fé, who gave him much assistance. The mules were locked in a typically Mexican, walled corral, and as he prepared to resort to legal means, the lawyer advised him that here the law was very uncertain, and if he went to replevy the stock, by the time he got the papers there would be nothing left to serve upon. The German, acting as agent, agreed to forego resort to law and leave the saddle mule upon delivery of the other animals, and soon Goodnight turned down the river for Sumner in possession of all his stock but one.

'When I was within thirty miles of Fort Sumner,' he recalled, 'I met a courier hunting me, who said that Mr. Loving had sent for me. Gangrene had set in and his arm must be amputated. Loving did not want the operation performed unless I was there, as he feared he might not survive it. I left the stock in charge of the hired man, in a few hours reached Fort Sumner, and the next morning set about to get the operation performed. The old doctor was in Santa Fé, at court-martial, and the young doctor put me off from day to day with various excuses. Loving became fretful, now realizing his serious condition, and said: "It looks hard to be forced to die in a civilized country, just for want of attention. I have always lived the life of a gentleman, and feel that I am entitled to treatment accordingly."

'I had not told him about the young doctor putting me off, but I replied that I would now go to him at once and see what could be done. Fortunately, I found him at the hospital alone, and told him briefly and in no uncertain words that I presumed he was putting us off because we were rebels, and that he must now either operate or make wounds on me.

"'All right," he said,"I will come and amputate the arm.'"

The doctor and two stewards came to the hotel, administered chloroform, and amputated the arm above the elbow. Loving came from under the anaesthetic and seemed to be doing well. Yet the artery was large and peculiar, and caused the surgeon concern. Goodnight dispatched a runner with relays of horses to Las Vegas for Dr. Shoup, giving the man five hundred dollars to make the trip. On the second night after the operation, Shoup arrived with a companion physician, and as Loving was resting easily, they sat in the hotel yard and talked with the young cowman. Presently the night nurse appeared and said the bandage had commenced to be stained with blood. Upon examination they found that the artery had broken, and it was necessary to chloroform him again and retie it. From the added shock he suffered a relapse and a gradual failing of strength. Yet he was a man of such splendid constitution that, in spite of neglect, starvation, and punishment, he lived for twenty-two days, perfectly rational to the last. He stated simply that he would like to have lived longer on account of his family, and to show his country that he was a man who could overcome difficulties.

For one thing he had in mind his indebtedness.

'The Confederate Government,' explained his partner, 'owed him a hundred and fifty thousand dollars for cattle he had delivered, which financially ruined him, and he asked me as a Mason to give him my word to continue the partnership for at least two years, until his remaining debts were paid and his family provided for. I told him that while I was willing to do this, his oldest son, who would be executor of his will, knew me only as an illiterate cowboy, and would be certain to object to my going on with the business.

"'I know that, but James does not know you, and I do. Ignore him. Your promise is all I want." I gave him the promise. Then his mind turned back to Texas, and at last he said:

"I regret to have to be laid away in a foreign country." I assured him that he need have no fears; that I would see that his remains were laid in the cemetery at home. He felt that this would be impossible, but I told him it would be done. He died September 25, 1867, and was temporarily buried at Sumner.'

OLIVER LOVING

Goodnight and the doctor who performed the operation became close friends, and one day the latter said:

'I want to tell you how ridiculously you acted. I am a Scotchman and have been in America only about two years, and I don't know a thing about your rebel government. I did not operate on Loving because I had taken a great liking to him, did not think he could stand an anaesthetic, and did not want to kill him. But I found I'd either have to kill you, operate on him, or be killed, and I decided I'd just take my chances on the old gentleman.'[4]

[4] The principal sources of this story are Goodnight's 'Recollections,' I, 39–50, and II, 102–14; Goodnight to J. E. H., November 13, 1926; April 8, 1927; December 3, 1928; and December 29, 1929. Supplementary details are given by Annie Dyer Nunn in the *Dearborn Independent*, August 30, 1924; J. Frank Dobie, *The Country Gentleman*, March, 1927; Depositions in Indian Claim Cases, Goodnight, No. 9133 (1899), pp. 215–16, and No. 8532 (1898), 28 pp.; Martin V. Scroggins, Bose Ikard, Wm. J. Wilson, and in Case No. 9133 (1893–1900); Cox, *The Cattle Industry of Texas and Adjacent Territory*, 306–08, 478–79; *Prose and Poetry of the Live-Stock Industry*, I, 62; J. M. Hunter, *The Trail Drivers of Texas*, II, 344–53.

After several months on the trail, the establishment of a ranch in southern Colorado, and the location of the herd driven by Joe Loving, at Bosque Grande, Goodnight again returned to Fort Sumner, placed W. D. Reynolds in charge of the outfit, exhumed Loving's body, and prepared to fulfill his promise. From about the fort the cowboys gathered scattered oil cans, beat them out, soldered them together, and made an immense tin casket. They placed the rough wooden one inside, packed several inches of powdered charcoal around it, sealed the tin lid, and crated the whole in lumber. They lifted a wagon bed from its bolsters and carefully loaded the casket in its place. Upon February 8, 1868, with six big mules strung out in the harness, and with rough-hewn but tenderly sympathetic cowmen from Texas riding ahead and behind, the strangest and most touching funeral cavalcade in the history of the cow country took the Goodnight and Loving Trail that led to Loving's home.

Their arrangements were sufficient. Down the relentless Pecos and across the implacable Plains the journey was singularly peaceful. Through miles of grazing buffaloes they approached the Cross Timbers, reached the settlements, and at last delivered the body to the Masonic Lodge at Weatherford, where it was buried with fraternal honors.

In the uncertain scale of human nature, there is no standard for the computation of the influence of one noble soul upon another. Though Goodnight was then thirty-one years of age, until his death, nearly sixty-three years later, he never spoke of Loving except in utmost tenderness, and his vibrant voice mellowed with reverence as he would slowly say, 'my old partner,' and raise his eyes to the picture that hung on the ranch-house wall.

XI. THE COMANCHERO TRADE[1]

ALMOST in a season the trace of Goodnight and Loving became a prominent trail. Drovers from the northwest border fell in upon it near Belknap and Camp Cooper; others from central Texas pushed out to intersect it near Chadbourne and the newly founded Fort Concho; and some from around San Antonio drove northwest toward the same intersection. Some turned off to follow the Butterfield Southern Mail road by the point of the Guadalupes and into El Paso, some kept on to the Indian reserves in Arizona, and others drove clear to the Pacific Coast. A few continued up the Pecos to the mouth of the Hondo, turned west through the White Mountains, skirted the White Sands, and kept due west for the same destinations. Still others kept north along the Trail to Wyoming, turned west along the Union Pacific, and scattered their drives through Utah, Nevada, and the Pacific Coast States.

By 1870, the trade along the Goodnight and Loving Trail was well established, and the amount of money handled by its Western bankers was noted as enormous. But mostly the drivers went to market and to range along the eastern edge of the Rockies instead of across the mountains; their camps soon dotted the water courses from the Big Missouri to the lower Pecos; and the drawl of the 'Texian' became as familiar on the Great Plains as the bellow of his longhorned steer.

Hitherto the traditional westward trend of migration had left this region in a wilderness state; the old animosities that

[1] A more extended treatment of this subject, with references, is given by the author in *The Southwestern Historical Quarterly*, Austin, vol. XXXVIII, pp. 157 ff.

sectionalized the eastern half of America had broken on the arid Plains. Now the trend of pioneering was reversed, and the cow country emerged from the fraying ends of northern trails. And what Goodnight and Loving's Trail was doing for its western edge, the Chisholm Trail was doing in even greater degree for its eastern and central portions.

As Texans strung out along these trails, the most superb of all the Great Plains Indians swarmed upon their flanks, and through the late sixties and seventies the toll that the Comanche levied was frightful. The greatest danger, as Goodnight observed, was on the frontier itself. Once away from the settlements, the hazards were less, but for a few years — from 1865 until 1875 — every man who drove was in danger of losing his cattle and having his 'hair lifted' besides. Nevertheless they drove, some recklessly, others cautiously, and month by month the Goodnight and Loving Trail broadened and deepened.

Goodnight and Loving's experiences with the Comanches were by no means isolated incidents. All along that trail were graves, now in forgotten places and holding forgotten men. W. H. Boyd, veteran of the drive of 1867, recalls many fresh mounds that 'had never been rained upon.' Astraddle of one near Fort Phantom Hill was a brand-new cowboy's saddle, both shelter and marker for the owner who slept beneath.

Sometimes the trail hands erected stones and scratched inscriptions thereon, hardly literary but often unique. In 1854, the *San Diego Herald* bore witness to the death of a young man on the trail, perhaps a cowboy driving a herd to the gold fields, and the epitaph was copied in Texas:

> here lies the body of Jeems Hambrick
>   who was accidentally shot
> on the banks of the pacus river
>   by a young man
> he was accidentally shot with one of the large
> colt's revolver with no stopper for the cock to
> rest on   it was one of the old fashion kind
> brass mounted and of such is the kingdom of heaven.

² *The Leon Pioneer*, November 29, 1854.

Years afterward, a trail outfit engaged in battle with Indians near the present site of Roswell, so the story still runs, in which another cowboy was killed. He was buried beside the Goodnight Trail, and the cow-camp poet, deficient in Biblical allusion, arranged a couplet to be carved in sandstone so that all who passed might read that:

> He was young, and brave, and fair
> But the Indians raised his hair.[3]

There is tragedy and yet something bravely and buoyantly significant in the fact that rather than their names and deaths, tradition commemorates their levity.

A few Texas frontiersmen still claim that Indians stole no cattle. Horses? Plenty of them! But what would Indians want with cattle when the Western World was alive with wild beef? To this pertinent question one may answer that they wanted them only for the purpose of trading to the *comancheros*, native New Mexicans who traded with the Comanches. Yet, through the years, evidence of their theft and trade has been as elusive as the thieves themselves. When Goodnight placed claims with the Government for cattle lost on the Texas border and on the Trail, he went to New Mexico, hunted down some of these old traders, and proved that what had hitherto been largely tradition was a matter of fact. Their evidence reveals incidents of the closing years of that trade, while its beginnings are truly lost among the mazes of Spanish legend.

The original trade was probably in robes and peltries, but soon the Indians learned that not only for personal use, but for purposes of barter, the stealing of horses was a profitable business, and they began to plunder the ranches of Texas and the *haciendas* of northern Mexico. Since most of this trade was in contraband, it soon swung away from the New Mexican settlements to be transacted in the open country — on the Staked Plains. From 1850 until 1870, the trade was at its

[3] R. T. Bucy to J. E. H., September 10, 1931

height, for during those twenty years thousands of head of livestock changed hands on the Plains. For years it wrought fearful havoc upon the Texas border.

When Goodnight, in 1876, came into the Panhandle from Colorado, there were at least three *comanchero* trails almost 'as plain as the wagon roads of today.' The most southerly left the Pecos near Bosque Redondo, and pointed east and south to the Yellow Houses, terminating in Cañon del Rescate, in the neighborhood of Lubbock. The upper trail left Las Vegas, followed the Canadian to the east of Tucumcari Mountain, and forked near the Texas line. The left-hand fork continued down the Canadian along the Fort Smith road to a trading ground at Las Tecovas, or Sanborn Springs, near Amarillo.

The right-hand fork turned southeast and pointed straight for the Puerto de los Rivajeños,[4] a day's drive from the Canadian. This Door of the Plains, as it was sometimes called, was a large gap in the cap-rock near the head of the Trujillo. Traders watered at the Trujillo, and next at the head of the Palo Duro, which they followed until near the site of Canyon. They turned south to strike the Tule above the breaks, proceeded to the foot of the Plains in the Quitaque country, and came to camp on one of the head branches of the Pease — Rio de las Lenguas, or Tongue River. Between these two major trails was another, which too led to the Tongue. Its travelers came by the government road from Santa Fé toward Fort Sumner, turned eastward a short day's travel before reaching the latter place, camped at La Laguna, proceeded to Laguna Salada, to Las Escarbadas,[5] and thence to the head of the Tule, where they fell in upon the northern trail to Las Lenguas.

Usually the trading was of a modest nature. During the

[4] *Rivajenos,* a contraction of *rio bajeños,* referred to those New Mexicans who 'lived down the river' from Albuquerque. This pass had evidently been used by them in trading or in hunting buffaloes.

[5] *Las Escarbadas,* 'The Scrapings,' were pits scratched out in a sandy draw from which seeped an abundance of water. One of the divisional headquarters of the XIT Ranch was later located here.

decade from 1830 to 1840, Josiah Gregg, historian of the Santa Fé Trail, wrote that the traders, 'usually composed of the indigent and rude classes of the frontier villages ... collect together several times a year, and launch upon the plains with a few trinkets and trumperies of all kinds, and perhaps a bag of bread and another of *pinole*,' to barter for horses and mules. Rarely did the entire stock of the trader exceed twenty dollars in value, but extravagant prices were placed on his articles and proportionally low valuations on the Indians' goods. In later years the traders enlarged their stores and brought ammunition, lead, muskets, pistols, paint, beads, knives, *manta* or calico, wines, whiskey, and breads of various kinds. Liquors were carried in gourd containers and the entire store of goods was usually packed on a few small burros, the *comancheros* walking beside and urging them along. The poorer traders bartered for only a few head of cattle, usually from ten to fifty, but the well-to-do carried their goods in *carretas* or wagons and sometimes returned with fair-sized herds. Stealing in wholesale measure from the northwest fringe of Texas settlement began shortly before the Civil War, when both horses and cattle were driven northwest by the Comanches to meet the traders in Cañon del Rescate, on Las Lenguas and the Quitaque, and at Las Tecovas and Tascosa.

Contrary to popular belief, said Goodnight, few Indians spoke Spanish. And yet Indians of various tribes and dialects, renegade Anglo-Americans, and Mexican traders gathered in the valley of the Tongues, where their negotiations called for the use of many *lenguas* — tongues. Hence the stream came to be known as Las Lenguas, though only its English equivalent is heard in that Anglican region today. To the north, in the region of Quitaque, was another valley where scattered bands of raiding Indians sometimes came together, and separated their captives to lessen the danger of escape, and to insure more rapid assimilation. Here mothers and children, torn from homes in Texas and Mexico, were scattered with the splitting of tribal bands, rarely to be ransomed by the traders. In that wild region it was known as a spot of heartache, of grief, and tragedy, and the Mexicans appropriately referred to it as Valle de las Lágrimas — the Valley of Tears.

And so down the trails from Santa Fé, Las Vegas, Puerta de Luna, and Anton Chico, to these places of rendezvous on the edge of the Plains, came the New Mexican traders, there to camp and wait the coming of the Indians after the light of the moon. There were times when the Indians sold, forcibly repossessed the animals before the unfortunate Mexicans had time to get away, and then forced them to buy again. That was one complication of the whiskey trade. But the profits were great. A loaf of bread might command a cow, but a keg of whiskey would retrieve a good-sized herd.

Juan Trujillo, of Old Tascosa, used to tell Jim East how he and his friends hid kegs of whiskey in the hills, perhaps ten miles from where they were trading. It entered prominently into consideration, but was not delivered until the cattle were two or three days on the trail. Then Juan and another Mexican, who had been left behind on good fast horses, piloted the Indians to the keg and rode *pá yá*. Though the trade was hazardous, the cattle were ransomed for a song. But in that day of scalping, the Mexicans did not want the Indians to sing it.

One of the most prominent traders was José Pieda Tafoya, who, backed by the commanding officer at Fort Bascom and a merchant at the Hatch Ranch, equipped with wagons loaded with enticing goods, and possessed of intimate knowledge of the face of the Plains and the nature of the Indian, continued to swing his great caravans out of the mountains and across the Plains. At the Quitaque, from 1865 to 1867, he traded for thousands of cattle, among them hundreds bearing the Sheek, the Loving, and the Goodnight brands — the CV, the Circle W, the WES, and the Circle road brand. From the colorful breaks and badlands of the Quitaque, his *peones* pointed them northwest to strike the Fort Smith road along the Canadian, trailed them west into New Mexico by way of Fort Bascom, and distributed them in the range country adjacent to the settlements at handsome profit, not only to José, but to his army friends besides.

When the Superintendent of Indian Affairs, A. B. Norton, reached New Mexico for the assumption of duty in 1866, he found the trade flourishing and unrestricted, and the Territory 'filled with Texas cattle.' He gave orders for the cancellation of all trade permits, and reissued licenses to but four citizen traders. These four nullified the restriction by subletting the privilege, and still others traded without permit, so that by 1867 the trade was at its height.

One day, as Goodnight waited with the wounded Loving, he looked up and saw six beef steers, lost from their herd at Horsehead, coming across the parade ground. They had been trailed north by the Indians, and were now driven openly and boldly into the settlements to be traded to the Mexicans. The military authorities did nothing about it. Perhaps they had worries enough of their own, as the Apaches and Navajos were still on the verge of starvation.

'In fact,' said Goodnight, 'they did not get half of what the Government appropriated. Many a time I saw the poor devils kill their whole week's issue of beef on the prairie and eat every ounce of the animal, paunch and guts included, at one gulp. That would be all they'd have for another week. When an animal was turned out, a dozen or so of the warriors would, after running it over the country and shooting up a beltful of ammunition, finally get it down. One time I persuaded them to let me make the kill. Twenty-five head of steers were let out, one at a time, and using my six-shooter, I killed them as they came out with just twenty-six shots. I won the respect of those Apaches right there.

'The Navajos used to slip away from the reservation, come down to our ranch at Bosque Grande and eat up our horses, which they preferred to beef. The dirty buggers ate up my own saddle horse one time — a cracker-jack — while there were plenty of cattle all around him.'

Again as he waited with Loving, the Navajos stole a number

of Mexican horses and brought them in to the reservation, where the owners, trailing them up, found and demanded them. Major Charles Jarvis Whiting ordered one Captain Thompson to take a squad of men and recover the animals, in which action the Indians attacked and killed six of his men before he got back to the post. And, furthermore, they kept the horses.

'Just after this,' continued Goodnight, 'probably three hundred Comanches came in at night and made a fight on the Navajos, who were camped just east of the post. I think the fight commenced about two or three o'clock. I was at the hotel where Mr. Loving was at the point of death, and I got on top of the building and watched the fight for some time. They did a great deal of yelling and shooting, and the blaze of the guns was quite an attractive sight. I understood the Comanches killed only two or three of the Navajos, but if any of the Comanches were killed I did not learn of it.

'At daylight the Comanches were just north of the reservation and post on beautiful level land, where Captain Thompson, with two companies of men, was ordered to attack them. I went to him, asked him to mount me, and let me show him how to kill a few Indians, but he refused. The next day he was kind enough to tell me why — he had not intended to fight the Comanches and was afraid I would go in and get killed. He said that since Whiting had not avenged the killing of his men a few days before, he wanted the Comanches to kill the whole bunch of Navajos and still hoped they would do so. Soon after this the Navajos stole a herd of my horses and mules that I had started down the Pecos to relieve Joe Loving's outfit, which was coming out from Texas. I was still with Loving and could not go. Afterward I found five or six of these horses on the reservation, and went to Whiting and asked him to get them. He refused by telling me it would make war, and he could not fight the Indians. "All right," I said, "I have three or four of my men and I'll get them myself." He informed me that if I made any disturbance he would put me in the guard-house and gave orders to the officer of the day to that effect.'⁶

For a while the herd that Goodnight and Loving had on the trail when Loving was mortally wounded was held at Eight Mile Bend, on the Pecos, but being too late for the letting of contracts at Santa Fé and Fort Sumner, Goodnight started the cattle toward Colorado. After Loving's burial he set out for Fort Bascom, where by report and in accord with their promise of the year before, the army officers had captured some herds from the *comancheros*. A decided and official movement was being made to suppress this illicit trade, and the soldiers had captured some seventy-three hundred cattle en route from the Texas trading grounds to the New Mexico frontier, and were holding them pending the arrival of claimants. Goodnight examined them thoroughly, recognizing by brands as well as flesh marks about two hundred and fifty head of his own, most of which had been stolen at Horsehead, but

⁶ According to a report in the Santa Fé *New Mexican*, July 28, 1866, the Comanches had, in that year, encamped within fifteen miles of the post for three days, then raided the reserve in broad day and driven off 'almost the entire herd' of Navajo horses. When Major McCleave sent troops after them, the Comanches sent word to the soldiers they would return in fifteen days and 'clean out' the Navajos. They opposed the reservation as being in their range, and sent word to General Carlton that they would take his scalp if he would but venture out.

some on the Clear Fork, and even a few from his and Sheek's home range. Besides his own, he recognized the brands of other Texas cowmen. Yet the officers refused to surrender any of the cattle to him because of his lack of legal authority to receive them. Before leaving home, he and Loving had armed themselves with powers of attorney from a number of Texans, but when the Indians captured Loving's horse these credentials were lost with his saddlebags, and thus their trouble had been for nothing.

He left Bascom and hurried west to intersect the trail and follow up his herd, while the *comancheros* stole back most of the cattle the soldiers had taken, and others were killed to keep them from going the same way. Goodnight passed the old Hatch Ranch, and nearby, in the valley of the Gallinas, about twenty-five miles southeast of Las Vegas, recognized some more of his cattle that still ran in the CV brand. He carefully circled in and out among the grazing herds, and estimating there were six hundred head of his own, hurried on to Las Vegas, hired a lawyer, and went into the United States Court to replevy his long-lost property. In spite of the fact that he proved by the *comancheros* themselves that they had brought some three hundred thousand head of stolen cattle and probably one hundred thousand head of horses from Texas into New Mexico, he was defeated, thrown in the cost of the court, and 'was lucky,' he said, 'to get out of the place alive.'

And thus it appears that the co-operation promised Loving and Goodnight at Fort Bascom, the strategic point for the control of the *comanchero* trade, was after all a half-hearted pledge. But down in Texas the cowmen were aroused and demanding less of theory and more of action on the part of the Government. At last the Eighth Cavalry was sent to eastern New Mexico for the purpose, one of its veterans still attests, of suppressing the traffic.

Slightly more than a month later, in August, 1870, William A. Pyle, Governor of the Territory of New Mexico, issued a proclamation against the trade and directed the judges of the border counties to 'arrest and bring to justice the guilty parties.' In particular he asked that civil authorities co-operate with the military by 'giving information to the commandant of Fort Bascom or of the picket line established on the eastern line of the Territory.'

Finally John Hittson, Texas cowman, deciding that even though the meek might inherit the earth, they would never possess its cattle, rode out to help himself in a truly 'Texian' way. He, too, armed himself with powers of attorney from various cowmen, but his faith was firmer in the persuasive power of Judge Colt, and he gathered an outfit of fighting Texans to guard against technical evasions and the right of appeal. Then he marched up the Goodnight Trail to New Mexico, invited the trail blazer to join him, and noised it far and wide that he came for Texas cattle and intended to have them, too.

Goodnight refused to sanction his moves, but Hittson moved on, repossessing Texan brands where holders lacked trustworthy evidence of ownership. And as he marched, he not only gathered cattle, but published notices to the Government as to how it might stop the trade by the disposal of well-organized companies of frontiersmen along the border. His operations were individualistic, bold, and colossal, and his contemporary press agent excellent. The work went on until he had recovered some ten thousand head, and when he laid down his guns, he continued the assault in the press, publishing in the *San Antonio Express*, in 1873, his previous indictments of the New Mexico trade.

In January, 1875, Governor Richard Coke, of Texas, called the attention of the Legislature to the demoralizing influence of this trade, and predicted no peace for the borderlands so long as Indians were granted permission to leave the reserves and barter with unscrupulous traders.

Not Goodnight and Loving's attempts at legal action, not the punitive Hittson campaign, not the proclamations and

speeches of Texan and New Mexican governors, nor the ineffec-
tive interest of the Federal Government, but rather the corral-
ling of the Great Plains Indians on Territorial reserves finally
broke the *comanchero* trade. The effective expeditions by
Mackenzie in the early and middle seventies, and the co-operative movements by Miles and Baldwin, removed the Comanches, Kiowas, and Cheyennes from the familiar haunts in the
Palo Duro, the Rescate, the Quitaque, and the Tecovas. When
the Indians were concentrated, the traders scattered, and a few
equally scattered incidents marked their passing.

General C. C. Augur, at this time in command of the Department of Texas, discovered, by 1872, that the western line of the
State was subject to depredations stimulated by this trade.
He decided that the time for action had come, and that efficient
frontier officer, Colonel Ranald S. Mackenzie, was sent to the
foot of the Plains. Using the *comancheros* as guides, he scouted
out the southern trail and followed it across to the Pecos. His
return by way of Fort Bascom and the head of Palo Duro
approximated the *comanchero* trail to the Quitaque, which trace
today is inappropriately referred to as the Mackenzie Trail.
In New Mexico he soon gave up his attempt to run down the
traders, and returned to the Panhandle, where, in the course of
his scouts, he captured old José Pieda Tafoya who was ventur-
ing across the Plains in pursuit of trade.

As a guide, said Goodnight, 'Tafoya was a wonder, and knew
the Plains from the Palo Duro to the Concho by heart.' Upon
his capture, Mackenzie, taking lessons in severity from the soil
itself, decided it proper to kill him. Thinking he might have
information of value, the veteran campaigner tried to get him
to talk, but José's lips were sealed by fear of the Comanches,
and all he knew was '*no sabe.*' Then, according to the story of
the buffalo hunters, Mackenzie propped up the tongue of a
wagon and hanged Tafoya to the end until he was glad to talk.
Hemp and a hangman's noose have long been conducive to
speech, and when Tafoya's feet again touched the ground he
really did *sabe*, and, furthermore, he agreed to lead the troops

to the Indian camp in the recesses of the Palo Duro Cañon. The well-known result was the defeat of the Comanche and confederated tribes, the killing of their horses, the resultant setting afoot of their warriors, and their broken retreat to designated reserves in the Territory. Quanah Parker, chief of the Quahada Comanches, heard of Tafoya's betrayal. When he met Goodnight in the Palo Duro in 1878, and learned that he too had knowledge of the great *comanchero*, he 'swore and be damned,' in the idiom of the range, that he would broil the old Mexican alive if he ever met him again. But Tafoya knew that the glories of his trade were done, and thereafter kept the broad Plains between himself and Quanah's Quahadas. As his ill-gotten fortune dwindled with the years, he sat and dreamed in the shadows of the Rockies, dreamed of rich caravans at rest on the Quitaque, of thousands of cattle loose-herded in its valleys, of tearful mothers and terror-stricken children in its camps, and of *oro* and *plata* at the end of the trail. He dreamed on, living in part on the charity of the man in whose cattle he had trafficked — whose cattle once again grazed in the Palo Duro, along the Tule, on the Mulberry, and in the Quitaque.

And so passed a trade that had developed through approximately one hundred and fifty years — a commerce as significant for the Plains as the buccaneer's trade for the sea. And in the fading of its trails it passed completely; passed from the memory of men and the stories of the range. Its names, too, are fading, for the Valle de las Lágrimas now sheds no tears unless for the past, and the tongues of Las Lenguas speak only from the dead in commemoration of the *comanchero* trade, hope and ideal of the outlaw West — cow thieving without odium, rustling without responsibility.

XII. THE GOODNIGHT AND LOVING
TRAIL

THE trace that led from Texas to Fort Sumner is generally known as the Goodnight Trail, while that which Goodnight later blazed direct to Cheyenne is called the Goodnight and Loving Trail, though sometimes the terms are used interchangeably. The course of this latter extension, which Loving made in the fall of 1866, which Goodnight used in 1867 and straightened in his drives of 1868, should be observed in some detail. Loving's course lay up the Pecos from Sumner to Las Vegas, up the Santa Fé Trail to Ratón Pass, and around the base of the Rockies by Trinidad and Pueblo to Denver. It was roundabout, and Goodnight swung fifty or sixty miles to the east, across the High Plains, keeping away from the settlements and shortening the drive.

Late in the fall of 1867, after his trip to Fort Bascom, he pushed up Loving's trail to overtake the herd as it drifted northward under the direction of 'One-Armed' Bill Wilson. After his unfortunate experience in Federal Court at Las Vegas, he hurried on, caught the outfit near Fort Union, and pointed the herd northeastward toward the Capulín Vega, where the remnant from the fall before was still being held by Foster and a devil-may-care boy by the name of John Rumans. Rumans was destined to leave his brand on the Goodnight outfit. From Missouri he had whacked a bull team across the Plains when only fourteen years of age, had freighted on the Santa Fé Trail, and had worked for 'Mad' Emory on the Cimarrón Seco at various odd jobs. As tough as bull-neck rawhide, as independent as a hog on ice, and as reckless as any drunk Indian, he was born to be a cowboy and a good one. He and Foster were camped with a wagon about two miles west of the Capulín crater, riding line on the Goodnight–Loving cattle. There was not another soul about.

JOHN MILTON RUMANS

Goodnight gathered his fat cattle from the Capulín, and with the combined herds turned northwest toward Ratón Pass, the gateway between New Mexico and Colorado. The outfit crossed through the high mesa country, pointed its herd up the Ratón Range, and as it passed over the divide and dropped down the Colorado side, came to 'Uncle Dick' Wootton's toll station and was forced to pay ten cents an animal for passage.[1]

Goodnight protested that the toll was too high. It was an

[1] In the winter of 1865, Uncle Dick Wootton applied for charters from the Legislatures of New Mexico and Colorado to build a toll road through the pass of the range dividing the two Territories, the pass most generally used by the mountain travel from north to south. Permission was granted, and in the spring of 1866, Uncle Dick moved down from near Pueblo, built a fairly passable road twenty-seven miles in length, and not only made money from tolls, but flourished from a roadhouse on the side. Howard Louis Conard, '*Uncle Dick' Wootton*, 417–26; Bess McKinnan, 'The Toll Road Over Ratón Pass,' *The New Mexico Historical Review*, II, 83–89.

old story with the mountain man, and he said positively that no rates would be given, whether a man drove one milk cow or three thousand Texas steers. Goodnight swore that if the toll was not reduced, he would find another pass and blaze another trail. Wootton laughed in his face — there was no other pass! But as Goodnight trailed down by pioneer Trinidad, he promised himself that Dick Wootton would pay.

From Ratón Pass the cowboys could see far to the north. On the right the mountains fell away to a great plateau that stretched in open, unbroken grasslands to the valley of the Arkansas; to the left the Rockies continued northward with the Spanish Peaks, the Greenhorns, Pike's Peak, and others on toward Denver. The streams that broke from the north side of the Ratón Range flowed north and northeast, cutting their cañons through the plateau as they approached the Arkansas. At the head of one of these cañons, the Apishapa, forty miles northeast of Trinidad, Goodnight established the first extensive cattle ranch in southern Colorado, in a beautiful cow country, where once again he had 'the world to himself.'

The Apishapa Cañon was about twenty miles long, and though not very deep was practically inaccessible except at the ends. It was lined with box elders and the water was full of decaying leaves which 'smelled something terrible,' probably giving the place its name, a word of reputed Ute origin meaning 'stinking water.' Though by day the stream played out in the sand, its waters rose and ran when the sun went down, and even if the leaves had killed out the fish, it looked good to these waddies from Texas.

To quote the vigorous John Rumans, Goodnight turned the cattle loose and left 'John Kutch, Fayette Wilson, me, and some other son-of-a-gun — who wasn't worth a damn, but whom he had hired as a boss — there in camp,' to cut pine logs, build a cabin, and locate the herd, while he turned on the long back-trail to Bosque Grande to meet Joe Loving, who was holding his drive at the partnership ranch. Joe was only twenty-one years of age when he started on the trail with his herd of thirty-two hundred head, and though he knew how to fight Indians, 'he was probably too young and inexperienced,' according to Goodnight, 'to handle such a herd. Anyway, I found it in bad condition when I met him at the Bosque. He was short a thousand head from various causes. Some had been lost and some had escaped in stampedes, and the Indians had got them before he did. I took out a thousand head of the strongest and best cattle, paid off the transient hands, and left Joe in charge of the remainder at the old Loving Ranch at Bosque.' Again Goodnight turned north with enough old hands to handle the herd, and on Christmas Eve, 1867, released his second drive on the Apishapa, after much suffering and trouble in getting through the snow in Ratón Pass.

At this time a famous outlaw band led by William Coe rustled and robbed throughout northeastern New Mexico and southern Colorado at its own free will. 'Coe, a nice-looking fellow but sure a game son-of-a-gun,' according to Rumans, was a power beyond the civil and military, and was scarcely opposed even by frontier ranchmen. With Goodnight's vigorously aggressive stand for order and honesty, it was as natural as the flow of the Apishapa down the plain that the two should clash. Foster, while camped with the herd on the Capulín Vega, unwittingly contributed to the approaching enmity.

He had hired three hands to help handle the herd, two of whom eventually told the reckless Rumans that they planned to drift down the Cimarrón to join Coe's band, and they wondered if he, too, would like to go. The youngster characteristically replied that he 'hadn't lost a damned thing down the Cimarrón' in the first place, and in the second, if he planned to steal he'd 'steal by himself, and then there'd be no whacking-up to do.' Dick Wootton, who knew the bad elements as well as the good, told Goodnight that the remaining hand was one of the outlaws, and upon their arrival at the Apishapa, the trail driver paid him his wages and told him to pull his freight. This independent action aroused the ire of Coe.

A few weeks later, a runner came from a prominent Mexican

at Trinidad with news that Coe and his men had taken the
town, were robbing the stores, appropriating the women, and
celebrating their arrival in high-handed style. Goodnight took
eight of his men and rode that night, covering the forty miles in
bitter cold, and reaching town at the break of day. The Mexican lived on the Purgatoire, at the edge of town, and 'seemed
to be expecting us,' said Goodnight, 'as he was standing at the
yard gate, and when I rode up said he had coffee ready for us in
the house. It is said that the Mexicans are noted for making
coffee, and this old man must have been the most noted of
them all, as I don't think I ever had such a good cup of coffee
in my life. We had ridden hard and needed it.' After a hasty
cup, Goodnight and his cow-hands rode into the village for the
purpose of running the outlaws out, or killing them if they
preferred to fight. Coe's men had wind of their coming, and
rode out on the south side of town as Goodnight came in from
the north. Coe, who was really no coward, afterward swore the
country over that he would kill the cowman on sight.[2]

Shortly the cowman met Dow Miller in Trinidad, and in
conversation learned that he was a Texan, of a prominent Titus
County family, 'courageous people, and fighters, so to speak,'
appraised Goodnight. 'He had been a gambler, miner, and
most everything else that was honest, from California to
Colorado. He said he was broke. I told him he was just the man
I wanted, and that I would arrange through what was known
as the Vigilance Committee — a body of the better citizens of
southern Colorado endeavoring to enforce law and order —
to have him made sheriff. He said he had nothing to be sheriff
with. I replied that I did, and gave him a mount, a Henry rifle,
pistols, and some money, and told him to go for them, which he
certainly did. This made war between me and the robbers, who
set out to kill me. I, of course, set out to see that they did not.
But this was the only place in a civilized country where I had

[2] Goodnight to J. E. H., August 21, 1929, 'Recollections,' II, 115, 119; John Rumans
to J. E. H., December 8, 1928, Deposition in Case 9133, pp. 180, 228; Horace Wilson to
J. E. H., February 22, 1930.

to dodge around, take the byways instead of the roads, and continually be on guard against my own race.'[3]

Again Goodnight took some of his hands and rode for Fort Sumner, which he reached about the first of February. Loving's

JOE HORN, A GOODNIGHT HAND

body was removed and sent to Texas, and the remainder of Joe Loving's herd left in charge of Rumans, J. C. Holloway, and Long Joe Loving. The Willburns had a herd to their west, and down the river John Chisum was in temporary winter camp holding some six hundred head that he had trailed from Texas the fall before. Except for these three outfits the country was unoccupied.

Never had Goodnight known busier and more trying times. His and Loving's cattle were now held at two widely separated

[3] Goodnight, 'Recollections,' II, 119.

places in a wild country, subject to raids of Indians and outlaws. The losses of the drive of 1867 had left the firm in debt, and Goodnight was faced, not only with the problem of paying the losses, but also with the fulfillment of his promise to Loving to continue the partnership, a serious obligation considering the problems and dangers.

Jim Loving, the old man's son, engaged in the mercantile business at Weatherford, agreed to gather the remainder of the Loving and Goodnight cattle in Texas, enlarge the herd with favorable purchases, and trail to Colorado in the spring. In the meantime Goodnight contracted to receive Chisum's drives at Bosque Grande on a fifty-fifty basis, allowing him a dollar a head extra for his risks on the trail from Texas. This agreement, in view of the subsequent history of the Pecos Valley, was a significant one.

Chisum, one of the most colorful characters of the cow country, operated with precision, and like Goodnight, covered a big country. Unlike Goodnight, he never went armed. He tolerated the criminal elements, letting them live, perhaps, as a surer means of staying alive himself. His aversion to arms may have been a protective measure in itself, for in that open country the code forbade the killing of a man without a gun at his side. By pure luck and good plainscraft, he escaped the Indians, who failed to grasp this subtle ethical distinction.[4]

Though Patterson was still contracting for the delivery of army and Indian beef, Goodnight was turning his attention to the range and speculative end of the business — the delivery of cattle to ranchmen and other contractors throughout the western portion of the Plains. Here again was the pioneer; others had followed his trail to the Bosque. The great range now was farther on, and his trails pointed the way. The abandonment of the Indian reserve at Fort Sumner sped his work.

From the beginning the reserve was bitterly opposed by the New Mexicans, and by the terms of a treaty in 1868 the Nava-

---

[4] For details of the life of Chisum see Cox, *The Cattle Industry of Texas,* 299-302; *The Northern Standard,* May 5, 1855; *Dictionary of American Biography.* IV, 77.

jos were returned to their old country in northwestern New Mexico.[5] When Goodnight came back for his next herd, 'the dirty buggers' who had killed and eaten his best saddle horse, and who had furnished his first profitable market for cattle, were gone.

Up on the Apishapa, Goodnight prepared his new ranch as a swing station on the trail. Bill Wilson and his brothers were anxious to pursue their individual fortunes, and cutting their cattle from Goodnight's herd, drew their wages and turned west into the Rockies, settling around the Spanish Peaks. So far as the records go, the Wilsons managed to live and ride in comparative peace for about four years, until February 2, 1872, when the boys rode into Trinidad, and George Wilson began gambling at the Exchange Saloon. In the course of the day he left the place, declaring he had been robbed. A little later he returned with his brother, Fayette, and a boy named Atwell, and demanded his money of the house. When Sheriff Juan Tafolla attempted to quiet him, George shot him through the stomach, Tafolla's gun went off into the floor, and the bystanders swarmed from the place into the street, 'some crawling across it through the mud, in their fear of the Texan's bullets.'

Frank Bloom was standing in front of his store at the site of the First National Bank, talking with one of his cowboys, when George and his brothers came running up. George, who had lost his hat in the scuffle, grabbed the cowboy's and called to Bill to 'come on,' while behind them swarmed a mob of perhaps twenty infuriated Mexicans. About a hundred yards east of the Thatcher Store there was, at that time, an arroyo, crossed by a footbridge, beyond which was the United States Livery Stable, where the cowboys had left their horses. When the Wilsons reached the bridge, the Mexicans were close upon

[5] *The Daily New Mexican*, February 16, June 8, October 27, November 24, 1866; July 22, 1868; May 30, 1870. *The Colorado Chieftain*, June 25, 1868; Bancroft, *History of Arizona and New Mexico*, 730–33.

On June 13, 1870, the buildings, stables, supplies of wood, and the fifty sections of land composing the reserve at Fort Sumner were offered at auction, and bought by Lucien Maxwell. See advertisement in *The Daily New Mexican*, May 30, 1870.

them, and 'One-Armed' Bill, stopping at the far end of the bridge, threw his rifle across his stub arm, and called to his pursuers: 'The first man that crosses that bridge is a dead one.' And though the posse knew no English, it understood perfectly, and 'the first man' did not cross. Then 'the desperadoes,' to quote the Trinidad *Enterprise*, 'mounted and . . . rode slowly out of town.' George Wilson is said to have been killed in Arizona, but Bill died peacefully, only a few years since, and if peace is ever the rightful reward of the warrior, 'One-Armed' Bill had earned it.[6]

In the spring of 1868, John Wesley Iliff, one of the greatest of early Western ranchmen, and a freighter named Fenton, came to the Apishapa, looked the Goodnight cattle over, and decided to take them if the owner would deliver them at Cheyenne. He agreed to do so.[7]

While Loving's drives had proceeded from Pueblo to strike the Platte at Denver, Goodnight's course was practically due north, across the Arkansas near Pueblo, and over the divide to the Platte, leaving Denver to the west. He hit the Platte at the mouth of Crow Creek, where Greeley now stands, and swam his herd, recalling that those old Texas steers, with only a portion of their heads and horns above water, 'looked like a million floating rocking chairs.' From there they trailed up Crow Creek to Cheyenne. Thus lengthened the Goodnight and Loving Trail across Colorado. It came into general use, though Goodnight delivered only one more herd in Wyoming — to the Chugwater, thereafter driving to Iliff's headquarters in the northeastern corner of Colorado, at the cottonwood grove known as Fremont's Orchard, where, in three years' time, he delivered from twenty-five to thirty thousand head of cattle for government contracts.

As soon as this herd was delivered, Goodnight and his outfit

[6] *The Colorado Chieftain*, February 8, 1872; Trinidad *Enterprise* quoted in the *Chieftain*, February 15, 1872; Frank Bloom to J. E. H., August, 1929; 'Frank G. Bloom — Pioneer Citizen,' in the *Chronicle-News* (Trinidad), August 18, 1929.

[7] For information on Iliff see *The Colorado Chieftain*, March 7, 1872, and the *History of Colorado*, Linderman Co., Inc., Denver, 1927, pp. 114–18.

turned back across Colorado and down through New Mexico to meet Chisum, as he trailed out from Texas. He and his cowboys worked hard and fast, long hours in the saddle and few on the ground, and were at Bosque Grande on the proper day. Often in the rush of work, in disregard of clock and calendar, they were uncertain of the date, but their arguments were finally settled by appeal to Bose Ikard, or any other negro hand that happened to be along, for the negroes alone never lost count of time.

In partial payment for the first herd delivered to Iliff, Goodnight took a ten-thousand-dollar note that Fenton held against Lucien Maxwell for the delivery of a train of goods to his store on the Cimarrón. Maxwell was unable to pay the note except by dribbles. Goodnight had counted on the money for meeting his contracts with Chisum, and since Maxwell could not pay, he took in John Dawson to help him handle the drives. Dawson was experienced but niggardly, and the partnership was not exactly harmonious.

At Bosque Grande they received their cattle, and Goodnight, by cutting out the original detours, blazed a new trail as straight toward his destination as water and grass would permit. Five or six miles above Fort Sumner, they left the river, turned due north to Alamogordo Creek, and pointed across the Plains by the Juan Dios and the Cuervito, down the latter to the Cuervo, and across the Canadian about twenty miles west of Fort Bascom.

When they reached the Canadian, Dawson told Goodnight, who was in camp, that he would cross the herd. He brought the cattle down to the river at a lope. At the bottom of the hill was a deep arroyo, into which the running herd crowded the leaders until they almost filled it, killing and crippling over thirty head. Goodnight was boiling mad.

'Hell, you don't know how to put cattle across,' he swore. 'Nobody that brings them into a stream at a lope, yelling at them, knows anything about cattle.' He took charge of the herd again and succeeded in crossing it that day, in spite of the chousing by Dawson, who 'was a good old man,' John Rumans mused, 'but didn't know the cow business much. He just thought he knowed it.' [8]

After crossing the Canadian, Goodnight pointed the herd up the Cinta, the Ribbon, a short day's drive to the foot of an

abrupt mesa, which still goes by the name of Goodnight Hill. They raised the mesa by a trail directly up its face, an elevation of some seven hundred feet in a quarter of a mile. Experienced trail drivers never attempted the climb except in the cool of early morning, when their cattle were well rested. Otherwise, the herd would balk. From here they pointed almost due north toward the Capulín crater, Goodnight attending strictly to the business of trailing while Dawson delighted in pottering around. One aggravating experience at the time was an amusing retrospection for Goodnight in later years.

Instead of sitting his tree in the dust of the herd, Dawson would 'fish, hunt, and potter along without doing anything.' As they moved northward, he heard of a bunch of dogies, and left the outfit to look them over and buy them.

'When he came back,' said Goodnight, 'he had so many lice that he could have taken his clothes off and driven them down the road. Everybody in the outfit got them. We got up on a creek in northern New Mexico and I told him I was going to

[8] Goodnight to J. E. H., May 22, 1929; Rumans to J. E. H., December 8, 1928.

stop and let the men wash up. He was a stingy old cuss and said we could get along all right. I told him I couldn't sleep.

"'Aw-w,'" he said, "turn your shirt wrong side out. It will take them all night to get back through, and you can get a good night's sleep."

"'You may do that,'" I replied, "but I'm going to stop and boil mine."

"'Don't you know it costs seventy-five dollars a day to run this outfit?'" he argued.

"'I know something about that,'" I said impatiently. "But I don't give a damn what it costs, I'm going to stop." It made him so mad that he went on ahead of us, and we didn't catch him until we got 'way up in Colorado.'[9]

Goodnight trailed by a course some fifty miles to the east of that followed by Loving on the first trip, and by himself in locating the Apishapa Ranch. He passed just west of Capulín, dropped down to the Cimarrón Seco, and turned up the South Trinchera to cross the Ratón Range full two days' drive east of Wootton's, and observed, in passing, the welcome spring that broke from the very crest of Trinchera Pass. From here Goodnight's new trail led north, out of the mountains, veered northwest to the Picketwire, and thence past the prominent Hog Back to the Apishapa, where for two years he maintained a swing station on the trail for holding his horses and recruiting his cattle.[10]

Trinchera Pass proved to be the outlet for which Goodnight

[9] Goodnight to J. E. H., May 22, 1929; Don H. Biggers, *Shackelford County Sketches*, pp. not numbered; Maxwell Land Grant vs. John B. Dawson, Case No. 520, Supreme Court, Territory of New Mexico, July, 1892, pp. 242, 265–69.

[10] The Goodnight and Loving Trail left Fort Sumner, passed Bosque Redondo about five miles above, and left the river to keep north to Alamogordo Arroyo, thence to El Cuervo, to Lagunas Coloradas, to the Canadian, and across it near the mouth of La Cinta. Ten miles up La Cinta to the north, it led up the mesa — Goodnight Hill, thence north to Black Lake, Carrizo, Palo Blanco Arroyo, Malpais Arroyo, west of the Capulín Peak to the Cimarrón Seco, and thence over Trinchera Pass. Down the North Trinchera the trail emerged from the mountains, pointed northwest to the Cola del Burro, Frijoles Arroyo, the Picketwire, Hole in the Rock, and on to the Apishapa. Jack M. Potter, of Clayton, N.M., has rendered much assistance in the establishment of its course. Goodnight to J. E. H., November 13, 1926, and August 2, 1928; Jack Potter to J. E. H., October 2, 1930.

was looking, since it was of easier grades, by a shorter trail, and free of tolls. And because of it, Dick Wootton did pay, for this trail caught the cattle trade from Texas and New Mexico that was beginning to pour into Colorado, Wyoming, and the Northwest. Immediately wily 'Uncle Dick' saw his mistake, and attempted to get Goodnight to shift back to the original trail, offering to pass his cattle free, knowing many others would follow his lead. But now it was Goodnight's time to laugh — there *was* another pass!

No sooner would he have one herd located, or well on the trail, than he would be looking for another, and day in and night out through 1868 and 1869, he drove himself relentlessly up and down the trail from southern New Mexico to Wyoming. He once observed that during the first few years on the trail, his longest stay in any one place was a four days' pause in Denver.

It is impossible to follow his meandering horse tracks, relate all his adventures, and consider all his problems. But his adventures and problems were symbolic of the life, and if he lived the full measure of his ability and time, if he adventured honestly and boldly, and if he met those problems bravely and vigorously, whether successfully or otherwise, then more than the man rides the trail of the past — the West itself rides there beside him.

In the fall of 1866, Loving had sold about a hundred head to a man named Collier, who planned to use them for work cattle. Then gold was discovered in the Sangre de Cristo of northern New Mexico, and before snow melted in the spring, prospectors were pushing up to the head of the Cimarrón, and assaulting the bleak crest of Old Baldy. Moreno Valley was soon alive with people, and Elizabethtown, 'E-town,' as the old-timers called it, sprang to lusty life in the evening shade of Mount Wheeler. Along with everybody else, Collier gravitated to E-town, and in spite of the prosperity of the time and place, failed to finish paying for the cattle before his own death settled the account.

Early in 1868, Goodnight learned the cattle were being killed by a local butcher, and, asking Bill Wilson to go with him, he crossed the Ratón Range, dropped down by the Maxwell Ranch, turned up the wild and scenic Cimarrón Cañon, and at the mines replevied the cattle.

'I was waiting around that night before starting back with them next day,' he recalled, 'when Bill said: "Let's go to a prize fight." I didn't know anything about fighting, but went with him. After it was over, a carpenter from Maxwell's, who was awfully drunk, was raising hell and wanting to kill somebody. We went from the fight to the stable where we had left our horses, and found this fellow there. The stableman was so afraid of him that he would not saddle our horses. We went to saddle them ourselves, and in doing so I leaned the fine, double-barreled shotgun that I carried against the adobe wall of the stable. The fellow, who was wanting to be a desperado and kill somebody, as everyone was killing everyone else, came in and started a row with Bill. I couldn't stand to see him jumping on a one-armed man, and started for him. He threw his gun down on me, and I backed across the stable from him, then drew my six-shooter like a flash and threw down on him. He wilted, threw up his hands and cried: "My God, man, don't kill me."

'"Get out of here then," I said, "and do it damned quick." He had some friends around, and I picked up my shotgun and told them if they didn't want him to get two loads of shot, to get him out.'

Next day Goodnight and Wilson started with the cattle, and just at the edge of the timber, near the foot of Baldy, met the sobered carpenter. The night before he had roundly cursed Goodnight, and this chance meeting was to the cowman's liking. Jumping from his horse he advanced toward the other's mount saying:

'You abused me last night without cause. Get off there and we'll have it out.'

'My God, Goodnight,' he exclaimed, 'you saved my life

once. Don't make me indebted to you for it a second time.' And the cowman recalled that 'he seemed, when sober, a rather decent fellow.'

In the summer of 1868, the famous Aztec Mine was discovered on the east side of Baldy, and Lucien Maxwell, expansive, liberal, and improvident, again had wealth commensurate with his gracious table and his far-famed silver service. He advised Goodnight that he could not pay the balance on the Fenton note in currency, but he could pay off in solid gold at the mine. They set out together from his ranch.

Maxwell, who had been with Fremont in the forties, was a striking character. His son, Pete, in charge of the mine, was not running things to suit him, and after looking over the works with mounting impatience, the old man finally exclaimed to Goodnight: 'Charlie, did you ever see a half-breed that was worth a damn?' And though the subject prompting the generalization was the old man's son, Goodnight, always impatient with disorder, heartily agreed: 'No, I never did.'

The mine maintained a little retort, melted the gold into chunks about the size of a guinea egg, and stored them in a hollow log. Maxwell pulled out the log and poured forth enough pieces 'to set a hen,' while Goodnight protested that he knew 'nothing about this gold business.' Maxwell was liberal in weighing it out, and when finally Goodnight got back to the settlements in Texas, he found he had about a hundred dollars in excess of the debt. After the payment, Maxwell reminded him of the thieves infesting the mountains, and asked if he thought he could get out.

'Why, yes,' he replied, 'I got in here. I've got to get out.'

The other spoke of the dangers of ambush in the cañon of the Cimarrón that lay for miles below them, and said he should have an escort. Some friendly Utes, under the leadership of the noted Ouray, who received their rations from the agency at the Maxwell Ranch, happened to be camped in the mountains nearby. Goodnight had seen Ouray at Fort Sumner and at Maxwell's where he had delivered the Utes some beeves, and Old Don Luciano, as the Mexicans knew Maxwell, delegated Ouray to escort him to the open country, some forty miles to the east. Off they rode, the Indians avoiding the pack-trail in the bed of the cañon for fear of waylays, safely keeping to the ridges, to the higher and more open ground. It was a unique experience for the young cowman — 'It was the only time in my life I ever had an escort.' [11]

As Goodnight rushed about his work in southern Colorado and on the trail, Jim Loving was making his plans to drive from Texas. He sold his mercantile business, gathered his herd, outfitted, and at last was ready to start. He decided against the Goodnight Trail in favor of that through Indian Territory and across the Plains of western Kansas, the course that his father had followed in driving to Denver in 1860. Even so, it was a trip that he never forgot.

The Indians were as bad as ever, having stolen the Sheek and Goodnight horses in 1867, and — just as Jim Loving was ready to start in the spring of 1868 — stole all his trail horses from the Black Springs Ranch. Frank Mayes, the negro cook who had been herding them, reported the loss of forty to forty-five head, and particularly bemoaned the theft of a fine saddle horse that belonged to Goodnight personally. Loving supplied his outfit with others by purchase, and on the twentieth of June pointed the herd north along the outer edges of settlement, four thousand head representing the combined drives of several ranchmen. The herd trailed on into the north, past the site of Wichita, and up the Little Arkansas to intersect the Santa Fé Trail.

When they met six to eight hundred Indians on the Arkansas, the boys from Texas thought their hair was gone. Big Black Beaver, a chief, rode out to meet Loving, who had bunched the herd and thrown most of his men around the

[11] Goodnight to J. E. H., July 10, and September 17, 1928; *The Daily New Mexican*, May 17, 1869; Twitchell, *Leading Facts in New Mexican History*, II, 415–16; anonymous pamphlet, *The Great Elizabethtown Gold and Copper Mining District*, pp. not numbered.
Chief Ouray died in Colorado, August 24, 1880. See *The Colorado Magazine*, I, 312, and VII, 187

wagon for defense. They conversed through a Mexican captive, and Loving, knowing their hatred for the Texans, claimed to be from the Cherokee Nation, driving on government contract, and argued the point almost to conviction.

But 'Nigger Frank,' taking in everything from the top of the trail wagon, recognized Goodnight's stolen horse in the hands of the Indians, pointed to the animal, and yelled: 'Yonder is Mr. Goodnight's horse!'

'Shut your mouth!' yelled Loving, 'the Indians will have your scalp on a pole.' 'And I hushed,' said Mayes.

Black Beaver let them pass, but stragglers hung beside the herd and soon proved there was no fooling the Comanches. One of them rode up to Billy Eddleman, a trail hand, saw the rawhide hobbles hung around his horse's neck in accord with the Texas custom, and knew only too well that they were lying. He pointed to the hobbles, severely twisted Billy's nose, and grunted: '*Tejano, no bueno!*'

After levying on the herd for a supply of beef, they let it pass on, while along the trail in front and behind them they took heavier toll from less fortunate travelers. Loving pushed his herd hard, keeping it jammed for protection, and reached Fort Dodge without incident. Between there and Fort Lyon the Cheyennes were on the warpath, and the military detained them. Wagon trains of emigrants were crossing the Plains, and when their force numbered about a hundred and twenty-five, they passed the final hazard together, and Goodnight met the herd at Lyon. Since it was badly done up from overheating, they rested a few days, and drove on to the Apishapa by the middle of September.[12]

Goodnight continued his deliveries to Iliff, and Loving sold some of the cattle locally. Several hundred head were delivered to a buyer in the Pike's Peak country, who failed to meet his

[12] Depositions in Indian Claims, Cases Nos. 9133 and 8532; Frank P. Mayes, 1893, pp. 47–52; John W. Sheek, 1899, p. 242; Aaron M. Lasater, 1893, pp. 22–24; Jeptha D. Crawford, 1893, pp. 41–42; Goodnight, 1898, p. 14, and 1893, p. 8; Loving, pp. 4–6; Goodnight to J. E. H., April 8, 1927; Cox, *The Cattle Industry of Texas*, 346–48; W. S. Ikard to J. E. H., January 26, 1932.

payments, and Goodnight had to take some of them back the following year. He found many had turned wild — almost as wild as the mountain buffalo which ran in small bunches in the Cripple Creek region. Seventy-five were too badly out-

OUTLAWED

lawed to gather, and he went off and left them. Among the bunch was one old crippled steer from which the creek is said to take its name.[13]

Late in December, 1868, *The Colorado Chieftain* observed that Goodnight, 'the well-known stock dealer,' passed through Trinidad on his way back to Texas, intending 'to bring his mother and her family to southern Colorado' for the purpose of 'fixing their permanent residence' there. Jim Loving was with him, their profits were packed in the wagon, and Bose Ikard, faithful Bose, sat on the driver's seat. Primarily, Goodnight was going back for the final discharge of Loving's

[13] Goodnight to M. S. Garretson, August 4, 1928, and July 28, 1918; Goodnight to J. E. H., April 8, 1927.

trust, after two years of the hardest work of his life, and other plans were to supersede those for the removal of his family.

He followed the usual trail down the bitter Pecos, and reached Weatherford in the early spring of 1869. 'When Jim Loving found I was making money,' he said, 'he wanted me to continue the partnership indefinitely. But I did not wish to do so. My promise was fulfilled and I settled with him, paying his family half of seventy-two thousand dollars that I had realized in profits since Loving's death.' [14]

At the same time Goodnight sold Sheek his interest in the remaining CV cattle, and prepared to 'go it alone.' He meant this simply in the matter of business, for before leaving Texas he made those arrangements which cowboys always make upon deciding to settle down. Yet he could not tarry. Grass was rising, and with it rose the obligations of the open range. Again he left his sweetheart and hurried back toward Colorado.

As the news of his profits spread, he expected a waylay by the Brooks band, which was in Weatherford at the time. Taking a good horse he headed northeast toward Indian Territory, and after crossing Red River heard rumors of the band. Somewhere ahead of him they tried to steal a race horse, and one of them was killed. Except for mud and rain, he rode to Baxter Springs, Kansas, without incident, where he was joined by Albert Dyer, and together they took passage for Kansas City. From there they railed to Hays and staged it, at the rate of twenty cents a mile, across the Plains to Pueblo. When his cattle began rubbing long hair off on the piñons, he was there and in the saddle, ready to continue his driving upon the Goodnight and Loving Trail.

[14] *The Colorado Chieftain*, December 24, 1868; Goodnight, 'Recollections,' II, 113–16.

XIII. TRAIL TROUBLES

GOODNIGHT's trail activity lasted nine years, during which time he usually handled from eight to ten thousand cattle annually. Numerous Texans handled more. Yet none so branded the West with the stamp of his character and the power of his personality. With a courage that recked not person or hazard, with a constitution of rawhide and a will of iron, he drove himself night and day as heartless others might drive their cattle. He blazed trails while others simply drove. Old John Rumans expressed it simply: 'We never asked anybody any questions, but told them where we were going, and went.'

Notwithstanding its economic significance, there was more in this movement than finding markets. Goodnight not only blazed a trail, but cherished an ideal, maintained a code, and — in spite of his rugged individualism, or more likely because of it — a high standard of responsibility to country and time. Consequently, the incidents which follow illustrate more than the adventurous rising of the tides of hot blood — they represent the cost of blazing a trail and making of a Western man.

Usually the relations of the native New Mexicans and the Texans were peaceful and cordial, but in the winter of 1868 a tragedy occurred on the Trail that caused much hard feeling and drew racial lines a little tighter. Frank Willburn, who had followed Goodnight out from Texas, still delivered cattle in Santa Fé from his ranch below Fort Sumner, and in November,

1868, two of his hands, George Fowler and Albert Nance, drove in a small consignment.

A Mexican, who thought they carried the money from the sale, slipped into camp and chopped their heads open with an axe, stripped and donned the clothing of one, took their horses and guns, and rode away. At the Willburn Ranch Dick Fowler, George's brother, gathered a band of Texans and rode for the scene, buried the bodies, and, after scouting around the Antón Chico country for a few days, fell in with old Sam Gholson, a noted warrior of the Texas border, coming down the trail. Together they discovered the Mexican culprit at a dance, stormed the place, and in a pile of wood in one corner of the room found Nance's gun. They took out the man who had hidden the gun and another one or two for good measure, and not finding a suitable tree — the piñons were scrubby little things — dropped a rope around the neck of one, handed it to Dick Fowler, who tied it hard and fast to the saddle horn — the Texans have never 'dallied' — and loped off and broke the Mexican's neck. They did the other — some say there were several — the same way, and then turned down the trail toward Texas.

In the meantime, Jim Loving and Goodnight were heading south toward the same destination. The news spread, and a posse of about thirty natives gathered at the old Hatch Ranch, on the Gallinas, and started down the river to meet the Texans, but when they reached Puerta de Luna the cowboys were gone. They turned back, met Goodnight's outfit on the trail, and spread out on either side as he rode up. And though racial feeling was high, and the Mexicans vastly in the majority, there was something about the cowman, as he rode down the line, eyeing them all, that caused them to keep their hands on their bridle reins.[1]

Goodnight said the trail drivers killed several Mexicans,

---

[1] Goodnight to J. E. H., September 30, 1929; E. C. D. Willburn to J. E. H., February 14, 1930; J. K. Millwee to J. E. H., July 3, 1932; *The Daily New Mexican*, December 17, 1868; *The Colorado Cheiftain*, January 7, 1869.

but was pleased to recall that 'among them they got the murderer. The same outlaw had stolen some of my cattle once before, and I would have got him if a snowstorm hadn't come and covered his trail.'

In northern New Mexico the Trail crossed the Cimarrón Seco at a little village called Cimarrón Plaza, long since passed away. As Goodnight drove one of his herds in the fall of 1868, his horse fell and severely injured him. When he camped near the Plaza one day for dinner, a half-breed named Fisher rode out and began looking for strays, and though all the cattle were in Goodnight and Loving's Circle, Fisher claimed several and began cutting them out. Goodnight, lying in the shade of the wagon, sick, sent Bose, who was cooking at the time, to stop Fisher from cutting the herd.

Next morning he saddled a horse, and though still too sore to wear a gun, rejoined the herd. Fisher rode up with a party of armed Mexicans, aiming to cut more of the cattle, and Goodnight let him cut a few head 'just to see what he would do. Every one of them was mine,' he said. 'I then turned them back into the herd, and not having a pistol, took after Fisher with my cow-whip, carried him out of the herd a-flying, and gave him a thorough going-over with it. His Mexicans ran into me with their knives, and would no doubt have done me much harm had it not been for one of my men, Holloway, who fell into the bunch with his six-shooter and stood them off.'

Upon Goodnight's return from Texas in the spring of 1869, he packed thirty thousand dollars in his saddlebags, and with a shepherd dog trained to sleep on the foot of his bed for the prevention of a fate similar to Fowler's and Nance's, crossed the Ratón Mountains and rode south, aiming to intercept the Texas herds that had wintered in New Mexico, before they started north. After a herd got on the move, it was always harder to buy than before it started.

'All the country was still wild and unsettled,' he explained. 'I crossed the mountains, and when I reached the Canadian, dropped into a Texan's cow-camp. He had wintered about two thousand steers there. I stayed all night, pretending I was going to the Bosque, where I always traded, to buy my cattle. The owner persuaded me to try and buy his herd, which I finally consented to do. In the morning we counted the cattle out, only a few miles from my Trail, and I bought some of his horses and hired three of his men to help handle the herd. I had instructed Rumans to follow me up as fast as possible with the outfit, and expected him to reach me the second day.

'I noticed that these three men gambled all night at the camp just before we started on the Trail. So when I hired them I told them I never allowed gambling, as I did not think it best. They readily agreed to this, so we packed our things on one of the horses and started. All went well that day and night, but on the first graze with the herd next day, they got down, went to gambling, and left me with the cattle to herd. I worked around to them as soon as I could, and told them they had agreed not to gamble, and they must mount and get back around the cattle, which they did. We drifted on, and the next day at noon they got down under a piñon tree and again went to playing cards on a saddle blanket. I got around to them as before, and tried to talk with them reasonably, but the fighter of the bunch, thinking he had me in a hole, looked up and said: "Well, by God, what're you gonna do about it?"

'"One thing I can do; I can pay you off."

'"What'll you do with your cattle?"

'"Listen here," said Goodnight, telling him what he was,

"that's none of your business. They're my cattle and I paid for them. See that trail. Get your horses and get on it damned quick." I happened to have plenty of silver in my pocket, and just pitched their wages down to them without getting off my horse, made them saddle their own, and saw that they took the back-trail then and there.'

Here, far in the wilderness, in the heart of outlaw domain, with a herd of two thousand steers that represented the sum total of the profits of three tragic years on the trail, Goodnight fired the only hands he had because of his rule that they should not gamble. True, he had plenty of horses, the country was open, and he expected John Rumans to meet him almost any time. But the outfit did not appear, and he and Shep kept the cattle drifting in the right direction, and being well grazed and watered by night, they scattered but little by morning. Again he directed their grazing and got them to the next watering.

On the evening of the second day he reached the Capulín Vega, where he happened to meet a Texan who had worked for him before. The puncher looked at the herd, and back to the owner with the natural question: 'Wher're your hands?'

'Here,' came the answer, as Goodnight pointed at himself.

'Oh, I mean the cowboys.'

When told there were none, he asked if some were not needed, and the owner said he thought so. A half-day's drifting brought them to the Cimarrón, and as the herd came down to water near the Mexican plaza, there stood the half-breed Fisher, 'the very man of all men,' said Goodnight, 'that I did not want to see. Supposing he would want to avenge things, I pretended not to know him. But when he made himself known, I of course asked him how he was getting on.

'"Do you need a *peon?*" he asked.

'"I think I do. Do you have a good horse?"

'"Yes."

'"When can you get him?"

'"Right now."

'"All right, come ahead." And he fell in with his horse, which made three of us and the dog. As we went up the cañon a few miles north, just before reaching the Trinchera Pass, we met Johnnie and the outfit, to my great relief. The snow had been melting rapidly in the mountains, the Picketwire had been out of banks, and he and the outfit had been held up for three days waiting for it to run down.'

Rumans looked at the herd in astonishment — a herd usually handled by ten to fifteen men. Then his eye fell on the half-breed.

'What in the hell are you doing with that Mexican?' he swore, while Goodnight pretended not to know him.

'Don't you know he is the damnedest thief in the country?' continued Johnnie, as he reminded his employer of the cow-whipping he had given the fellow the year before.

'All right,' Goodnight finally rejoined, 'but just leave him alone. We need him.'

While Rumans always thought Fisher was planning to kill the trail driver that night, 'The strange part of it is that he stayed with me until fall,' the cowman mused, 'worked for me two successive summers afterward, and never did refer to the incident. And he made me a good hand.' [2]

Vigilante justice was at work in southern Colorado, and as the gold rush gathered speed into the Moreno Valley, its protagonists organized at the mines. In spite of their operations, however, William Coe and his men operated too, and so powerfully that they deserve particular mention. They built a rock house, near the corners of Colorado and New Mexico, a regular fortress far from the nearest settlements, from which to operate against travelers on the lower Santa Fé Trail, the settlements in Kansas, and ranchmen in Colorado and New Mexico. They boldly rode into Fort Union and drove off government buckboards and teams, imposed on the Mexicans, killed, robbed, rustled horses and cattle, and in total depravity some even stole sheep. Detectives sent after them were

[2] Goodnight to J. E. H., February 27, 1929; Rumans, as cited.

killed, they flouted the civil and military, and their Robbers'
Roost on the Cimarrón was a place of refuge that the surrounding world duly respected.

They prospered for full three years, during which time Coe's
and Goodnight's enmity grew apace, though they had never
met. Time and again the cowman heard of the outlaw's
threats to kill him, but he already knew the rewards of vigilance, and kept his eyes on every man that rode to meet him.

Once, as Goodnight came north from the Bosque to the
Apishapa with a winter herd, he rode ahead toward the Cimarrón in an attempt to secure corn for his horses. On the Capulín
Vega he met two well-armed horsemen shortly before he turned
down the Cimarrón to 'Old Mad' Emory's, who lived some
ten or twelve miles below, to get him to deliver a load of corn
at the Trail crossing. Emory met him at the gate, and inquired,
excitedly, if he had met a couple of riders.

'Yes, in the Vega,' said the trail driver.

'That was Coe and one of his best men. They stayed all
night with me and said they would kill you if they ever met
you,' Emory answered.

'Their not knowing me undoubtedly saved my life, as I
surely would not have stood much chance against two bad
men,' Goodnight later explained, 'as it is a fact that law-
abiding men do not shoot until they have to, but the outlaw
shoots without cause.'

Goodnight caught 'Fingerless' Jackson, one of Coe's men,
on the Pecos, and sent him north by stage to be tried at Denver. As the stage passed through old Colorado City, above
Pueblo, the Vigilance Committee stopped it, took him off,
and hanged him for crimes that had been committed there.

Coe made a custom of stopping at the Emory Ranch, turning his horse in to feed, eating his meals, and making himself
at home. One time he came by soon after a troop of soldiers
from Fort Union had been there looking for him. After eating,
he lay down for a nap at the bunkhouse, and Mrs. Sumpter,
who kept the ranch, sent her boy to catch the soldiers. They

returned and took Coe prisoner while he slept, forwarded him to Pueblo, where he was thrown in jail to await trial, and kept under guard of troops. Luke Cahill, an old trooper, was on guard one night when some men called and said it was necessary to change Coe's quarters. As the jail was opened, someone, with a touch of Western irony, advised the outlaw that he had better take his blanket, but Coe, knowing the change of climate would be warm enough, answered: 'No, I won't need it.' Cahill watched the Vigilantes put him in a wagon, tie a rope around his neck, and drive the wagon from under a limb. The next morning his knees were touching the ground, but death by strangulation was quite as final as by more graceful and finished hanging.[3]

One of Coe's men called 'Tex' was notoriously known around Ellsworth, Kansas. When he and a couple of his *compadres* gave some emigrants trouble, they were arrested and turned over to the military at Fort Wallace, and though they had hounded the wagon train for days, they were released. Two of them again took up the trail, and on the Arkansas, about sixty-five miles below Pueblo, stole the stock from the entire train of thirty or forty wagons, leaving the owners stranded.

This was late in the summer of 1870, while Goodnight was returning with his bride from the States, staging across the Plains from Abilene to Pueblo. He happened by on the day of the theft, and observing no stock with the train, called to the stage driver to stop. He walked over to the teamsters, learned the story of their loss, agreed to send them some help, and resumed his journey to Pueblo, where he and his wife stopped at the old Drovers' Hotel, kept by Harry Pickard 'and his good wife, a very kind, motherly woman.'

There he reported to the Vigilance Committee, and the thieves were caught at Randall's Crossing on the St. Charles,

[3] Goodnight, 'Recollections,' ɪɪ, 120; Luke Cahill to J. E. H., August 23, 1932; Rumans, as cited; *The Colorado Chieftain*, July 23, 1868; Stone, *History of Colorado*, ɪ, 509–10; A. W. Thompson, 'Early North-Eastern Part of New Mexico,' in *The Clayton News* (N.M.), December 22, 1927.

by the sheriff of El Paso County, and placed in jail at Pueblo. About midnight the sheriff requisitioned the prisoners because it was 'cooler traveling in the night,' but they did not have far to go. After trotting them down to the site of the First National Bank, the Vigilantes hanged them to a tele-

BRANDING

graph pole 'but a stone's throw from the tree upon which Coe came to an untimely death under similar circumstances,' cheerfully recorded the contemporary *Colorado Chieftain.*⁴ Coe's band gradually dispersed, and some measure of security was thereby attained. In four years' time the change was so great that Goodnight gave away faithful Shep, the dog trained to sleep on the foot of his tarp, and there was more than racial significance in his remark that the region 'had become a white man's country.'

Sooner or later, on most of the Texas trails, determined and bitter opposition arose against drivers on account of Texas or splenetic fever, a dread disease later discovered to be transmitted by the tick. At that time it was only known that the wintering of cattle away from the lower portions of Texas removed the danger. The feeling engendered by the trailing

⁴ Goodnight, 'Recollections,' II, 117; and to J. E. H., June 15, 1929; *The Colorado Chieftain*, August 4, 1870.

of cattle was accelerated by two incidental conditions: the fact that Texas cattle were not affected, and hence the belief of many of the drivers that their cattle were harmless, and the natural opposition of resident stockmen to flooding the markets with cheaper stock. On the other hand, the trade brought much money to the territories in which it centered, and naturally had its local champions among merchants, bankers, and livestock dealers. Almost as soon as Loving and Goodnight pointed the way for the Texans, opposition arose to the trade.

While Colorado prohibited the direct introduction of Texas stock, trailing continued, partly on account of the fact that many of the herds had been wintered on the Pecos, but mainly because of the impossibility of proving that the others had not been 'wintered' too. In the summer of 1869, longhorns were selling for $27.50 a head at Las Animas, admittedly 'a high price for that kind of stock.' The next year an estimated forty-five thousand head of Texas cattle were wintering in the valley of the Arkansas alone.

Hence it was apparent that the law prohibiting the introduction of Texas cattle was not being enforced, and this influx sent the high prices of beef that had obtained after the war to lower levels, which, though still manna to the Texans, was disappointing to the natives. 'It caused many of our ranchmen,' recorded the local paper, 'to dispose of their American cattle and invest in the Texas,' in order 'to be able to compete with the prices of Texas stock. . . .' [5]

Feeling against the Texas trade grew until there were outbreaks of violence along the Trail. When the herds cut through the settled districts of Colorado, where stockmen had a better grade of cattle, distinguished from the Texas breed by the term 'American,' the owners often met the drivers in armed force, and told them they would have to take some other course.

'Some men met us at the trail near Cañon City, one time,'

[5] *The Colorado Chieftain*, November 5, 1868, May 20, 1869, September 15 and 22, October 27 and December 8, 1870; April 20 and 27, 1871, and August 7, 1873; Mose Hays to J. E. H., November 8, 1931; Bancroft, *History of Nevada, Colorado, and Wyoming*, 248, 544.

Rumans recalled, 'and said we couldn't come in. There were fifteen or twenty of them, and they were not going to let us cross the Arkansas River. We didn't even stop. The Old Man got a shotgun loaded with buckshot and led the way, saying: "John, get over on that point with your Winchester and point these cattle in behind me." He slid his shotgun across the saddle in front of him and we did the same with our Winchesters. He rode right across, and as he rode up to them, he said: "I've monkeyed as long as I want to with you sons-of-bitches," and they fell back to the sides, and went home after we had passed. If they had done a thing, we would have filled them so damned full of lead they'd never have got away.'

At another time, on the divide east of Denver, the settlers shot into one of Goodnight's herds at night, and stampeded and killed a number of his cattle. Among those helping to stampede it was the noted Chalk Beeson, who located at Dodge City, and who, upon meeting the cowman many years later, reminded him of the incident.

'Do you know, Chalk,' came the hearty rejoinder, 'you fellows done such a good job that the damned herd is running yet.' [6]

Early in April, 1869, as his late associates, Joe Curtis and John Dawson, were trailing a herd of sixteen hundred head across the divide between Cherry Creek and the Bijou, 'they were attacked,' to quote the Pueblo *Chieftain*, 'by a gang of marauders estimated to number about fifty men. These men shot and killed quite a number of cattle, wounded many others, and stampeded the entire herd,' claiming that they feared Texas fever, while the paper affirmed that their object was 'doubtless plunder.' Frank Pape, who had just passed through from the Taos country, sent back from the Fountain for reenforcements, and planned, with about thirty men, to take his herd of twelve hundred head on by fighting, if necessary.

The trail blockers from El Paso and Douglas Counties re-

[6] Rumans, as cited; Oliver Loving, Jr., to J. E. H., February 19, 1930; Merritt Beeson, *Scrapbook*, Beeson's Museum, Dodge City.

plied to the Pueblo paper by saying that the Texans were attempting to force passage through the most thickly settled portions of both counties, after being asked to go around 'on a perfectly feasible route, where they would not come in contact with American cattle, nor graze on their range,' and claimed the Texans defied them, saying they would drive 'where they d——n pleased.'

For some time there had been an organization in Boulder, Arapahoe, El Paso, and Fremont Counties known as the Colorado Cattle Association, whose object, the citizens argued, 'is simply to keep such stock away from the settlements as they consider dangerous to American cattle,' and unless the trailmen drive outside the line of settlements, they warned, 'they will encounter serious difficulties; because there are at least fifteen hundred men who have pledged themselves that no herds of Texas cattle shall pass over the main thoroughfare between the Arkansas and Platte Rivers, unless they have been at least one year within the limits of the Territory.' Their last line of legal defense was the law that forbade the importation of 'any Texas cattle, for any purpose whatever.' [7]

Goodnight had diverted his trail to the east of the troubled areas, and continued to drive without serious conflict with the settlers. In a test case the quarantine law was held an invasion of the rights of Congress, and in the fall of 1870 'the Denver newspapers,' so Pueblo observed, make 'quite a parade of a judicial decision' by the judge of the Second District to the effect that the law 'is unconstitutional and void. The joke of this able decision comes in when it is known that the law in question never was enforced in the Territory, and was repealed by the last Legislature. . . .' [8]

Goodnight continued to drive by the usual route until 1875, when he found it to his advantage to blaze the New Goodnight Trail, which left Fort Sumner along the course of the old Good-

[7] *The Colorado Chieftain,* April 15, 22, and 29, 1869.

[8] *The Colorado Chieftain,* October 27 and November 3, 1870; *Dallas Herald,* December 3, 1870.

night and Loving Trail, and at first followed it to the Cuervo, branched to the east by Laguna Colorada, and crossed the Canadian about ten miles below Fort Bascom. It turned up Ute Creek about three days' drive, passed the Rabbit Ears, near present Clayton, and the Cimarrón Seco near Robbers' Roost. From there it bore a little northwest to Freeze Out and to Two Butte, and down it to Granada, Colorado, on the railroad. Though straightened by later drives, it was always known as the New Goodnight Trail.[9]

Upon this drive a storm struck the outfit in the Tucumcari country, near the Canadian. It resulted in a terrible stampede and a flood that caught them soon after they had broken camp. 'After a few miles trailing we came to the Charco, a creek probably twenty feet wide, with banks six to eight feet high, and level with flood water,' Goodnight recounted. 'We put our leaders against the creek, head on. After about three hundred head had passed over, something caused the leaders to stampede, and they whirled in their tracks, right back the trail. The distance was short and we failed to control or stop them. They simply took the water, met those in the stream behind them, actually filled the creek with cattle, and crossed the water on their own bodies.

'I put my horse in upstream, just above the mass of cattle, and crossed in dead water. I expected a heavy loss from drowning, but it happened so quickly that all came out alive, and in less than ten minutes we had them moving across the creek again in the right direction. This sounds unreasonable, but it is true just the same.'[10]

[9] According to Jack Potter, its course in later years was away from the old trail at Bosque Redondo, five miles above the fort, and up the Los Truches, a dry creek, for twenty-five miles, across the Plains for about thirty, and thence off the cap-rock just east of the Cuñeva. It led to the Plaza Larga, and to the Blue Holes, on the Pajarita, a total of eighty miles without water. It passed down the Pajarita through the Tucumcari country to Deadman's Crossing, about ten miles below Fort Bascom, led out by way of Los Carros Creek, thence to and up Ute for thirty miles or more, thence up the Muerta a day's drive, and north by east to the Tramperos, and bore east of the Rabbit Ears. After crossing the Cimarrón at the mouth of the North Carriza, it led by Carriza Springs to Freeze Out, to Two Butte, and down it to Granada. Jack Potter to J. E. H., September 29, 1932.

[10] Goodnight, 'Stray Notes,' 5-6.

This was the last trail to bear Goodnight's name. Though he laid out a practicable route from Pueblo to the Palo Duro the next year, its course was never thoroughly broken, and comparatively its use was inconsequential. Another year and his men laid out the Palo Duro-Dodge City Trail, which likewise had its troubles and problems, but they are another story. The blazing of the New Goodnight Trail in 1875 ended the driver's operations in New Mexico, and marked an epoch in his life — the passing of his most restless activity, and, in spite of the troubles, his happiest days.

THE characters along the way were as varied as Goodnight's troubles. Some of them have already trailed across these pages: 'Honey' Allen with his bees and pecans, Rich Coffee with his watermelons, John Dawson and his graybacks, and many another of equal attraction. Others — Mexicans, Indians, negroes, and whites — crossed these trails and left memories deeper than their tracks. Following the Goodnight and Loving Trails out from Texas, up through New Mexico and across Colorado, these characters, quaint and bizarre, strong and masterful, fall in with the historical procession at the proper time and place.

From the border of Texas to the settlements of New Mexico there were no friends except in the chance meeting of infrequent travelers. In 1867, John Chisum came out from Texas and located on the Pecos at Bosque Grande, occupying the range that Goodnight abandoned. For years he remained the first friend on the Trail west of the Texas settlements, and though his arrival was subsequent to Goodnight's driving from Texas, he was an intimate friend of the young trail-blazer for a number of years.

Chisum was born in Madison County, Tennessee, August 15, 1824, and at thirteen came with his parents to settle at the site of Paris, Texas. With money furnished by S. K. Fowler, of New York, and with cattle cheaply purchased in the coast country, he left the office of county clerk to engage in the cow business near Denton. During the Civil War he delivered cattle to the Confederacy, and moved stock to the Pecan Bayou country, near present Brownwood, where the village of Trickem evolved, so named, according to legend, from the practices of gamblers who stopped there to shuffle their cards.

JOHN CHISUM

After the war, Chisum entered upon a strangely contradictory career, and his motives and character are still matters of reminiscent conjecture. His name has been confused with the Texas trail to Kansas — the Chisholm Trail — the confusion being the result of contemporaneous incident and phonetic similarity.

Chisum drove no herds to the north, but immediately after the war took three small bunches of cattle to Little Rock and sold them to a packing-house owned in part by himself, the Fowlers, and others. Their packing processes were crude, their beef spoiled, and the firm went into bankruptcy. Chisum is said to have charged the loss to experience and turned his face toward the Goodnight Trail. The creditors of the enterprise, finding that he, of all the incipient packers, had not resorted to bankruptcy, took judgment against him alone.

But his assets were wild Texas cattle, inaccessible for attachment and inconvertible into cash, and Chisum went his way by other trails while the judgments went on file in the North.

Then he started his drives to the Pecos and became well established at Bosque Grande, delivering thousands of beeves to Goodnight, the Pattersons, and others, and locating his unsold stock cattle on the Pecos. He secured powers of attorney to drive many Texas brands, which, ostensibly, were to be paid for upon his return to Texas. He even, by one account, executed notes for the payment of many of these cattle, which notes continued to repose in Texas while he established permanent residence in New Mexico, and watched his cattle, under the 'long rail' brand and the 'jingle-bob' mark, grow into one of the greatest herds, grazing one of the most extensive ranges, of the Southwest — a range one hundred and fifty miles up and down the Pecos, and as far to either side as a long-legged cow could graze. Indeed, he flourished, and the lower Pecos, from Fort Sumner to near the Texas line, was almost indisputably his by the time he shifted his headquarters to South Spring River, near the site of Roswell.

In the meantime, Goodnight was receiving many of Chisum's drives at the Bosque and trailing them northward, maintaining friendly relations until Chisum, losing a herd to Indians, turned back to gather another on the Texas frontier without regard for mark and brand, and drove them in place of his original herd. Goodnight refused the stolen stock, but the genial Chisum took no offense, though Goodnight took him to task and then went his way.

Tom Catron, young and ambitious Territorial attorney, brought suit against Chisum on account of the stolen cattle. Upon appearing in court at Las Vegas, Chisum pulled his powers of attorney from a long zinc tube and spread them before Catron, who, seeing he was whipped, forthwith asked for dismissal of the charges. Yet Catron was no quitter. Accepting the packing-house judgments for collection, he stayed close on Chisum's trail, and in the course of litigation over stolen cattle and legal indebtedness, Chisum was thrown into jail at Las Vegas, where he passed the time writing a defensive statement. After his death in 1884, the court in chancery at Roswell held the packing-house judgments valid and due, and they were at last collected from 'Uncle John's' estate.

At one time Chisum was supposed to have sixty thousand head of cattle on the range. In 1875, he sold thirty thousand head to Hunter and Evans, commission men of Kansas City; by 1880 his deliveries to them had totaled fifty thousand; and he estimated that the Indians and rustlers had stolen ten thousand head. During the seven years prior to the Hunter and Evans sale he had annually delivered about ten thousand head to Goodnight, besides many thousands to Patterson and other contractors. Perhaps his bitterest disappointment, and conviction for the moralist that justice is sure, though laggard, came in his settlement of the Hunter and Evans deal. Hunter, it is said, had gone to Texas and bought up the old Chisum notes from frontier cowmen for a few cents on the dollar, carried them to Las Vegas in a satchel, and after the herds were on the trail under care of well-armed outfits, met Chisum and paid him in his own notes at par. In Chisum's later years the fortunes of war levied heavily upon him, his business suffered from thieves from within and without, and broken in health he saw the impairment of his estate, the crowding of his range, and the loss of his power.

In his environment his sense of humor, fortunately, did not leave him. A strange chuck-line rider dropped into the ranch one day, gravitated to the kitchen, and found, in the absence of the regular cook, the owner himself filling the rôle. After helping himself to a cup of coffee, the sweater turned and said: 'Working for Old Chisum, eh?' And with a slight smile the coosie agreed: 'Yes, working for Old Chisum!'

Chisum was tall, angular, plain in his dress and tastes, and on the ranch was at times mistaken for an ordinary waddie. Though his room was furnished with a comfortable bed, he always pulled off a blanket and slept on the floor. A genial, well-poised bachelor who had suffered the caprice of a woman, he handled a battalion of dead-hard fighting men without resort to a gun.

'He was a great trail man,' appraised Goodnight in later years. 'No one had any advantage of him as an old-fashioned cowman, and he was the best counter I ever knew. He could count three grades of cattle at once, and count them accurately even if they were going in a trot.'

His life was truly hard and in his death passed one of the most distinctive characters that ever drove the Goodnight Trail from Texas.[1]

While making their monthly deliveries of beef at Santa Fé during the winter of 1866, Goodnight and Loving drove up the Pecos past the ancient Indian ruins and the old Spanish church, through the Apache Cañon by the Pigeon Ranch, and into the capital town. After one delivery Goodnight rode up the cañon of the Rio Grande to Taos, and became acquainted with Standing Deer, the venerable chieftain and medicine man of the Taos Pueblos. Not only was this old man versed in herbal lore, but he was learned in native ritual, and once in conversation with Goodnight referred to the mission church at the Pecos ruins.

At one time, he related, many years ago, the Indians kept an immense snake in this sacred place. Periodical human offerings were made to it by way of atoning for native transgressions and keeping the snake alive. And there was a distinct if short-lived honor, he said, in being chosen for sacrifice.

'Was this necessary, then?' asked the cowman.

'*Si, señor!*' replied the chief gravely. '*Muy necesario.*'

'Well,' interrogated the other, 'if it was necessary then, why isn't it necessary now?'

[1] Goodnight to J. E. H., January 18, 1926; August 2, 1928; 'Recollections,' II, 116; *The Colorado Chieftain*, December 9, 1875; Siringo, *A Lone Star Cowboy*, 96, 158; Cox, *The Cattle Industry of Texas*, 299–302; Conard, '*Uncle Dick' Wootton*, 442; *The Standard* (Clarksville, Texas), May 5, 1855; J. Phelps White to J. E. H., March 2, 1933; *Dictionary of American Biography*, IV, 71.

This was most unexpected, but the old chief scratched his head awhile and rose to the occasion.

'In the first place,' he said more gravely still, to translate his vernacular to English, 'there are no snakes big enough to eat anybody. In the second, there isn't anybody who wants to be eaten.'

STANDING DEER

On the upper Cimarrón lived Don Luciano Maxwell, a native of Kaskaskia, Illinois, who had learned the West in the employ of the American Fur Company. He was adventuring with Fremont in the early forties, later married a daughter of Carlos Beaubien, and bought out the other heirs to the million-acre Beaubien and Miranda Grant, in northern New Mexico, after the former's death in 1864. This grant, rich in timber, minerals, water, and irrigable lands, had perhaps as varied and interesting a history as any in the Southwest. It was alleged, in the sixties, that Maxwell's stock and lands were policed by five hundred Apache Indians, who, 'faithful and trustworthy, had reduced stealing from his herds and flocks to a minimum.' Approximately a thousand Mexicans lived on the estate in virtual peonage, while Navajo squaws, ransomed from raiding Apaches, served the great ranch home. With its store, shops, grist mill, racing stables, and the many hands that operated them, the headquarters was a bustling village.

For many years Maxwell prospered at trading, farming, mining, and ranching, and at his home on the Cimarrón lavished his hospitality in a truly baronial style, living expansively and boldly as long as fortune willed. He entertained many famous guests at his table, where covers were daily laid for more than two dozen people, served them with sterling silver, and sent them up and down the Santa Fé Trail happier than when they came. His ranch was the agency for tribal divisions of the Apaches and Utes, and when he sold out in 1870, the Indians, so disgusted that they threatened to kill him if he offered 'to leave the grant,' claimed that the English company could never take possession, and that they would go on the warpath rather than leave. A correspondent wrote to complain that 'this tribe has lived upon Maxwell's bounty so long that they have come to think that he is bound to feed them and let them loaf round his ranch the rest of their lives.' Maxwell left for Fort Sumner, and though his last years were spent in comparative poverty, his broad grant perpetuates his name, and northern New Mexico cherishes his tradition.[2]

Goodnight sold cattle to Maxwell and often stopped at his ranch, where came many mountain men famous throughout the West — Colonel Phieffer, St. Vrain, Tom Tobin, the Bents, Kit Carson, and his right-hand bower, Charlie Autobees, Zan Hicklen, Tom Boggs, Dick Wootton, Robideaux, Ouray, and many others of almost equal luster. Goodnight

[2] Twitchell, *Leading Facts in New Mexican History*, II, 300, 415; *The Colorado Chieftain*, July 23 and November 26, 1868, and September 3, 1870.

met them there and on the trail from Vegas to Denver, and, always inclined to hurry, was impatient with them for the time they consumed at gambling and loafing around. Though all possessed the qualities of leaders, they were not driven by exceptional ambition, and hence enjoyed a care-free life in which leisure still had a part. And finding leisure they found desire for entertainment, and delighted not only to gamble but to string the greenhorns from the States.

In spite of the colorful array, Goodnight was always restless to move on about his work, and soon was pushing on the bridle reins up the trail to Ratón Pass, on the north side of which lived the inimitable Dick Wootton, sly, crafty, and self-sufficient, as wise in the ways of the Rockies as any Ute Indian. According to Henry Inman he ranks next to Carson as scout and frontiersman. His camp was almost an institution, and 'Uncle Dick' watched over it with philosophic prudence.

After long years of adventurous life in the West, he saw the strategic possibilities of Ratón Pass, and in the winter of 1865, as we have seen, obtained permits from Colorado and New Mexico to construct a toll road across the Ratón Range. In the spring of 1866 he constructed his road, put up a tollgate, and built a roadhouse besides. Except for much cursing at this restriction of Western freedom, business went peacefully for a couple of years, and the old settlers still like to tell how frequently 'Uncle Dick' hauled a whiskey barrel full of silver dollars into Trinidad for safe-keeping, but mention not the size of the barrel. However, at that day, the barrels were big enough. After two years of rough roads and prosperity, the Commissioners' Court of Las Animas County, Colorado, decided the toll was too high and ordered it reduced. 'Uncle Dick' complied, but, to quote the contemporary *Colorado Chieftain,* 'raised the toll on the New Mexico end of his road so that the aggregate amount charged for passing over it is now just what it was before. "Catch a weasel asleep."' And so operated the individualistic Richard Lacy Wootton until the Santa Fé Railroad built through in the late seventies, and, in retiring, the old frontiersman gracefully explained that he merely 'got out of the way of the locomotive.'[3]

From 'Uncle Dick's' the Santa Fé Trail led north by the base of the Rockies to the Greenhorn, a small stream leading out of the mountains to the Arkansas, where another trail stand was kept by a mountain man almost as widely known as Maxwell and Wootton — old 'Zan' Hicklen. According to the meager records, he was born in Lafayette County, Missouri, came to New Mexico with a merchant's train in 1846, was mustered into the army, and joined Colonel Doniphan's expedition to California during the Mexican War. After residence in California and New Mexico for several years, he came to Colorado and settled on the Greenhorn to live from 1859 until his death, February 13, 1874. He married a daughter of Charles Bent, the first Territorial Governor of New Mexico, and being generous, kind, sympathetic, and hospitable, numbered his friends by a wide acquaintance. 'There was a knack of story-telling and a quaint, original kind of wit about the man that made him a welcome member of many a campfire party.'

When a number of tenderfeet stopped at his ranch one time for dinner, and all were seated at the table, Zan turned to one of his employees, who apparently did the hunting, and pointing to a dish of meat asked:

'What kind of meat is this?'

'Buck,' answered the hand.

'Ah, yes, I thought so,' said Zan, as he speared off a piece, 'squaw ain't good this time of year.' And he was pleased to note that the pilgrims from the East ate but little meat.

Again three travelers stopped to spend the night, sat around the fire until bedtime, and then inquired as to where they might sleep. Turning to one, Hicklen asked:

---

[3] Henry Inman states the given name as Richens, in *The Old Santa Fé Trail*, 241; Conard, as cited, 417-26; *The Colorado Chieftain*, May 20, 1868, and files through 1876; *The Colorado Magazine*, January, 1930, pp. 77-78.

'Do you have any blankets?'

'No!' replied the unfortunate.

'You can sleep in that corner,' Hicklen directed, pointing to the barren spot. Turning to another he asked the same

question, and when he received the same answer, indicated another empty corner. And so, too, he inquired of the third, who readily spoke up:

'Yes, sir! I have a pair of blankets.'

'Then you can sleep with me,' concluded the host.[4]

Once as Goodnight trailed north toward Fremont's Orchard he found a settler's camp at the crossing of the Arkansas, and rode by to drink at the well. A good-looking young woman drew a bucket of water, and asked if the herd was Texas cattle. The cowman replied in the affirmative, adding that the hands were Texas men.

'Oh, Mama, come here!' she cried. 'Here's a lot of live Texicans.' They were very much alive, according to Goodnight,

<hr />

[4] *The Colorado Chieftain*, February 19 and 20, 1874; Goodnight to J. E. H.; *The Colorado Magazine*, IV, 183–85.

and turned out to be 'the thirstiest sons-of-guns' he ever saw.

The buyer of this herd, John Wesley Iliff, was a native of Ohio, educated at Wesleyan University. As a young man he had refused the paternal offer of a farm with the cryptic suggestion: 'No, give me five hundred dollars and let me go West.' He stopped in Kansas, but when gold was discovered in Colorado, he invested everything he had in a stock of goods and proceeded to Denver in 1859. After less than two years as a merchant, he bought a small herd, launched back upon the Plains, and in ten years was one of the largest operators in the West, grazing some eighteen thousand head of cattle on the North Platte, fifty miles east of Denver. Goodnight's delivery to him on Crow Creek in the early spring of 1868 is said to have been the first Texas herd in Wyoming, and the new owner was known as the first 'cattle king' of the northern Plains.

He transferred his residence to Cheyenne, where he lived until 1874, returning then to Denver, and dying in his prime, February 9, 1878. He was noted for his friendliness toward the Indians, for his abstinence from drink, and his aversion to arms. 'He was a wonderful cowman,' said his friend Goodnight, 'and ranked next to Chisum as a counter of cattle. He was the only man I ever saw who could count and keep books at the same time.' Alex Swan, impressed by his clean-cut character, declared that 'he was the squarest man that ever rode over these plains.' [5]

Quite naturally the closest friends of a man upon the trail were his hands, and Goodnight was fortunate in the loyalty he commanded from his men. Among the most notable of these were 'One-Armed' Bill Wilson, whom his boss described as 'the coolest man in the outfit,' John Rumans, 'the most reckless rider I ever saw,' and Boze Ikard, 'one of the best night hands I ever had.' Though he would as soon his own

[5] *The Colorado Chieftain*, March 7, 1872; Goodnight to J. E. H., April 8, 1927; *History of Colorado* (anon., 1927), 114–18; E. S. Osgood, *The Day of the Cattleman*, 18; *Letters From Old Friends and Members of the Wyoming Stock Growers Association*, 54.

name were forgotten, it was his master's wish that this old slave might be tallied out in history.

Bose was born to slavery in Noxubee County, Mississippi, in June, 1847, under the ownership of Dr. M. Ikard. He was brought to Texas along with Ikard's family and belongings some five years later, and grew up on the Cross Timber frontier, at Ikard's place on Grindstone Creek, nine miles west of Weatherford, where he learned to farm, hunt cattle, and fight Indians. In 1866, Loving brought him out to the wagon, and he stayed on the trail until 1869, when he came back to Texas with Goodnight. He was anxious to return to Colorado, but as there were so few negroes in that country his master advised that he stay in Texas and buy a farm.

He was a good bronc rider, an exceptional night herder, good with the skillets and pans, and according to his boss, 'surpassed any man I had in endurance and stamina. There was a dignity, a cleanliness, and a reliability about him that was wonderful. He paid no attention to women. His behavior was very good in a fight, and he was probably the most devoted man to me that I ever had. I have trusted him farther than any living man. He was my detective, banker, and everything else in Colorado, New Mexico, and the other wild country I was in. The nearest and only bank was at Denver, and when we carried money I gave it to Bose, for a thief would never think of robbing him — never think of looking in a negro's bed for money.

'We went through some terrible trials during those four years on the trail. While I had a good constitution and endurance, after being in the saddle for several days and nights at a time, on various occasions, and finding I could stand it no longer, I would ask Bose if he would take my place, and he never failed to answer me in the most cheerful and willing manner, and was the most skilled and trustworthy man I had.'

In his declining years Goodnight kept in touch with this faithful friend and often sent him needed money. He died in

1929, was buried at Weatherford, and just before his own death his master erected a marker and inscribed thereon:

Bose Ikard

. . . .

Served with me four years on the Goodnight–Loving Trail, never shirked a duty or disobeyed an order, rode with me in many stampedes, participated in three engagements with Comanches, splendid behavior.

C. Goodnight

And so to the end of his long days Goodnight subscribed his greatest debt to man still due this negro who saved his life several times, this superb rider, remarkable trail hand, and devoted servant. He too added life, and friendship, and color to the Goodnight Trail.[6]

[6] Bose died January 4, 1929. Goodnight to J. E. H., June 15 and September 30, 1929; Goodnight, Deposition in Case 9133, Indian Claims, pp. 180–81; Bose Ikard, Deposition, February 17, 1900; *The Daily Herald* (Weatherford), June 8, 1929; W. S. Ikard to J. E. H., January 26, 1932.

XV. MANAGING A TRAIL HERD

THE successful venture of an outfit upon the trail meant much more than the mere following of cattle from range to market. The proper management of a herd was an exacting process, a science, even an art. Rare knowledge of animal psychology, quick and keen anticipation of what might happen under varying conditions of topography and weather, proper evaluation of horses and men, and even intimate and individual acquaintance with the cattle being handled, were qualities of an efficient trail boss.

Furthermore, the job demanded the utmost patience with cattle and horses, physical durability, mental alertness, caution, and courage — always courage. A good trail boss was a thorough outdoor man for whom the vagaries of the seasons held few secrets and no fear. He knew the value of good bed grounds, the necessity of discipline, the bearing of good cooks on high morale, the best grasses, good water, and the time of day to throw his herd upon it. He was a naturalist as well as a commander; a ruthless driver of himself, but not of his cattle.

He received his herd on the range in Texas, where it was road-branded, counted, and pointed toward its destination, a thousand or two thousand miles away. In spite of drought, storm, flood, Indian, outlaw, and the uncertainties of grass and water, it was his sacred obligation to turn it over intact, and in as good — even better — condition at the point of delivery. It was not a job for the timorous, and be it said to his general credit he 'bellied up to the lick-log' like a man.

Years ago at the general roundup in northern New Mexico, a shorthorn from the States asked Uncle Bill Follis, wagon boss for the 101, how long it took a man to learn the cow business.

'Well, son,' came the measured words, 'I've been at it sixty years, and I learn something new every day. You never get any diplomas in this business.'

And so a good boss was not only a combination of intelligence, action, stamina, and courage, but a product of long and close communion with cows.

From the vigorous breed that settled the West, and the rigorous life that tested their mettle, came many good trail bosses whose names, for the most part, are now obscured by the dusts of time. Yet Goodnight has essayed rather complete expression of the technique that made them successful, declaring first:

'When I made up my mind that I was going to drive, I set about collecting my outfit. My first step toward this was to round up fifty or sixty good horses. Then the mess-wagon was made ready with provisions. For instance, when the Goodnight Trail was laid off, I had to prepare for a six-hundred-mile stretch between settlements. Meantime, I informed my neighbor stockmen that I was to drive to a northern market, and would receive any cattle they wanted to go with the herd, arranging for the concentration of the herd at some given point, where the cattle were driven through a chute and branded with a trail or road brand. I was never over three days in putting the average herd of three thousand head together.

'Owing to the danger of Indians and stampede, I always got out of the settlements as soon as possible, for cattle that were scattered were much easier traced on the trail than in the settlements, and the danger of meeting Indians was less. Our outfits consisted of sixteen to eighteen men, a mess-wagon drawn by four mules, driven by the cook, and a horse wrangler who had charge of the horse herd. We aimed to have as many experienced men as possible, and after a few years there developed on the trail a class of men that could be depended upon anywhere.

'These men were thoroughly drilled regarding their places and duties. I always selected two of the most skillful to be my pointers, to handle the front of the herd and keep it on the course given out by the foreman. They were never changed from their positions at the head of the herd. I always selected three steady men for the rear, to look out for the weaker cattle — the drags. Since the speed of the herd was determined by the drags, it was their duty to see that the stronger cattle were kept forward and out of the way, so that the weaker cattle would not be impeded. This was called "keeping up the corners." It was necessary to see that the rear was no wider than the swing — that part between the leaders and the drags — else loss would be occasioned from overheating, for the heat from so many moving cattle was terrific. If the pointers found the swing getting too long, they simply checked up until the herd was the correct length — one half-mile.

'The rest of the men were divided along the sides, the swing. Except for the corner men they were changed each morning, as the nearer the point the lighter the work, and a system of rotation divided the labor on men and horses. Besides, three hundred miles of the Pecos was bad with alkali dust, and the men not only shifted their positions daily, but reversed their sides of the herd. If you were first behind the pointer on the right today, you would be second on the left tomorrow, third on the right the next day, and so on until you dropped back to the drag man on the corner, and then you began working back toward the lead again. Each man knew his place and took it each morning.

'Trail hands were well disciplined and were governed entirely by signals, being too far from the leader to receive orders any other way. The handling of the herd in the least time and at the least expense of horseflesh caused a system of signals to come into use — signals mostly derived from the

Plains Indians and well adapted to the purpose. They were all made from horseback, and movements of the hat were the principal features.

THE TRAIL BOSS

'The signal to break camp and move upon the trail, simply a motion with the hat in the direction to be followed, was repeated by the pointers and passed along to the rear. About eleven o'clock the signal to graze was passed along the line. Then the men ate dinner, which had been prepared while breakfast was cooking. When the cattle began to lie down, the manager knew that they had grazed long enough, and gave the signal to resume the trail. The pointers guided the herd in the right direction, and if it were snowing or storming, the foreman rode ahead to indicate the course.

'The column would march either slow or fast, according
to the distance the side men rode from the line. Therefore,
when we had a long drive to make between watering places,
the men rode in closer to the line. Under normal conditions
the herd was fifty to sixty feet across, the width being governed
by the distance we had to go before resting. Narrowing the
string was called "squeezing them down." Ten feet was the
lowest limit, for then gaps came, and the cattle would begin
trotting to fill up the spaces. The pointers checked them in
front, for they were never allowed to trot. After a herd was
handled a month or two, they became gentler, and it was
necessary to ride a little closer to obtain the same results.

'We always tried to reach water before sundown. This gave
us ample time to have the cattle filled and everything arranged
for a pleasant night. The herd was put in a circle, the cattle
being a comfortable distance apart. At first, when the cattle
were fresh, I used a double guard; that is, half the men guarded
the first part of the night, the other half the latter part. In
storms or stampedes we were all on duty. After the herd had
been out for fifteen days, it was "trail broke," and four men
were sufficient to guard three thousand head of cattle, and
after two or three months two men at a time were sufficient.
It was my practice to use standing guards; the men who had
first watch the first night would have it all through the drive.
If you left the choice to the old hands, they invariably chose
the standing guard. Ordinarily each guard stood two hours
at a time and a little over. We never had any watch to go
by, but divided the time by the dipper. The last guard was
the shortest, for each relief stood a little overtime to be sure
they were not calling the next guard too soon. After we had
been out awhile the men could easily stay awake; in fact, the
habit became so firmly fixed that if in camp they would wake
at the regular time, and would not be able to sleep during
their watch. They rode around the herd facing each other,
and in this way passed twice in one complete circuit.'

If the choice of bed grounds was little short of scientific

judgment, the location and pitching of a cow-camp was next to an art, particularly in Indian country. Experienced Jack Potter tells a story illustrative of Goodnight's skill.

'When the Government was moving the Jicarilla Apaches from their reservation to the San Juan country, in western New Mexico about 1886,' he recalled, 'they came by Fort Sumner where they were once held in captivity by the United States soldiers. While they were camped there, I got acquainted with an old gray-headed Indian by dividing my Star tobacco with him. When he found out I was a *Tejano*, he got into a talking mood. He told me that Charley *Tejano* (meaning Goodnight) was too wise for the Apache. He squatted down and made a map on the ground, showing *novillada*, *remuda*, and *cocina* all together, with the *remuda* held between the herd and the wagon for protection. And then he showed how careless John *Tejano* (John Chisum) was in getting his outfit scattered, and how easy it was to steal from him.... He told me that, after the Goodnight and Loving Trail was well established, the people brought stock to their country, which saved them the trouble of having to go to the Conchos and the Colorado to steal them.'[1]

'It was a rough, hard, adventurous life,' Goodnight continued, 'but was not without its sunny side, and when everything moved smoothly the trip was an agreeable diversion from the monotony of the range. But things did not always move smoothly. The stampede was especially guarded against during the first ten days or so of the drive. The cattle were nervous and easily frightened, and the slightest noise might startle them into running — some were stampeders by nature. Hence everybody was on the alert, and if we succeeded in holding the herd together the first two weeks, we seldom experienced trouble from stampedes farther along on the trail. The men slept on the ground with their horses

---

[1] Jack Potter to J. E. H., April, 1933. 'The next time I see you,' Mr. Potter wrote, 'I will expect you to reimburse me the value of one half pound of Star Chewing. It taken just that amount to get his story.'

staked nearby. Sometimes the demands were so urgent that our boots were not taken off for an entire week. Nerves became so tense that it was a standing rule that no man was to be touched by another when asleep until after he had been spoken to. The man who suddenly aroused a sleeper was liable to be shot, as all were thoroughly armed and understood the instant use of revolver and rifle.'

The psychology of a stampeding herd was difficult to fathom. A well-managed herd ordinarily gave little trouble, but once it started stampeding it was hard to stop. Its running almost became chronic. In the beginning, as in the case of Indians, the cause of a run might be obvious. And though in the first stampede the cattle might have run themselves to exhaustion, their nervous tension did not necessarily subside. Night after night they have been known to run, taking fright at 'something,' as we on the range say, which was apparently nothing, yet 'something' too subtle for the sophisticated sense of man. Often three thousand steers have been dozing in peace — only a few restless old fellows on their feet — with the night riders circling around them at an easy gait. Then 'something happened,' and with unbelievable suddenness, as quick as the flash of a wakeful eye and as unexpected as the flush of a covey of hidden quail, with an unearthly roar that was the blending of innumerable hoofbeats, with the distinct quaking of the earth as if in fear itself, the cattle were up together and gone. A moment, a second, an instant ago they slept in peace, comfortably scattered and headed to every point of the compass. And yet they rose, they flashed to their feet, apparently all headed in the same direction, and in impenetrable but perfectly co-ordinated mass, they stampeded.

At that electric instant the horse was keener than the man above him. Through his flesh ran a tremor of excitement, his ears came up, his eyes flashed, and his breath came quick as he instantly calculated the course of the herd. And before the man could think that gentle, dozing horse had whirled, sprung, and charged into the night as a part of that wild race to — God Himself did not know where. At first the man was helpless, and the horse alone rose above that riot of animal nature. Goodnight declared:

'In the excitement of a stampede a man was not himself, and his horse was not the horse of yesterday. Man and horse were one, and the combination accomplished feats that would be utterly impossible under ordinary circumstances.'

When the night was unfathomably dark, the rider felt the utmost helplessness as he sat in his saddle and blindly rode through treacherous prairie-dog towns, across ravines and knolls and gullies, wildly rode into obscurity and sometimes into oblivion. It was an unforgettable, elemental experience that weaklings could not relish nor timid men endure.

As the cattle strung out and the fastest and strongest animals pushed to the lead, the night herder judged their course by the noise as his horse raced along in the darkness for the point of the herd. Once having gained this necessary but dangerous vantage, he pushed beside the lead animals, until, almost imperceptibly, perhaps, they veered to one side. Those immediately behind veered with them, and others behind gave way too, and still the horse crowded in until the herd was describing an arc. Even if the man could not see the cattle, a well-trained horse — and night horses were carefully chosen for sure-footedness, good eyesight, and sense — held the cattle to the arc until the swift animals in front closed the circle and caught the tail of the long-strung, stampeding herd, and thus threw the cattle into a mill.

'They invariably circled to the right,' said Goodnight. 'If any old trail driver ever knew of a herd milling to the left, I would like to hear from him.'

Around and around they raced, as the cowboys squeezed the circle smaller, kept the wildest ones from flying out at tangents, and finally brought the mill to a stop, though often a few head broke out and scattered far and wide. When the cowboys failed to throw the herd into a mill, the stampede sometimes passed entirely from control, and the herd which left the bed ground in volume, scattered, and lost its form.

Those wild rides in the lead of two or three thousand big steers, into the night sometimes so dark the riders could not see their horses beneath them, were the most nerve-racking experiences of exciting range life. Not the fact that falls would come, for they came almost every day, as any stove-up

cowboy can attest, but the fact that they could not be seen as they did come was the thing that shook the staunchest nerve. A gully, a bluff, a precipice — these loomed up in the mind of the man who was riding blindly, and these took their toll of cattle, of horses, and of cowboys. Some few may have placed their faith in God, but not many would have bargained His assistance for a clear-footed night horse, and most all would have sworn by everything unholy that 'the Lord wasn't out on a night like that.'

After the stampede was over and the herd was gathered, the hands laughed, joked, and enjoyed it in retrospect. And usually the more distant the incident, the more they enjoyed it. Frank Mitchell, veteran of the JA ranges, tells of an old-timer at Clarendon who entranced his listeners with a wild tale of a terrible stampede years before. 'In the darkness,' he concluded, 'the herd headed for a sixty-foot bluff and poured over the top like hell after a preacher. I was ridin' on their fetlocks when my night horse — and God, he was a good one — went over the top with them. And I was still a-settin' in the saddle like a reg'lar hand when he hit on his all-fours and bogged three feet deep in solid rock.'

'The heat developed by a large drove of cattle during a stampede was surprising,' said Goodnight, 'and the odor given off by the clashing horns and hoofs was nearly over-powering. Sometimes in cool weather it was uncomfortably warm on the leeward side of a moving herd, and to guard against loss in weight and muscular strength from the effects of this heat, the experienced trail manager always aimed to keep his cattle well distributed while they were in motion. Animal heat seems to attract electricity, especially when the cattle are wet, and after a storm I have seen the faces of men riding with a herd scorched as if some furnace blast had blazed against them.'

Goodnight had a feeling that a herd of cattle tends to attract electricity until enough rain has fallen to wet it. Lightning struck one of his herds on the Platte, and killed 'a big old black steer that was bad to stampede,' an 'act of God' for which Goodnight was grateful. At the same time it knocked down Tom Brannon, the worst swearer the driver ever had on the trail, 'and he didn't swear any more for two months.' 'If a man is struck by lightning and is not killed,' said Goodnight, 'wet him and stretch him out, and ten to one he'll come to and get well.'

Perhaps only the night herders have experienced in their full and awful sublimity the electrical displays of the High Plains country, when men were struck and 'turned black as niggers in five minutes' time,' when horses were killed and bridle bits melted in their mouths, conchos from their saddles, and shoes from their hoofs; when the lightning struck the earth 'and rolled along the ground in balls of fire'; and when the luminous display shone from three thousand sets of horns in the darkness, flashed back and forth on the night horse's ears, and glowed on each man's gloves and hatbrim. Some men were mortally afraid of lightning, and Goodnight remembered a camp near the Platte where one of his hands — 'the toughest old nigger I ever saw,' he explained — rode into camp and said: 'When the lighten' gits on mah hawse's years,

I throws mah gun away.' In such storms, often accompanied by terrific winds, the horse beneath the cowboy was more comforting than plenty of life insurance, because as the old cowman said: 'A horse will stand on the ground when the wind is so strong that it will blow a wagon away. I have been on horses and have seen everything in camp blown away, but never a horse went down.'

'After a stampede we generally spread the cattle out to settle down, but never took them back to the same bed ground, for we knew they would run again. We always tried to find the highest ground, where, once settled, they would generally become quiet, though it took several days to rid them of the effects.

'I had system on my drives. My friends often laughed about it, but the most successful drives were always systematically ordered. We ate breakfast just as day broke. The pointers and two other men, who were to relieve the last night guard, ate at once. If there were no signs of Indians, the herd was started from the bed grounds and put to grazing as soon as possible; when in danger of an attack, the herd was kept on the bed ground until all hands were mounted and around them. The cattle were always headed toward the course we were taking. The men ate, saddled, and fell into place promptly. It is remarkable that during my years on the trail I rarely had a man who would shirk his duty; had he been so inclined he would have been ridiculed out of it. It is certain that no deadheads ever stayed in a cow-camp any length of time.

'In laying off a new trail the foreman or owner would, after roping a good horse from the cavvieyard, start out to prospect the country twenty or thirty miles ahead — that is, if he did not expect to find water sooner. If he found that he was striking a desert, he would return to the herd and inform the men that the cattle were to be moved with all possible speed without actually crowding them. He would then change horses, ride on ahead until he found water, and go back and signal to the men. From an eminence he would ride rapidly in a circle and turn his horse broadside to the herd. If he kept the horse standing in one position, he meant "move ahead," but if the course were to be changed, he would lope off until he reached the line of the new course, where he would stop and signal "come ahead" in that direction.

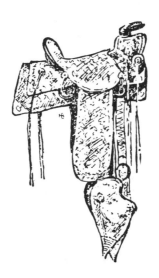

'I was the only trail man I know of who used steer leaders. I conceived the idea after the first trip and found it to be of great advantage. I used two steers. The bells I put on them were of the very best type and were arranged with a strap which would easily stop the clapper. When the signal to graze was given, the man in charge of the lead steers would fasten down the clappers and turn the steers off the trail. After we had been out a month, should a clapper come loose at night the whole herd would be on its feet in no time. The lead steers were of great advantage in swimming rivers and in penning, for the cattle soon learned to go where the bell called them.

'When calves came to have a cash value, I had special wagon

beds built with sixteen-foot frames that would haul thirty to forty calves. These calf-wagons would go right along with the herd and pick up calves as they were dropped. At night the calves would be turned out with their mothers, and then in the morning, after they had walked until tired, they would be roped and put in the wagon. But a cow knows her calf only by scent, and we were liable to make a mess of things, as the calves would rub together until the cows couldn't tell their own because of the mixture of scents. To solve the problem we put each calf in a sack, and numbered the sack so as to get it on the same calf every morning.'

Any treatment of trail technique would be incomplete without reference to the driving qualities of the Texas longhorns, and Goodnight summed up their excellences:

'As trail cattle their equal has never been known and never will be. Their hoofs are superior to those of any other cattle. In stampedes they hold together better, are easier circled in a run, and rarely split off when you commence to turn the front. No animal of the cow kind will shift and take care of itself under all conditions as will the longhorns. They can go farther without water and endure more suffering than others.

'They can be handled on the trail for less expense. Blooded cattle will actually run over you if you don't get out of their way, but the longhorns never do if they can possibly turn. I have never handled any cattle on the trail which space themselves in march as well as they do. They have less tendency to lose weight in trailing; thus it does not require near as much skill and patience to handle them on the trail as it does the blooded races. From my observation they have at least double the endurance, and their period of life and usefulness is also about double that of any other. They never shed their teeth from age, as most other breeds do, and all ranchmen would do well to retain their blood in the improved herds as far as practicable.'

Trail life, with its hot, dusty days and its tense, sleepless nights, placed a heavy strain upon the men who followed it.

In the course of troublous times the nerves of all were on edge, and a man could find a fight by not half trying. Most owners and bosses drove without any particular code except such generally recognized niceties of the cow country as that each man's mount was wholly his own, the cook was master of the wagon and everything about it, and all hands should turn out on a stormy night. But a few trail drivers adopted rules for the conduct of their outfits. When the firm of D. H. and J. W. Snyder, counted among the most extensive operators on the Western range, took the Goodnight Trail in 1868, Dudley, who was of a religious nature, hired Colonel W. C. Dalrymple to go along and kill Indians, but warned the veteran warrior, who is said to have liked his dram, that there would be no drinking on that trip, and drew up three rules for the cowboys:

You can't drink whiskey and work for us.

You can't play cards and gamble and work for us.

You can't curse and swear in our camps or in our presence and work for us.

The firm kept these rules as long as it was in the cattle business, but out on the Delaware, in New Mexico, old Colonel Dalrymple broke over. The outfit had neither tents nor tarps, and while camped one night in that desert region, a heavy rain came up. George Wulfjen, the cook, and the only favored one in camp, was sleeping beneath the wagon-sheet. In the middle of the night Dalrymple roared:

'George! Oh, George! Get up, George! They say it doesn't rain in this country, but this is the damnedest dew I ever saw.'

Among Goodnight's hands in 1866 was a school-teacher from East Texas named Thomas Brooks, and a young fellow by the name of Snyder, who, in working opposite each other on the point, fell out while making the burning drive across the Plains. They passed the 'damned lie' across the herd, 'which meant they must shoot.' Snyder rode on to Goodnight, who was out in the lead, and asked permission to fight the duel. 'I sent him back to his place,' said the cowman, 'telling him I was trying to run the herd and I'd do the fighting for the bunch. Then Brooks came up, and being a school-teacher made quite a talk, saying it was impossible for them to go on together the rest of the way. I said: "Mr. Brooks, I'll just give you your time and loan you that horse to ride back to Texas," which was then a small distance of some four hundred miles through the wilderness and Indians. He said this was not practical, and I replied: "All right, then. You will go on as you are, but just below Sumner we will strike the Bosque Grande, where I shall rest the herd and give the hands a chance to wash their clothing and clean up. There I'll pay you both and you can get out of my camp and shoot. There is a fort nearby where you can get medical aid if needed." He said it was a fair proposition and he would accept it. Eventually we reached the grove of timber and I called them up, told them I was ready to pay them off, and that they could settle their affairs. They informed me they had already settled and were now good friends.'

Usually when cowboys quarreled on the trail they shot it out then, and their friends explained the deaths later. The explanations were usually laconic and sufficient, as in the case of the old-timer who was interrogated on the witness stand as to why he killed a neighbor: 'Because he was a thief,' came the Texas drawl, 'an outlaw, and just a little slow.' And yet the strong character of Goodnight so dominated these fighting Texans that he held their natural passions in check. Why Brooks and Snyder were so considerate of the boss's views can best be explained by observing his code.

'Before starting on a trail drive, I made it a rule to draw up an article of agreement, setting forth what each man was to do. The main clause stipulated that if one shot another he was to be tried by the outfit and hanged on the spot, if found guilty. I never had a man shot on the trail. In over seventy years on the range and in the handling of hundreds of cowboys, the most serious trouble among my men was a couple of fist fights. But in passing over the desert between the Concho and the Pecos, I used to see two graves, and at Horsehead Crossing there were thirteen others, all the result of pistol shots but one. I shall never forget the impression made upon me by those lonely graves, where rested cowboys killed in battle with one another after having fallen out while crossing the long stretch without water. I thought then, as I think now, that all foremen and owners should have been responsible for the lives of their men, not only against Indians so far as possible, but against each other in all cases.'

These incidents occurred and this code was formulated long ago. Though the Goodnight Trails continued in use for many years after their blazer quit following them, the traces now are either plowed under or erased by the slow-growing sod of the sinuous Pecos — 'graveyard of the cowman's hopes.' The stream still drains a dry land devoted to the raising of cattle, Bosque Grande is still nothing but a cow-camp, Pope's Crossing a forgotten ford, Horsehead a desolate memory. But even as the land is saturated with its alkaline salts, so are the traditions of the soil impregnated with the genius of its individualistic men — Chisum of the Jingle-bobs, Loving of the Trail, Maxwell on the Cimarrón, Wootton at Ratón Pass, Hittson on the Arkansas, and Iliff on the Platte. And out of all his troubles, losses, and disappointments, the most enduring impression of the greatest of all cattle trail-blazers is not without significance.

'All in all,' one could hear the old man say, 'my years on the trail were the happiest I have lived. There were many hardships and dangers, of course, that called on all a man had of endurance and bravery; but when all went well there was no other life so pleasant. Most of the time we were solitary adventurers in a great land as fresh and new as a spring morning, and we were free and full of the zest of darers.'[2]

[2] This chapter is reconstructed in large measure from my notes of many interviews with Colonel Goodnight, from a brief remarkable document he dictated bearing this chapter title, and from his account of trailing found in *Prose and Poetry of the Cattle Industry*. I have drawn from a number of feature articles written about him, notably those by J. Frank Dobie. In a few cases the quotations are composites of several observations Goodnight made upon the subject.

XVI. THE RANGE IN SOUTHERN COLORADO

DURING the winter of 1869, Goodnight acquired a location on the Arkansas, above Pueblo, with a view of making it his home. About five miles west of the town the river cuts through a narrow rock cañon, below which the high bluffs recede from the stream for approximately a mile before again closing in, thus forming a sheltered valley below the level of the surrounding plains — an ideal location for his headquarters, typical of the many he chose.

Here the Arkansas had broken into the Plains, and on both sides of the river lay an immense virgin range. With no shelter to the north, sweeping blizzards drove cattle into the stream, but on the south side of the river the Rockies bore farther to the east, and driving winds forced cattle into the shelter of the wooded foothills. That was as it should be, and Goodnight's practiced eye saw the lay of the land at once, for here the forces that wore down the Rockies to level the Plains had designed a perfect range in the form of a triangle, with about twenty-five miles of the Arkansas as the northern base, Hardscrabble Creek the western side, and the crest of the Greenhorns, together with the St. Charles River to its junction with the Arkansas, the longer leg. Well-watered, sheltered, and covered with uncropped grama that put the tallow on a steer like corn, it was a sizeable and inviting range, even for the questing Goodnight, and here he invested his earnings after closing up the Loving partnership.[1]

[1] *The Colorado Chieftain*, February 24, 1870.

He abandoned his camp on the Apishapa and made the Rock Cañon Ranch his swing station on the trail for wintering of horses, recruiting of cattle, and holding over of his steady men. He entered his brand on the county records early in

MRS. CHARLES GOODNIGHT

1870, and not only were the P A T cattle soon familiar, but the country became aware of the driving force of the man who owned them. He began the improvement of his ranch, launched other herds on the trail, and left for Hickman, Kentucky, where he was married to Mary Ann Dyer, July 26, 1870.

Molly Dyer, as she was called, was born in Madison County, Tennessee, September 12, 1839. For years both sides of her family had added to the bounty of a noble heritage — there were statesmen, among them a governor, and noted military leaders, one in particular distinguished at the battle of New Orleans. And though her background was distinctly Southern, Molly had learned the hard practicality of the West. She was the only, the gifted and adored, daughter of Joel Henry Dyer, and the chief stabilizing force among a large family of boys.

In 1854, her father, prominent lawyer of Tennessee, came

West and eventually settled in the Texas Cross Timbers.
Rumor is that some personal difficulty or tragedy sent him
westward and ruined a promising career. Five of her brothers
served the Confederacy in arms, one dying in the ill-advised
Dove Creek fight near the site of San Angelo. They were
not particularly noted, but Molly, darling of the open range
and 'mother of the Panhandle,' is enshrined in cowboy memory
the breadth of the Plains. After long acquaintance on the
border, after courtship during the war and a few meetings
later, she and the young trail driver became engaged in the
spring of 1869.[2]

The trip to Texas was round about and hard, and they
arranged to meet at the home of her relatives in Hickman.
After the ceremony they immediately took boat to St. Louis,
from where they journeyed to Abilene by rail — at that time
probably the 'hardest place in the United States.' After a
night at the Drovers' Hotel they left by stage for Pueblo — a
long grueling ride across the sun-baked Plains. Before they
reached their destination, the slight little woman was feeling
the strain, but at the Drovers' Hotel at Pueblo, they were
hospitably received by the owners, Harry Pickard and his wife.

Next morning the two Coe men were swinging from a telephone post nearby, and Goodnight, knowing that his bride
felt lonely so far from home, was anxious that she should
not hear of the incident immediately. Mrs. Pickard learned
the news, rushed to the room and told her, and she at once
sent for her husband, who admitted the report was true.

'I understand they hanged them to the telegraph pole,' she
exclaimed in distress.

'Having been married such a short while, and not accustomed to making excuses,' Goodnight recalled, 'I hardly knew
how to reply, but finally stammered out in a very abashed

[2] Phoebe K. Warner, 'Mary Ann Goodnight,' typed copy in hands of author, and
'Story of the Plains' First White Woman,' *Southwest Plainsman,* January 9, 1926.
Goodnight, 'Recollections,' I, 49, and II, 32, 139–40; Goodnight to J. E. H., August 2,
1928; John Marlin to J. E. H., February 18, 1930; F. C. Varner to J. E. H., January 22,
1932.

manner: "Well, I don't think it hurt the telegraph pole." This seemed to irritate her very much, and she said: "I used to think I knew you in Texas, but you have been out here among the Yankees and ruffians until I don't know whether I know you or not, and I want you to take me back to Texas. I won't live in such a country." I agreed to this, but insisted that she must first have a rest, and during the next few days made it a point to acquaint her with all the good ladies of Pueblo, whom she found quite as human as herself, and the trip back to Texas was soon forgotten.' [3]

As a diversion from the four-hundred-mile trip across the Plains, a party made up of the Goodnights, Thatchers, Stones, and other friends made a trip to the Colorado Springs country. They spent one day in 'visiting the picturesque falls of the *Fontaine qui Bouille*,' another in exploring the Garden of the Gods, and another the Pike's Peak approaches. On the return Goodnight's spirited team bogged down in an *acequia*, and as he tried to get them out he was kicked in the mouth, the blow cutting his lower lip and loosening several of his teeth. He was treated by Dr. P. R. Thombs, a member of the party, after which all happily drove on to Pueblo. [4]

Pueblo, then about twelve years old, was launching upon a period of rapid growth. It appears that in 1858 some settlers squatted on the east bank of the Fontaine and began 'to call their ragged little hamlet "Fountain City."' Prospectors, bound for Pike's Peak in 1859, described the village as consisting of 'forty or fifty log and mud cabins, inhabited by Americans and Mexicans.' On the first of July, 1860, the village of Pueblo was laid out. 'The first saloon and grocery was opened in the spring of 1861, ... soon afterwards another store was opened by Dick Wooten,' and John A. Thatcher freighted a small stock of goods from the Missouri in 1862. By December, the town was beginning to grow, and a small hotel accommodated every guest who brought a blanket and

[3] Goodnight to J. E. H., June 15, 1929; 'Recollections,' II, 117.
[4] *The Colorado Chieftain*, August 11 and 18, 1870.

'would lie down in what served the double purpose of a dining-room and sitting-room.'

By 1866 the trend toward conventional life resulted in a legal trial when two citizens claimed the same team. The lawyers elicited evidence while the empaneled jury of six men, impartial and true, sat in the box and heard witnesses gravely reflect upon the veracity of either side. After testifying, they repaired to settle their differences, and just as Henry Thatcher was making his plea, someone yelled 'Fight.' Judge, jury, litigants, and Constable Joe Cox ran out. The combatants were down, but one, a witness and a good friend of Cox's, happened to be on top. The constable, mindful of his duty, yelled above the din: 'I command the peace!' Then, mindful of his more fundamental personal loyalties, he leaned over and called to his friend in a low voice: 'Give him h — l, d — n him!' But when the man on the bottom turned his friend under, Cox deputized a bystander to 'pull the scoundrel off,' after which 'several of the jury were so disgusted . . . that they pulled off their coats and threatened to thrash him for his efforts in discharging his duty as a citizen.' Thus came the dignity of established law to southern Colorado, while the boasted 'moulder of public opinion' was not far behind.

Upon June 1, 1868, Dr. M. Beshoar, Wilbur F. Stone, and George A. Hinsdale established *The Colorado Chieftain*, which heralded, in an exceptionally attractive style, the passing of the frontier days. Eighteen months ago, it recorded in its salutatory, there were 'scarcely seventy-five inhabitants in Pueblo; now, its population is but little less than five hundred souls.' By the time Goodnight arrived with his bride, Pueblo had grown from a drab little village to a 'progressive' town.[5]

A few days after their arrival the young couple went to their

[5] *The Northern Standard* (Clarksville, Texas), December 10, 1859; *The Colorado Chieftain*, June 1 and 11, 1868, December 28, 1871, January 7 and 14 and March 4, 1875; Raymond Thatcher to J. E. H., August 24, 1929; Mike Studzinski to J. E. H., August 24, 1929; Frank Hall, *History of the State of Colorado*, 477; Jerome C. Smiley, *History of the State of Colorado*, 241, 439; W. S. Stone, *History of Colorado*, I, 152; Wilbur F. Stone, 'Early Pueblo and the Men Who Made It,' *The Colorado Magazine*, VI, 199–210.

ranch home, where, as the groom said simply, they 'resided happily' for the next six years.

The three thousand cattle he had on the range were not yet located and had been giving serious trouble. Shep West had been left in charge, and Rumans was still one of the hands.

'Shep was a windy, white-shirt, pretty fellow,' complained Rumans in later years. 'He spent most of his time in town, and left me to do all the riding. I got up about four o'clock each morning, ate breakfast, and went to riding. I came in about nine o'clock at night, ate supper, and went to bed, and I rode at a run all the time. I rode down eighteen head of horses and then bought a mule. West raised hell and said he'd make me pay for the mule. I told him Goodnight had left me there to look after those cattle, and I was going to look after them or somebody was going to haul me off. When the Old Man got back I had the steers. I told him that the pretty fellow had been spending his time in town, while Shep told him that I had bought a mule without authority, and he ought to make me pay for him.

'"I'll pay for the mule," the Old Man said, "and fire you." And he did.[6]

'The Old Man worked like a nigger all the time. He just lived on a horse. I worked with him six years and never had a cross word. He was the finest man I ever saw. When he'd get ready to leave the ranch, he'd say: "You just stay with this outfit until I get back."'

Among Goodnight's neighbors on the range was a Canadian named H. W. Cresswell. Broad-framed and broad-gauged, he had organized 'H. W. Cresswell and Company' by the winter of 1868, and was giving the long slash as his brand. Two and a half years later, he placed the Bar CC on record, a brand that came to distinguish him as surely as the nickname, 'Hank.' He and the Thatchers joined Goodnight in buying out squatters, and, operating together they shared the country between the St. Charles and the Hardscrabble.

[6] John Rumans to J. E. H., December 8, 1928, and April 12, 1931.

Besides Hittson, others were coming into the country whose names still connote horses, cattle, and extensive ranges: George Reynolds with the Spanish Gourds, Pollard brothers with the PO's, Robert Moody and P. T. Barnum with the Dippers, R. E. McAnulty with the Turkey Tracks, and H. S. Boice with the LK's connected.[7]

With his usual zest for life, Goodnight settled himself to the work of converting his location into an attractive frontier home. He ditched the valley for irrigation, imported apple trees from the States by stage, and set out the first large orchard in southern Colorado — some of his trees may still be seen today. As corn was commanding five cents a pound on account of freight charges from the East, he saw the need of local crops and turned to farming, realizing good profits until the railroad arrived in 1872, and the prices slid to the bottom.

His work on the trail continued, and he wintered many cattle on 'the Goodnight range,' as it was called. Leigh Dyer, his brother-in-law, was placed in charge of his outfit, and camps were kept on the St. Charles and at Babcock's Hole, on the Hardscrabble, from which the boys rode the designated lines.

He shipped in a few shorthorn bulls and thoroughbred cows soon after the coming of the railroad, branded them P A T M for his wife, and placed them at Babcock's Hole. Within a couple of days a Mexican from the St. Charles rode up and claimed one of the bulls. Goodnight, digging post-holes with a spade at the time, was in no particular humor for haggling, but asked the Mexican if he was sure he knew the bull.

'*Si, muy bien!*' he replied. The cowman made one swing with the spade, and this neighbor lost all interest in bulls.

Though Goodnight, Cresswell, and the Thatchers maintained line camps, their cattle often ranged far beyond the St. Charles, to be gathered by the general roundups that worked the Arkansas Valley. In 1874 a prolonged storm swept

---

[7] *Brands*, Pueblo County, I, 32, 47, 49, 80, 82, 91, 143, and 173; *The Colorado Chieftain*, December 8, 1870, October 17, 1872, and June 26, 1873.

out of the mountains and drifted their cattle eastward into the point formed by the junction of the Arkansas and the St. Charles, where high bluffs prevented their crossing the rivers. They could not be drifted back in the teeth of the wind, and as they faced starvation the combined crews of the cowmen cut down the bluffs, scattered dirt across the ice, and drifted them over to shelter and grass. The next spring some of them were gathered from as far east as the Kansas line.

The cowmen, showing a co-operative bent, met at Fort Garland in the fall of 1868, organized for the purpose of making 'local regulations as to the grazing of stock,' and decided that cattle should be herded from the middle of May to the first of November, but that they might run 'without let or hindrance' the rest of the year.[8] In November, 1871, they met again and formed a Stock Raisers' Association; planned the arrangement of roundups and the recording of brands; condemned the driving of cattle except by owners; condemned, too, the running at large of Texas, Mexican, and other inferior bulls; and advised the sheepmen to 'pay due and proper regard to existing claims of cattlemen to ranges already occupied by them.' They recommended fencing of fields against stock, and the branding of calves by the time they were six months old. While no open-range cowman needed the latter advice, mavericks, always to be sought and found by the dishonest, caused much trouble. Many devices for their peaceful disposal were tried throughout the cow country, and the State of Colorado finally authorized a commissioner to attend the annual roundups, seize and sell the mavericks, and deposit the proceeds to the benefit of the common school fund.[9]

Important functions of the association were the establishment of a code of ethics and the maintenance of the unwritten laws of the range designed for the common good, the most

[8] The meeting took place November 28, 1868. John Wilkins was chosen president of the association and Oliver Beeman secretary. *The Colorado Chieftain*, December 10, 1868.

[9] The same, November 30, 1871; Bancroft, *History of Nevada, Colorado and Wyoming.* 545.

important of which was the sanctity of property rights. Naturally there were the ordinary cow thieves, with whom Goodnight soon clashed, as usual.

FOREFOOTIN'

Among the settlers he had bought out of his range was a family by the name of Crouch, members of the Baptist Church, but hard characters who bore the name of gamblers and thieves. They moved out of the range and settled at its western edge, on the Hardscrabble, where they began furnishing beef for coal miners, nearby. For a year or more Goodnight thought they were killing his cattle, and placed a detective on Hardscrabble to watch them. Instead of apprehending, he joined the thieves in stealing from Goodnight and the Bar CC's. When his duplicity was discovered, he caught Goodnight's best horse, left, and was never heard of again.

Next a man named Aikens, a relative of the Crouches, turned up from Illinois, and the latter, having 'got in pretty good shape financially, gave him the cold shoulder because he had nothing.'

Aikens complained that he was in need of work, and Goodnight sent him up in the mountains to peel some poles for construction of a fine corral, making a point to see him frequently, and always pretending to doubt the stories of rustling, which spurred Aikens to tell all that he knew.

When the main roundup reached the mountains, Aikens came down to spend a night with the outfit. He told Goodnight that the Crouches had killed a fat, barren cow that belonged to his bookkeeper, that the meat was hanging in the old man's barn, and that the hide was thrown over his fence. On the Hardscrabble, Aikens continued, was a large thicket into which they had cut a lane, cleared a space, and built a corral. They had been butchering cattle there, he said, and had fourteen hides on hand which they planned to market next day. Cresswell swore there was nothing to it, and advised that the work proceed.

'Never mind,' replied Goodnight, 'we will change the program, and instead of going east we will go west today on the roundup — up to the Crouch neighborhood.'

He arranged for the outfit to pass immediately by the corrals and barn. As they approached, the Crouches rode off, and Goodnight told Ben Davis, the bookkeeper, to drop off his horse, examine the hide and signal him if it was in his brand. Davis identified the hide, gave the signal, and Goodnight went after them. George Crouch escaped, but Dick was captured and turned over to the authorities. Goodnight took his wagon to the thicket and packed out the hides, closely observing the beef heads scattered about, from which the ears had been cut to destroy the marks, and then took his wagon back to the range near where the magistrate lived. Nine indictments were found against both suspects, and the cases went to trial in Fremont County, before Judge Baker, 'a nice old chap from the States.'

Goodnight swore on the stand as to the mutilated hides and their brands. Lawyers for the defense made the usual plea that the plaintiffs were rich cowmen, persecuting poor little men, and H. C. Thatcher, the cowman's lawyer, feared not only their ability to get a conviction, but a sufficiently heavy bond to hold the culprits, because Judge Baker, though 'an honest man, belonged to the same Baptist church as the Crouches, and couldn't believe they were guilty of stealing cattle.'

'Now you get up a good dinner at the wagon with your cow outfit,' said Thatcher to Goodnight, 'and I'll invite the old Judge to a cowboys' dinner. I think he would like it. Then you must get him on to the hides.' Goodnight dumped the hides into a nearby irrigation ditch, while Thatcher purposely delayed the trial for another day to give them time to soften. Arrangements were made, and the next day at noon the hides were hanging over a fence near the encamped wagon. As the Judge came out in company with Goodnight, he passed them unnoticed, had a good dinner with 'a nice set of boys,' as Goodnight appraised his men, and then started back to court.

'Knowing him to be a refined gentleman,' said the cowman, 'I was racking my brain for all that was in it for a way to draw his attention to the hides. I was at my wits' end when he looked up and said:

'"By the way, are those the hides in controversy?"

'"They are! Would you like to have a look at them?"

'"Indeed, I would," he answered.

'I walked over and lifted off the first hide we came to, and took him behind it, leaving it between us and the sun. It happened to be a Bar CC hide, and it had soaked until the brand showed plain. He at once said: "What is that?"

'I pretended not to see it. He put his hand on it, saying: "Bless my life, that's a Bar CC."

'I took him down the fence and showed him all the hides, and he read more than half of the brands, while I explained the rest. As we walked back to court, he said to me:

'"There's one more thing I'd like an explanation of, but it's very delicate and I don't want to hurt your feelings. You swore positively that those ears were cut off after the animals were killed. The lawyers pounded you unmercifully and did not move you. How could you swear to that?"

"'It's easy enough when you understand it," I said. "You are aware the skin is a little thicker on the outside of the ear than it is on the inside, are you not?" He said he did not know anything about it, so I said: "It *is* thicker on the outside, and on the inside of the ear it is very thin. Now, when you cut the ear off after the animal is dead, it will not bleed. As it dries, the skin on the outside will shrink back from the gristle of the ear about one eighth of an inch, while the thin part on the inside of the ear will shrink back farther, a quarter of an inch, leaving the gristle projecting like your finger-nail. Now it is a fact, Mr. Baker, that if you cut the ear off when the animal is alive, and let it go an hour or two, the blood will dry on the edge of the ear — in other words, adhesion sets in. Shoot this animal down after the blood has dried and the gristle will not project. This is one of nature's facts and cannot be denied."

"'It's clear to me, sir," said the Judge, and he went and gave us a bond so damned high that they couldn't see daylight.'

His brother escaped, but Dick Crouch was convicted in Judge Moses Hallett's court at Cañon City, and sentenced for a term of two years, beginning May 10, 1875. In December, 1881, after Goodnight's removal to the Panhandle, the other indictments were dismissed by agreement.[10]

Soon after his removal to the Arkansas, Goodnight bought an interest in a grant of approximately three hundred thousand acres made by the Mexican Government to Gevacio Nolan,

[10] Goodnight to J. E. H., February 27, 1929, and April 8, 1927; D. R. McCormick to J. E. H., May 22, 1932; *District Court Record*, iii, 127, *General Docket*, Nos. 250–58, pp. 96–100, and C. Goodnight to Mr. Lobach, December 7, 1881, all in the Fremont County Court House, Cañon City, Colorado; and *Record of Convicts When Received into the United States Penitentiary of Colorado*, Cañon City.

Among those who should be remembered for their work of bringing law to southern Colorado, Goodnight thought Governor C. M. Hinsdale, Judge Wilbur F. Stone, H. W. Cresswell, J. A., M. D., and Calvin Thatcher, Perry Baxter, Si Smith, Harry Pickard, Judge Moses Hallett, J. M. Fosdick, Daniel Boone and P. K. Dotson were particularly deserving. Goodnight to J. E. H., September 16, 1927.

of Taos. After various transfers, the land passed to people interested in the Denver and Rio Grande Railway, who subsequently organized the Central Colorado Improvement Company for the purpose of acquiring the properties, digging a

JIM OWENS, JA COWBOY

canal twenty-five miles in length, planting 'no less than five hundred thousand trees,' conversion of the land to small irrigated farms, and final disposal to actual settlers.[11] Railroads were then building across the Plains and development was catching.

In the fall of 1871, Goodnight and the Pollards incorporated the 'Goodnight and Pollard Ditch, Flume and Milling Company' for the purpose of constructing an irrigating and milling ditch on the St. Charles. With Goodnight acting as manager, the ditch was built, but three years later the milling privileges and site were disposed of. Goodnight reached an agreement with the Improvement Company for the use of water from ditches passing through his land, built fine rock corrals and

[11] *Records*, County Clerk's Office, Pueblo County, vol. 2, pp. 456, 489–510, 582–85. and vol. 3, pp. 722–23; *Mortgage Records*, I, 250; *The Colorado Chieftain*, June 18, 1868 July 14, 1870, December 21, and 28, 1871, August 15, and September 26, 1872, and March 25, 1875; *Miscellaneous Records*, Pueblo County, vol. 10, pp. 27–28.

barns, and became one of the most extensive farmers in the section.[12] He invested heavily in city lots and farm lands, and attempted to divert the Arkansas River from its natural course to one he had chosen for it, in order to keep it from cutting away his orchard and to give himself more room, giving rise to the old settlers' jest that 'Goodnight went broke trying to change the course of the Arkansas.' Only after he left the country did floods divert its channel along the direct lines that he had indicated.

During this time the growing village of Pueblo gave thought to the adornments of settled life. Goodnight pledged a thousand dollars to help start an educational institution intended to be 'independent of all religious creeds and sects,' and Mrs. Goodnight led in building the first Methodist Episcopal Church, South, in southern Colorado. Dave McCormick, their irrepressible Irish cowboy, recalls that he gave the better part of one month's wages to the project, but that shortly after its completion a storm tore much of the structure away, and Dave, feeling that the Lord was displeased with his contribution, never made another one afterward.[13] But he did leave his accumulated wages on deposit with Goodnight, who paid him interest at the rate of two per cent a month.

This alone was indicative of the dire need of credit facilities, and in September, 1873, Goodnight joined in organizing The Stock Growers' Bank, which opened by advertising six per cent interest on three months' deposits, seven on six months', and eight on twelve months'. The loans Goodnight personally negotiated were then costing him from one and a half to two per cent monthly.

'The panic ... wiped me off the face of the earth,' he once said. 'I had loaned $6000 on a half block of ground on which was the only brick building in the town; I also owned the opera

---

[12] *Records*, Pueblo County, vol. 3, p. 535; *Miscellaneous Records*, vol. 10, pp. 337–38, 480–81, and 628–29.

[13] *The Colorado Chieftain*, March 14, 1872; Phoebe K. Warner, 'Mary Ann Goodnight,' as cited; and Dave McCormick to J. E. H., May 22, 1932.

house and all the vacant buildings in the place, [which] would just about pay the taxes in 1873.' He sold the half block for $2000, and 'was mighty glad to get it,' though two years later the iron works located there, and the Yankee buyer sold the place for $25.000.

'When the panic came,' Goodnight explained, 'Thatcher brothers owned half of Pueblo, but they deeded it over rather than pay taxes on it. Afterwards they went back and redeemed it, and it made them rich. I've heard men talk about their foresight in holding on to Pueblo property — they didn't have any more foresight than a rabbit.' [14]

A number of meat-packing-houses were built at Las Animas, the terminus of the Santa Fé Railroad, and Goodnight and John W. Prowers, his prominent neighbor down the river, established a plant of their own. By the spring of 1876 there was a decided revival from the crash, and the faithful *Chieftain* noted the growth of the business.

> We have interviewed Mr. Charles Goodnight, one of the oldest and most experienced cattle men in the country, a member of the firm of Prowers & Goodnight, who have been slaughtering and shipping cattle from West Las Animas during the past season. Mr. Goodnight informs us that during a portion of the winter the warm weather spoiled some of the beef, occasioning considerable loss to the firm, but during the last two months of the season . . . all losses were made good, and the profits of the season quite satisfactory.
>
> From the stock grower's point of view Mr. Goodnight thinks this revival of the cattle trade will be of immense advantage to the country. All of the rough cattle, which would have brought little or nothing alive, have been slaughtered and sent to eastern markets, bringing good prices. This kind of stock has been effectually cleaned out of the country, along with thousands of good cattle, and the herds are reduced in number and composed of a better quality of animals. Small herds of good cattle will require less range to feed them, and will be far more profitable to the cattle grower. . . . [15]

[14] *The Colorado Chieftain*, September 4 and November 13, 1873, and October 22, 1874. Clipping, 'Trailing the First Herd to the Panhandle,' from the *Southwest Plainsman*, n. d.

[15] *The Colorado Chieftain*, March 16, 1876.

In spite of its freshness, this matter of range in southern Colorado was already becoming important. Goodnight's losses in the panic had been disastrously heavy, and overstocking of the ranges, which were slow to recuperate, meant that once again grass was the prime consideration of the man of affairs. He returned to the trail to counteract the adversities of fortune; strong lust for virgin range came upon him; and again he turned his face toward the Plains of Texas.

XVII. THE HOME RANCH OF THE PANHANDLE

BEFORE returning to the trail in the spring of 1875, Goodnight placed Leigh Dyer in charge of an outfit, and instructed him to drift his stock cattle eastward along the Arkansas and locate on Two Butte Creek, south of Las Animas. Cresswell prepared to move his cattle toward the same territory, as Goodnight headed for the lower Pecos to receive a herd. After laying out the New Goodnight Trail, he back-tracked to rejoin his men on Two Butte Creek.

As fall approached, he gathered his herd of sixteen hundred head and drifted them toward the Llano Estacado, that great plateau of New Mexico and Texas, a wilderness, arid, unsettled, and then almost unknown. As a ranger he had explored its far edges during the Civil War, and had learned something of the country in which he intended to locate.

Though fifteen expansive years had passed since he began to learn its terrain, it was yet unclaimed even by pioneer stockmen. Traditionally, it was the Great American Desert, and for Gregg, Marcy, and other early travelers it was truly 'the dreaded Llano Estacado ... the great Zahara of North America.' Even in this year, 1875, the *Texas Rural Register and Immigrants' Handbook* advised the world that it was improbable that the Staked Plains could 'ever be adapted to the wants of man,' adding that this was 'the only uninhabitable portion of Texas.' But Goodnight recalled its miles of unbroken buffalo turf, its rich grama grasses, and its scattered waterings. Besides, he never read guide-books, and hence moved with confidence. He found the land the same as Albert Pike found it forty-three years before, and so aptly explained that:

> No man can form an idea of the prairie, from anything which he sees to the east of the Cross Timbers. Broad, level, grey and barren, the immense desert which extends thence westwardly almost to the shadow of the mountains, is too grand and too sublime to be imaged by the narrow contracted, undulating plains to be found nearer the bounds of civilization.
>
> Imagine yourself ... standing in a plain to which your eye can see no bounds. Not a tree, nor a bush, not a shrub, not a tall weed lifts its head above the barren grandeur of the desert; not a stone is to be seen on its hard beaten surface; no undulation, no abruptness, no break to relieve the monotony; nothing. ... Its sublimity arises from its unbounded extent, its barren monotony and desolation, its still, unmoved, calm, stern, almost self-confident grandeur, its strange power of deception, its want of echo, and in fine, its power of throwing a man back upon himself and giving him a feeling of lone helplessness, strangely mingled at the same time with a feeling of liberty and freedom from restraint.[1]

The principal features — streams, cañons, and springs — that break the sameness of the plateau were named by New Mexican *comancheros* and *ciboleros*. They knew the land intimately for a hundred years before another white race came, and being capable plainsmen, crossed it at random while other frontiersmen thought it an impassable barrier. The naming of the Staked Plains, according to early American chronicles, is due to the staking of a road across its unbroken surface by Spanish travelers, which legend probably has some basis in fact, for even yet, along the western edges of the Plains, cowboys sometimes see the white stone *mojoneras* — mounds or stakes — which not only guided the hunter and trader along his way, but indicated a nearby seep of water.[2]

[1] Albert Pike, 'Narrative of a Journey in the Prairie,' *Publications of the Arkansas Historical Association*, IV, 71–73.

[2] Francisco de Baca to J. E. H., August 26, 1932; see Gregg's comment in Thwaites's *Early Western Travels*, XX, 239.

Toward this land Goodnight's outfit pointed his herd, down by Two Butte to the Cimarrón, past the ruins of Robbers' Roost, Coe's old rendezvous, and to the Canadian, on the south bank of which, in a wild portion of eastern New Mexico, they went into winter camps late in 1875, locating one on Rano Creek and another ten miles west.

DOWN THE PALO DURO

At that time the swarthy natives who lived in the settlements far to the west engaged principally in sheep-raising. Each winter their *pastores* drifted huge flocks toward the edge of the Plains, and back toward Las Vegas for shearing in the spring. Goodnight's outfit was well armed and strong in men, and it was an anomaly in the usage of the range when, that winter, approximately a hundred thousand sheep were drifted in around it for protection. A few renegade Indians and whites still made life hazardous, and as the Western World was large, Goodnight told his cowboys not to molest the *pastores* as long as they stayed outside the designated range for his cattle. He established the camps for his cowboys; then he returned to Colorado.

Though there were no fences enclosing the interminable Plains, custom established the lines of a cowman's range as firmly as steel wire. And yet custom may be broken even as wire fences may be cut, and down from the high country to the west drifted the sheep of a native New Mexican Governor. On they came, like a cowman's plague, grazing the land bare and polluting the water holes they used, to locate inside the cattle range.

Among those with the cattle was James T. Hughes, son of the noted author of *Tom Brown's School Days*, and a Scotchman, J. C. Johnston, later a director of the Matador Land and Cattle Company, Limited, of Dundee, who, like the balladist from Arkansas, was actually 'learning how cowpunchin' was done.' In the upper or western camp, adjacent to the hated sheep, was the fighting Irishman, Dave McCormick, and a Mexican *vaquero*, Panchito — Little Frank.

In riding line Panchito discovered the Governor's sheep and reported to McCormick, who rode out and told the *mayordomo* that he must move outside their range. Next morning he rode back, and found that instead of moving, the herders were building a cedar tepee for shelter. Immediately he and Panchito rounded up the sheep, and by cursing and throwing rocks at the *guias*, the goats that led each flock, forced them into the Canadian. Four or five hundred drowned and died in the quicksand, but the cowboys, feeling there must be plenty of sheep where these came from, happily went back to their accustomed work. Winter wore on without incident until a Mexican deputy appeared, arrested Johnston, who owned a slight interest in the cattle, and haled him before court at Las Vegas, where Goodnight was forced to pay the damages.

Besides Indian traders, buffalo hunters, and herders, the mustanger, another Mexican type, frequented the Plains. Frank Mitchell recalls that the mustangers sometimes drifted milk cows along with their outfits, caught mustang colts, fed them milk by hand, and drifted back to the settlements with their strange pastoral relations. According to the story Goodnight used to relate to Mitchell, one of these strange characters told him of a wild gorge that cut the Llano in two, a wonderfully sheltered place for a ranch that he had once seen. Goodnight was wanting a permanent range, and together they set out to find it, drifted too far down the Canadian, cut southward below the breaks, and after considerable riding, turned back northwest, along the foot of the Plains.

There were many cañons, and the confused Mexican had almost despaired of finding the place until, one day, they rode up on the brink of the Palo Duro, near the mouth of the Tule. The guide clapped his hands above his head in joy, and shouted:

'*Al fin! Al fin!* At last! At last!'

And so when spring of 1876 came, the Goodnight outfit drifted down the river into the Texas Panhandle, and summered on the pleasant Alamocitos, a short tributary of the Canadian. The sheepmen came in around them, and in the fall Goodnight, having decided to move again, made a treaty with the *mayordomos*. He would leave the Canadian Valley, with its hundreds of miles of well-watered, rugged, and sheltered range, to them. They in turn agreed to stay off the headwaters and out of the colorful cañons of the Palo Duro, where he had decided to locate. It was a simple matter to split those vast Plains in two. Two hundred miles from a village and from legal authority, Goodnight and the *pastores* naturally were the law unto themselves, and the land was theirs to rule.

Only one Mexican transgressed this agreement. Leigh Dyer took the double of his rope and whipped him off the range, and it is authoritatively said that he never came back. In time another flock came from the west — sixteen hundred head of sheep owned by some Americans, named Casner. Their story is more tragic still.

Among those caught in the California gold rush were John Casner and his three grown sons, who, after making quite a stake, decided to leave California. They spread a map, and after some deliberation over its vacant spots, decided to locate upon the headwaters of Red River, in the Panhandle of Texas. They separated, the father and one son, Lew, turning south to prospect Arizona and New Mexico. The other boys took the bullion and set out for the mint at Carson, where they had it minted into twenty-dollar gold pieces — a thousand pieces in all. As they made their way east they purchased some sheep, and sold the clip at Trinidad. They pushed on across the high, dry plains of northeastern New Mexico, and settled in camp to graze their sheep on the broad clean ridges along that jagged gash, that wild gorge torn through the surface of a placid land, the Palo Duro Cañon.[3]

Before treating with the sheepmen, Goodnight had sent Dyer and a Mexican guide across the Plains to the south to scout out the Palo Duro and the approach thereto. After they returned, the outfit moved down the river to the future site of Old Tascosa. Two miles below was the camp of Nicolas Martínez, a *comanchero* now engaged in running sheep, and his notorious brother-in-law, the outlaw Sostenes Archiveque, who had recently been run out of the Rio Grande settlements of New Mexico, and who, the old herders claim, had killed twenty-three Americans. As a trader bartering with the Comanches for years, Martínez knew the Plains like a book. He knew the boundless wastes, the arroyos, the cañons, the trails, and the waterings. And, he assured the trail driver, he could pilot the herd to the Palo Duro and into its yawning depths — the ancestral camping place of the Comanches — by a trail the Indians had used for ages.

Late in October they left the Canadian and proceeded to Las Tecovas — the springs northwest of Amarillo where the Frying Pan Ranch was later located — crossed the divide, forded the narrow waters of Red River, just below the junction of Palo Duro Creek and the Tierra Blanca, turned east, paralleling the course of the cañon, now to their north, and

---

[3] Goodnight, 'Recollections,' I, 7 and 28; Goodnight to J. E. H., November 13, 1926, April 8, 1927, August 2, 1928, September 29, 1929; H. T. Burton, *History of the JA Ranch*, 25.

intercepted the old Indian trail due east of the site of the town of Canyon. They approached from across the tablelands, gazing over the gorge to the plain on the other side, unaware the cañon was near until they were almost on the verge of the cap-rock. And there, of all places, the four-mule chuck wagon

'HELL, LET 'EM RUN!'

team became frightened and ran away, heading straight into the chasm with the terrified cook loudly calling for the cowboys to stop or turn them. Those joking devils, knowing mules and perhaps hating cooks, only whooped and yelled in glee:

'Hell, let 'em run! You never saw a prettier place!'

The cattle moved slowly, in single file, down that ancient trace probably never before cut by the cloven feet of domestic animals. The cowboys took the wagon to pieces and packed it down the seven-hundred-foot wall on the backs of the very conservative chuck-wagon mules, and supplies of provisions and corn were transported in the same way. Since buffaloes stayed out of narrow gorges there was water and grass in plenty, and the cattle grazed at their own free will. After two days the portage was done.

As the cowboys worked the cattle down the cañon to where it widened, they began coming upon bands of grazing buffaloes

In the lead rode Goodnight, Dyer, and Hughes, pushing the great shaggy animals along in another herd, an awesome experience in a wild, strange land that Goodnight never forgot. By taking their Sharp-shooters and knocking up the red dust beside them, they stampeded those animals that grazed high on the cañon sides down to join those in the drive. The roar of the herd was awful, and as the stragglers crashed through the brittle red cedars in mad stampede, the cañon walls re-echoed their flight as with the rattle of distant musketry, and the little black bears, startled from usual peaceful retreats, loped off to other shelter in the sandstone ledges. By the time they dropped the wild herd, Goodnight estimated they were driving ten thousand buffaloes. From the thousands of flinty, grinding hoofs, the fine red dust of the Palo Duro rose as a vast streamer behind them, rose for a thousand feet to the cap-rock, to the level of the Plains and to the skies beyond, almost as significant as the column of an Indian's signal fire.

Leaving the buffaloes, they turned back up the cañon and chose a spacious park on the south side, beside which ran a little stream from a spring near the cap-rock, far above. There Goodnight designated a location for corrals, a house, and a picket smokehouse, and established the Home Ranch, the first within the bounds of the Staked Plains.

The Palo Duro, the Prairie Dog Town Fork or headwaters of Red River, received the drainage of the northern portion of the Staked Plains, and cut a colorful system of cañons nearly sixty miles long. Nearly a thousand feet in depth, and varying from a few hundred yards in width to extensive bad lands fifteen miles across, it furnished shelter from the northers of the bleak Plains, and water and grass sufficient for many thousands of cattle. Its cottonwood, wild china, hackberry, and cedars had been fuel and shade for Comanche camps from time long past, and a *comanchero* told Goodnight that he had once seen twelve thousand Indian horses grazing therein. It was an unexcelled winter range, with the high bluffs of the cañon, the cap-rock, more effectively fencing the animals in than posts and wire.

A hundred miles toward Kansas, Jim Cator had a buffalo camp on the North Palo Duro; about a hundred miles to the east and a little north, Fort Elliott was staked out on the Sweetwater; Fort Griffin lay a much longer journey southeast; and the nearest settlements in New Mexico, Kansas, and Colorado were from two hundred to two hundred and fifty miles away. Here at last was plenty of room. But Goodnight had to hurry back, as other affairs in Colorado still demanded his attention.

The outfit again took up the routine of a well-ordered ranch, while 'Colas Martínez and Goodnight rode up the cañon to the Comanche trail, passed out over the rim, and headed northwest across the brown, sere Plains. As they crossed the divide and turned down into the Canadian breaks, along the Rios Amarillos they met the two Casners with their ox-wagon, a few head of cattle and horses, their sheep, and a Navajo boy for a herder, headed south to the Palo Duro.

Goodnight engaged Martínez to accompany him to Las Animas for the purpose of bringing back additional supplies for the ranch. It was a long wilderness ride, three hundred miles of Plains that seemed to reach on and on to infinity; a land where the eye rested on an illimitable level, on a horizon rarely static, but imperceptibly moving back with the advance of the rider, as the horizon at sea advances with the sailor, apparently always the same and yet never the same. On they rode, sleeping together on sweaty saddle blankets at night, broiling their meat together on bull-chip fires by day. The awful vastness of that land, like a glimpse of eternity, broke down their racial differences and bound them close together. This, and the powerfully dominant personality of Goodnight, may explain the action that followed.

The cowman thought of the hazards of his boys, their extreme isolation, and their exposure to outlaws and thieves. He thought, too, of the dangerous Sostenes Archiveque, and he talked of him to the faithful 'Colas, who promised to help put law into the Panhandle. The cowman need have no fear of his outlaw brother-in-law, 'Colas reassured. He would kill Sostenes himself if he continued his career of crime. With this reassurance, Goodnight proceeded from Las Animas to Pueblo, and 'Colas turned back with the extra provisions for the Palo Duro Ranch.

Goodnight may well have been uneasy, for it was an active day for horse rustlers and outlaws. Fort Elliott, in the extreme eastern Panhandle, had just been established for the purpose of maintaining the dignity of established order, and keeping the reserve tribes out of Texas. While it hardly did either, it had the distinction of furnishing the region with one of its most gifted outlaws, an officer who secretly directed one of the bands which established a new Robbers' Roost on the Canadian, some miles below Tascosa.

Beneath this officer the active leader of the band was a fellow most seriously known as Goodanuff, and it is supposed that he, coveting the Casner property, induced the blood-thirsty Sostenes to raid their camp. Sostenes mounted himself on a race horse, and with a Mexican boy from Tascosa to accompany him — probably to herd the sheep — rode over to the Palo Duro.

After some maneuvering he induced one of the Casners to go down the cañon on a hunt, and as they passed through a thicket Sostenes dropped behind and shot him through the back of the head. He returned to the sheep camp without arousing suspicion, got the drop on the other, killed him, and then mounted the Mexican footman on his horse and sent him on the menial errand of killing the Navajo. Having seen enough excitement for one day, the young *pelado* rode out of camp and hit a high lope for peaceful Tascosa. Sostenes must have been exasperated, as he had to walk out and shoot the Indian himself. The Casner sheep dog attacked him viciously, and in attempting to kill him Sostenes shot out one of his eyes. Perhaps the outlaw got the money they had received for the wool; the twenty-dollar pieces have never been found. The damnable part of the whole episode, from Sostenes's point of view, was that a real *caballero* should be forced to walk the forty-odd intervening miles to Tascosa.

Long before he arrived, the boy had reported to 'Colas, and as Sostenes walked into his house about midnight, he was stabbed to death by the *comanchero* and his friends. Respectfully and religiously enough, the Mexicans buried him on the crest of a hill south of the river, where, with characteristic Latin devotion, they raised a cross above his grave. Though the cross has long since rotted away, and Tascosa itself has fallen to 'dobe dust, the name of the eminence, *Sierrita de la Cruz* — Little Mountain of the Cross — may still be heard.

Hardly a week later Dyer and Hughes, exploring the upper reaches of the cañon, saw the loose stock, and found the camp and the body of one of the men. The wounded dog, near starvation, was still faithfully holding the sheep in herd. They drifted the stock down the cañon to the ranch, and perhaps there was a sort of pastoral, poetic justice in the fact that Dave McCormick had to help herd them.

Dave had been keeping a lonely camp on the east line, holding the cattle in and the buffaloes out of the upper cañon. For months, until the buffalo slaughter was done, he or another cowpuncher daily rode this line, turning from eight to fifteen hundred buffaloes in order to save the grass. Reduced from one extremity to another, the Irishman now had a horned frog as a pet — an appreciative reptile that gorged himself on the green blow-flies that Dave caught as his own supper broiled on the fire. And as long as the cowboy had plenty of buffalo meat, the horned frog had plenty of flies, for the hide hunters were out, the slaughter at its height, and the world was teeming with billions of flies that hatched from the thousands of decaying carcasses — flies swarming so thickly that only by smoking them away with smudges of buffalo-chips could the camp-men eat their meals.

And so the winter wore on, until Goodnight became uneasy

about the boys. Letters were few and far between, and, fearing the outlaws might kill his hands and take the cattle, he decided to make his way down from Pueblo and look after them. Through his banker friends, the Thatcher brothers, he got let-

ON THE BUFFALO RANGE

ters to the post traders of Fort Dodge, Camp Supply, and Fort Elliott, and in February, 1877, went to Dodge by rail, and there got government transportation on the ambulance to Camp Supply, in the Territory.

When he reached Supply, 'so many officers and dogs got on' that they crowded him out, and as another ambulance would not run for a week, he hired an old military guide to bring him through by pack to Fort Elliott. On Commission Creek, in the Panhandle, the most noted highwayman of the Plains and eighteen of his men were camping near the trail. Goodnight did not know them, but the guide informed him that it was Dutch Henry's band.

'All right,' he said, 'stop the pack. I want to talk with him.'

In astonishment the guide asked if he did not know who Dutch Henry was. Replying that he had some knowledge of him, but wanted to see him, nevertheless, the cowman rode over and asked to see Mr. Henry.

A good-looking young German said:

'I am the man.'

'I am settling on the upper Red River,' Goodnight stated, 'and am trying to make it a peaceful and lawful country. I much prefer to have no trouble with anyone, and I want an understanding with you. If you depredate in that country we will have to clash. I have a bunch of good men, well armed and good shots, but I dislike to be compelled to use them in that way. I would like to divide territories with you. If you keep out of my part of the country, I will never cross the Salt Fork [a stream about twenty-five miles north of the Palo Duro].'

'Well, old man,' he answered, 'you are damned plain about it, but it is a fair proposition and I will do it.'

'I suppose,' Goodnight concluded, thinking of a bottle of fine French brandy in the guide's pack, 'that you boys have been on a long trip and might enjoy a good drink.'

'Just try us,' Dutch Henry said pleasantly.

They sealed the bargain with a drink, and parted good friends. While they never came in contact again, the outlaw kept his word and never gave Goodnight any trouble.

From Fort Elliott a partner of old Bill Koogle, a buffalo hunter, brought Goodnight to the head of Dry Creek, where he met one of his boys. He found his own property in good condition, and investigated the matter of the sheep and their owners. Finding no trace of identification, he again rode back to Las Animas, and at Pueblo gave the story of the killing and a description of the property to the local paper, and inserted a request that other Western papers should copy. Gradually the story sifted throughout the West.

John and Lew Casner were prospecting near Silver City, New Mexico, in company with an old Quantrell man named Berry, and another scrapper called Bell. It happened that neither of the Casners could read, but when one dropped into town for provisions, the merchant wrapped some articles in a paper containing the story. Back at camp the purchaser unwrapped the articles and pitched the paper down. Either Berry or Bell picked it up, happened to read the account of the killing, and the Casners knew it must be the other two boys. With their two friends they struck out for the Staked Plains, some weeks later arrived at the Home Ranch, where they easily satisfied Dyer that the property rightfully belonged to them, and upon its delivery made reward for its keep.

When Goodnight arrived in the summer, the Casners were running their sheep on McClellan Creek, nearby. He soon concluded that John and Lew were rather 'tough *hombres*,' and though Dave McCormick disagrees, the reader may judge for himself. Up the Tierra Blanca west of the Palo Duro, toward the New Mexico line, were a number of Mexican *pastores*, and the Casners decided to kill them all. Goodnight advised that he would permit no such outrage, and when told that they were going anyway, he simmered their tempers by saying that he would open up on them with his own men if they did. So instead, they rode over to Tascosa to commit a leed as wholly unjust.

By account they killed old Nicolas Martínez, who had avenged the original murders, claiming they found him in possession of some of the Casner effects. They hanged his wife by her thumbs, attempting to make her talk. They learned of the complicity of the Robbers' Roost band, and set out to get Goodanuff, its leader, who was supposed to have incited Sostenes to the murders. By the time they found him at Fort Elliott, he had heard they were on his trail, had given himself up to the military authorities, and was safely imprisoned in the post guard-house. When they demanded his delivery the authorities refused.

The Panhandle was then under the jurisdiction of Clay County, and recourse to legal procedure necessitated a trip to the border town of Henrietta, over two hundred miles to the

east and south. Bell and Berry went after the sheriff, who refused to come, but who deputized Berry to receive the prisoner
and deliver him at Henrietta. Berry presented his papers and
received not only the prisoner but a government ambulance to
haul him in, and an escort of five soldiers to help guard him —
greater generosity than he desired.

The first night out they camped twenty miles down Sweetwater Creek. About midnight several negro buffalo hunters
suddenly appeared at the camp, though negro buffalo hunters
had never been seen on the range before, pointed their big
Sharps guns at the party, and said they wanted to talk with the
prisoner alone. Next morning the innocent Berry and the excited soldiers found him tied to a cottonwood tree, 'but,' as
Dave McCormick concluded the story with a mighty pleased
look on his face, 'they tied him so high his feet wouldn't reach
the ground.'

During the winter, Hughes, who along with Johnston had
bought a slight interest in the cattle, kept a journal and trans-

mitted excerpts to his father in England. Some were published in English newspapers and helped to arouse English interest in the cow country. Upon the first of January, 1877, Hughes wrote of their new location, and observed that now

Everything went on much as usual — with the exception of two snow storms, one on November 13 and the other on November 22, as we had no house, and doing everything, especially getting out of bed, in a snow storm is 'bracing' to say the least of it — until December 11, when riding along down the river alone on 'Cubby,' I espied a bear. I immediately threw the persuaders into 'cubby' and ran him up to the bear.... I had ... only my six-shooter. I shot fourteen times before I got him to stop, but, I think, I only hit him three times. Shooting 'on the dead run' (the way they say 'at full gallop' out here) is very good fun and exciting.... On the 5th I struck 'an outfit' hunting a cattle range. They ... were thirty miles out of their reckoning, and they did not even know the name of our river, although they knew that it was somewhere in the country. The next day I struck two fellows hunting cows, or rather, traveling over the country on the spec. of finding cattle which a large company lost on the drive from Texas to Kansas.[4] ... On the 15th we finished the first room of our house, and so felt easy about future storms. On the 16th we went down the river to kill some turkeys for Christmas; ... we got fourteen....

On the 22d I washed all my clothes, a very great undertaking ... not having washed my clothes since we left the Canadian. On the 23d and 24th it snowed. We all shaved and 'greased up' with bear oil for Christmas — the only thing we could think of doing, as we had run out of all grub except flour; but then flour, bear, buffalo and turkey is pretty good living. On the 25th, Christmas Day, Ley started up-country to find what had become of our provisions, and corn for our horses, as they were overdue nearly a month. It snowed again on the 28th, and the snow is on the ground yet.... Yesterday we repeated the shaving and greasing-up for the new year.... They say Johnson and I look like 'winged outfits' about the head, as nobody wears side-whiskers out West.

[4] These were Frank McNabb and another Hunter and Evans cowboy. McNabb went into the Lincoln County War soon after this and was killed at the Spring Ranch, on the Bonito. D. R. McCormick to J. E. H., January 11, 1933; *Ford County Globe*, Dodge City, Kansas, May 14, 1878.

> ... I did hope to get off a letter in time for Christmas. These
> fellows, the lost cattle hunters, who in their travels of six weeks
> struck Fort Elliott, with the exception of which they never saw a
> white man till they came here, say it is one hundred miles any
> way you make it.... I don't think I told you about the first
> buffalo I killed. I was, luckily, on 'Cubby,' who, as you know, is
> my favorite and exclusively my own horse ('doesn't belong to
> the concern,' as Goodnight would say). I ran 'Cubby' right up
> alongside the buffalo, within about ten feet, and commenced
> firing with my six-sho ter. I brought him down at the sixteenth
> shot, having, of course, to load and throw out the shells 'on the
> dead run'; very exciting and jolly, and not at all dangerous, as
> long as you don't tumble off your horse at any sharp turn after
> the buffalo is wounded.[5]

And so the jolly son of the author of *Tom Brown's School Days*
learned the use of a six-shooter and the ways of the West.

Soon after locating, the outfit sent the cook to Trinidad for a
load of corn and provisions. The winter wore on with the cook
long past due, and finally the hands were 'out of provisions of
all kinds,' as Dave McCormick recalled, 'and lived on nothing
but meat for six weeks — bear, turkey, and buffalo. Often I'd
shoot a buffalo and take nothing but the tongue, the marrow
bones, and the tenderloins. I'd broil the tenderloins, roast the
marrow bones, and crack them. They were fine. I would bury
the tongue in the coals, roast it overnight, and tie it on my
saddle or put it in a *morral* and carry it along for lunch. Those
who used tobacco seemed to suffer most. At the ranch there
was a big mesquite stump in front of the mess-house that the
cook used to knock the grounds out of his coffee pot on, and
they had accumulated around it for weeks. The boys scraped
all of these up and smoked them.'

They learned later that the cook picked up a confederate at
Trinidad, and after starting on the return trip, decided to sell
the wagons, provisions, and teams, and light out. The theft
was discovered, and he was apprehended near Cañon City,
Colorado. Meanwhile, the boys in the cañon daily expected his
arrival until Walter Dyer came in from Pueblo, and Hughes
wrote the good news to his folks in England.

[5] Cox, *The Cattle Industry of Texas*, etc., 100–01.

Walter got into camp with letters and tobacco, so you can fancy what a jolly evening we had. You should have seen the boys going for the baccy — they got it off his saddle before he had time to get down.... Four days ago Ley and I started down the river on an exploring expedition, and he took it into his head to rope ... a buffalo. He threw his rope onto a buffalo cow, and

THE OLD HOME RANCH

shot her twice. The cow then commenced 'coming for' him, and his horse getting scared 'let into bucking,' and spilt Ley on a stump. He got very badly shaken, and can do nothing yet, but I hope there is nothing else wrong. For two or three hours he lay and could not move at all, and I had to move him when he had to change positions. The first thing he said was... 'I tell you, Hugh, this thing of life is a mighty uncertain kinder business.'

Things have never looked so well for us before, as now we have got the cattle into a place where they can hardly get out, and the only thing we have to fear are horse and cattle thieves.... In this life there is a very happy combination of business and pleasure, as a fellow is always running across game which other men have to hunt, and then very often don't get.[6]

Thus was founded the Old Home Ranch, first in the Panhandle-Plains country of Texas. Two hundred and fifty miles from a railroad and a base of supplies, a hundred miles from the

[6] Cox, as cited, 101.

nearest transient neighbors, in a land where a cowboy could ride for six weeks without seeing another white man, Goodnight chose a range that Nature had designed, fenced, sheltered, and watered. The Palo Duro Ranch, perhaps his greatest pioneer venture and the object of his dearest affections, was destined for unusual success.

XVIII. FOUNDING THE JA

AMONG prominent Britishers interested in Western range life was John George Adair, owner of a large estate at Rathdair, Ireland. After training for the diplomatic service he found the work not to his liking, and having a leaning for finance, instead, visited New York in 1866, established a brokerage firm, and prospered by negotiating large loans in England at a small rate of interest and lending to creditors in America at a high rate. About 1869 he married a remarkably attractive widow of New York, Cornelia Wadsworth Ritchie, whose ancestry for two hundred years before had claimed, and whose relatives for seventy years since have occupied, important places in American life.[1]

Both Adair and his wife had their share of sporting blood, and in 1874 they engaged in a hunt on the Kansas prairies in which Adair killed no buffalo, but did manage to shoot his saddle horse in the top of the head, killing the animal and almost himself. This trip seems to have interested him in Western life, and in 1875 he moved his brokerage business to Denver.

In March, 1876, Goodnight found it convenient to borrow thirty thousand dollars from Adair's agent, George W. Clayton, giving in security his lands near Pueblo, and paying interest at the rate of eighteen per cent a year. As the country gradually swung back from the depression of 1873, and popular interest

[1] The Wadsworths were prominent in early Connecticut, during the Revolutionary and Civil Wars. James W. Wadsworth carries on the tradition in New York. See H. T. Burton, *A History of the JA Ranch*, 17–23; Cornelia Adair, *My Diary*, August 30 to November 5, 1874; and H. G. Pearson, *James S. Wadsworth of Geneseo*.

in cattle and lands continued to mount, Adair became anxious to get into the cow business himself.

After running all over the country looking for a favorable situation, he came back to Denver, where, in 1877, his friends advised him that they knew of only one man to get, and, said Goodnight, 'they brought us together. I was very desirous of starting into the cattle business on a large scale, first to better my financial condition, but mainly to hire men enough to protect and sustain a business.' This meeting resulted in their decision to visit the Palo Duro together, and make plans for an extensive ranch.[2]

Mrs. Goodnight was in California awaiting the time when her husband's unsettled affairs would permit them to be together again. Goodnight was working back and forth from Colorado to the Panhandle, and for want of mail facilities, except by the hundred-mile ride to Fort Elliott and resort to government post, was able to communicate with her but infrequently. Dissatisfied with the arrangement, she wrote that she wished to come to the Panhandle, and finally advised her husband to meet her in Denver on a certain day, 'which, of course,' he said, 'gave me time to go to Trinidad horseback. She gave me the ultimatum either to leave the Panhandle and come out to civilization, or she would go to the ranch in the Palo Duro. By this time I had contracted to enter partnership with the Adairs, and could not honorably leave the Panhandle if I had wished to do so.'

'Very well,' she said, 'I will go home with you.'

Along with the Adairs they made their way to Trinidad, where they outfitted for the trip to the cañon. Goodnight bought a hundred head of the best Durham bulls in Colorado, loaded four wagons with six months' supply of provisions and equipment, secured a light ambulance, horses and hands, and set out. Six were in the party, besides two cowboys, who made much fun of the fact that they were starting a ranch with a herd of bulls.

[2] Goodnight, 'Recollections,' I, 21, and II, 121–22.

They crossed the Ratón Range, came down by Cimarrón Plaza, and from there launched into the wilderness. Mrs. Adair, an accomplished horsewoman, rode all the way, while Mrs. Goodnight drove the team to one of the wagons. They came south to the Canadian, crossing at Tascosa, which had

THE GOODNIGHT SIDE-SADDLE

just been founded, and passed south and east along the divide between that stream and the Palo Duro, aiming to describe a half-circle and enter the cañon from the northeast, opposite the Home Ranch. On the divide water was inaccessible because of the precipitous walls of the cañon, and the caravan was two days without. In the afternoon Goodnight said to his wife:

'Mary, we've got to reach water tonight. The cattle and mules are famishing. I am sure we are within ten miles of a pool of water, but we cannot afford to miss it a foot. We must reach it before dark, so I'll ride on ahead and locate it exactly, then come back and meet you. I want you to take charge of this outfit and keep everything moving. Watch me as far as you can see me and aim toward that point on the horizon where I disappear.'

He rode off and disappeared beyond the oval of the Plains, while the stock and teams wearily trailed along behind him. Then of a sudden one of the cowboys came up to Mrs. Goodnight in a long lope, and stated that he had seen Indians in the distance. She trained her field-glasses in the direction indicated, and apparently saw Indians bedecked in head-dresses, and on the warpath. Quickly they corralled the wagons, threw the stock inside, and made preparations for defense. The Indians came no nearer, so they decided the party had camped. Shortly before sundown, Goodnight, having located water, returned and found the wagons still within a mile of where he had left them.

'What in hell's the matter, Mary?' he swore in exasperation. 'What have you been doing here?'

'Oh! Charlie! Charlie! The Indians!' she cried. 'They are nearly out of sight now, but we were afraid to go any nearer.'

Goodnight took the field-glasses, glanced through them, and turned back impatiently.

'For God's sake, Mary, that bunch of Indians is nothing but a patch of bear grass in a mirage.'

Only one wagon succeeded in reaching the lake that night — the teams were unhooked and driven to water. After resting for two or three days they pushed on to the brink of the cañon, where the Adairs, who were in the lead, came hurrying back to Goodnight saying that through their 'glahses' they had discovered another bunch of Indians.

Goodnight observed that they were soldiers, likewise seen through a mirage. He did not understand their presence until Adair told him that he was expecting an escort, from Fort Elliott, for Mrs. Adair. In retrospection, Goodnight said:

'When we reached the cap-rock the bulls were put into the cañon, where they would need no herders, and all hands were put to road-building, keeping all within rifle range. The third day we reached the mesa which overlooked the entire cañon.

The large park below us held some thousand or fifteen hundred buffaloes grazing, at sundown.

'The night that followed I shall never forget. The volume of sound from a herd of buffaloes is great, and it being mating season, the sound was great, indeed, with numerous stampedes making it appear to be very close. Mrs. Goodnight, not being accustomed to such scenes, became greatly alarmed for fear they would run over the wagon. I utterly failed in convincing her that the herd was miles away. It began to rain. The down-pour was terrific, and the lightning a blaze of light, intense, with thousands of flashes on the wagon-sheet. While knowing it would be useless, I got up, to pacify her, and made a great fire with dry cedars, assuring her that buffaloes would be easier turned by a light than by a cavalry regiment.' [3]

Within a few days the party had built a trail which enabled them to get their wagons to the bottom. For many years the only wagon-road into the recesses of the cañon, it was four miles long in its meanderings from the cap-rock to the bed of the river. The Goodnight and Adair party camped at the ranch and put up at the two-room log cabin about the middle of May, 1877.[4]

Adair spent some time seeing the country and the cattle, and enjoying a frequent hunt for buffaloes on the Plains above the ranch. He came out to the corral one morning while the outfit was hastily catching mounts preparatory to getting off on a work down the cañon. Buffaloes were on his mind, and he called over to Si Sheek, who was roping horses: 'Si, catch me a horse.'

'All right, Mr. Adair, as soon as I can.'

Adair retreated to the ranch, but in a few minutes came out again, repeated the order, and then strode back to camp.

'Boys, catch Old Idaho,' Si directed.

[3] Goodnight, 'Recollections,' I, 7–8 and 21–23; Mrs. Phoebe K. Warner, 'The Wife of a Pioneer,' *The Cattleman*, March, 1921.

[4] According to a commemoration tablet at the JA headquarters, Goodnight entered the Palo Duro with his herd, October 23, 1876, and the Adair party came May 15, of the next year.

Now, Old Idaho was an outlaw horse that never failed to throw a wall-eyed fit and pitch all over the country every time he was saddled. They roped him out of the *remuda*, and pulled him up to the snubbing-post in the middle of the corral tc saddle him. They threw Adair's 'slick fork' into place, tied

THE ADAIRS

his cannon beneath the stirrup leather, hitched Idaho to the fence, and in spite of their hurry, retreated into the cedars beyond the corral to watch the fun. When Adair returned, rigged out for his buffalo hunt, Old Idaho eyed him suspiciously, shied to one side, and snorted like a mustang stud. Goodnight had honestly advised Adair that there was much harmless snorting in the Texas cow-horses, and so he innocently threw the reins over the horse's neck, wallowed into the saddle, and, Si Sheek sadly concluded, 'If Old Idaho didn't stand perfectly still until he got on, and walk off like the gentlest horse in the world, then I'm not sittin' here.'

In spite of frequent clashes between the conventionalism of the Old World and the freedom of the New, the inspection of the lands and cattle went forward, and after two weeks Adair was ready to leave. The outfit had moved out on the Plains and was camped near the Koogle Jump-Off, above the present JA headquarters, when the final unpleasantry came.

In the course of their work, Hughes and Dyer, Goodnight's brother-in-law, had fallen out, after which Hughes advised Adair that Dyer was stealing from Goodnight. In Hughes's presence Adair mentioned the matter to the cowman, who asked his authority for the charge. Adair refused to divulge his source, and Goodnight, in mounting anger, replied:

'We Southerners expect a man who makes any such statement to cite his authority, and if he refuses, we figure he's a damned liar on his own account.'

Thus they passed the matter up, but when he was ninety-three years old, Goodnight would berate himself in reminiscence:

'He was an overbearing old son-of-a-gun, and would have been beat up several times if it hadn't been for me. I don't see why I took it. I ought to have challenged him to fight, and if he wouldn't, I should have pulled him off his horse and beaten him up.'

When the tally was complete, Adair departed for civilization, and left the cowboys to the peaceful pursuit of keeping out buffaloes and riding line against outlaws and Indians. They all breathed easier after he was gone, though the prejudice that caused the ill-feeling was not one-sided.

June 18, 1877, the Adair and Goodnight partnership was effected, a five-year agreement providing that Adair should finance the enterprise while Goodnight should furnish the foundation herd and direct the ranch. He was to receive a salary of twenty-five hundred dollars, which, along with operating expenses, was to be paid from current proceeds. He suggested the JA brand, Adair's connected initials, and agreed that the herd might be limited to fifteen thousand, if desired. Additional cattle and twenty-five thousand acres of land should be bought, all with cash; Adair's investment, with ten per cent interest, was to be repaid in full; and at the end of five years the residual properties divided, one third going to Goodnight and two thirds to Adair. Adair further agreed to withdraw no money from the enterprise until the contract expired.

Apparently Goodnight was making a reckless bargain to assure himself the means of extensive operations, and though he observed that 'it was mighty high interest...I did not mind it, because I knew I had a fortune made.' In looking ahead to the day of settlement, he attempted to induce some of his best trail hands to come to Texas with him. One objected that there was 'too much land and too few people,' but Goodnight replied, 'the land will stay and the people will come.' By the end of the five-year contract his prophecy had come true.[5]

Almost coincident with the formation of the Adair–Goodnight partnership was the appearance of Jot Gunter in the Palo Duro, noted land man of the firm of Gunter, Munson and Summerfield, surveyors and locators, of Sherman, Texas. He seems to have put in a blanket survey covering most of the cañon, and Goodnight's original negotiations for land naturally took place with him.

Texas, owning her own lands, had granted certificates to railroads, corporations, and individuals for millions of acres, such certificates to be located by the grantee upon any of the

[5] Contract between John G. Adair and Charles Goodnight, June 18, 1877, copy in files of author; Burton, as cited, 27; W. A. Bronaugh to Charles Goodnight, November 19, 1929.

unclaimed domain. Throughout the seventies there developed an extremely active trade in lands and certificates, and this firm was among the largest speculators in the field. Gunter and John Summerfield, the surveyor, looked after their interests on the frontier, while W. B. Munson, the lawyer, devoted his time to the office. They located certificates at a specified rate per section, and often took their pay in kind, locating one certificate in turn for another. They virtually cornered the market, and Goodnight found that the firm had surveyed him in. But his splendid judgment of the necessities of a successful range stood him in good stead, and in meeting the provision for the initial purchase of twenty-five thousand acres, assured the great success of the JA Ranch. He has himself told the story of his negotiations with the astute Gunter:

'To begin with, Adair furnished only money enough to buy twelve thousand acres. I knew that would not monopolize the ranch business on the Palo Duro, but I wanted to stay. However, the bad part of it was that Adair got mixed up with Gunter and Munson, and they were too smart for him, and the result was that they tried to hold me up for one dollar and twenty-five cents an acre. I had to get it through them or take my chances, and I *wanted that cañon*. I finally got them down to six-bits, and closed for twelve thousand acres, provided they would let me set the compass and they would run it. That is where the *Old Crazy Quilt* comes in. I took all the good land and all the water I could get, and under the contract they were to let me designate twelve thousand acres more that I was to take the next year at my option. Well, I scattered that all over the Palo Duro Cañon; every good ranch in the country, every place a man was liable to come, I took. It cost like the devil to survey it. We surveyed for four or five days, and Gunter got to kicking and said:

'"Why don't you take *this* land?"

'"I don't want it," I said.

'"I ain't going to run this outfit all winter for you."

'"You contracted to, didn't you?"

'"No, I didn't."

'"You had better get your contract out and read it." It stated just what I claimed.

'"Now, Jot," I said, "behave yourself and get along with the contract and I'll tell you where you can get another chunk of country. There's a country over there at Quitaque that is vacant."

'"That ain't vacant," he said.

'"I know it is. It's the next best thing on earth, and you can locate that with these certificates you have and make a fortune."

'"I'll do it," he said.

'Well, we ran all over this country, and kept surveying, and designating, and taking, spotting it up so they couldn't sell it to anybody else. And then he entered into a contract with me that he wouldn't sell to a cattleman unless he bought a ranch.

'"Now, if you'll go into this," I said, "and not sell to a cattleman unless he buys a ranch instead of a section or two, I'll make this the best country in the world."' [6]

Adair soon authorized Goodnight to make more extensive purchases than the contract called for, and he said:

'I bought land anywhere and everywhere I could get it, provided I could get it right. I paid different prices for it. Some land cost me twenty cents per acre, some twenty-five, some thirty, and some thirty-five cents per acre. The largest amount I ever bought at one time was one hundred and seventy thousand acres in the Tule country at twenty cents per acre, which necessitated the formation of the Tule Ranch.'

For awhile Goodnight and his outfit had a camp on Turkey Creek, but as the need of range arose they extended their lines down the cañon, and in 1878 established a camp at the spring where the present JA headquarters stands, another on

---

[6] Burton, as cited, 33–34. This apparently arbitrary action was designed to prevent speculators from acquiring small tracts inside a range and extorting fancy prices from the established cowmen.

Battle Creek named for hard-working, reckless Frank Mitchell, and another on the Mulberry; border outposts 'whose responsibilities were twofold — curtailing the wanderings of stray cattle and watching for rustlers.'

Goodnight and his cowboys settled down for the second winter in the Palo Duro with Mrs. Goodnight to share their troubles. She patched their clothes, sewed on the buttons, doctored the sick and injured, and sympathized with those rough but tender-hearted cowboys, isolated by the Plains. Her first woman neighbor was the wife of T. S. Bugbee, the second ranchman of the Panhandle, who came in on the Canadian, about eighty miles to the north, a few months after Goodnight. 'For six months she and Mrs. Goodnight lived the most isolated life I have ever known in all my frontier experience,' said Goodnight. 'Neither could have seen any women associates for from six to twelve months, but they both claim those to be among their happiest days.' Goodnight arranged for Cape Willingham to bring his wife and two children to the Panhandle, but the first women who entered the cañon after Mrs. Goodnight were Comanche squaws, with Quanah Parker's band.

The solitude and the wind were trying for a woman, and it was quite a domestic blessing when one day a cowboy rode in with three chickens in a sack.

'No one can ever know how much pleasure and company they were to me,' Mrs. Goodnight once said. 'They were something I could talk to, they would run to me when I called them, and follow me everywhere I went. They knew me and tried to talk to me in their language. If there had been no outside dangers, the loneliness would not have been bad.' [7]

By the fall of 1877, other ranchmen were coming into the country; besides Bugbee were Bates and Beals, H. W. Cresswell, George W. Littlefield, Mose Hays, the Reynolds brothers, and others on the Canadian. Fort Elliott was well established, with Hide Town, which was first called Sweet-

[7] Phoebe K. Warner, 'The Wife of a Pioneer Ranchman,' as cited, 67–71.

water, and then Mobeetie, growing up on the creek below it. Tascosa expanded in the western Panhandle, and the next year, 1878, L. H. Carhart, a Christian preacher who speculated in lands, established a prohibition settlement in Donley County, and called it Clarendon, after his wife.

CATTLE ON THE BUFFALO RANGE

All went well until the fall of 1878, when a large band of Indians left the Territorial Reserves and headed back into Texas, ostensibly upon a buffalo hunt. They passed Fort Elliott and struck into the cañons of the Palo Duro, expecting to find game on the way. Five years before, the killing of the vast herds had got into good swing, and in spite of its serious interruption by the Indian battle at Adobe Walls in 1874, the slaughter was practically done by the winter of 1878. Disappointed at not finding game, and having many hungry mouths to feed, the Indians found and began killing JA cattle in the lower reaches of the Palo Duro.

The line riders on the east side 'sent me a runner,' said Goodnight, 'stating that Indians were coming in considerable numbers. I at once mounted a good horse and started to meet them.

'The weather was bitter cold, with snow on the ground. Before I could meet the Indians, they had entered the cañon, where they split into three bands. There being no buffaloes at this late year, they were killing cattle at a fearful rate. The Kiowas seemed to be in one band, with two bunches of Comanches co-operating. When I met the Kiowas, they were in an ugly mood, and it looked like trouble. I met one bunch of them north of the Tule, another on the Tule, and Quanah and the Comanches passed up the cañon behind me while I was after these. I followed them up, and at sundown found them making camp in the main cañon, five or six miles below the ranch. I rode up and inquired for the *principal*, as among them were a renegade Mexican and a *captiva*, a woman captive, who spoke beautiful Spanish. Designated as the *capitán*, Quanah, upon my asking his name, made this reply: "Maybe so two names — Mr. Parker or Quanah." Quanah meant odor or perfume, and he was named from the fact that he was born on the prairie, among the flowers.

'I told Quanah I wanted him at headquarters, up the cañon, for the purpose of making a treaty. He pointed out that it was late, his ponies worn, and his papooses tired, but agreed to report in the morning. In the forenoon the setting for the parley was laid. They came up, ten or twelve of the old heads and a few of the young ones. Eight or ten of the outstanding braves were selected as inquisitors. They formed a circle and the interpreter and I were in the middle.

'"Don't you know this country is ours?" one asked. I answered that I had heard they claimed the country, but that the great Captain of Texas also claimed it, and was making me pay for it, as they could see by the land corners they had passed. The controversy, I declared, was a matter between them and the State of Texas, and if they owned the land, I was quite willing to settle with them. Quanah said this was fair.

'"Where are you from?" they asked. "Are you a *Tejano?*" Knowing their bitterness toward the Texans, and knowing that they knew little about the United States as a whole, I told them I was from Colorado — which was in a sense true. I was in a trying position, never knowing from which inquisitor would come the next question.

'"What are you doing here?" and every face was on me.

'"Raising cattle."

'"Aren't you killing buffaloes?"

'"No."

'"Aren't you killing them to eat?"

'"No. I have plenty of fat cattle, and buffaloes aren't much good."

'Then, being suspicious, they started in to prove whether I was a Texan or not by testing my knowledge of the Western country.

'"What are the nearest mountains?" they asked.

'"Sierras de Ratónes," I answered.

'Then they asked me where the Cimarrón was; the Capulín; the Tucumcari. Finally they questioned me about the Pecos River, and what I had been doing on it, saying that they used to handle cattle on that stream.

'"Yes," I said, "you damned pups licked me once and stole my cattle."

'Though this was a false statement, the interpreter translated it, and they just roared. They were finally convinced that I was "*no Tejano*" and said they were ready to negotiate a treaty.

'"What have you got to offer?" they asked.

'"I've got plenty of guns and plenty of bullets, good men and good shots, but I don't want to fight unless you force me." Then, pointing to Quanah, I said:

'"You keep order and behave yourself, protect my property and let it alone, and I'll give you two beeves every other day until you find out where the buffaloes are."'

And so they treated and settled down together in perfect peace. The cowman kept his word in regard to the beeves, and Quanah — ? Goodnight says he never knew an Indian who failed to keep his.

The Kiowas were in an uglier mood, and Goodnight dispatched Frank Mitchell to report the outbreak at Fort Elliott. Mrs. Goodnight, fearing for the boy, asked her husband to send an older man. He refused, saying that Frank was light, and durable, and could ride farther than a man. Early next

QUANAH PARKER

morning, Mitchell crossed the parade ground and handed Goodnight's message to the commander of the post, John P., 'Dobe,' Hatch. Meanwhile, the citizens of Clarendon were agitated, and petitioned the Government for protection from 'about two thousand Indians in this part of Texas.'

On December 29, Lieutenant A. M. Patch started to the Palo Duro with a detachment of cavalry, and a few days later loped up to the ranch. When Quanah saw them, he turned a little whiter, and asked Goodnight their business, which question the other evaded.

Patch rode up and asked what he should do.

'Get down,' advised the cowman, 'and turn your horses loose.'

'Without guard?' he said.

'Yes,' came the reply. 'I've reached an agreement with them, and they won't bother your horses.'

'They would court-martial me for that,' he said.

'Well, what are your orders?'

Patch reached in his pocket and handed them to Goodnight, who read that the soldiers were to report to him for orders.

'All right,' added Goodnight, 'get down and turn your horses loose.'

Patch did so, and on the twenty-second of January, 1879, reported back to his adjutant the status of Indian affairs on the JA Ranch. At the head of Battle Creek were fifty Apaches under the chief, Taho; at and around the Home Ranch were sixty-four Comanches under Quanah, and sixty-seven Kiowas under Tapedeah; and seventeen Pawnees under Spotted Horse and Running Chief were camped at the mouth of Cañoncito Blanco. Six more Comanches and squaws were reported farther up the cañon, and Patch believed there were not more than two hundred and fifty in all the Panhandle, though two hundred and sixty-three Comanches alone had just passed an army camp on Buck Creek, to the east, on their way back to the Territory.

The chiefs complained bitterly of the agencies, saying they were hungry and wished to hunt buffaloes. Quanah assured Goodnight that he had no intention of returning, and though he kept the Indians in check, he continued living on the cowman's bounty, while making no effort to conceal his contempt for Patch's negro troopers.

Down the cañon and on the Mulberry, the Kiowas were causing the cowboys some worry, particularly a little band under an old Indian called White Wolf, who wanted to be neighborly with Frank Mitchell and Jake Quick — an experienced old frontiersman who had worked for the Bents, in Colorado — who were keeping camp together.

'White Wolf stayed until spring,' Mitchell said. 'He had three squaws with him, one of whom he offered to Jake, and said he had a sixteen-year-old girl at Fort Sill that he would give to me. Before leaving, they wanted to give a big feast for us, but I had to ride my line that day, and Jake, who could eat half a beef in a week, explained that he had stomach trouble, and the doctor had told him not to eat meat. So they left with their dogs and we missed the feast.'

JAKE QUICK

Captain Nicholas Nolan came to the ranch with a detachment of the Tenth Cavalry, and began negotiations with the Indians for their peaceful return to the Territory. White Wolf tardily arrived at the tent where he was holding a pow-wow, and stood at the flap a few minutes before being noticed. Finally Nolan observed his arrival, and advised him, through McClusky, his interpreter, to be seated on a stool. Somewhat nettled, White Wolf squatted to the ground, saying:

'Tell the white chief that the earth's my mother, and I'll sit on her bosom.'

Inside two weeks the Indians agreed to return with the troops, which brought to an end their last large migration into the Panhandle. Goodnight cherished his friendship with Quanah until the chieftain's death in 1910, and to the end of his own life was a benefactor of the red men in a country he had wrested from them! This may be the irony of history, though the way of the truly brave![8]

[8] Goodnight, 'True Sketch of Quanah Parker's Life,' *Southwest Plainsman*, August 7, 1926; Goodnight to J. E. H., November 13, 1926; April 8, 1927, and September 29, 1929; Goodnight, 'Recollections,' I, 50; II, 22, 26–27; Burton, as cited, 14–17; *Frontier Times*, December, 1926, p. 42. Frank Mitchell to J. E. H., December 22, 1929; Silas Sheek to J. E. H., January 23, 1932; *Farm and Ranch*, April 17, 1926, pp. 2 and 22; Petition of Citizens of Clarendon, December 30, 1878; Nicholas Nolan to Post Adjutant, Fort Sill, I.T., January 8, 1879; John A. Wilcox to Assistant Adjutant General, Fort Leavenworth, January 17, 1879; A. M. Patch to Post Adjutant, Fort Elliott, January 22, 1879; all in the Adjutant General's Office, Austin, Texas.

THE JA Ranch entered upon a period of expansion, intensive organization, and remarkable growth in range and in herd. In spite of further Indian scares, the spring came peacefully enough, and the restless Goodnight was in his element and at his prime as a range manager. By the time he needed more grass, the hunters had killed out the buffaloes, though for two years afterward the JA's had all the well-cured, wild beef they could use.

Settlement of the Panhandle, which had begun from the northwest, now flowed from the east, and the natural outlet to the world was through Henrietta in that direction, and Dodge City on the north. Goodnight decided to move head-quarters twenty-five rough miles nearer the eastern, outside world, the railroad and supplies. George Osborne, a Casner associate, cut the logs for the new ranch-house, and Goodnight, an old master at the work, so carefully mortised their ends that the results of his skill can still be seen, as stable today as when done in 1879.

After leaving the JA's, Leigh Dyer moved the Baker bro-thers' herd into the Quitaque country, directly to the south, and then left to go into business for himself at the junction of the Tierra Blanca and the Palo Duro. There Archie Argo helped build a cedar-log house in the winter of 1877-78, which pre-emption, a year or two later, was relinquished to Gunter, Munson, and Summerfield, who owned the surrounding range and started the GMS. This ranch soon became the well-known T Anchor. Dyer moved down Red River, below Goodnight, and joined L. G. Coleman in founding the Shoe Bars. And yet, except for the village of Clarendon, there were few neighbors between the Palo Duro and Bugbee's Quarter Circle T's, on the Canadian.

In addition to the two-room log house for himself and wife, Goodnight had dugouts made for the boys, another for the cook and his wife, a shop for the blacksmith, and work was soon started on a big bunk-house and mess-house combined. Barns and corrals were built, and eventually the great rock house was constructed for the use of the Adairs and the manager of the properties.

Near the headquarters the cap-rock recedes to the north, and fifteen miles or more away to the south is a point of the High Plains called Schott Hill, where the other rim of the cañon recedes southward toward the head-breaks of Little Red and the Quitaque. The headquarters stands at the upper lip of the broad mouth of the Palo Duro Cañon, looking eastward across seven miles of short-grass tableland known as Mulberry Flat, which is bounded on the north by broken badlands, on the east by Mulberry Creek, and on the south by Battle Creek and Griffin Hills — long, grass-covered ridges that divide the good waters from the bad. Away down in Hall County, Deep Lake was, roughly, the far boundary of their range. From headquarters east the country assumes a gentler tone, but back up the cañon the original range is so rough the ordinary cowboy can't find his saddle-seat with a forked stick.

Besides the original supplies brought from Pueblo and Las Animas, provisions for the ranch were freighted by ox-team from Trinidad. When the outfit again exhausted its supply of flour, the boys lived upon beef for six weeks, roasting liver until it was perfectly dry, and eating it in place of bread. Finally, Frank Mitchell took a boy and a four-mule team and set out to meet the long overdue freight outfit, which, luckily, they encountered on the Plains west of Amarillo Lake, and soon sour-dough was brewing in the kegs again.

After 1880, the ranch began getting its supplies from Lee and Reynolds, sutlers at Fort Elliott, who operated extensively in the government and the buffalo and cattle range trade. They had immense crews, working a thousand head of steers when grass was rising, and six hundred mules when

MULE-FREIGHT

snow began to fly, and did most of the hauling for the Panhandle country. Goodnight contracted their delivery of six months' supplies for fifty men, corn for a hundred horses, and sixty-seven miles of barbed wire at the ranch from Dodge City, promising, in part payment, to load them back with cedar logs. Ten drivers swarmed into headquarters with thirty wagons loaded to the bows, and the cedars they took on the return trip left the Mulberry barren of its noblest trees, and Goodnight sick at heart over the devastation. Their wagons cut a distinct road from the Palo Duro to Fort Elliott, and the logs were used in the post there.[1] Already the Panhandle-Plains were throbbing with life, and in 1881 freighters were spoken of as the 'scarcest article in the Panhandle.' Though Hamburg and Company alone kept a bull train continually on the road to Dodge City, hauling one hundred and forty thousand pounds at a load, and making a round trip

[1] Goodnight to J. E. H., April 8, 1927; *Ford County Globe*, March 19, 1878, and July 1, 1879.

every twenty-four days, they could not meet the needs of booming Mobeetie.[2]

After the Texas and Pacific Railroad reached Colorado City, in 1881, supplies were sometimes freighted from there, but when the Fort Worth and Denver reached Wichita Falls the next year, that village became the point of supply for the JA's. At first there were two classes of freight; mule in the winter and ox in the summer. Oxen were far better if subsisting on grass alone; but during the winter mules foraged and were fed besides. The regular rate of ox-freight was one cent per hundred pounds per mile, and at Tascosa the merchants explained that merely the high cost of freight made ordinary sewing needles sell for ten cents apiece. If a hundred pounds of corn cost a dollar at Dodge, it cost three dollars and a half laid down at the ranch.

With the late seventies and early eighties a new day was dawning for the cattle industry of the West — the day of foreign investments, improvement in breeds, artificial watering facilities, barbed-wire fencing, and permanent ranges owned in fee. Goodnight had read the signs long before, and again moved in the lead.

In accord with the original plan, he bought cattle upon the trail and off the range, adding to his own herd in the Palo Duro. He segregated his blooded cattle from the first, retaining them in the upper reaches of the cañon, placing his best bulls there, and culling out his inferior stock to place with the common or main herd. Cattle bought from the outside were carefully culled. Serviceable cows were placed in the main herd while inferior grades were cut out, spayed, fattened on the range, and trailed to market with the beef herds in the fall. Thus, by cutting at both ends, Goodnight doubled the speed of improvement of his herds.

A number of the first cowmen coming from Colorado had well-bred shorthorn cattle, and some, like Goodnight, brought fine bulls of the same breed. J. L. Driskill and Sons placed

[2] *Fort Griffin Echo*, September 17, 1881.

imported sires on their Cimarrón Ranch in 1880, and Cresswell, Bugbee, and others ran beef breeds far superior to the
old Texas longhorn. In the spring of 1881, Goodnight bought
two hundred head of registered shorthorn bulls and three

JUD CAMPBELL

hundred heifers at Burlingame, Kansas. O. H. Nelson, noted
breeder, shipped them to Dodge City, where they were met by
Jud Campbell, Goodnight's trail foreman, and headed south.
Upon meeting a South Texas trail herd on Wolf Creek, and
knowing the danger of Texas fever to high-grade cattle,
Campbell thought up 'the only sensible thing he ever did
while working for me,' said Goodnight. He turned his herd
into Wolf Creek and drove straight upstream until he was
west of the trail left by the Texas cattle, thus avoiding con-

tagion. And so with the basic Texas stock, Goodnight continued grading with Durham sires, realizing blockier and heavier
animals, with good beef qualities.

Though a strong believer in blooded cattle, he early decided
that the pure-bred shorthorn was not best adapted to that
range. In the winter of 1871, he had seen some Aberdeen
Angus on the Laramie Plains, and though lots of cattle froze
in that high cold country, these black polls came through with
straight backs and good flesh. Upon inquiry he learned that
foundation stocks were scarce and high, and he turned to the
Hereford. At Las Animas, in 1876, he had first seen a few
inferior Herefords belonging to T. L. Miller, who attempted
to sell them to Goodnight, and who 'got as hot as a wolf'
when the latter turned them down with the remark that his
'damned cattle were no good.'

It is said that upon a trip to the Philadelphia Centennial
in 1876, W. S. Ikard, of Henrietta, became interested in the
breed, and a few years later brought the first Herefords to
Texas, though this honor is contested by an early importation
by William Powell. Powell told Nelson of bringing five head
to Fort Worth in 1878 that he almost had to give away; Lee
and Reynolds brought seven carloads of Herefords to their
LE Ranch, west of Tascosa, in the summer of 1880; Towers and
Gudgell, of West Las Animas, placed a few Herefords on the
Cimarrón in 1881; and the next year Nelson threw a bunch
upon the JA range. In 1883 he brought a fine herd to the
upper Tule, and located it near 'Mackenzie's old boneyard.'
In this bunch were twenty-five bulls for which he had paid
two hundred and fifty dollars each, about six hundred and
twenty-five cows, and some four hundred calves. Goodnight
went out from the JA's to look at them, and agreed to take
the lot at seventy-five dollars around, counting calves. As a
sandstorm was blowing, they waited to count the herd, and
seven more calves were on the ground next morning, provoking
from Goodnight the terse observation of 'a damned expensive
night.'

Many old Texans wagged their heads at such prices, and the suspicious know-it-alls felt sure that the two were conniving to 'skin' Adair out of some money. Yet these herds proved to be the cheapest the ranch ever bought, for they early established the quality of the JA cattle, the first in the

DYER'S DEHORNING

country to sell as high as twenty dollars as yearlings. One registered cow in the bunch that would fight a circular saw had killed a couple of horses, and Sam Dyer, who was put to herding, roped her and chopped off her horns. When she was nineteen years of age, she was seen on the Quitaque with a big fat calf at her side.

In eight years Nelson imported over ten thousand purebred bulls to the Panhandle, thereby doing more than any one man, perhaps, to establish the breed on the Great Plains, and earning for himself the nickname of 'Bull.' In the meantime, Goodnight proceeded with the improvement of the JA blood; as a range breeder he came to be recognized as a man without a peer, and he is generally accredited, as Alvin H.

Sanders records in his *Story of the Herefords,* with revolutionizing the blood of the Panhandle.

Goodnight always felt sure that the best beef herd he ever had was that on the JA's after the lapse of eleven years. The trace of the Texas stock contributing trail, open-range, self-reliant characteristics, with the shorthorn blood adding extra weight and bone to the dominant Hereford strain, was a beef combination, he felt, that has never been excelled among the highest bred cattle of later years.³ In spite of a few scattered champions of the Aberdeen Angus, the Great Plains, today, is predominantly a white-faced country.

Along with the improvement of range breeds came the barbed-wire fence, and no one factor in the West so affected the grading of cattle as did wire, for with enclosed ranges each man had exclusive use of the fine sires he placed with his cows. Before fencing, each outfit maintained its established lines by camps, riders daily patrolling to hold in the home herd, and to keep out neighboring or stray brands.

Early ranches suffered severely from the blue blizzards of the High Plains, and the winter of 1880 drifted cattle far from their home ranges, covering the Panhandle with thousands from the Arkansas and the Platte country, hundreds of miles away. With spring, outfits came from Kansas, Nebraska, and Colorado, and outside men even from Wyoming, to join the general works on the Canadian and the Red. In turn ranchmen there were sending men to the Blanco, Brazos, and Colorado country, to bring back their drifts and save their calves. Many of them maintained floaters, or floating outfits — chuck-wagons with a few men, grub and horse feed — that floated around the range catching and bringing back, after the abatement of blizzards, the drifts that broke through their line riders.

Drifts from an open country piled up in sheltered places,

³ Goodnight to J. E. H., May 22, 1929; O. H. Nelson to J. E. H., same date, and February 26, 1927; *Fort Griffin Echo,* November 27, 1880, and November 19, 1881. *Ford County Globe,* August 10, 1880, November 1, 1881, May 1 and December 11, 1883.

and the Canadian and Red River were eaten clean by cattle that came in with the storms. The first fences of note were drift fences, to hold back cattle from, or within, a given range, and perhaps the most famous of all was that built, largely in

1882, by co-operating ranchmen north of the Canadian. It spanned the Panhandle from east to west for approximately two hundred miles, and saved the grass of the Canadian the next severe season, 1884, but its length was a chain of carcasses where entire herds drifted into it to starve and freeze to death.

Probably the first bit of wire fencing in the Panhandle-Plains country was a short line across the bed of the cañon above the Home Ranch, which cut off that portion of the range for the JJ, or pure-bred herd, and served besides as a weaning pasture for the calves. In 1881 and 1882, the T Anchor put up the first big enclosure, fencing in two hundred and forty thousand acres of grass, with posts eighty feet apart, so that when mustangs and antelopes hit the fence full tilt, the wires would 'give' considerably instead of breaking. Then Goodnight began erecting a sixty-mile drift fence from the edge of the Plains, near the Armstrong County line, along the divide between Salt Fork and Mulberry, to Coleman and Dyer's Shoe Bar range on the east. When connected with the Shoe Bar fence, which ran east by south to near the site of Memphis, it was a hundred miles long. The first fall after its completion, a blizzard drifted herds of antelopes into a pocket of the fence, and the settlers at Clarendon killed fifteen hundred of them. Bates and Beals, of the LX's, lost three hundred cattle against it, and in one blizzard twenty-five to thirty thousand head streamed down from the north. The Plains lakes were frozen, and the JA cowboys were sent to water the drifts on the Mulberry, and after the storm to throw them back upon the Plains. Spring came early, the depressions were full of lake grass, and by the last of March these cattle were fat.

Goodnight fenced the Quitaque Ranch in 1883 — the freighters bringing out wire and profiting on return loads of buffalo bones — and the Tule in 1884 and 1885. Throughout the early eighties fencing spread far and wide, and the land that had once been free and open passed into the limbo of the good old days, while men turned their attention to long-time leases and ownership in fee. Despite its excessive cost, the prejudice against it, the troubles it caused, and the revolution it wrought in the life of the West, 'bobbed' wire had come to stay. One amusing and somewhat pathetic incident is significant of the passing of a life that was high, wide, and lonesome.

For years the Pueblo Indians had made periodical buffalo hunts to the Plains to supply themselves with robes, with meat, and especially with tallow for their religious rites, and hence knew the land thoroughly. Soon after cowmen began stringing the range with wire, the old Taos chieftain, Standing Deer, dropped into the village of Clarendon upon his return from a trading trip with the Kiowas. He was having difficulty finding his way, and the Clarendon settlers, knowing nothing of Indians, thought his men were Comanches and were about to kill them. The Casners were working in the lead, and there was great excitement just as Goodnight happened in, rode up behind the party, and sat unnoticed for a few minutes as the wrangling continued. The chief was trying to tell the settlers, who understood no Spanish, that he was not a Comanche, and was asking for Goodnight and telling his excited listeners, without avail, that: '*Yo conozco un hombre se llama Buenas Noches. El tiene muchas vacas, muchos caballos, y muchas todas.... —* I know a man called Goodnight. He has many cows, many horses, and much of everything....' But the mob understood no more of this, and apparently would have killed the Pueblos if Goodnight had not appeared, and called Standing Deer by name. The old man's face brightened with joy as he turned and recognized the cowman, who explained to the settlers that these were not warriors but peaceful Taos Indians.

Standing Deer asked a question that dumbfounded him: 'How do you get back to Taos?'

'You surely know the way back to Taos,' answered Goodnight. 'Haven't you lived in this country all your life?'

'*Si, señor!*' answered the Indian. '*Pero alambre! alambre! alambre! todas partes!* — but wire! wire! wire! everywhere!'[4]

In 1877, Goodnight began buying lands up and down the cañon. He realized that the twenty-five thousand acres called for in the Adair contract would not command the range the partnership needed. Knowing it was a good time to buy, he pressed the matter with Adair, and by 1882 they had bought ninety-three thousand acres and were ready to buy more. Besides these purchases, Goodnight had bought the Quitaque, the fine range adjacent to the south, for Mrs. Adair. At the time of the purchase, O. J. Wiren, the manager, and two Wisconsin lumber men, Kellogg and McCoy, were partners in the business. They branded the Lazy F, the Square-Topped Hat, and the Dipper. Some one hundred and forty thousand acres were bought at twenty-two cents an acre, but the ranch, approximately thirty-five miles square, contained about twice this much land, as the alternate sections still belonged to the State. Delivery was not effected without high feeling on either side.

---

[4] Goodnight to J. E. H., April 8, 1927, and September 30, 1929; R. E. Baird to J. E. H. June 26, 1926; L. Gough and Vas Stickley to J. E. H.; Burton, as cited, 92.

Goodnight considered Kellogg and McCoy as straight as a string, but he had little faith in Wiren. After the contract for the purchase of the Lazy F's was signed in 1880, cattle advanced sharply in price before delivery was made, and it was rumored that Wiren planned to break the contract by squeezing the cattle in on Goodnight faster than he could receive them,

and then declare the deal off. Goodnight took his hands, constructed a big corral with a long chute, and at the beginning of the delivery put his best men at the irons and trained hands in the crowding pen. In the spring of 1881, Colonel McCoy was on hand, the irons were hot, and Wiren, handling the Quitaque outfit, had two thousand head of cattle bawling at the gates. With hot bars the Palo Duro hands tallied each animal as the chute was jammed full, and counted them out at the end into another corral, so that in case of a miscount they could immediately be counted again. Goodnight watched Wiren like a hawk and drove him relentlessly. If he made a mistake in the count, Goodnight suspected his doing so on purpose, and rimmed him out unmercifully:

'If you can't count,' he would yell, 'get to hell out of there and get somebody that can!'

And so, amid the heat and roar of the corral, the din of bawling cattle and shouting men, the fogs of pungent smoke, and the flash of cherry hot irons through the bars of the chute, the evening, as we say in Texas, wore on, but long before night the two thousand cattle were branded and out on the range. Goodnight turned to Wiren:

'Why in the hell don't you have some more cattle here? Where are they? Farrington, get your outfit out there and help that son-of-a-bitch bring in some cattle.'

Wiren knew that he had met his match, and old Colonel McCoy, watching from the top rail of the fence, called down to the buyer:

'Goodnight, they can say what they want to, but you know your business.'

And so Goodnight bought the Quitaque and the Lazy F cattle for Mrs. Adair, and protected her interests throughout the deal. According to the JA contract, Adair was to draw no money from the enterprise during the term of agreement, but after purchasing the Quitaque he declined to advance the needed money, and advised Goodnight to pay for it out of the earnings of the JA's. This, to the amount of about one hundred thousand dollars was done. Goodnight resented the breach of contract, but paid the money and never recovered his share.

In 1883, Goodnight bought the Tule Ranch as an addition to the JA properties, though it was organized and administered as a separate division. He purchased one hundred and seventy thousand acres of beautiful cañon and adjacent Plains land, established headquarters on Tule Cañon, about twelve miles east of the site of Tulia, and began fencing it. Other lands were bought from Gunter and Munson, from railroads, and from the State, and the combined ranches grew to more than 1,335,000 acres, ranging above one hundred thousand cattle, as the decade of the eighties passed the meridian. Fine herds of beef strung out for the railroad corrals at Dodge City, and money poured into the bank accounts of Adair and Goodnight.[5]

When the first contract expired in 1882, they had — after allowing for repayment of all moneys advanced by Adair, plus ten per cent interest — a clear profit of more than $512,000. Adair urged extension of the partnership through another five years, and by the new contract the indebtedness to himself was secured by a mortgage upon the entire property; neither was to draw any money from the enterprise for private use except by consent of both; additional real estate purchases were to be financed by Adair; and Goodnight was to be paid seventy-five hundred dollars a year for his management of the ranches.

Again it is apparent that Goodnight took all the risk, personal and financial, securing, through the ranch and cattle, the repayment of Adair's advances with eight per cent interest, and risking not only his original third, but all his labors to this end. In 1885, Adair made his third and last trip to the ranch, having with him a servant to attend his personal needs. Goodnight inquired of the man as to why Adair brought him along: 'To curse me, sir, when he stumps his toe,' the valet answered — 'which he did, beautifully,' added the cowman. Adair left the ranch while Goodnight was struggling with the depression of the middle eighties, and on his way north died at St. Louis, May 14, 1885, by the terms of his will leaving all his range properties to his wife, Cornelia Adair. Goodnight continued the partnership with her.

His work of development was almost done, a work minutely appraised by an 'explorer' sent out by the *Galveston News* in the winter of 1885, who observed not only the character of the ranch, but of the man who founded and directed it, and who wrote:

> It is a century ahead of the free-grass longhorn ranch of the past few years. It was constructed by a bold pioneer and a man

[5] Burton, as cited, 37, 59; *Hall County Deed Record*, Wheeler, Texas, 13–15; *Deed Records*, Donley County, I, 200, and following.

of native genius and miraculous energy and industry. He has had to be a ranger captain, his home for years a fort and his cowboys his soldiers; he has made his rails, built his houses, working as a laborer and carpenter; he has excavated his dugouts at his stations in early days; he has engineered his road making along the gorges and mountain sides and handled the pick and spade; Winchester belted to his back he has built dams and made his tanks, shod his horses, and mended his wagons, imported from abroad his fine bulls, made great land trades and little ones, parleyed with the Indians, and stood off the rustlers. . . .

JA HEADQUARTERS

He has built . . . nearly fifty houses, large and small, hundreds of miles of roads, twenty or thirty large water tanks, and as many large corrals. The ranch has hundreds of miles of wire fence, has a fine hay farm, inclosures separate for beeves, for bulls, for horses, for poor cows to be fed, for calves weaned. . . .

The improvements at the main headquarters of the Palo Duro ranch are better than those of most of the other Panhandle ranches. . . . The main house is a commodious two-story wooden structure of large logs and planks. . . . Water for domestic purposes is brought down through iron pipes from a large spring at the foot of the brakes, which rise into the broad Llano Estacado 1000 yards above this abode. . . .

The mess-house is a large and very substantial structure. . . . Near this house is a dairy, where the butter is made and stored during the summer in sufficient quantities to last headquarters during the entire year. . . . A short distance from this house is the poultry yard and house where the largest and finest breeds of fowls are kept. They supply eggs by the gross for the residents

of this village, and the cook who takes care of them says that at
least 1000 chickens a year are appropriated for table use. Across
the street is the large blacksmith shop, where wagons are mended
and horses shod.... Adjoining this structure is the tin shop,
where all the tinware used on the ranch... is manufactured
from the best and heaviest quality of tin....

On the farm, some twenty miles from the headquarters... last
year, 300 tons of hay were saved.... The water at this farm is
strong with gypsum, very unpalatable to a stranger, and in warm
weather can discount a double dose of Epsom salts....

... one bunch of Hereford bulls, about sixty in number...
cost $27,000, being the finest imported stock. The bulls alone on
this ranch are valued at $150,000 and number 2000 head. Tanks
are made every few miles and at each tank a corral.... Some
fifteen tanks on this ranch, with the corrals, probably cost
$20,000. Everything of this kind is let out by contract....

Young men... do the cooking.... Many employees save their
wages, and I was informed that this ranch company has $26,000
cash on deposit belonging to the boys.... They are permitted to
buy horses and stock and keep them on the range, and encouraged
to invest and keep their money.[6]

Thus had the Palo Duro wilderness been transformed from
an Indian's camp-ground and a buffalo and wild-horse range
to probably the finest and best-managed ranch in the Great
Plains region when the depression of the eighties came. The
industry on a large-scale basis was being fought by politicians,
and on June 30, 1886, Goodnight wrote Mrs. Adair that he
felt the interests of both would be best served by a division of
the properties at the expiration of the contracts; that he was
having maps made showing three equal divisions; that construction of a division fence and a tally of the herd would be
necessary; and that, as the work would take until the end of
the season of '87, they must plan far in advance. Mrs. Adair
was slow in decision.

Meanwhile, inventories were made, and in the fall Goodnight wrote:

We have no time to lose.... If it is inconvenient for you to
come to New York yourself, if you will send Maquay with proper

[6] *Galveston News*, January 10, 1886.

authority it will do as well. I will there make every reasonable proposition for settlement. I will come prepared to take either end of the range. . . .

Division will be absolutely necessary on my part as I see you and me will never agree on sale. Of course you have a perfect right to your own views as regards your own property. I do not wish to interfere with you in the slightest way in view of these rights. Neither will I stand with you in a matter that I think will be my ruin. I am now getting too old and worn out to think of losing what I have and undertaking to make a new start. There will be 2 railroads in here by next September. Their junction will be about 25 miles west of our pasture on the plains. When this is done the settlers will come by hundreds. They will annoy us so we cannot make money in our business. I wish to sell my interest before this occurs. Nothing shall defeat this if I can find a buyer. I can sell if divided. Besides the handling of these properties is very unpopular and prejudicial to my interests and not very profitable to you or me.[7]

Certainly he saw the trend of events with their impending dangers. While he believed cattle had 'at last struck bed rock,' and there would be a good boom within three years, 'I have made up my mind to sell and not undertake to hold for the rise [he wrote]. I am afraid to hold on account of the settlement of the country.'

Late in December, he observed that 'Clarendon is now full of land squatters. . . . The Fort Worth & Denver & the Southern Kansas R. R.'s are booming, they are grading all winter . . . [and] will form a junction . . . in Carson County in Sept. I think they will build the biggest lumber town in the shortest time of any town in the West.

'Every school section anywhere near the supposed junction will be taken in the next few days. If the 7 sec. bids fail to hold and the legislature should fail to give us relief in the way of leases I think we are pretty well gone up. Having hell would be putting it lightly.'[8]

William Henry Plunkett Maquay, banker of Florence, Italy,

[7] Goodnight to Mrs. Adair, December 10, 1886, *Letter Book*, Panhandle-Plains Historical Society, Canyon, Texas.

[8] Goodnight to Wm. Maquay, December 29, 1886, *Letter Book*, as cited.

and alleged illegitimate son of the late partner, was designated
by Mrs. Adair to act as her agent in division. By Adair's will
he was beneficiary to the extent of one hundred thousand
dollars, and in Goodnight's opinion was interested in nothing
but the money. In the midst of hard negotiations with him,
Goodnight was contending with litigation brought by the
State of Texas over leases and alleged illegal fencing; he was

THE WYLIE MORRISES, JA RANCH

trying to lobby measures through the Legislature guaranteeing, by lease, reasonable tenure of alternate sections of school
land; and alone was financing their operations when the Western World was crashing about them.

By the terms of division he agreed to take the Quitaque
Ranch, one hundred and forty thousand acres of land and

twenty thousand cattle, in exchange for his one-third interest in the Palo Duro, thus leaving Mrs. Adair in possession of it and the Tule. Her indecision had driven him into taking the losing end to assure the trade's going through. But the partnership had not been pleasant, conditions were terribly adverse, and he was anxious to close out while he yet had time. To ease the strain, he sold, in the course of division, a one-half interest in the Quitaque to L. R. Moore, of Kansas City. Mrs. Adair and Maquay, uncertain as to the future, seemed to wish his continued management of the Palo Duro, and he assiduously devoted his time to her interests, going to Kansas City in the summer of 1887 for the settlement of ranch notes and the borrowing of operating funds. It was a heart-rending task, for the middle and late eighties were tragic years for the cow country. Cattle firms were 'still tumbling,' the summer 'uncommonly dry,' grass and water were short, and, he wrote, 'a good burglar stands a better chance to get money in Kansas City than a Western cattleman.' But he succeeded, and on the thirteenth of August wrote Maquay, characteristically:

> Upon reaching Kansas City I commenced wiring you for the money to pay notes. The failure of Curtis & Atkinson, Ikards and others occurred while I was there and the Kansas City Banks and others lose heavily making them exceedingly uneasy and compelling me to stay right there till the debt was paid. I am satisfied if the money had not come to pay the notes our property would have been at once attached....
>
> I succeeded in selling 4000 JA yearlings to be delivered at 2's between 15th Apr and 15th May 1888 at 12.50 per head — (delivered at 2's) and getting 15,000 cash down — 25,000 to be paid Nov. *1st* and 10,000 upon delivery of cattle. This was the very best I could do and more than can be done again this year. This money enabled me to get all the notes out of bank.
>
> Regarding the purchase of west end do not inconvenience yourself for it does not matter in the slightest whether I get it or not. It is only a matter of time about the ranch being sold. If things are not exceedingly well handled here [he added, significantly] it will sell too soon....
>
> Cattle are falling in value continually.... They will go lower

before the change comes. At least half if not more of the pastures that are solid land east and south east of us are now under attachment and will pass under the sheriff's hammer during the next 90 days. The banks are so loaded with cattle and land that they cannot lend them. Hence you can put yourself in shape to undergo a hard deal. This is why I wrote Mrs. Adair a few days ago I would not retract the trade made with her and Moore for 25,000 not that I had got a fair or made a sharp trade in Quitaque but it put me in shape to be out of debt and from under the sheriff's hammer. I believe I will make up the losses I have sustained out of someone else's misfortunes before the thing is over with.

Speaking of expenditures and money this immensely dry weather shows me the importance of having 5 or 6 windmills put up in this pasture. Will you order it done or would you prefer to have the money and blow it in on that side? It is perfectly immaterial to me — therefore I am perfectly willing to carry out your wishes. Count of the ⌐ [the Lazy F] cattle will commence on Oct. 1st. You can so notify your men. I shall soon place Jack in charge of Quitaque ranch so he may have a fair chance to cause a clean collection to be made, leaving no stone unturned on my part to give you all you have and all that is fair.[9]

By this time Goodnight had established the JA brand as a mark of excellence, and though 'the shadow of the great catastrophe' hung over the West, John Clay, who bought these cattle, describes them in his autobiography, *My Life on the Range:*

> In the hundreds, nay thousands, of cattle deals I have had, this was the best I ever made. This was a magnificent bunch of cattle and as I looked at them in after years, saw them grow on the range, my admiration of Goodnight as a cattleman soared skyward. These cattle had a Texas foundation, several crosses of Shorthorn and then a Hereford top. They retained their rustling ability, they had bone, breadth across their loins and a mellowness of coat that caught a buyer's eye. The same brand of cattle in later years could not touch them.[10]

When Goodnight closed the books upon his administration of the properties, they showed that he had handled more than

---

[9] Jack Ritchie was Mrs. Adair's son, then working on the Palo Duro Ranch. Goodnight to Maquay, August 13, 1887, *Letter Book,* as cited.

[10] John Clay, *My Life on the Range,* 194.

three hundred thousand cattle, with a total loss of only six-teen hundred head in the eleven years of operation. These figures, reached by actual count, have probably never been approached by anyone else running an outfit on the open range, or for that matter within an enclosure. They, alone, are proof of the cowman.

On December 27, 1887, Goodnight left the Palo Duro Ranch — the creation of his own genius, product of his hardest labors, and the object of his dearest affection — to move over on the railroad and settle at the station called in his honor. His health was bad, his stomach shot to pieces, and several times he was at the point of death. With the coming of the nineties, farming settlers, turning toward the Plains with freshened zest, began locating alternate State lands in the Quitaque, and the vexatious troubles of loose granger stock, eating of stray beef and branding of mavericks, burning of ranges, and destruction of fences — all of which he had fore-seen — impressed upon him anew his original acuteness in blocking the Palo Duro ranges, and his misfortune in division. His greatest mistake was in leaving the rugged JA's.

Eventually he disposed of the entire Quitaque to L. R. Moore to follow adventure further in Mexico, zestfully and courageously as ever, but eventually unhappily.

That he chose wisely and well in pioneering on the Plains is seen in the fact that the JA's continue today as one of the greatest ranges of the West, embracing nearly half a million acres, grazing twenty-five to thirty thousand cattle, watched over by fine Texas cowboys who still know the use of open-reined bridles, ropes, and branding-irons. In spite of the trying times at which they closed it out, it is remarkable to observe that through the ten years of Goodnight's direction it paid an annual profit of seventy-two per cent on the capital advanced by Adair. More important, still, is the record Goodnight gave it as an institution of high-hearted action, square shooting, and fair dealing — truly old-fashioned virtues of the horse and buggy days.

XX. FIGHTING FOR ORDER

A CASUAL survey of Goodnight's action must impress even the rabid reformer that outstanding representatives of individualism cherished the ideals of law and order and the sanctity of property above the hazards of life. The most individualistic men usually have led in the establishment of those amenities and standards by which complicated social development proceeded.

As he had been on the Western trails, and as he was in southern Colorado, so in the Panhandle-Plains country Goodnight became the dominant personality. There were other capable and forceful contemporaries, but Goodnight, before law came and before the cowmen organized, as well as after law came and after the cowmen organized, was the most positive fighter for order and the most relentless hater of thieves. Still sturdy of physique, commanding of eye, masterful of intellect, and fiery of spirit, he was a man feared by the lawless and respected by all. He was always the first to back his convictions with his money, his men, and his guns.

While only in regions of sparse settlement can rustlers ply an easy trade, in the West of even thirty years ago great, broken, and unsettled stretches of country offered them necessary refuge. Soon after cowmen began taking the grass for their longhorned cattle, organized bands of thieves stole from the settlements to the east of the Staked Plains, and sold their horses in New Mexico, Colorado, and Kansas; then stole others there and sold them back in Texas.[1] This organ-

---

[1] See the *St. Jo* (Texas) *Times*, September 23, 1882; *Tascosa Pioneer*, December 15, 1888 and September 13, 1890; Goodnight, 'Recollections,' II, 122; *Galveston News*, January 7, 1886; *Ford County Globe*, February 4 and June 10, 1879.

ized cycle continued until cattlemen and peace officials broke it up, but not before outlaws had depredated upon the frontiers for several years. The reason was obvious. At first each cowman interpreted the law to suit himself, and exacted justice when that law was infringed upon. Successful thievery, on any extensive scale, is a matter of co-operation. The outlaws were organized; the resistance was individual.

Among outlaw bands were those led by three noted bad men. John Sellman, fugitive from Fort Griffin, was working back and forth from the Canadian to Devil's River, and was alleged to have one hundred and seventy-five confederates; Billy the Kid led a smaller but really efficient following of desperadoes on the west; and Dutch Henry's band was almost equally desperate and probably the most numerous — Charlie Siringo said he had three hundred followers.[2]

Henry Born, Dutch Henry's official name, was a buffalo hunter who stole from Indians and soldiers at every opportunity, but who solemnly swore that he had never touched 'a white man's horse.' In 1867 he was scouting with Custer; in 1874 he fought with the beleaguered buffalo hunters at Adobe Walls. Sometime later, when Indians stole his horses near Fort Dodge, he appealed to the post for help, was refused, and told the officers that thereafter he would steal every government animal he found.

During the next few years, Dutch Henry, 'with a wider range than all the rest,' was gathering government horses and building a reputation. Now he struck near Fort Hays, again he stole government teams near Fort Elliott, next he was trading in Las Vegas or Taos, resting up at Trinidad, or devising other raids in the shadows of Fort Sedgewick.

When arrested at Trinidad late in 1878, he was a 'rather genteel-looking man,' to quote the local *Enterprise*, 'for a horse thief, road agent and murderer.' Bat Masterson brought

[2] Siringo's notation on a letter, Henry Born to Chas. A. Siringo, July 6, 1920, copy in files of the author; Affidavit of J. McIntire, Wheeler County, June 30, 1879, Adjutant-General's Office, Austin; W. E. Payne, 'Dutch Henry's Raid Near Fort Elliott,' *Frontier Times*, January, 1924, pp. 24–27.

him to Dodge City for trial, which he faced with perfect poise, and after acquittal frankly admitted that he was 'even with the Indians and the Government' and was 'ready to smoke the pipe of peace and bury the hatchet.'

This was the man whom Goodnight met near Wolf Creek, in 1877, and with whom he formed a treaty whereby the outlaw agreed not to deprecate in the lower Panhandle. True to his word he stayed out, but in the Spur country to the south a post-oak motte served as a holdout for another band said to have been forty in number, but thought by Goodnight to have been only twenty-nine strong. In the fall of 1877, six Mexican freighters brought a train of merchandise from Trinidad to establish the village of Tascosa. These outlaws, who happened to be camped nearby, stole the Mexican stock and put out for the south, leaving the teamsters stranded. The Mexicans came over to the Palo Duro and began working for Goodnight, cutting cedars and helping to build the ranch corrals, in order to buy teams for their return.

They gave Goodnight and his men descriptions of the stolen stock, and while Dyer was locating his ranch at the head of the Palo Duro, Henderson, one of the outlaws, rode up on a big blue horse and asked for work. Dyer, recognizing the animal from the descriptions, merely advised that his outfit was small and needed no hands, but that Goodnight and Adair were putting in a big ranch down the cañon, and he might get work from them. As he was going to the JA's, Henderson rode with him to where the outfit was building corrals on Mulberry. A nod from Dyer caused Bill Koogle, the buffalo hunter, and the hands, to throw down on him. They turned him over to the Mexicans, who inquired as to his disposal. 'Hang him,' came the reply, and the Mexicans did, thoroughly.

By one account he died maintaining his innocence, but according to Goodnight, he confessed he had been sent to spy out an approach to the cañon before returning with his band for the purpose of killing the outfit and stealing their cattle and horses. Goodnight's enemies claimed that he had the hanging done — though he was away from the ranch at the time — 'the origin of the story,' he recalled, 'that I had hung ten men. If there had been a hundred hung, it would not have hurt the country.' [3]

At first there was no law except that which cowmen enforced arbitrarily, and their actions were often illegal, as they denied culprits *habeas corpus*, or the privilege of evading extradition.

In 1878, three horse thieves miscalculated their course and inadvertently passed by the JA Ranch. They rode in after night with a bunch of mules, ate a late supper at the mess-house, and stopped in the flat south of the headquarters. As day was breaking, Goodnight saw the grazing stock and the three men arising from their bed rolls. After getting his gun, he came back by the blacksmith shop, and asked Jack Watson if he had seen the men the night before. He replied that he had, and knew one of them to be a thief. By this time they had ridden off, and Goodnight, knowing nothing definite about their operations, decided to let them go.

Near noon a man named Foster came in, hell-bent from the west, on a 'give-out' horse, wanting to know if anyone had seen some mules.

'Your men and mules both stayed over in that flat last night,' Goodnight advised him.

Foster, excited and full of talk, began telling Goodnight that he wanted horses, he wanted help, he wanted grub, and he wanted this and that.

'Oh, damn it, shut up,' the cowman finally exploded. 'Go over there to the mess-hall and get your grub. I'll attend to the rest.' While the pursuer was eating his breakfast and telling the cook that the mules were stolen from his grading crew on the Atchison, Topeka and Santa Fé, north of Las Vegas, Goodnight had two fresh horses saddled. Foster came out of the mess-house still blabbing about what he wanted to

---

[3] Goodnight to J. E. H., June 25, 1925, and January 26, 1927; Goodnight, 'Random Notes'; T. D. Hobart to J. E. H., September 8, 1932; Goodnight to Mrs. J. C. Nunn, April 12, 1928, copy in Goodnight Papers.

do, and Goodnight impatiently told him to get on the extra horse and come along. They loped down the trail where John Mann's outfit was branding calves on Battle Creek, seven miles below the ranch, and heard from Mann that the thieves had passed him as he came in off the roundup. Goodnight told Mann to take three or four choice men and hit the trail at once, and in a few minutes they were on the go, Foster with them.

JOHN MANN, WAGON BOSS

The thieves kept a southeast course to the Rath Trail crossing, on Red River, a course that would have carried them into the Millett Ranch, a hard lay-out near Seymour. Mann made good time, covering the forty intervening miles by dark, and when he could no longer see their tracks, he and his men lay down and waited for day. They outrode Foster in the evening, and he lay out by himself. In fact, he had lain out every night since leaving New Mexico, and 'had some grit,' Goodnight remarked, 'even if he was a damned fool.' At the break of day, Mann took the trail again, and soon came to a dry creek, just west of the Milliron headquarters. The thieves had camped under its bluff, staked their mules to graze, and were still in bed when Mann rode up and stopped his horse on the bank, ten or twelve feet above them. One waked and started to reach for his gun, but changed his mind when Mann told him to leave it alone.

'You don't want me?' he queried.

'No, I haven't a damned bit of use for you myself,' Mann answered, 'but there is a fellow right behind me that has.'

'Is his name Foster?'

'You've guessed it,' said Mann.

Late that night they reached the JA headquarters, and the boys took charge of the prisoners. One was supposed to be a very bad man, and Foster, fearing he might have trouble in getting him through, wanted to have him ironed. Jack Watson made handcuffs from discarded buggy tires, and riveted them in place, after which Goodnight called Jud Campbell, told him to pick a man to accompany him to Bugbee's ranch, on the Canadian, eighty miles to the north, and purposely gave them their instructions before the prisoners.

'Take these prisoners direct to Bugbee's ranch with this note. Make them as comfortable as possible, but do not allow them to get within six feet of you, and you are not to get within that distance of them. Take them there dead or alive — don't allow any foolishness.'

The trip required a couple of days, and up on McClellan Creek one of the prisoners got off his mule and told Campbell he would not go a step farther.

'You heard my instructions,' replied the cowboy as cool as ice, and pulling his gun, continued, 'Now, damn you, get on that mule, or I'll put you on him, dead.' The prisoner got on!

Goodnight asked Bugbee to escort the prisoners to the next

ranch west, with a request that it in turn forward them to
the next, and so on until they reached the Bell Ranch, from
where they would be sent to Las Vegas.

During the winter of 1878, a couple of rustlers stole twenty
head of saddle stock out of the Palo Duro, and upon discovery
of the loss, Goodnight sent Frank Mitchell to Fort Elliott to
wire a description of the stock to officers throughout the
country. About a month later, the sheriff at Las Vegas wired
back that he was holding the men and horses.

'Frank,' said Goodnight, 'you've got to go to Las Vegas.'

'Goodness alive, Mr. Goodnight,' he exclaimed, 'I can't go
to Las Vegas.'

Mrs. Goodnight interceded for the boy, asking: 'Why don't
you send Farrington?'

'Why, he'd get drunk at Tascosa,' replied her husband,
'and if he ever got to Las Vegas, he'd get drunk there, and
never get back.'

After they had 'chawed the rag' awhile, as Mitchell recalled,
he saddled Rondo, his big sorrel, and set forth on 'the lone-
somest ride' he ever made. He swung up the Palo Duro to
Dyer's, crossed the Plains to Tascosa, and the next night
stopped at Ledgard and Campbell's sheep camp on the Alamocitos, where twenty-five thousand sheep were lambing.
Mitchell was not interested in them, but he was intrigued by a
couple of New Zealand dogs that, by working back and forth,
were herding two flocks each. From there he went to Banta's
Store, forty miles to the west, a tough dive run by an Irishman
and his Mexican wife. Next day he rode into Fort Bascom,
and, getting a sack of biscuits and beef and a *morral* full of
corn, started on the hundred mile ride to Las Vegas. When
dark came, he lay out with the dry stock, and went to sleep
on his saddle blanket.

'I staked my horse near that night, and he was as smart as
a man,' Mitchell praised. 'Every little bit he'd come in and
smell of me, where I lay under my slicker, to see if everything
was all right, and then go back and graze. A horse doesn't

lie down until near morning. About four o'clock he lay down and slept an hour — I could hear him snore. We thought as much of our horses as the best friend on earth, because they were the best friends we had.'

Mitchell carried a letter to the Mexican sheriff, who treated him well, and, after the thieves had been tried and sentenced, started with the horses for the ranch. He begged a couple of New Zealand puppies at the Alamocitos, and with one in each of his spacious saddle pockets, started across the Plains toward the head of the Palo Duro.

Near Amarillo Lake he saw three riders driving some horses toward him from the east, and, suspecting they were thieves, veered his horses to pass behind them. They turned to meet him, and, riding to the lead of his horses, Mitchell resorted to the old Western practice of waving them around. As they disregarded the warning, he slid to the ground, pulled his Sharps muley from the scabbard, and dropped a couple of bullets ahead of their horses. On they came, and as final warning he knocked up a cloud of dust under the lead-horse's nose, and slipped in another shell for business purposes. But they heeded the injunction, and turned into the west while he pounded his charges on the tail toward Dyer's ranch.[4]

In April, 1880, the JA outriders heard of two men who passed up the Tule with a bunch of horses, making their way westward across the Plains. They reported at headquarters, and two days later a man named Smith, foreman of the Stevens and Worsham Я2 Ranch, on Wanderer's Creek, and some of his hands came up, hunting the men and horses. Fourteen head had been stolen, and the *Fort Griffin Echo* took notice of the theft, commenting that 'the good citizens in the Panhandle are about sick of these "rustlers" and the time is near at hand when there will be men "lost in the sand hills" or a judicious hanging inaugurated by Judge Lynch's court.'

Goodnight offered to send Farrington with Smith after the rustlers. Since they had passed up the Tule, Farrington knew

4 H. F. Mitchell to J. E. H. December 22, 1929, and September 4, 1932.

he would not have to bother with trailing them, for they must surely cross the Plains on the old *comanchero* trail by way of Escarbadas. The season was early and range horses still poor, and Farrington had to take one of Goodnight's private mounts, a fine blood-bay but a bad bucker, as mean as the devil. He told Smith they would not need his men, and the two pushed across the Plains by the Indian trade road, intent upon discovering where the thieves had crossed the Pecos.

Goodnight addressed a note to Stevens and Worsham by their men, advising that he had sent Farrington after the rustlers, and so confident was he of their capture that he asked them to send the sheriff of Clay County to Vegas promptly, as 'Farrington will have the men by the time he gets there.' He further advised that there was virtually no law in New Mexico, and, since convictions were scarce and the outlaws powerful, attempts might be made to release the captives by writ of *habeas corpus*, and hence there was need of hurry. He was writing Charles Kitchen and Dr. Shoop, friends of his there, to prevent this if possible, yet advised that the sheriff take no chances, but be there on time and take the prisoners.

Farrington and Smith, learning that the horses had been crossed at Sumner, headed toward a notorious ranch in the foothills, where they found one of the thieves, a fellow named Snow, helping to dig a well. It was a fortunate break, for they simply called down to him to come out. He was a tough one, however, and begged the JA puncher to give him a six-shooter and they would fight it out, but Farrington replied that was not at all necessary. Upon discovering that Stockton, the other fugitive, was out in the hills hunting deer, Farrington, fearing someone might slip out to warn him, took a little turn in hope of seeing him. Fortunately, he met Stockton, who immediately opened fire, and Farrington's bay broke in two. But Farrington was a real cowboy, and in spite of the pitching, jerked out his Sharps and took a shot, anyway, fortunately nipping Stockton, who gave up, wanting to know what kind of a gun the other carried, with 'bullets that sang like humming-birds.'

Smith took the horses and headed for Texas, while Farrington pushed hard for Las Vegas with the prisoners, slipped into Kitchen's Hotel, eased on the train to chain them to the

FARRINGTON AND THE RUSTLER

seats, and sent them back to Texas without benefit of preliminary hearing or evasion of extradition. Snow was sentenced, but Stockton broke jail at Decatur, crossed the Rockies in Colorado, and upon his first break the Vigilantes got him and ended his career without benefit of law or clergy.[5]

Thus, even as late as 1880, the Panhandle knew almost nothing of the sovereignty of Texas, but politically might have been another domain. Goodnight's successive, if arbitrary, strides had each time carried his country nearer peaceful occupation. First he had succeeded in keeping transient sheep.

[5] Goodnight to J. E. H., April 8, 1927; *Fort Griffin Echo*, April 10, 1880.

men out of the Red River country, an intrusion which, aggressively pushed, would have led to strife. Then he divided the country with Dutch Henry's outlaws, pushing them off his own range as the first move toward pushing them off the Plains. At various times he captured outlaws and deported them into sections of organized law, sending his men far into New Mexico after renegades on the west, and into Indian Territory for fugitives to the east.

At times he detained suspicious characters by giving them work until their identities could be established, or papers could be sent for their arrest. One notorious individual, who was given a job pending arrival of definite information, grew wary, came to the ranch office, and asked Goodnight if he could get his time. The cowman, dictating letters to the bookkeeper, agreed, and asked him to be seated. Dictation aside, he settled for the work, after which, for some unexplained reason, the man asked for a letter of recommendation. Again Goodnight agreed, and, turning to the secretary, dictated:

> To Whom It May Concern:
>   This will introduce you to the damnedest horse and cow thief that ever left southern Texas...

At which juncture the man sprang to his feet, exclaiming that he did not think such a letter would help him.

'It's the only kind I can write,' snapped Goodnight, and immediately one more thief was headed toward the Territory.

Goodnight had long realized the need of established range credit, whereby ranchmen might finance their operations without being forced to pay the extortionate rates of one and a half to two per cent a month that he had paid in Colorado. The cow country was hardly established in centers of credit, but Goodnight urged its importance upon Adair and other foreign financiers, and the Texas Land and Mortgage Company was organized in England in the early eighties, with C. E. Wellesley established as manager of its Dallas office. The company did a thriving business, met a decided need, and at times had as much as three hundred thousand dollars loaned to the JA Ranch. In addition to lending money, it became a sort of clearing-house for British interests in the Southwest. With unlimited confidence in the integrity of Goodnight, and vast respect for his intelligent grasp of the range industry, Wellesley often called upon him for expert advice and help when the general Western tendency seemed to be to 'unload on the foreigners.'

South of the Quitaque the expansive Espuela Land and Cattle Company was sold, in 1885, by the organizers, A. M. Britton and S. W. Lomax, to an English concern which became the Espuela Land and Cattle Company, Limited, briefly called the Spurs. In accord with a rather general practice of that day, the buyers accepted the range on book count, with the proviso, it seems, that an actual tally of the cattle would be made on demand. Britton and Lomax had organized an immense project, beginning with their original purchase of the Spur cattle, and had taken in many little men whose herds were branded into the Spur, the owners taking stock in the company proportionate to the value of their cattle. More and more they expanded until, by their books, they had one hundred and twenty thousand cattle on the range at the time of delivery. For some reason the buyers became suspicious and demanded a count of the cattle by a disinterested party.

Wellesley asked Goodnight to count them, but he replied that his own business demanded all of his time. Asked if he could recommend a man, Goodnight replied that he had a foreman who was competent, and who could neither be bought nor scared.

Upon his return to the ranch, he sent a note to Farrington, at the Quitaque, to the effect that he wished him to count the Spur cattle, and asking him, in case he would accept the job, what he would charge. The courier found him on the range, branding, and Farrington tore a leaf from his daybook, and in substance wrote Goodnight the following:

'You had better have nothing to do with the deal, for your

neighbors are mixed up with it in a way that will cause you
hard feelings, and I know you well enough to know that you
are not going to get anything out of it.   There is about $500,000
difference between their range delivery price and an actual
count.   But if you require me to make this count, I'll do so to
the best of my ability, provided you let me pick six men from
all your outfits, the Tule, Palo Duro, and Quitaque, for which
I will charge them $5000.'

JOHN FARRINGTON

Goodnight agreed to his choice of men, and the matter was
dropped until Wellesley wired that a gentleman by the name
of Walker would arrive on a certain date, on his way to receive the Spurs.   Walker, a Scotchman, came by rail to Dodge
City, buck-boarded it to Mobeetie, and thence to the Palo
Duro, where he stopped for the night.   When they were comfortably settled after supper, he asked Goodnight if he had his
'mon' ready, and the cowman simply handed him the note he
had received from Farrington.   Walker read the note, looked
awfully serious, and re-read it.   Turning to Goodnight he said:
   'Indade, this charge seems to be very great.   But I rather
like the way the young mon puts it.   He seems to know his
business.   While I cannot agree with him, as I have Mr. Brit-

ton's sworn statement as to the number of those cottle, but if the young mon is right as to his conclusions, he would be a very cheap mon after all. Now do you think he would count the cottle on a pro-rata basis?'

'That I cannot answer,' replied the host. 'I simply leave it to you and Mr. Farrington.'

Next day Goodnight drove Walker to the Quitaque behind a team of fine little mules, and, after reaching an agreement with the foreman, Walker proceeded to the Spurs, where Britton tried to induce him to take the cattle without count.

'No, sir,' he said. 'I have come thousands of miles to count these cottle, and they must be counted.'

'Then, Mr. Walker, who is to count these cattle?'

'I'm not in shape today to tell you who's to count the cottle,' he prudently answered.

'Is Charles Goodnight to count them?'

'I can assure you, sir, that Mr. Goodnight is not to count these cottle.'

'All right,' said Britton, apparently relieved; 'anybody but Goodnight will be satisfactory to me.'

Two or three days later, Goodnight's foreman turned up with a wagon and a crew of six of the most expert cowboys in the Panhandle, and hell began popping as the counting began. A fence was built across the range, everything thrown to one side, and with the gates tied and watchful riders patrolling the line, Farrington began to tally the great herd back to the other side. The arbitrary measures aroused bitter opposition among some of the Spur stockholders, officials, and hands, but were necessary and rigidly pursued. One night the line riders reported to Farrington that the fence had been torn down, and a small bunch of counted cattle run out to the uncounted side. He immediately went to the place, and, after mending the fence, estimated, from the tracks, the number of cattle that passed, and notified the owners that he was charging them with six hundred head against the final tally. Later he admitted that he thought there were about four hundred driven across, but said he wanted to be sure to charge off enough in justice to the buyers, and also to penalize the sellers sufficiently to discourage such measures.

The work went on, the tally indicating to many of the little stockholders, who had placed their fortunes in the enterprise, that the count would fall far short, and they in effect were ruined. Grimly but honestly they saw the deal through, for they were men of strength and of sand. But Walker, scared almost to death, felt sure there would be some killings, and went to Farrington, advising: 'I think we had better compromise and settle this the best we can.'

'No,' came the answer, 'I can't make any settlement. If I do, Goodnight will give me my time, and I don't want it. I've got to count these cattle.'

And so he did, to the satisfaction of the English buyers, and without bloodshed on the range. The final tally was said to have been for some sixty-two thousand cattle, in place of one hundred and twenty thousand which the company claimed. Bad winters, theft, loose management, and inflated assets — apparently these had taken their toll.

Farrington rode back to the Quitaque and divided the five thousand among the men, but the pay was insignificant, for Goodnight and his outfit had embittered neighboring cowmen. This, too, was the reward of character, of honesty, and an ethic of aggressive action.

And yet he sent his men off to count the T Anchors, which were being sold to another foreign concern, the Cedar Valley Land and Cattle Company, Limited, where, too, rose the question of strays and shortage, the tides of high feeling and of danger.

The Clarendon Land Investment and Agency Company, of England, promoted and locally managed by L. H. Carhart, the founder of Clarendon, collapsed after the memorable winter of 1886, and was reported to have had only fourteen thousand cattle left, when its books represented from twenty-five to thirty thousand head. George Tyng was sent out to investigate, and Count Cecil Kearney, representing the stockholders, wanted Goodnight to send an outfit to make the count. But he, knowing the tremendous personal and business cost from long contact with the West, avoided a meeting until the Count came to him at the ranch. Then he demurred with

MITCH BELL

the remark that he had already made two sets of enemies in the country by just such procedure, without a cent of profit to himself. Kearney feared trouble and bloodshed, and was at a loss as to his course if Goodnight turned him down. The years had been hard and the cowman was wanting to slow up, but the appeal touched both his sense of pride and justice, and with fierce determination he assented: 'Rather than have the word go out that there is not enough justice and honesty in this country to count cattle to a stranger, I will take the job and count them.'

Farrington and Henry Taylor swung over the divide to the north and counted the Quarter Circle Hearts peacefully and well, thereby adding another modicum of character to the Western cowman's dealings with foreign capital, and more enemies to the JA roster.[6] With this act Goodnight's direction of the outside relationships of the Palo Duro Ranch practically came to a close, for the dissolution of the Adair partnership was near at hand.

In addition to his innate desire to see fair dealings the rule of his country with native and foreigner alike, Goodnight knew that one thing the land then needed was more and cheaper capital, and he did all he could to encourage its honest investment. When the astute and capable Scotchman, Murdo Mackenzie, left the Prairie Cattle Company to take charge of the Matadors, the neighboring range south of the Quitaque, Goodnight, knowing rocky roads were ahead of the new management, advised his foreman that if he ever heard Mackenzie was in trouble to drop his work, no matter what he was doing, and go to his aid.[7]

If he was particular of the rights of his cowboys abroad, he was downright jealous of their conduct at home, and generally the Plains demanded the most exact code of range ethics of all the cow country. Constant fidelity to duty, solicitous care of horses, unquestioned bravery in every crisis — such was the least expected of every Texas cowboy. But readers of popular Western literature may be dismayed to know that on the JA's, the Shoe Bars, the XIT's, and many other ranches west of the one hundredth meridian, the moral requirements for ordinary waddies was more rigid than are those for matriculants in the leading universities today. Good-

---

[6] Goodnight to J. E. H., June 15, 1929; *Tascosa Pioneer*, September 1, 1886, June 11 and July 9, 1887; M. E. Bell to J. E. H., December 19, 1929; H. W. Taylor to J. E. H., September 3, 1932; *Galveston News*, January 6, 1886; Goodnight to Wm. Maquay, June 18, 1887, *Letter Book*, as cited.

[7] Murdo Mackenzie to J. E. H., November 22, 1932.

night made three rules for his ranches: no gambling, no drinking; and no fighting. With S. W. Lomax, manager of the
Spurs, and H. H. Campbell, of the Matadors, he agreed that
between their ranches they would employ no hand 'discharged
elsewhere for theft or drunkenness.'

BREAKING JA BRONCS

Goodnight went farther. With the help of neighboring cowmen he declared all the country south of the North Fork of
Red River — his country — under a state of prohibition. 'No
whiskey was ever allowed,' he said. 'It was kept out by force
until the law reached here. Up to the time of the organization
of Donley County there was not a murder in the whole country
south of Mobeetie, or, in other words, in all that kept free of
whiskey.' [8] Though these ideals and rules of conduct were
formulated on the trail and brought to the JA range in 1876,
they are still in force, not because of puritanical standards on
the part of owners and managers, for some relished the qualities of good cocktails themselves, but because they realized
that whiskey, cards, and cows mix but poorly.

[8] *Galveston News*, January 7 and 10, 1886; Burton, *A History of the JA Ranch*, 83,
103; Goodnight, 'Recollections,' I, 13; Holden, *The Spur Ranch*; *Tascosa Pioneer*, July
31, 1886, and March 30, 1887.

One may wonder if these rules were enforced. A characteristic incident illustrates the Goodnight discipline. Among the recruits from the old country sent over, not only for regeneration but for education in the cow business, was Jack Ritchie, son of Mrs. Adair by her first marriage. With him Goodnight seemed unusually patient, hoping that he would become engrossed in range life and make an efficient manager for his mother, even writing, in the fall of 1886, that he had 'raised Jack's wages to 50 per month, not that he can possibly earn it but to make him feel better and to feel like he was of some importance as you suggested.' During the course of the next year he mentioned that Jack seemed satisfied, was doing well, and was in charge of the Tule Ranch. As he prepared to give up the management of the properties, Goodnight, hearing the rules had been broken, wrote:

Jany 8 88

J. W. Ritchie
   Tule
   It gives me great pain to write you this letter but I feel it my duty and I will perform it.
   During the last week ... my manager of Quitaque got on a general drunk, gambling and so on in Clarendon. In having the matter looked up, ... I found the men had been gambling on Tule in your presence and in your room.
   This was the greatest surprise to me and it is with the greatest regret that I write you this as I had the week before, only, written your mother that you were clear of those things since being with me and that I believed you would succeed as a business man and that I had made you foreman of Tule ranch at a salary of $100 — per month. I now write to say to you that you will not be foreman of the Tule ranch at least not by my authority but you will remain second foreman for at least six months at a salary of sixty dollars per month. Your raise then will depend upon your conduct. I hope it will be such as to enable me to put you in charge but never will I raise you while you know of or permit gambling to be done on the ranch.
   I would gladly step out of the management of this ranch at this hour and shall do so at the earliest opportunity but as long as I run it or it is run with my name in its connection I will not sub-

mit to this gambling. I hope you will take this in the friendly feeling in which I mean it as I assure you I pity you more than blame you. Why do you let your enemies get the advantage of you so easily. You can and should defeat them. Why don't you do it. I have put Beverly in entire charge of the ranch for six months with positive instructions to discharge every man interested in the game of cards at or on the ranch except yourself. If you was only an ordinary foreman you would go with them. If Beverly fails to carry out this order I shall discharge him and keep on discharging till nothing but the harmless cows are left. I regret that I did not have the time to come and see you personally but inasmuch as my own ranch is without foreman or management, I feel it my duty to first go there as I got the worst of it in purchase and continue to get the worst of it ever since. I will be there 8 or 10 days and will be happy to meet you there. Should I not however I will endeavor to come by and see you before I leave the country.

Your friend

C. GOODNIGHT

He immediately discharged his brother-in-law — 'my manager of Quitaque' — and except for his desire to guard Mrs. Adair's interests, Ritchie would have gone too. After this letter he addressed himself to Beverly.

Jan 8 88

L. C. Beverly and Whom it may concern and especially the employees of the Tule Ranch —

This is to certify that I have this day appointed and made L. C. Beverly General Ranch Manager of the Tule Ranch giving him full and all control as ranch manager until further orders to be given by myself or my successor.

1st To discharge all men who have been gambling on the ranch except J. W. Ritchie.

2nd Not to permit or allow any gambling to be done.

3rd To discharge all men who drink on the ranch or come there drunk.

4th If Beverly does not obey these orders I will send a man there who will.

Yours

C. GOODNIGHT
Manager for Mrs. C. Adair.[9]

[9] *Letter Book,* 95–98.

Upon the same date he addressed Mrs. Adair:

It is with the deepest regret I write you this especially so as I have recently been compelled to discharge some members of my own family for like offences. On January 1st I placed Jack in charge of Tule ranch. On January 5th on having looked up some of the acts of the Quitaque men Walter Dyer among the rest who was manager and who I discharged on the spot, I found that Jack had been gambling with his men. . . .

CHARLES GOODNIGHT, AT SIXTY

When thoroughly convinced of this matter I have placed the old foreman . . . in charge and made Jack second man as before for six months at which time with good conduct I will again raise him but if he gambles again upon the ranch . . . I shall discharge him. But I hope this will not be necessary. I really do not think it will but I am certain to discharge my duty if it becomes necessary. I as much regret to write you this as I do to meet Mrs. Goodnight . . . after discharging her brother who I know she loves so well but business and my duty to the same demands it and I will do it if it costs my life. Do not think that I will meet Jack in any unfriendly way. On the other hand I am sorry to be disappointed by him.

Let this trouble you as little as possible but rest assured I will do the best I can for you and him, and as soon as you possibly can find someone to take my place here. I am heartily sick of men and ranches.[10]

And so his final duty on the JA's, both as to internal management and outside relations, was the maintenance of his code at severe personal cost. Responsibility never sat lightly upon his shoulders, and though he knew his trade was bad and destiny was against him on the Quitaque, he still cherished the interests he represented, and wielded the axe with savage determination, though the chips fell close at home.

[10] *Letter Book*, 253–54.

XXI. THE PANHANDLE STOCK
ASSOCIATION

COWMEN who early followed Goodnight into the Panhandle
for permanent range were mostly men of honesty and integrity.
But whether they killed their own calves or ate a neighbor's
beef, they were all men of force and courage. How each held
his portion of free grass and water without title and without
fence, merely by the unwritten laws of the Western range;
how each looked after any of his neighbor's cattle that strayed
among his own; how one and another banded together in
general roundups to work the ranges from New Mexico to the
Indian Nation, is a matter of fairly general knowledge. The
detailed story of their organized fight for law has never been
told.

Back of their co-ordinated endeavor is the story of an
attempt at legal organization, and the establishment of order
through regular channels. The first officers to reach the Plains
were Texas Rangers, members of the famous Frontier Battalion under the command of that fire-eating little Captain,
G. W. Arrington. A veteran of Mosby's guerrillas, outlawed
under the carpetbag régime of Alabama, adventurer in Hon-
duras, and officer on the Texas frontier, he was a hyena on
the heels of bad men. Quick-tempered, soft-spoken, black-
eyed, he handled his men with unrelenting discipline, even as
he hunted outlaws with ruthless resolve. After service on the
lower frontier, he was given a company to operate westward
from Fort Griffin across the Plains to New Mexico, and from

Tobacco Creek and the head of the Colorado through Greer County and the Panhandle to the Canadian.

By February, 1879, citizens of Mobeetie had petitioned for organization of Wheeler County, and prayed likewise for a company of Texas Rangers. Arrington scouted north to Mobeetie in June, 1879, and incensed over Indian hunting privileges granted by the military, and the resultant raiding and devilment thereby caused on the side, soon became embroiled in a quarrel almost to the point of armed conflict with the commander of Fort Elliott, Colonel J. W. Davidson. Upon deciding his handful of men would not get to fight the army after all, he packed his outfit, headed west by Clarendon to the Palo Duro, and leaving his men behind, dropped into the ranch, alone, without establishing his identity.

In the custom of the country he was welcome, but the next day Goodnight, suspecting he was a ranger spying out the place as a possible refuge for outlaws thus far in the wilderness, expressed his suspicion. Arrington readily admitted the imputation. Then he headed south to Blanco Cañon, and upon his return to Fort Griffin addressed a letter to Major John B. Jones, Adjutant-General, that Goodnight, having lost heavily to the Indians the winter before, had assured him 'that he was not going to stand it any longer — that if he did not get some protection he would go to fighting Indians himself — that he could raise 75 well armed men any time — and for me to call on him at any time for men or means....' [1]

The region was a fertile place to work, and Arrington's company was said to have made hundreds of arrests, of which number, Goodnight understood, only about two and one half per cent were Texans — the rest were from every State in the Union. The rangers, though in the prime of splendid frontier organization, were operating over a vast territory, and consequently could not catch all the wrongdoers.

In the three years since Goodnight's arrival at the Palo

[1] G. W. Arrington to John B. Jones, June 18, and July 12, 1879; Goodnight, 'Recollections,' II, 125; *Ford County Globe*, February 4, June 10, and July 22, 1879.

Duro, cowmen had drifted into the virgin ranges along the breaks of the Plains like their herds before a storm. From the LS's on the Canadian, at the western fringe of the Panhandle, to Mose Hays's outfit at old Springer Ranch, on the Government Trail, the river and its tributaries were running thousands

A PLAINS DUGOUT

of cattle. From Jim Cator's Diamond K, on the North Palo Duro, to the U Ranch, on the head of the North Concho, the escarpments of the Plains sheltered longhorned stock and some grades. No longer were the nearest neighbors eighty to one hundred miles away, as in the first days of the JA's and the Quarter Circle T's, but now the traveler might spend each night beneath a dugout roof by thirty- and forty-mile rides, or if fortunate even stop for dinner at some meager camp on the way.

Mobeetie was growing: Mark Huselby established a hotel, Lee and Reynolds held the sutler's concessions, trading houses were established, and saloons flourished in picket houses, with dancing and gambling on the side. While it was 'only a trading settlement of four or five houses covered with dirt' in 1876, it had lost much of its indigenous character four years later as frame houses were erected among the sand hills along the peaceful stream. The county was organized in the summer of 1879, although most of its citizens were gamblers, dance-hall people, and buffalo hunters, many of whom bore such names, if the *District Court Minutes* are trustworthy, as Butcher Knife Bill, Feather Stone Jones, Matilda Wave, Frog Mouth Annie, and Fly Speck.

Goodnight declared his conviction 'that the intention of the county organization was to prevent law and order rather than to enforce it.' Though one hundred and fifty qualified voters were necessary for legal organization, there were probably no more than that in the entire Panhandle. The names of cow-punchers on the JA and LF ranches, some of whom were a hundred miles away, were used in petitioning for organization without their owners' knowledge. In fact, the county was organized before ranchmen even fifty miles away heard of the move, though the sutlers, Lee and Reynolds, bitterly fought the measure.

It has been claimed that most of the county officials were living with prostitutes when they were elected, but for some unexplained reason this motley citizenry chose an honest, if long-winded man, Emanuel Dubbs, as judge, and an educated, respectable gambler, Henry Fleming, as sheriff. Fleming elevated his station and did some good work, but there were no convictions during the first two years. In 1880, Judge J. A. Carroll, sent from Denton to hold the first court, made his way by rail to Emporia, Kansas, thence to Dodge City, and took the stage to Mobeetie — a trip of eight hundred miles. The next year the mammoth Thirty-Fifth Judicial District was created, and Frank Willis, who was appointed District Judge, secured the first convictions, finding true bills, according to Goodnight, 'against every officer except himself, Dubbs, and Fleming.' [2]

On the Canadian River, in Oldham County in the western Panhandle, Tascosa came to life in the spring of 1877 to contest, in a truly bucolic style, the supremacy of Mobeetie. Strictly a range town offering an interesting retreat for good people as well as a comfortable refuge for bad, it seems to have

[2] Goodnight, 'Recollections,' II, 126; Goodnight to J. E. H., September 3, 1927; *Fort Griffin Echo*, August 7, 1880, July 23 and November 19, 1881; Gammel, *Laws of Texas*, IX, 100; G. W. Arrington to John B. Jones, June 18, 1879, Adjutant-General's Office, Austin; *Ford County Globe*, July 20, 1880, and April 26, 1881.

exceeded its eastern rival, one hundred and twenty-five miles away, in downright depravity and devilment. In spite of Goodnight's antipathy for Mobeetie — heightened by the killing of a brother-in-law there — and his conviction as to its unexcelled wickedness, Arrington's belief that Tascosa was 'the hardest place on the frontier' seems well founded. In 1881 the county was organized, Cape Willingham was elected sheriff, and with a double-barreled shotgun, undertook, somewhat successfully, the cultivation of those conventions of settled life the environment had hitherto discouraged. If these settlements were typical of frontier range towns, the two succeeding villages in the Panhandle-Plains country were not without philanthropic precedent.

In the fall of 1878, as has been noted, Carhart founded his Christian Colony in Donley County, brought in good Methodist farming settlers from the Middle West, sold them lands, issued the deeds with prohibition clauses, and thereby established the first temperance experiment on the dry, dry Plains. Compared with Tascosa and Mobeetie, Clarendon, with its few farming settlers and a half-dozen preachers, was a more proper though less aggressive place, which the cowboys referred to as 'Saint's Roost.' [3] A hundred miles south of Clarendon, Paris Cox colonized a number of Quaker families in Crosby County in the fall of 1879, and appropriately called his village Estacado, the first settlement above the cap-rock of the Staked Plains. [4]

Notwithstanding this infiltration, the more astute observers soon saw that whereas the first cowmen came for grass, many of those who followed came for 'climate' as well, and with the increase in settlement there was an increase in the number of riders who swung wide loops and carried running-irons upon their saddles. In spite of the efforts of individual cow-

---

[3] *Tascosa Pioneer*, June 12, 1886; Goodnight, 'Recollections,' I, 11; Burton, as cited, 84; *Deed Record*, I, 3, Donley County; A. R. Carhart, MS., 'Clarendon,' Goodnight Papers.

[4] See Burton, as cited, 84; Roger A. Burgess, 'Pioneer Quaker Farmers of the South Plains,' *Panhandle-Plains Historical Review*, 1928, pp. 116 and following; *Clarendon News*, August 2, 1879.

men and the work of Texas Rangers, the toughs practically controlled the country, and Goodnight decided the cowmen must organize. He urged the idea of protection with Bugbee, Nelson, Cresswell, and other important cattlemen, and when the problem of fever added a pressing and even greater danger, cowboy couriers passed the word from ranch to ranch, carrying the call to all the better class of people from the North Plains to the Matadors. In March, 1880, they met at Mobeetie, and under the leadership of Goodnight attacked the trail problem with speed and precision, chose him as president, and about a year later more formally organized The Panhandle Stock Association of Texas.[5]

Goodnight's individual troubles continued, and he not only held herds out by force of arms, but wrote the cattlemen of the lower country and advised them that they could not come through his Panhandle ranges. He addressed a blanket warning to one of his old frontier friends, George T. Reynolds, who in turn handed it to the editor of the *Fort Griffin Echo* with the comment that, though it was so plain as to 'require no explanation,' he desired 'its publication that stock men generally may know how overbearing prosperity can make a man.'

Que Ti Qua Ranch, Aug. 20. [1881]

Dear Sir:

I send Mr. Smith to turn your cattle so they will not pass through our range. He will show you around and guide you until you strike the head of this stream and then you will have a road. The way he will show you is nearer and there are shorter drives to water than any route you can take. Should you come by here you will have a drive of 35 miles to make.

I hope you will take this advice as yourselves and I have always been good friends, but even friendship will not protect you in the drive through here, and should you attempt to pass through, be kind enough to tell your men what they will have to face as I do not wish to hurt men that do not understand what they will be very sure to meet.

I hope you will not treat this as idle talk, for I mean every

---

[5] 'The Panhandle Stock Association of Texas,' Archives, Secretary of State, Austin, Charter No. 2721; *Ford County Globe*, December 28, 1880, and February 22, 1881.

word of this, and if you have any feeling for me as a friend or acquaintance, you will not put me to any desperate actions. I will not perhaps see you myself, but take this advice from one that is and always has been your friend.

My cattle are now dying of the fever contracted from cattle driven from Fort Worth, therefore do not have any hope that you can convince me that your cattle will not give mine the fever, this we will not speak of. I simply say to you that you will never pass through here in good health.

Yours truly,

C. GOODNIGHT [6]

Thus Goodnight laid down the principle of the Winchester Quarantine, by which extra-legal procedure the Panhandle, for several years, protected its cattle against fever-bearing herds.

In a three-day session, held at Mobeetie early in 1881, the Panhandle Stock Association was formally organized, the constitution and by-laws were drafted and approved, and a reward of two hundred and fifty dollars for anyone rustling Association cattle was posted. The Northwest Texas Stock Association, organized at Graham in 1877, and destined to become the Texas and Southwestern Cattle Raisers' Association, made little attempt at first, according to J. F. Evans, to enforce its resolutions against stealing. Much theft was by big men, and members of the executive committee of the latter organization shook their heads and told Evans that the Panhandle could not enforce its drastic measures without bloodshed. Goodnight and other old-timers had anticipated opposition to the rigid enforcement of this resolution, not only among strictly dishonest men, but among some of their old Texan members, inured, as they were, to the Texas tradition of free grass and free beef. Hence they considered it good policy to elect a Texas man as president, and J. F. Evans, who had just come from Sherman to locate the Spade Ranch on the Salt Fork, near Clarendon, was elected, not because of his experience with cows, but because he was an honest man 'from Texas.' Con-

---

[6] *Fort Griffin Echo*, October 8, 1881.

servatism could not then reasonably charge innovation by outside men.

In contrast with the Northwest Texas Association's executive committee of twelve, theirs was constituted of only five members, and purposely kept small to permit of an easy

CHARLIE MURPHY, PALO DURO COWBOY

quorum and expeditious handling of business. Its power was almost arbitrary. Charged with the general interests of the Association, it might hire inspectors, detectives, and legal counsel, spend any amount of money it thought wise in the promotion of the welfare of the members, and to keep the nature of its operations strictly executive and hence unknown to thieves, was required to make no report as to the nature of expenditures. With the establishment of order this generous, executive policy was restricted by an amended charter and constitution in 1886, limiting the expense fund to five thousand dollars.[7]

[7] J. F. Evans to J. E. H., December 31, 1930; 'Constitution and By-laws, Panhandle Stock Association,' Panhandle-Plains Historical Society, Canyon; 'Amended Charter,' Archives, Secretary of State, Austin, under date April 26, 1886.

The Association had no capital stock, but in 1886 its aggregate of credits, lands, and cattle was estimated at ten million dollars. Operating expenses were raised by fees, by annual dues, and primarily by assessment upon the membership herds, either at rate of from one to three cents per head, or one dollar and a half upon every thousand dollars' valuation. The organization grew rapidly, and though its membership represented some three hundred thousand head of cattle, it was by no means a big man's affair. In emphasizing this point, Goodnight said that 'we organized for the purpose of mutual benefit, co-operation, and protection, taking in any settler that would join us, whether he had one cow or ten, guaranteeing that our attorneys would take care of his legal battles and our inspectors would take care of his cattle interests.' Throughout the life of the Association the man with one cow or saddle horse had equal rights with the man who counted his cattle by the tens of thousands.

'It worked very well, brought the good people together, pitted them against the bad, and put order into the country.' Most of the settlers were poor, and whenever one went into court the Association took his case off his hands, furnished him its attorneys, and bore all the expenses. Yet this arrangement was subject to assault. In the early eighties English, Scotch, and Eastern American capital was being poured into the cattle business, and invested in immense outfits in the Plains country. These companies usually sent lawyers to represent them at the Association meetings, who, along with sophisticated ideas of business and careful routine, brought a conviction that voting strength should be adjudged on the basis of stock.

'At one meeting they made some smooth talks,' explained Goodnight, 'in favor of granting extra votes on the basis of the number of cattle owned. They made it sound pretty good, and it looked like the members were going to vote it through.' Under such an arrangement, it should be observed, Goodnight and Adair would have had the most powerful voting strength of any member of the Association. Yet the organizer thought this subversive of the original aim, and characteristically took the bull by the horns.

'I knew nothing about oratory,' he continued, 'but I got up and told them plainly that such a move would defeat the purpose of the Association, which was to give the little man equal right with the big man, and before I'd see such a rule passed, I'd disband the whole organization. But,' he concluded, 'the rule did not pass.' [8]

O. H. Nelson followed Evans as president, Goodnight came in again, and feeling he could be more helpful outside, declined re-election. He was succeeded by Robert Moody, who had ranched with P. T. Barnum, in Colorado, before coming to the Panhandle to establish the PO Ranch near the site of Canadian. These wheel-horses, with Nick Eaton, Thomas S. Bugbee, and H. W. Cresswell, often served on the executive committee. Obviously it is impossible to follow the adventures of each administration through the various ramifications of its work, such as building the two-hundred-mile drift fence above the Canadian, the 'Winchester Quarantine,' the problems of the general works, sheep, wire, and so on. An attempt to sketch the cultural influence of the Association must be guided by its primary purpose — protection.

At first the Panhandle was attached to the Tenth Judicial District, and anyone with official business journeyed upwards of four hundred miles to Gainesville, or some equally remote North Texas point. Small wonder that the plainsmen talked of 'going to Texas' as of going to Colorado or Kansas! In an attempt to reduce these limitations of distance the cowmen succeeded, in 1881, in securing the creation of the Thirty-Fifth Judicial District, embracing the entire Panhandle and part of Indian Territory. Senator A. L. Matlock, from the Montague District, introduced the bill, and 'Spade' Evans, present to help push it through, suggested to Governor Roberts

[8] Goodnight to J. E. H., July 2, 1929; 'Proceedings, the Association,' 24 and 29; *Ford County Globe,* August 30, 1881.

the appointment of I. N. Roach of Weatherford as district attorney. But Roach had voted his county's instructions against
Roberts in political convention, and hence was hardly accepta-
ble.

'I don't buy my enemies!' Roberts answered. 'What that
country needs is young men.'

'Governor Roberts,' Evans replied, 'you never were so mistaken in your life. The only women we have in that country are
lewd. What we need is married men — men with families,' and
so led into an argument of the home as a moral influence.

The Governor stood up, slapped him on the shoulder, and
said:

'Mr. Evans, you are correct and you shall have them.'

Evans next proposed J. N. Browning, of Albany, whom
Roberts appointed. Matlock dropped by and the Governor
asked his preference for district judge, and when Frank Willis,
of Montague, was proposed, Roberts asked:

'Well, how did he stand for me in the last election?'

'Governor, I believe he is about the only man in the county
who did vote for you,' Matlock replied, and Willis got the
place.

He and Browning moved to Mobeetie and entered upon
their duties, the first eschewing not a friendly game on the side,
nor the latter a gratuitous drink. The political ambition of the
former was eventually to cause both trouble, but now they co-
operated in launching the local ship of justice where the ports
of conviction were in inverse ratio to the hazards involved.
Except for their home town, Tascosa was their only worry, and
while Oldham's county judge was allowed but 'one hundred
and twenty dollars per year for his services,' the town boasted
other accessories of justice in a husky blacksmith who held its
inquests, and the finest Boot Hill Grave Yard south of Dodge
City.[9]

[9] Evans, as cited; A. L. Matlock to J. E. H.; Nelson, 'The First Panhandle Stockmen's Association,' as cited; *Senate Journal*, 1887, Appendix, 49; *Fort Griffin Echo*,
April 8, May 14, July 9 and 23, 1881.

The fees of office were so small that men of ability could not afford the jobs, and in order to put and keep capable men in important official position, the cattlemen began paying bonuses above the regular fees of office, raising this money by the usual assessment against themselves. They paid the sheriff of Wheeler County a bonus of five hundred dollars annually, and when W. H. Woodman — a brilliant, eccentric character who loved liquor and commanded psychology when lacking in law — was elected district attorney, he was paid an annual bonus of fifteen hundred dollars.

The politicians of the State, coming from timbered and well-watered sections, had little conception of the particular needs and problems of this isolated and essentially different land. Goodnight told Evans that he would like to bring Senator Matlock to the Panhandle at his own expense, show him over the country, and acquaint him with its problems, but hesitated to extend the invitation for fear Matlock would consider the offer a bribe. Evans assured him that he knew the Senator as an intelligent, high-class man, and that the letter might be written in perfect propriety, without fear of offense. Goodnight wrote, but receiving no answer, feared Matlock had misconstrued his offer, and so informed Evans.

Evans vigorously reassured him, and promised to mention the matter to Matlock as soon as they met. Later the occasion presented, and Evans questioned his friend:

'Matlock, do you remember a letter you got sometime ago that neither you nor anyone else in the Senate could read, which you finally threw in the waste-basket?' He did, perfectly. Evans advised him of its contents, but the reconnaissance was never made.[10]

At the first session of the Legislature following the creation of the district, some members favored its abolition on account of the thinly settled nature of the country. Of the twenty-seven counties in the district, besides Wheeler and Oldham,

[10] Evans to J. E. H., January 1, 1931; A L. Matlock to J. E. H.; Goodnight to Evans, January 30, 1882, Evans Papers.

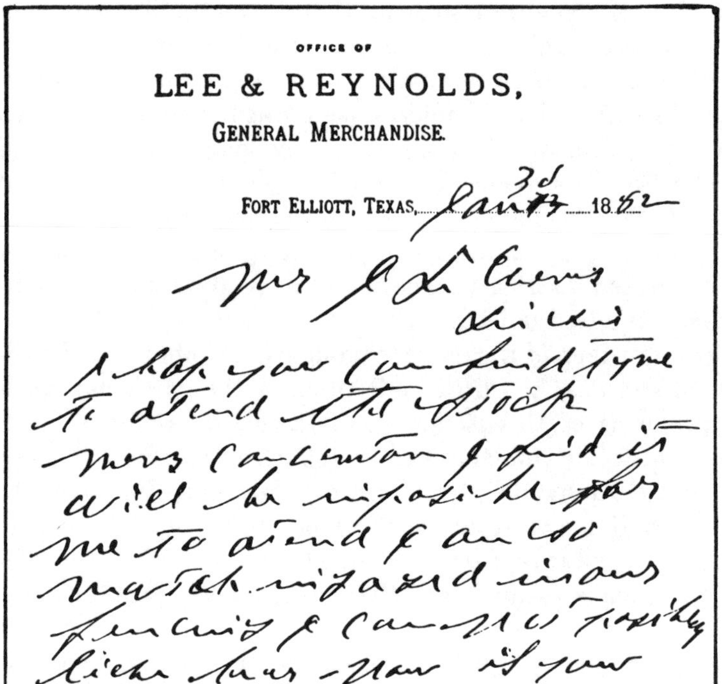

OFFICE OF

LEE & REYNOLDS,

GENERAL MERCHANDISE.

FORT ELLIOTT, TEXAS, Jan 3d 1882

Mr J L. Evans
Dear Sir

I hope you can find tyme
to attend the stock
mens Convention & find it
will be imposible for
me to attend & am so
much engaged in our
fencing & can not posibly
leave hear — Now if you
can go down & will see
that your expences are
paid it have our the
A Socistian dogs not
pay you I will pay
you have at yous
expences my self
I think it of very great
importence that we are
represented if you go
their do all you can

GOODNIGHT'S LETTER ABOUT MATLOCK

OFFICE OF

LEE & REYNOLDS,

GENERAL MERCHANDISE.

FORT ELLIOTT, TEXAS, ...18......

for the School bill we
want that passed at the
next meeting of the legislator if posible & on the
most favorable terms we
can git. Try & show the
Northern delegates that
our grass does not
support as many cattle per
acre as the northern can
nothing as we dont have
but 2 months growing
spring weather & the
grass is short & thin
on the ground I have
not heard from some
man Lock yet in
any way I hope the child
never miss construe my
letter I remain in haste
faith your friend
C Goodnight

only Donley possessed a town, and Goodnight wrote Evans, who had previously opposed its organization, that it might be well to organize so that the Plains could 'show some progress' before the Legislature. What was more important, he wished to reduce the distance to a legal seat, and get away from the toughs at Mobeetie.

Thereupon Evans, from his home at Sherman, wrote to his friends in the Christian Temperance Colony, whose earlier efforts at organization he had forestalled, that the cattlemen would support the petition praying for organization if the colonists would agree to their naming the sheriff, judge, and commissioners. L. H. Carhart and J. T. Otey, a merchant at Clarendon, to whom he addressed the letter, agreed to the proposition, and the colonists prepared the petition and started it over the country.

As in the case of counties already organized, they had to go beyond their political bounds to muster the required signatures. The procedure was slightly irregular, but what was a county line between Western friends? Goodnight's cowboys on the Palo Duro, though most of them were in Armstrong County, were asked to sign; of course those on the RO and the Spade ranches were solicited; and finally the citizens looked toward a political convention and actual organization upon March 22, 1882. So far there had been no manifest opposition toward Evans's proposal, but now L. N. Nall, his foreman on the Spades, wrote that:

> the town *click* is doing all they can to get all the oficers we will Mix it with them　do you care if I run for Comishiner it is just as you Say　let me hear from soon godby.

Verily, there was growing opposition, for according to Evans, most of the county offices had been tacitly assigned among the colonists, even before they came to Texas. So Judge J. G. Murdock, who it seems had never been a judge, but planned to be, aroused some indignation against the arbitrary Evans proposal, and called a county nominating convention, claiming, and probably with cause, that Otey and Carhart had no right to make such a contract for the colony on the one hand, and that Evans had no right to dictate on the other. Rowes's and Evans's cowboys attended, and Goodnight brought his men up from the Palo Duro.

Murdock was elected chairman of the convention and immediately the question arose as to who might vote. The chairman opened the *Texas Statutes* and read the law clearly defining that only qualified voters might participate in county conventions. Hence it was quite evident that were the law adhered to, Goodnight's cowboys, and — on account of the drifting nature of the breed — many of Rowes's and Evans's would be barred, which meant certain victory for the colonists. Goodnight arose to state that the initial steps toward organization had not, of necessity, been altogether by regular procedure, and presented a motion that the only requirements for voting in the convention be the appearance of the individual's name upon the petition. Murdock admitted some irregularities in the past, but now insisted that they proceed only in strict accord with the law. Naturally the colonists supported his ruling, and he refused to put the motion to a vote.

'Well, if the chair won't put the motion,' said Goodnight, rising, '*I put the motion*. If a man can be legal voter for the purpose of petitioning for the organization of a county, he ought to be a good voter in its convention. If you look at it like I do, if a man's name is on the petition as a voter, then I'll be damned if he doesn't vote here.'

The cowboys voted in the convention at Clarendon, nominating G. A. Brown as judge; Al Gentry, sheriff; a freighter, two ranch foremen, and Goodnight, as commissioners. 'Of course that was a six-shooter vote,' said Evans in later years, 'but we were standing on the petition, and I think we were right.' At any rate, it is interesting to observe their management of the county's affairs.[11]

[11] Evans to J. E. H., December 31, 1930; Goodnight, 'Recollections,' II, 126-27; I. N. Nall to J. F. Evans, February 20, 1882, in files of author.

The commissioners served without pay, advanced the needed money themselves, ran the county on a cash basis until the first year's taxes came in, and kept public business in the hands of responsible people. Here, too, the pay of county officials would necessarily have been parsimonious had not the cowmen subsidized the offices. An attempt had been made to get John Farrington to offer as sheriff.

'No, thank you,' he replied to a solicitor. 'I make more where I am, and I'm not shot at *all the time.*'

Both the county judge and sheriff were paid annual bonuses of one thousand dollars during the first two years, half of which was paid by Goodnight alone. After Judge Brown retired, the office was allowed eight hundred dollars annually until the country settled; Browning resigned as district attorney because the office would not support him; and his successor, Temple Houston, brilliant but erratic son of the old General, besides being paid a bonus was furnished a law library.

Since there was no doctor nearer than Fort Elliott, the cowmen, to induce a good one to Clarendon and to insure against his starving before the country filled with people, paid Dr. W. H. Stocking a bonus of eighteen hundred dollars for five years.

In 1881, Judge B. H. White, of Clarendon, called Goodnight's attention to the fact that a number of the nesters had children of school age, but were too poor to educate them. Since there was no provision for a public school, Goodnight discussed the matter with the Association, and was instructed to provide the school and assess the cattlemen south of the North Fork for its support. The secretary, W. L. R. Dickson, pro-rated the needed amount and the school was maintained for two years, though not a cowman had a child in attendance.

The first teacher, Tom Martindale, to quote Goodnight again, 'was really a roustabout; kind of thought to be a head of the thieves. He was well educated and as smart as he could be, so when we got to looking for a teacher, I said: "Here's this son-of-a-gun! We ought to hang him. Let's put him to teaching school." We did, and he made a good one too.' [12]

In the winter of 1880, the cowmen sent John Poe, late from the buffalo range and the marshal's office at Fort Griffin, to join Pat Garrett, sheriff of Lincoln County, in hunting down Billy the Kid, who was depredating upon the cattle of the western Panhandle. Largely through his cool, calculating work, Garrett succeeded in locating and killing the Kid at Fort Sumner in the spring of 1881.

As the most effective means of fighting outlawry, 'Spade' Evans, small and rotund but virile enough, with a high resolve born of youth and lofty purpose, favored the initial and relentless prosecution of big thieves. In accord with this policy, the Association first arrested the driver of a Spur trail herd, who, in passing, killed a JA calf for beef, in harmony with a long-established practice of the open range. Arrington arrested him seventy-five miles up the trail, and unceremoniously haled him back to Mobeetie for trial. The country roared for this handling of a big cattleman 'like an ordinary cow thief'; a bold move that cut deep into the long-cherished creed of some old-time Texas cowmen — 'not cheap thieves,' as Evans explained, 'but six-shooter men who saw no harm in eating a neighbor's beef.' And though no bill was found, the action exercised a marvelous psychological effect in showing that the fight on theft was to proceed from the top.[13]

The Capitol Syndicate, or XIT, had not yet entered the western Plains to take up its long and vigorous fight for law, and around Tascosa dead-hard men continued to give trouble. One of the first and largest outfits in that section was the LX, owned principally by Bates and Beals, wealthy Massachusetts men. Its manager, outlaw Bill Moore, stole wherever it was profitable, especially from his employers. Around him

[12] Goodnight, 'Recollections,' I, 16, and II, 127; Nelson to Goodnight, May 30, 1927; Burton, as cited, 88–89; Goodnight to J. E. H., May 22, 1929; 'Cattlemen Established the First School,' clipping from *Southwest Plainsman*, Goodnight Papers; *Senate Journal*, as cited, 33, 69, 73; *Fort Worth Gazette*, January 11, 1884, and February 17, 1887.

[13] Evans, as cited; *The Globe Live Stock Journal*, August 5, 1884.

were cowpunchers ready to maverick the company calves or steal from their neighbors, and the Association soon thought that Deacon Bates, as he was called, was trying to make up the deficit by gathering strays himself. In the winter, when hair was long and brands were hard to read, he trailed the LX beeves, and strays that fell in on the way, into the Cherokee Strip, from where, after fattening in the spring, they were shipped to market, and the owners in the Panhandle, unaware of their fate, marked up heavier winter losses. Such was the belief of many of the cowmen in the eastern Panhandle, and when a trainload of LX cattle were driven into Caldwell for shipment, the inspector cut approximately one-fourth of them as strays

Martindale, the school-teacher, turned inspector, was alert when the next LX shipment arrived. He carefully examined the cattle in the corrals, found no strays, but upon crossing the river into Illinois discovered seventy-two that had, apparently, been unloaded outside St. Louis and crossed to the other side. Warrants were sworn, and Arrington, now sheriff of Wheeler County, traveled to Massachusetts to arrest Deacon Bates, but found, in that conventional commonwealth, that extradition was necessary. Governor Ben Butler was out of the State, and Arrington was kept running from pillar to post in an attempt to get his papers. The Southern gentleman thought little of Butler, who, as military guardian of New Orleans, was extremely unpopular. Little could be hoped from a conference with the partisan Arrington, but the sheriff was persistent, and upon the Governor's return was successful in securing the papers. Bates, it seems, was a political enemy of Butler's and the latter is reported to have approved the papers, saying: 'I never signed another document with the same amount of pleasure.'

Arrington hurried his prisoner toward Texas, detouring from his contemplated route to evade the service of a writ of *habeas corpus,* and placed Bates in jail at Mobeetie. The case was continued; District Attorney Houston had resigned upon the outbreak of the cowboy strike at Tascosa to run for the Legislature; and Lucius Dills had been appointed to fill out the term. The case was again continued in November, 1883, and Dills wrote Bugbee, then living in Kansas City and one of the principal witnesses, urging expedition of the trial. Bugbee indignantly answered, according to Dills, that he had written Houston months before that the cattle had been paid for, and he now had no complaint. A year later, Willis dismissed the case on Dills's motion, because, the attorney said, he had found no evidence to sustain 'any allegation in the indictment,' and because he had learned that Bugbee would exonerate the defendant. Yet the cowmen were displeased with Dills's work, and after the next election W. H. Woodman was in office, and Dills was on his way to New Mexico, nursing a decided antipathy for Goodnight.[14]

The RO Ranch, on the Salt Fork, owned by Alfred and Vincent Rowe, fine English gentlemen, was managed by John Petrie, good cowhand, likable college graduate, evident gentleman, and, so his neighbors claimed, a shrewd rustler. Following the discoveries of a cowboy detective hired by Evans, the executive committee charged that he and his men were rustling. The Rowes were not convinced and kept him on the ranch. According to Association by-laws, the employment of a known rustler by any member was cause for expulsion, and in August the Association met in executive session and called the Rowes before it to show cause why the rule should not be invoked. They were finally convinced, and agreed to discharge Petrie. But on the outside, wild rumor was flying across the ranges.

On account of the impossibility of convictions, a strong minority in the Association had been favoring the formation of a vigilance committee, though the dominant spirits opposed it. Now, while the Association was in executive session at-

[14] Nelson to J. E. H., February 26, 1927; Evans, as cited; Goodnight to J. E. H., April 8, 1927, and August 2, 1928; Jas. H. East to J. E. H., September 27, 1927; Lucius Dills to J. E. H., March 3, 1933; *Minutes, District Court,* Wheeler County, I, 254–55 and 280; II, 44–45, 54 and 98.

tempting to dispose of the Rowe case, rumor had it that the
cowmen were organizing the long-anticipated committee.

The speed of news by the grapevine telegraph is always
marvelous. In the Argentine the gauchos used to say that
'a man without a horse is a man without legs.' Even so,
where the fastest means of locomotion was the flying feet of
a cow-pony, forty miles was a fair day's ride — sixty a long
day's ride. The gauchos said, too, that 'a stolen horse carries
you well,' and in forty-eight hours after the meeting, news
had traveled two hundred miles across the Panhandle. In
only thirty-six hours, twenty-four well-known rustlers had, in
cowboy parlance, pulled their freight for parts unknown.

Early in July, 1883, following the work of Evans's detective,
John Petrie and four of his men were arraigned before the
bar at Clarendon to stand trial for theft, and some of their
friends came down from Tascosa. Sympathizing with the
lawless element, directing, co-operating with and encouraging
it, was a man of unusual craftiness who was never found
responsible. His name was Jenkins — nickname Hoggie —
and his particular section of Tascosa, that adobe portion
down the river sheltering dance-halls and saloons, was called
Hogtown in his honor.

It seems that Jenkins and his cohorts set out to see that
there should be no courts in the Panhandle, or, if courts, then
no convictions. The country was full of perjurers who almost
made a business of going from court to court, where, with the
help of sympathetic jurors, they swore thieves from under
convictions in spite of incontrovertible evidence. In regretting
the difficulty, Goodnight simply observed that in court the
dishonest had one decided advantage — he can swear whatever is necessary while the man of integrity is limited to the
facts. The evening before court convened at Clarendon to try
Petrie and his friends, Jenkins showed up with 'two wagons,
plenty of whiskey, five or six noted rustlers and perjurers, and
two or three bad women, and camped just across the creek from
the courthouse, or rather the old shack in which court was held.'

Though he had no particular business in town, Goodnight happened in with the JA outfit, and other men came in from the Spades and the Shoe Bars.

JESS STEEN, JA LONGHORN

During the night the Tascosa renegades cartooned Judge Willis most shamefully, sending him the skull and cross bones, and made some threats against the court. Next morning he met Goodnight on the street, and excitedly told him that it would not be safe to open court.

'Well, Judge,' Goodnight answered, 'I know very little about your courts, but I do know a great deal about these ruffians and thieves. As you see, my mess-wagon is over there on the creek, in which we have our sharp-shooters and pistols.

I have eighteen good men. You go and open the court. At the proper time, if necessary, order me to fire, and in ten minutes I will have the hill clear, even to their wagon spokes.'

Willis thought it a splendid suggestion, and as court opened without disturbance he was wont to construe this as the turning point in law in the Panhandle.

When he came to the jury selection, Willis properly ruled Association members ineligible, since they were paying for the prosecution. But veniremen were scarce, and in order to make cowboys eligible, they were deeded lots in town and the jury was eventually completed. 'Through sympathy or fear,' Evans wrote, 'the jury material was with the indicted. Both sides were playing for high stakes. It's difficult to envision the surroundings, or realize the tension. With testimony to waste, Goodnight and I knew that conviction could not be had. We were playing a big bluff — to wear them down.'

One suspect was released, but as many indictments as possible were brought against each defendant so as to break him financially, if not convict him. Petrie saw the plan, and knowing that it would work, said that the defendants would leave the country if the cases were dropped. This was agreed upon, and a formal judgment of banishment, perhaps the first in the history of the State, was signed by the defendants and entered upon the records of Donley County. 'We ... do solemnly swear [it reads], that in consideration of certain cases now pending ... being dismissed, and the further consideration that no more bills of indictment shall be filed against us, we each of us hereby agree to leave the Panhandle of Texas within ten days, and never voluntarily return. . . .' [15]

As the band filed out of the shack and walked to the hitching-rack for their horses, Goodnight met them, and though every man was armed to the teeth, the cursing with which he sped them on their way cannot be given in print.

[15] Evans to J. E. H., February 6, 1931; Goodnight to J. E. H., April 8 and September 2, 1927; Nelson to J. E. H., February 26, 1927; Burton, as cited, 85–87; Henry Taylor to J. E. H., September 3, 1932; Certified Affidavit of Abner Early, Doc Thompson and Bud Stevens, from District Clerk, Donley County, 1884; *State Docket*, District Court, i, 4–6; *Civil Record*, i, 49–54, all at Clarendon, Texas.

And thus passed the first years of the Association's work, with diligent prosecution of big men but with no convictions for theft in the entire Panhandle. Up at Mobeetie the government butcher, who had been killing Laurel Leaf, Bar CC, and Springer Ranch cattle, and piling the hides into a ditch, was caught and prosecuted by the Association. District Attorney Houston, sober as a judge, closed his eloquent plea to the jury with Lord Nelson's injunction to his men before Trafalgar: '"England expects every man to do his duty," and,' he implored, 'Texas expects the same of you.' It was a beautiful appeal, and they sent the defendant to the penitentiary like men. One extra-legal incident has not been forgotten.

Mose Hays, owner of the Springer Ranch, after lying around town several days expecting to be called as a witness, arrived that morning, late. Judge Willis imposed a fine. They left the courthouse together, Mose imploring the Judge to remit it, and offering various excuses, to all of which his Honor turned a deaf ear. On the way downtown they passed a saloon where the familiar clink of glasses and the pervading aroma invited the thirsty inside. Forgetting his appeal from the law, Mose turned to his stocky friend: 'Judge, let's go in and get a drink.' For the first time his Honor heard him, and, turning, slapped the suppliant on the back, exclaiming: 'Now, Mose Hays, you've said something,' a classic expression, which for years thereafter was the invariable response to such a proposition anywhere on the Plains. It was really an occasion for celebrating, for after six years of relentless work the first cow thief had been sentenced from the Panhandle, and that, too, was 'saying something.' If it did not mark the millennium, it presaged another day, for with the multiplication of county organizations and the definite assignments of rangers, the old order was changing, as indicated by another incident.

One fine summer day in the eighties, the Turkey Tracks had thrown a herd together on the Canadian, and the cowboys were cutting cattle when the apparently honest range boss looked up and saw two men coming over a hill in the distance.

He took them for rangers, but said nothing about that, only remarking to one of the hands: 'Look after the herd until I get back.' Reining his horse in the opposite direction, he loped out of sight, and, though that was fifty years ago, the weathered Woods Coffee, who took charge of the herd, concludes this story with a whimsical smile: 'He hasn't got back yet.' [16]

With detectives riding the ranges, inspectors watching the trails and markets, and responsible men holding the public offices, wholesale theft became both hazardous and difficult, and rustlers of cattle scattered beyond the Plains, or worked in petty fashion.

And as he paused at Christmas time in 1885, and thought back on the last ten years of individual and co-operative effort, the leader of the Panhandle Stock Association observed to a critical stranger:

'Certainly, we have quiet, peace and order here now and the law is enforced better than down below. We sleep with our doors and windows unfastened, and even the store on this place is not locked, the lock not being used, having got out of order.' [17]

[16] Mose Hays to J. E. H., November 8, 1931; T. D. Hobart to J. E. H., September 8, 1932.

[17] *Galveston News*, January 7, 1886.

XXII. THE LEASE FIGHT

THE disorderly processes of Panhandle life, centering around the rough-and-ready villages of Mobeetie and Tascosa, were only slightly counterbalanced by Clarendon, the sedate temperance colony on the Salt Fork. The two first 'bellied up to the bar and took their pizen straight,' while 'Saints' Roost,' timidly perched in the crotch of Carroll Creek, drank gyppy water, and hoped crops would grow where they had never grown before.

Though Clarendon had the refinements of a paper, the *Clarendon News*, printed in Sherman and mailed out about once a month, the country was too dry even for prohibitionists, and its devotees soon dwindled away. With the coming of the Fort Worth and Denver Railroad, in 1887, the old site was abandoned for one on the railroad, occasioning regret at Tascosa because never again could a neighboring court sentence a prisoner to '"ten days in Clarendon" as the nearest approach to solitary confinement.'

Those were hard, frugal days, trying the resources and ingenuity of the settler who first attempted to till the soil. Usually he lived in a dugout in the ground, packed or hauled water from great distances away, burned cow-chips for fuel, and otherwise adapted himself to the rigorous clime if he stayed on his claim. Yet along advancing railroads washed that restless tide of immigration symbolized by the man with the hoe. Washburn, Panhandle City, Amarillo, and other villages dotted the Plains with unpainted board structures, and by the fall of 1887 there were ten newspapers in the Panhandle, each booming its particular location as the promised land, though two years before only three counties had reported election returns — one hundred and fifty votes at Mobeetie, one hundred and twenty-five at Tascosa, and eighty-four at

Clarendon. Far out on the Staked Plains, Deaf Smith County made preparations to organize, and though it had not yet dreamed of a courthouse of Georgian marble, certainly not again would its voters hold their election in the shade of a haystack, as initially done, and report the total returns as 'two Democrats, two Republicans, and a sheepman.' [1]

Agitating the lower country at this time was the old conflict of range versus grange. Yet in the Plains country intimidation of honest little men and nesters seemed remarkably infrequent. When, in 1885, a reporter asked for the cowmen's attitude toward settlement, Goodnight answered that:

> They are indifferent. They don't think it much of a farming country, but they are willing for anybody to try it who wants to

[1] Files of the *Tascosa Pioneer*, 1886–89; G. R. Jowell to J. E. H., January 17, 1927.

do so. They say that stock-farming does not conflict with them, and that if it is a farming country farmers will occupy it and the cow must go. It is natural and it is right, and nobody is foolish enough to fight the inevitable.[2]

But 'down in Texas' rumor was wild, and generally the press joined the politicians in branding cowmen as trespassers on the range, enemies of settlement, and dictatorial usurpers of 'the children's grass.'

When asked for advice, Goodnight emphasized, not the breaking of all the sod, but stock-farming instead. In 1892, when the tide had flowed to his pasture fences, a representative of the *St. Louis Globe-Democrat* put the usual question:

'Can a farmer make a living as far west as this?'

'Yes,' came the more mature answer of the cowman. 'But he can't make money. He may, by hard work, do a little better some seasons than a living, but he can't get rich. The only way a farmer can do well here is to combine stock-raising with farming.'[3]

Almost as he spoke there hung over the Plains the shadow of the memorable drought of 1893 to 1895, which practically depopulated the country. Though the booster of the early twentieth century claimed such opinion the mark of moss-back cowmen, it may still be pondered, for in spite of splendid scientific development of dry-farming the droughts of recent years saved the Government the trouble of withdrawing these submarginal lands from cultivation. Nevertheless, the papers of his country unjustly branded Goodnight as the greatest enemy of settlement, and lent color and conviction to the attacks made down below. Desire for a degree of stability in range tenure did not imply unreasoned opposition to settlement.

In 1880, Panhandle cowmen met to discuss Texas fever and the trail, and looking toward the problem of control, agreed that leasing of the public domain was indispensable to their

[2] *Galveston News*, December 14, 1885, and January 7, 1886.
[3] Walter B. Stevens, *Through Texas: A Series of Interesting Letters*, 16.

interests, unless the State would sell the lands. In 1881, they sent a lawyer to Austin for the purpose of assuring the Legislature that they wanted to pay for the lands they were using 'in order to hold possession and not be subjected to intrusion.' They were already pouring their cash reserves into land, but soon saw that their 'investment would be thrown away ... unless the policy of leasing the school alternates should be adopted,' and Goodnight himself journeyed to Austin to urge leasing of the public domain,[4] but a lease act failed of passage because of the opposition of the free grass element.

Instead, the Legislature passed the Land Board Act of 1883, which provided for the competitive sale of as many as seven sections to the individual; that ranch lands 'may be leased ... for not less than four cents per annum' for not more than ten years; and that leases were to be let competitively upon such terms as the State Land Board, set up by this act, might designate. The Board was to be composed of Governor John Ireland, Attorney General John D. Templeton, Comptroller W. J. Swain, Treasurer F. R. Lubbock, and Commissioner of the General Land Office, W. C. Walsh.[5]

Early in February, 1884, the Board provided for county surveyors to receive bids for both sale and lease of public lands, but that the competitive features of leasing were inapplicable should have been apparent from the beginning. The ranges were already occupied by cowmen who had usually bought portions of their range, had built tanks and other improvements thereon, and had fenced their grass for protection and conservative tenure. And though they held the public lands or free range by priority or range right, by the unwritten laws of the open country, they held it on terms of good will with one another and by a code superseding the dictates of formal government.

[4] A few years later, cowmen on the national domain were urging the Federal Government that leasing was 'necessary to bring system into the cattle-raising business.' *Fort Worth Gazette*, January 20, 1885; *Report*, Bureau of Animal Industry, 1884, p. 242; *Galveston News*, January 7, 1886. For comment on the railroad lobby for leasing, see the same issue and the *Fort Worth Gazette*, July 2, 1884.

[5] Gammel, *Laws of Texas*, ix, 394–95; *Report of State Land Board*, 1885, p. 5.

Infringement upon another's established range was so indecent and unneighborly as to be tantamount to war. Hence, after the country was stocked to capacity it was not done, and, quite naturally, when leases were let, Goodnight did not bid against his friends on the Shoe Bars or the Spades, and neither did they attempt to lease the range from under him. Each went to the designated agent and tendered bids on his established range at the minimum prescribed by law, the bids were forwarded to Austin, and the Land Board came to life.

'Discovering' that range law nullified the competitive feature of the legislative act, it met and arbitrarily resolved that — the law to the contrary, notwithstanding — it would lease no more land for less than eight cents an acre; that it might refuse to lease watered lands 'for any reason ... good and sufficient'; that sales should be made only to actual settlers; and that no watered lands should be sold. The spectacle of a board revising the provisions of the act it was created to administer might have been an amusing bit of Western humor except for the consequences.

The country rose in arms while range security jostled in political laps, and the ensuing fight, shot through with political ambition, ignorance, and prejudice, waxed high and hot in the local forum, in the press, and at the capitol. The cowmen carried their case to the courts and the Board was finally whipped into compliance with the law. The entire battle centered on Goodnight as the greatest of the 'bullionaires,' as the most powerful 'usurper of the children's grass.' It was an unfortunate episode in the history of Texas, and a bitter experience that he never forgot and never forgave.

This was the situation in 1885. Conservative plainsmen had aligned themselves in favor of leasing, lobbied for a law to that end, and had complied with its provisions. The Land Board had doubled the rate of lease, and many ranchmen, already caught on the verge of another depression by the backwash of the boom, and struggling under high interest levies and tremendous outlays for fencing, saw they could not pay. Some made no tender of bids at all, but most of those of the eastern Panhandle joined Goodnight in sending Gib Brown and Temple Houston to Austin, through whom they maintained their original tenders of lease.[6]

'Grass Commissioners' were sent out to investigate violations of the Board's rulings. General Henry E. McCulloch said eighteen million acres were being grazed free. W. T. Gass reported five million acres of school lands illegally fenced in the Panhandle, and added that 'the law cannot be enforced, at least by civil process, in the Panhandle counties.'[7]

By the first of December, 1885, 'the theme most talked about in government circles,' a correspondent wrote, 'is the question of using physical force for the ejectment of illegal fencers from the public lands.' Swain argued that the Government should send the rangers to tear down the fences, and Lubbock wished them first to make an example of the seven hundred and fifty thousand acres of the Goodnight and Adair pasture. Governor Ireland demurred for fear of constitutional authority, but intimated that if the sheriffs of the country took no action he would order the military out.[8]

The hectic year drew to a close with Goodnight seeking the best counsel in the State as to the legality of the Land Board's action; that body in the position of having to admit it was wrong or immediately take steps to enforce its decisions; and the range country watching to see what Goodnight would do. Early in December he went to Austin and again tendered his lease at the minimum. It was indignantly refused,[9] and Attorney-General Templeton served notice on W. H. Woodman to bring suits against the cowmen for illegal enclosure. He wrote:

I think that criminal prosecutions should be instituted.... I do not think that the courts below should undertake, whatever

---

[6] *Galveston News*, January 31, 1887; *Report of State Land Board*, 1885, pp. 6–11.

[7] *Fort Worth Gazette*, December 2, 1885.

[8] *Fort Worth Gazette*, November 24 and 29, 1885.

[9] *Fort Worth Gazette*, December 1, 1885; *Galveston News*, January 8, 1886.

may be their views, to pass upon the validity or constitutionality of the statute in any respect. I say this with a good deal of hesitation, and with all due deference to the courts; but I do think the grave duty of overturning the statute, for any reason whatever should be left to the courts of final resort. Should decision be against the State on the Statute, of course the State is without remedy; but, on the other hand, the defendant has his remedy by appeal, and as a general thing, there is no difficulty about those who would be prosecuted giving bonds and appealing in both civil and criminal cases.... Perhaps it might be necessary to resort to extraordinary means in some cases to hunt up evidence ... to send some one, not as a spy or detective, but openly, for the purpose of seeing and ascertaining that there is an illegal enclosure or that there is line riding so that he can go back and testify before the jury intelligently to that fact. If you can suggest any method by which you can be assisted from here, I think the Land Board, and perhaps the Governor, would take steps to furnish the assistance.[10]

Upon Christmas Eve, Templeton wrote Judge Willis expressing a hope that the law was enforceable; hazarding a belief — though 'the validity of the law has been gravely questioned' — that if a conviction can be had below, 'the court of appeals will sustain it'; and finally assuring the Judge that 'a question of so much gravity as the validity of the law should be left to the court of final resort....' [11] Willis did not answer.

Meanwhile, the Land Board and its commissioners spread the impression that the cowmen were fighting for free range and were decidedly hostile to leasing in policy, to which Goodnight answered, through the *Galveston News*:

'I am on record as the first man in the West who offered to buy and lease lands ... every man who knows me knows the charge to be false. After twenty-eight years experience in the cattle business I am strongly against the free-grass idea. It simply means the use of the grass to the strongest arm. The six-shooter and free grass go hand in hand, and as long as it is free so long the ranger is a necessity. There is more

[10] *Senate Journal*, 1887, Appendix, 100–01.   [11] The same, 125.

money for the cattleman in a fair lease than in free grass. The reasons are: 1. That he is able to systematize his business and improve his stock, the real secret of profits. 2. My next neighbor, who leases with me, must assist me in protecting my cattle to protect his own. To monopolize free grass a man must have a tough set of hands, whom he has to keep around him all the time, and they will eat up the profits and make every blade of grass cost him more than if he had it leased and fenced. I mean this to apply to a country settled by cattlemen, and not a wilderness. And then again, did anybody ever hear of any country being anything where the people did not own the soil? Properties of no kind can be safe where the people are not fixed to the land.' [1]

The public defense seemed futile. Templeton had advised the local officials to act, and when the village of Clarendon was enlivened with the opening of court in January, District Attorney Woodman appeared before the grand jury of cowmen, drawn the previous July, and asked for indictments. Thereupon the jury, of which Goodnight was foreman, found true bills against many of the Panhandle cowmen for illegal fencing, several of whom, like Goodnight, were on the grand jury themselves. The first bill was against the foreman for 'Unlawfully fencing and herding on Public School Lands,' and two days later, January 9, six more were found against him for the same offense. A total of seventy-six were found in all, and after several days for the clerk to write them out, Goodnight brought them to court in a basket and the jury was discharged.[13]

Judge T. J. Brown, of Sherman, whom Goodnight summoned in defense, came north through the Territory, to Dodge City by rail, and thence to Old Clarendon on the stage. This capable jurist favored the retention of Browning on account of his standing with the nesters, and Goodnight deferred to his wishes. The suits were tried before a jury made up — of neces-

---

[12] *Galveston News*, December 14, 1885.

[13] The author's detailed account of this trial, fully annotated, is to be found in *The Southwestern Historical Quarterly*, Austin, July, 1935, xxxviii, 1–27.

sity, on account of the sparseness of people — of some of the cowboys working for men being tried. Templeton came out to see the job well done, staging his way through a country noted for its gyppy water. He was unused to its properties, the more he drank the more he wanted, and by the time he reached his destination he was somewhat the worse for wear. He and Goodnight met in Clarendon, sat down on a convenient cottonwood log, and discussed the impending litigation.

CLARENDON COURTHOUSE

According to the cowman, the Attorney General's remarks soon developed that he was there actually for the political support of his friend Browning; and he offered to drop his fight on Goodnight, if Goodnight in turn would support Browning for district judge. Goodnight bluntly told him that he could not do so on account of Browning's record, whereupon Templeton indicated that, if he refused, prosecution of the enclosure cases would proceed. As Goodnight thought of the fifty-two cowmen involved in the fight with him, and the tender of exception by Templeton, his blood boiled, he screwed about on the log, and faced the official of State:

'I know nothing about law,' he said bitingly, 'but I do know one thing — if I've committed a crime, you can't remit it. Now I have two guns and you have none. If an outlaw comes up here and shoots you down and I just sit here, what does it mean for me?'

'It would make you accessory to the crime,' answered Templeton.

'You're mighty right, it would. And if I compromise with you, I have incriminated fifty-two men. We have disobeyed no law. Four cents was the minimum!'

'Then there is no hope of compromise?' asked the Attorney General.

'Not a God-damned bit! I'd see you in hell first, farther than a wedge would fall in twenty years.'

Thus the conference ended as T. S. McClelland, the surveyor, came their way.

It happened that sometime before, J. P. Weiser, of Canada, had sent a barrel of Canadian Club whiskey by express, all the way to the JA Ranch, in appreciation of some kindness Goodnight had rendered him and his herds. Since liquor was not allowed on the ranch, Henry Taylor had immediately dispatched it back to Clarendon, where it had fallen into McClelland Brothers' real estate office, and where, during the depression, the drought, and the troubles with the State, it served materially in reviving the drooping spirits of cowmen, district judge, and assembled lawyers. Templeton's stomach was shot to pieces with alkali and gyp, and as McClelland happened by, Goodnight turned to him, saying: 'I have been quarreling with this stinker, but he is sick and needs a drink of good whiskey. Kindly take him over to your office and fix him up.' McClelland followed instructions and reported that the Attorney-General, after imbibing for his stomach's sake, was feeling mighty good when he left.

The suits were tried on an agreed statement of fact, the cow-men admitting enclosure while the State admitted legal tender of bids, and though — according to the Clarendon *Northwest Texan* — they were 'ably prosecuted by the eloquent district attorney, W. H. Woodman,' they were likewise argued 'ably, ... exhaustively, and successfully' by the Honorable J. N. Browning, W. H. Grigsby, and G. A. Brown for the defense. The attorneys contended that defendants had bid four cents an acre for the enclosed lands; that leases had been awarded by the county surveyors; and that lessees had 'tendered the money for them to the Land Board, and had kept up such tender yearly.' Judge Willis charged that if this defense was found true, the jury should render a verdict of not guilty, and they forthwith rendered their decision in accord.

It was an amusing situation which the frontier enjoyed. Woodman, appreciating it fully, took occasion to excoriate the jurors for their decision. Addressing them individually, he 'expected no more' from old McFrogge and other cowboys, but when he came to W. A. Allan, a sort of itinerant preacher then running the White House, he took him to particular task:

'But Parson Allan, *I am surprised at you.* I had expected more of you — a leader in the moral and spiritual life of your community,' and so kept on until Allan was thoroughly angry.

After the trial the cowboys 'rigged the Parson up to whip Woodman' for this manifest injustice, and he jumped on the lawyer with a truly ministerial zeal. Woodman laughed him down with the truth: 'Oh, bless your soul, Parson Allan. Don't you know that was all for the benefit of the Attorney-General?'

In the meantime, Goodnight had secured opinions from ex-Governor J. W. Throckmorton, Judge T. J. Brown, Silas Hare, and Buck Walton that the action of the Board was insupportable by law. Significant at this time, and coincident with the announcement of the unofficial opinions of this counsel, was Governor Ireland's letter, which 'fell like a bombshell on the Board,' suggesting that they reduce the lease to four cents. Lubbock and Swain were said to be weakening, and a week later the Texas Live Stock Association met in Austin, and again recommended that leasing be continued as a solution of free-grass troubles.

Templeton was not satisfied, and thought the questionable procedure in court at Clarendon was ample for the disposal of both Goodnight and Willis. Besides, this was election year, political fortunes were at stake, and the Board felt it had to go forward.

Browning himself was aspiring to Willis's office, which he hoped to achieve through the combined support of the administration and the reactionary element around Mobeetie and Tascosa. Knowing that a bitter political fight would precipitate greater burdens on the already distressed frontier, Goodnight went to Mobeetie and requested Browning and Houston, legislative protagonists of the open range, to refrain from making an issue of the subject.

But Browning's sympathies were really with the other side. A month before the trials, Templeton had urged his retention by the State, pressing upon Governor Ireland the facts that he 'had held office in Northwest Texas, had been a cattleman himself, and was thoroughly conversant with their ways and habits.'

Goodnight sued out a mandamus to force the State's agent to accept his tender of lease at Clarendon, but the official pulled out overnight and the writ was not served. Thereupon the State employed Browning to assist against Goodnight, and to fight similar mandamus proceedings at Colorado City. Templeton's temporary injunction enjoining Goodnight from maintaining his original fence and from line riding was discharged in July, and Goodnight was awarded costs against the State. Templeton and Browning gave notice of appeal to the Supreme Court.

In April, Goodnight had again gone to Austin, had confronted the Board in stormy session, and had made a written proposition to take all school lands in his range at four cents from the date of his application in 1884, 'before the inclosure act went into effect.'

As lease tenders were made in cash, Goodnight joined Buck
Walton and W. B. Munson, of the T Anchors, went to Colonel
George Brackenridge's bank, and drew seventy-two thousand
dollars for the JA's, while Munson drew the amount his firm
owed. After employing a husky porter they loaded more than a
hundred thousand dollars in a wheelbarrow, strapped on their
six-shooters, and with the negro wheeling the money before
them, marched up Congress Avenue, over to the old Land
Office, and tendered the money to Treasurer Lubbock. He refused to accept, but Walton pushed a receipt for tenure under
his nose, and Lubbock affixed his signature. The cowmen
wheeled the money back to the bank, Goodnight paid one hundred and seventy-five dollars for its use, and the State had lost
its chance forever.

Of the bitter sessions held in Austin between the Board and
the cowmen, the memory of at least one might be recalled. It
was a decidedly hostile atmosphere that Goodnight experienced
in the consultation room, tempered no bit by the queer group-
ing of political animosities — East Texans now hating the
Board for a policy claimed to favor big cowmen, West Texas
free-grassers hating it because of the passing of open range, and
conservative cowmen generally hating it for arbitrary usurpation of power and vacillating policy. And the Board — Ireland,
Lubbock, and Templeton particularly — must have hated this
stubborn cowman who refused to knuckle under to their rulings,
who stood firm and determined against the usurpation of his
constitutional rights. The East, where the votes were heavy,
looked to the Board to make an example of this 'glorious Goodnight,' this 'usurper of the children's grass,' this 'feudal baron,'
this arch 'bullionaire,' as the *Galveston News* derisively called
him. The West looked to him for leadership, a representative
cowman who could not be bought, intimidated, or bluffed. He
made his tender, the Board again told him it was unacceptable,
and Goodnight informed the group that he would stand on
legal rights.

'You cannot legislate for me,' he said. 'I was on the frontier

carrying a gun when I should have been in school. I served the
State as a ranger for four years. I put in my life to make this a
free country and haven't been paid a cent for it. Now, if this
Board can legislate for me,' he glared at the Governor, 'I'll
leave your damned State.'

'Where will you go?' one asked.

'Russia,' he spit out; 'it's the next meanest place I know.'

'You'll have to pay,' came the answer.

'Before I pay the lease, I'll see you all in hell,' he swore.

The conference closed, and as Goodnight left Austin by
train, a member of the Board, en route, too, dropped down
beside him.

'I didn't know you were an old frontiersman,' he said. 'If I
had known it, I would not have favored getting you up before
the Board. I thought you were an Englishman, and we had you
up as the leader of the bunch.'

'I'm sorry you told me that,' answered the cowman. 'It
makes me feel mighty bad.'

'Why?' inquired the official.

'Well, I like to live in a country where every man's liberties
and opportunities are the same.'

Templeton published his official report for 1885–1886, quite
erroneously stating that the Panhandle country was 'hostile to
the idea of paying for the use of lands. . . . I will describe the
farcical judicial proceedings shamelessly carried on under the
. . . pretext . . . of punishing the illegal enclosure of these lands,
but it would appear in fact for the real purpose of securing
immunity against punishment by preordained verdicts of not
guilty.'

Then he told of the suits brought in Judge Willis's court, not
mentioning, however, that he had served notice upon the district attorney that they must be brought. He pointed out the
ridiculous spectacle of a grand jury finding bills against itself,
and cowmen being tried by their own cowboys. Manifestly,
rings the innuendo, here was intimidation of the court, incom-
petency on the bench, and collusion between the accused and

those sitting in judgment. Perhaps here at last was vindication for the Board's arbitrary action, and the saving grace for the beleaguered administration. They jumped upon it like a road-runner upon a June bug.

— HDBugbee —

CHARLES GOODNIGHT

Around Mobeetie and Tascosa a considerable element of free-grassers supported Browning and Houston in their contentions for the open range. Willis was popular in the 'Jumbo District,' and Browning hesitated to run for the bench, but his partner, Colonel Bill Grigsby, decided to make the race. Goodnight threw his support to Willis, and, holding the balance of power, elected him.

When the votes were in, Grigsby was angry with Goodnight, and when a year later, Goodnight was taken ill in Kansas City, came near dying, and the report reached Mobeetie that he was dead, Colonel Grigsby was not among the mourners. Meeting T. D. Hobart, capable representative of the New York and Texas Land Company, and reminding him of what a curse Goodnight had been to Texas, he began giving him down the country. Of a sudden he stopped with a precautionary thought: 'But understand, Hobart, if Uncle Charlie isn't dead, this talk doesn't go.'

Thus Willis remained in office, but most of the State officials prominently connected with the administration of the public domain were swept aside. Browning returned to the House and Houston to the Senate; Sul Ross was inducted as Governor in January, 1887; Jim Hogg inherited the fight on Goodnight from Templeton; and on the twenty-first, Willis addressed the Legislature requesting an investigation 'of such charges and reflections as are made against me' in Templeton's report.

Finding both Houston and Browning against him, Willis got into a terrible sweat. He asked Browning to see Hogg and request a delay in the investigation until he might have time to consider 'tendering his resignation.' Goodnight, boiling at this turn of affairs, got hold of his letter of resignation, kept Willis under his eye, and refused to let him present it.

By early February a special committee was considering impeachment, and Goodnight sent Major W. M. Walton before it. Old Buck Walton, as he was known, was a real 'Texian,' an individualist and a warrior, ejected from the Attorney-General's office when the carpetbaggers took control in 1866. He mixed his law with a judicious amount of liquor, and wrote the life of Ben Thompson, noted gun-fighter, on the side.[14] Walton read a letter stating that Grass Commissioner Gass, instrumental in bringing the charges, had said that he knew 'nothing could be made of the present charges, but that he was going up in the Panhandle to hunt up proof that would show that Judge Willis was in collusion with Charles Goodnight.' Walton asked the committee to recall him and deal with him as it thought best. Attorney General Hogg was quite willing for Gass to 'be dealt with and disgraced' if the statements proved true, but he was for vigorous prosecution of the charges against Willis.

With evidence being heard by the House committee, with

[14] Goodnight admired him for his courage and ability. See *Fort Worth Gazette*, April 24, 1884.

the ambitious Hogg rising in the political world and vigorously pushing the investigation, with all but two lawyers in the 'Jumbo District' and the Panhandle's own representatives in the Legislature hostile to him, Willis's prospects were anything but promising. Browning told Nelson that 'there were about forty lawyers in the House and the balance were grangers, and that Judge Willis stood about as much show as a stump-tailed bull in flytime.'

Before the House committee upon February 18, General Hogg arraigned Willis's conduct and actions upon two main counts:

'1. They were collusive, fraudulent and farcical.

'2. They were irregular and invalid as to the defendants, but estopped the State.'

If the Judge were knowingly responsible, Hogg argued, 'he was corrupt, [and] if he did not know, then he was guilty of criminal negligence.' Upon the first count he was 'impeachable for a high crime,' and upon the second he 'would be guilty of an official misdemeanor.'

The evidence was heard only in committee. Upon its report to the House, Judge J. H. Davis, Buck Walton, and Judge J. A. Carroll spoke in defense. Hogg argued for the State, and upon conclusion of his speech 'the friends of the majority report, by concerted action, cut off all debate' from the floor and forced a vote by moving the previous question. In spite of the vigorous dissenting minority report declaring none of the charges substantiated, the resolution for impeachment was adopted, sixty-seven to twenty-one, with Browning declining to vote. And though the vote lacked four of being the constitutional two thirds necessary for impeachment, the resolution was declared passed, and Willis's case was sent to the Senate for trial.

In the course of proceedings, Nelson had testified that Temple Houston, during his term as district attorney, had 'demanded and received the sum of $600' from the Panhandle Stock Association as a bonus above the fees of office. Houston took umbrage at this statement, because he claimed 'that chastity of honor which feels a stain like a wound,' and asserted that this was an independent fee.

'I will not stand upon this floor [he said to the assembled Senators] and in this high presence, and bend my privileges to the abuse of any man, but I say, sir, that anything contrary to what I have said, is utterly, unspeakably and abominably false ... and he who feels himself wronged may right himself how and where he chooses. I hold myself personally responsible wherever I may be, either in or on the outside of this hall. Less than this I should not speak; more than this I could not say.'

He was supposed to be a fire-eater, as this eloquent challenge might indicate, and Colonel B. B. Groom, one of the Panhandle cowmen present, rushed to Nelson in a heavy sweat and exclaimed: 'O. H., you had better run up to Fort Worth for a day or two.' Nelson inquired as to the trouble, and Groom told him of Houston's statement. Later, cowman and senator met in the lobby of the Driskill, and according to report, Nelson said: 'I hear we're going to have to fight it out.' Houston asked him to explain, Nelson did, and the genial orator replied: 'Hell, I had to say something. Let's go get a drink.' [15]

Before the Senate, Hogg argued that the facts showed 'willful corruption,' and asked for Willis's removal. Willis pleaded his own case, and even the *Galveston News*, generally hostile, admitted 'his legal argument was very ingenious and forcible.' Houston, who had at last been touched, stressed the fact 'that the judge had no appeal' from their decision, and urged 'the necessity therefore for a calm and impartial verdict.' A vote of twenty-two to five for acquittal followed, and Judge Willis and the remaining cowmen happily left for the dry, sunny ranges of the Panhandle.[16]

The prejudice aroused and the ill-feeling engendered died

[15] Houston's statement and explanation of the 'fee' is found in the *Senate Journal*, 1887, p. 256.

[16] For adverse comment in the Panhandle see the *Tascosa Pioneer*, March 2 and April 13, 1887.

out only after many years, but the State was whipped on every
score. A House bill introduced 'to validate the acts of the
State Land Board,' ignominiously conceived, was properly
killed, and the State's case against Goodnight for illegal enclosure finally resulted in a decision of the Supreme Court in
favor of the defendant, long after the political issues were dead.

Yet the land legislation impending in both Houses was still
such as to cause Goodnight and other cowmen much worry, and
the bills that caused them to shudder were introduced by
Browning and Houston, both free-grassers. Browning proposed
the abolition of leasing; Houston proposed not only to prevent
but 'to make the maintenance of existing unauthorized en-
closures' penal, punishable by fine and penitentiary imprisonment. Enactment of Houston's bill would have forced the
destruction of all fences, thrown the country back into an open
range, bankrupted the straitened industry, and brought on the
utmost confusion and strife.

Knowing that if his fences were removed, the Canadian
drifts would eat out his range each winter, Goodnight was in
a stew to see the bill killed. Indirect battle was a new thing to
him, and after two weeks of sweating without other visible
results, it still looked to him as though the measure would pass.
He appealed to Buck Walton for action, and Walton finally
told him he knew of one man who could stop it.

'Get the wires hot and get him here,' snapped Goodnight.

And the next morning George Clark, 'a big pussy man' from
Waco, as the cowman recalled, walked into the office. Walton
explained the situation, and the cowman asked what he would
charge for his lobby.

'Five thousand dollars!'

'If you kill it, I'll pay you your price,' came the crisp answer,
and Clark struck off toward the capitol. Goodnight sat around
the office until finally Clark came puffing back to report that
everything was all right, that he had got the bill tabled, and
needed only one more day to finish it.

'The next day he went back,' recalled Goodnight, 'and when

it came up those old East Texas fellows jumped on it and just stomped the hell out of it. Houston looked like lightning had struck him. When Clark came back to the office, I said:

"'Look here, Clark, how did you do it? I've been here two weeks and didn't do a thing."'

Clark sat down and explained:

'I went up to these old corncob pipe fellows, from down in East Texas, and, referring to the enclosure bill, said:

"'What are you going to do with Goodnight's bill?"

"'Goodnight's bill?" they would say; "that's not Goodnight's bill. That's Temple Houston's bill. I understand that Houston and Goodnight don't even speak."

"'Why should they speak? Don't you know Houston is working for Goodnight, and that that old son-of-a-gun wants this law passed because he wants free grass?"

"'O-o-h-h," the old corn-cobber would say, "is that so?"

"'Of course it's so! Aren't you a hell of a fine fellow to be up here trying to serve the State!"' Clark would answer with simulated, biting sarcasm.

And so from one to another the suggestion had its effect. The Legislature tore the bill to pieces, George Clark went back to Waco to resume his practice, and later to run against Hogg for Governor in one of the bitterest campaigns the State has experienced, while the Legislature returned to a disposal of the lease question.

At the meeting of the Texas Live Stock Association at Dallas, in January, Goodnight went on record with other leading cowmen favoring a ten-year lease system 'to the end that lessees may be secure for a term of years in all improvements they may make . . .' and in March he pulled out of Austin for the convention of the Northwest Texas Stock Association to urge better organization, because 'there was a deep-seated feeling against cattlemen in the State . . . gaining strength, while cattlemen were doing nothing comparatively for their own protection. . . .' And after all, what was the cowman's hope for a new lease on life? G. A. Brown answered the question — a long lease on his range, because 'with a settled lease policy, and an absolute tenure for a long term of years, and . . . a low rental, so as to justify the enclosure of the lands, destroying of prairie dogs, and making of tanks, digging of wells and erection of windmills thereon, I believe stockmen will take new courage and that every section of school land in the Panhandle could be leased.'

Too many members of the Legislature thought the West would settle immediately for the ten-year lease proposal to pass, but a law was approved for five-year leases at *four cents* an acre. A few days before, Goodnight had left Austin for the JA's, wiring Mrs. Adair's agent on the way that the 'session of the Legislature is not yet ended but our lease Bill will pass. I have paid for it and should know. . . .' The lease fight and the Willis impeachment had cost him twenty thousand dollars. 'It cost me lots of money, but we upheld the honor of the Panhandle.'

Thus finally the troubles of lease and fencing worked themselves out to peaceful ends, though those inspired by ambition and politics are perennial. Browning became Lieutenant-Governor, and Judge W. B. Plemons went to the Legislature from the Panhandle. One day as he sat at dinner with Goodnight at his new ranch to the north of the JA's, the old warrior suggested a 'four section' law for the western part of Texas, which would allow settlers sufficient land for stock-farming, and which might be effective in a semi-arid, agricultural economy. Thinking of the settlers it would precipitate into the country, Plemons exclaimed: 'Why, Mr. Goodnight, it would ruin you.'

'Nothing will ruin us that settles the country,' he said, and the suggestion resulted in the 'four section act' of 1895, which did much to settle the West.

XXIII. JA LONGHORNS

BENEATH the saddle sheds at the JA headquarters stands the old chuck-wagon, battered, beaten, and worn, apparently resting its creaking frame through the early months of each year. For sixty years, now, from the stirrings of spring's first grass until the snows fly in the fall, it has been the mobile home of the JA boys. Before 'bobbed' wire slashed the range to pieces, it cut its ruts from the sand hills of the Canadian to the breaks of the Brazos; it loosened its wheels in the heated drifts of Greer County, and soaked them tight again on the upper Palo Duro. From the coming of wire until the late eighties, it regularly rolled its cheerful way from the Salt Fork to the Quitaque; from Bitter Creek to Pleasant Canyon. The roads on this rough and colorful range were ground into being by its broad-tired wheels, engineered by the wagon cook and his four-mule teams.

From the commissary, with its store of extra provisions in the front end, to the chuck-box and the modernized 'cooney' on the rear, it is a vehicle loaded with the mellow connotations of an age. What tons of Arbuckle's coffee have been stored in its spacious depths; how many hundreds of beeves have been swung from its wagon spokes; how many barrels of sour-dough have brewed between its side-boards!

Many cooks, crabbed and grim, genial and expansive, have worn the paint off that high spring seat; have put the dents in the chuck-box lid. Great herds have been bedded within its easy range to rest the long nights through. Many drive horses, at the end of distant stake ropes, have snorted their crisp welcomes to shadowy but familiar forms, radiating from it in the dim light of many false dawns. Hundreds of cowboys have topped off their bad ones in its comforting nearness of early day, and many more have successfully kicked-out much worse horses while resting in its welcome shade of an evening.

The wagon, though somewhat more elaborately equipped, is, from the snaggle-toothed comb that hangs on the side-board to the horseshoe nails in the bootleg, essentially the same in usage and tradition as it was fifty years ago. The qualities of a good cowboy are the same; the principles of handling stock are no different; the etiquette of the cow-camp unchanged.

And whoever will saddle a good horse and jog up the cañon on a summer day may see the outfit on the move, a picture something like this. Here drifts the wrangler with his *remuda* of a hundred and fifty head; behind comes the cook with his bed rolls piled high; and trailing him is the hoodlum wagon with its odds and ends, from drinking-water to worm medicine. They make camp at a surface tank on Coyote Flat, from where they can see far beyond Pleasant up the Palo Duro, and down toward Gyp in the other direction.

The cook and hoodlum roll the beds off on the clean grama turf, drive stakes, raise the fly, and dig a pit for the fire. Coosie sets his coffee pot on the flames, pulls a quarter of beef from the cool depths of the wagon, and slices it into steaks; he places dried fruit to stew; a skillet of grease to heat, empties a third of a sack of flour into a dishpan, hollows the center, and pours in a gallon of fragrant sour-dough. He washes his hands, if his conscience isn't clear, throws in a fistful of baking powder, a pound or so of lard and the other essentials, and dives into the bubbling white mass with a right good will. While some cooks are as meticulous and clean as any old maid, others seem to know the virtue of soap and water only in a distant sort of way. No matter! For when they wipe their hands on the seats of their breeches, straighten up from over the coals and roar their welcome 'Chuck,' every mother's son stampedes for the box like a bunch of wild mockies for the open range. And whether their steaks are perfect, or their biscuits squat to rise and bake on the squat, they are unquestioned bosses of the camps as though to the manor born, and woe to the man who transgresses their prerogatives.

Among the most colorful cooks on the JA's was Jerry Shea, government teamster who came to the ranch with the troops from Fort Elliott in 1878 to induce Quanah's tribe to return to the reserve. Irrepressible Irishman flourishing in any environment, he withheld corn from the government mules to peddle out to the JA boys. Later he returned to the ranch and took his place at the hind-end of the wagon, a good teamster and a splendid cook — some say the best they ever saw. He could prepare a meal for forty men in half an hour, and he held his own in any company. Once when the outfit was camped on Battle Creek during the branding season, Jerry made a big pot of soup, thickened with rice. It proved an inviting dish, and after three platefuls Colonel Goodnight appraised its quality:

'This is mighty good soup, Jerry.'

'It's taken you a hell of a long time to find it out,' growled the old campaigner.

Jerry broke the rules of the ranch and got drunk, and though he was prized as highly as a fine saddle horse, Goodnight had to let him go.

'I hate to fire you, Jerry,' he said sympathetically.

'By God,' said Jerry, 'I hate for you to, too.'

Of all the cowboys that have trailed across the JA ranges, Frank Mitchell cut the widest swath and left the boldest tradition behind him. He came to the ranch in May, 1878, a smooth-faced boy of quick retort, reckless as a locoed horse, and as energetic as a sand-storm. Today, in his advanced seventies, he knows the capacity of horses and men; he can tell what a cow will think and do before she knows herself; and his stocky frame is still driven by seemingly boundless energy. 'I got my training from the greatest of them all,' he said simply. Thus is the tradition perpetuated.

In the winter of 1879, Mr. and Mrs. Goodnight returned to Pueblo to clear up their unfinished affairs, and Mitchell was left at headquarters. The Colonel wrote back instructing him concerning many things that should be done, but upon his return in the spring was annoyed to find the work unfinished, and inquired of young Frank why he had not done this, and that, and the other.

'You never told me to,' came the reply.

'I wrote you to.'

'Maybe you did,' retorted Frank, 'but nobody on the ranch could read your letter.'

'Where is that letter?'

'Down there in my bed roll.'

'Go get it.'

Mitchell went after it and the Colonel took it, studied it a long time, and finally swore:

'Damn it, if I could think of what it was I wanted to say, I could read it.'

At that time it was the custom to rustle horses immediately after breakfast, which job Mitchell assumed himself. The country was open, but horses have favorite ranges, which the rustler soon learns. Upon his return to the ranch in the spring of 1880, Goodnight brought six mules that he had bought from a surveying crew. The two big wheelers, having become attached to the Dodge City range, were continually hankering to go back, though they were two hundred and fifty miles away, and one morning they showed up missing.

'Where are those mules?' Goodnight inquired of Frank.

'I couldn't find them,' he answered. 'They've been trying to go back to Dodge ever since they've been here.'

'They're shod and you can trail them,' said the boss. 'Go out and strike their trail, and don't come back without them.'

Frank followed instructions.

'I started out in my shirt sleeves,' he recalled, 'expecting to catch them in a few miles. I cut a circle for their trail, soon found it, and started out on it, nearly due north. I followed it all day. The mules would graze along for a little way and then they would strike a lope. Jim Burdick had shod them with calks and most of the time I could follow their trail at a lope. Night found me near the Canadian, and I laid out, built up a fire, and tried to keep warm. Next morning I started on, got across the river near the Turkey Tracks, and turned in there for something to eat. I hadn't had a thing since breakfast the morning before. I borrowed a fresh horse and took the trail again. Those mules took a course for Dodge as straight as any Indian ever went to the brush. I followed them for nearly two hundred miles, until I struck a haying outfit on the Cimarrón. In their corral were my mules, with their heads sticking over the fence on the north side, looking towards Dodge, and braying.'

The same spring Mitchell had another adventure at headquarters that is still a favorite topic of conversation around the JA's, an experience rooted deep in the cowboy tradition. As long as Texas cowboys have been tying their ropes hard and fast to their saddle horns, they have been roping any and everything that wore hair, and a good many things that don't, both as a part of their daily work and for the sport it has given them. They have smeared their magueys on everything from panthers to buffaloes, from fence staves to locomotives, and they have spent the rest of their days telling how they and their favorite roping horses turned this thing and that through its tail. Truly, one may say, the lore of the range is tied together with catch-ropes, held down by thousands of good horses settin' on their haunches

BILL WILEY, JA ROPER

This particular morning Mitchell took a circle for the horses and met a nice black bear. To expect him to pass up such a chance was like expecting a hungry cow to pass up a beargrass bloom. Frank jerked down his rope, shook out a little loop, and took after the bear as he leisurely drifted down the flat, lifting up big bull-chips and pulling fat grubworms out for his breakfast. Frank dabbed the loop around him, jerked up his slack, whirled his rustling horse toward the ranch, and came up the hill to find Burdick starting a fire in the forge. Another cowpuncher roped the bear's heels and they stretched him out between their horses, and settled down while Jim 'het' an iron. Then Mitchell ran the JA on Bruin's hip, and turned him loose. He started up the draw toward the spring, his course bringing him by the big dugout that served as a kitchen and mess-hall, which with open door appeared a likely cavern, and he turned inside.

Mrs. Devier, who with her husband was doing the ranch cooking, was standing at the stove washing the breakfast dishes, her baby resting in its nearby crib. When the bear broke into the door, she grabbed the child, and in panic pitched it out at the window, fainted, and fell into the woodbox behind the stove. Old Bruin passed into the mess-hall, jumped up on the long table, and went out through the window at the end of the room, carrying the sash with him. Jim Burdick came running up the hill, circled the dugout, and stepped on the baby, as the bear ran up the trail toward the spring and met an old boy from the cotton country, with a bucket of water in either hand and another on his head. He left his water and went out over one rim of the cañon, while the bear made his escape by the other. He came near breaking up the ranch, and anybody else would have been fired for causing such a commotion, but Mitchell escaped with a good rimmin' out.

In the summer of 1881, Goodnight sent Mitchell and a wagon to attend the general roundup to the east, and bring back the JA strays that had drifted down the river. He took 'Johnnie Come-Lately' as his cook, 'Bat Cave Dude' Stewart— so named from a hole in the corner of one eye — as one of his hands, and stray men from the F's and Shoe Bars joined him, so that he was handling a sort of pool outfit before the work was done. They drifted with the general roundup from the Deep Lake country, through the Diamond-Tails, down into Indian Territory, and turned back up the North Fork, holding the JA strays with the regular cut. After about four months, Goodnight sent a hand to help them in, a scrapping old bugger who had been in the war, who was said to have killed a couple of men down around Fort Griffin, and who was known to the country as 'Club-Footed Jack.'

Among the outside men who had thrown in with the JA outfit was one named Bud Roberts, who had a sleepy little buckskin pony that looked harmless enough in a *remuda*, but was greased lightning when turned on a track. Up near Mobeetie and along McClellan Creek were a lot of little men, inveterate gamblers, who when told that the dun was a race horse, would not believe it at all, and staked their money on their judgment. So it happened that by the time the roundup reached the head of North Fork, Mitchell had most of their loose money in a sack in the JA wagon, as well as a bunch of cattle with burnt brands in the cut.

In accord with custom he informed the assembled outfits that he would start home next morning, so that they might come and check his cut. He was particularly careful to have a clean herd — remembering the fearful cursing Goodnight had given him when he and Joe Horn branded some mavericks — and had cut only those burned brands that he felt positive belonged to the JA's. It happened that one of these cows had a yearling in the brand of John and Lew Casner following her, and the owners had been bragging around that when it came to a show-down, they were going to cut the cow and yearling. Mitchell knew their background, and they were the only ones he feared might give trouble, for when he had cut the cattle from the roundup, Lew Casner had said: 'That yearling isn't yours. She's in my straight mark and brand.'

'You'll play hell gettin' her,' Mitchell retorted.

And so on the morning the outfit was to leave, Mitchell threw his cut together, and called to the assembled outfits: 'There they are, boys,' in invitation to look it over. All thought of the Casner threats, but old 'Club-Footed Jack,' sitting his horse ominously near, with his Sharps muley under his leg and his forty-five on his hip, growled: 'The first son-of-a-bitch that cuts a cow will never cut another one,' and it is needless to say that the pool outfit trailed into the JA's with its entire gathering. The news of the dun horse had preceded them, and when they reached the ranch Goodnight glanced at the stock and then fixed the young wagon boss with his piercing eyes.

'What do you think I sent you down there for?'

'To work the country and gather the cattle,' came the laconic answer.

'From what I hear you've been doing damned little but running horse races,' complained the old man.

But they had gathered some burnt cattle in addition to the strays, and secretly he was pretty well pleased.

The Plains of Texas probably developed more good horses and more good cowmen than any portion of the West. A man or a horse must work cattle to learn the cow business, and granting the average intelligence of each, the more cattle he works the more he learns. In the open country men and horses handled many times the cattle that the same crew could have handled in timber or brush. Besides, the Plains was a good horse country, and with no lack of horseflesh it was quite easy for an outfit to work fifty to a hundred square miles of country in a day. Work in a herd makes good cutting horses, lots of roping makes good ropers as well as trained horses, and long communion with cows is bound to teach a man their nature. In reckless spirit a cowboy is born; only in long, hard training is he made.

A ranch that has run anywhere from twenty-five to more than a hundred thousand cattle annually for sixty years is bound to produce efficient cow-hands, and no one can name them all. Among those who come to mind are Frank Mitchell, vigorous and reckless; Joe Horn, who swung a vicious little loop; Mitch Bell, sensitive and genial; Lem Brandon, a top hand whom they all circled around; stocky Jim Christian; thin-flanked Fred Scott; and so many others. Perhaps the two most noted men on the Palo Duro range were John E. Farrington and Old John Mann.

Farrington was brought to the Quitaque from the Bells by Leigh Dyer, in 1877, and came to the JA's after Wiren took charge of the F's. He held the position of range manager with Adair and Goodnight for many years, and served a brief period on the JA's in similar capacity after the partnership was dissolved. He was cool and trustworthy, 'a good man for the times,' said Goodnight, 'but the sort who didn't belong to a civilized country. He ought to have gone out when it settled.' Wayman Brown put it in another way when he said that 'Farrington was a good man, but always looking for "two pair."'

Henry Taylor recalls him most vividly; his pants were always too long, sagging around the heels of his boots, and an old tow sack might hang to his spurs half a day before he would stoop to pull it off. On the ground or on a horse 'he was the slouchiest man I ever saw.' He rode deep in the saddle — 'four or five joints of his backbone below the cantle.' Exceptionally long bushy hairs grew out of his ears, and when a Mobeetie barber, in addition to giving him a hair-cut, trimmed the growth out of one ear, Farrington rose in rage and gave the fellow a terrible beating. He 'lowed the Lord had put those hairs there, and no good purpose could be served by cutting them out. When he first came to the JA's he ran the wagon, but soon became range manager, riding from camp to camp overseeing the regular work, checking up on the condition of the cattle, and spending some time with the wagon, thus relieving Goodnight of much riding.

Before coming to the Palo Duro, John Mann had worked for Hank Cresswell at the Bar CC's above the Canadian, and no better range man ever drank alkali out of the Red. Cows — he knew cows as a professor knows books! He came from away down in Texas and had studied them in all dimensions, and the psychology of a herd of steers was as clear to him as the Panhandle skies. While working for Cresswell he had drifted into Dodge, got thoroughly organized — for liquor was his worst failing — and when his employer suggested they return to

the ranch, Mann told him he was not ready. A few days later
he sheepishly turned up at the Bar CC's, and Cresswell told
him he would have to drift on, but gave him a letter of recommendation to Goodnight, who hired him, and it may truly be
said that cow work on the JA's was never the same thereafter.

JOHN MANN

'He was the best range man I ever had,' Goodnight recalled.
'He had been in the business ever since he could ride a horse —
in fact he couldn't remember when he did begin. A range man
must know how to handle men; the handling of the cavvieyard
is very important; and he must handle breeding cattle carefully, without loss and without leaving motherless calves. A
careless foreman let the boys tear out and throw everything
into the roundup. A careful man had his hands cut out weak
calves with their mothers at the start of the drive. If a cow

is taken off several miles she will return to her calf. But if both are moved, and get separated, the calf may not go back, especially if it is weak and tired-out. The Texas calf would always go back, but the higher-bred an animal is, the less of this instinct it has. Motherless calves were never seen on Mann's range.'

Mann was as neat as a pin, says Henry Taylor, but a very peculiar man who was not always liked by his hands. One reason, according to Mitch Bell, was because he kept them from being wild — he handled his herds quietly and easily, he allowed but little roping, and he stood for no abuse of horses. They all agree that he could clean up a herd better than anybody on the range, quickly and smoothly too, and though he seemed sour and glum, he was always well pleased when he shaped a herd so thoroughly that Goodnight cut no cattle from it on final careful inspection.

Cows have certain ranges that they prefer, and can often be found in the same locality. As he rode the ranges Mann spotted the cows in their favorite places, and when working that region a long time later, remembered them like old friends, watched for them in the roundup, and if any was missing he knew it and bawled out the hand who had driven her range. Much like Goodnight himself, he remembered the composition of a herd from its flesh marks, and if any cowboy dozed on guard and lost a few head from a herd of two thousand, Mann always knew it without making a count. He worked the JA ranges cleaner than they have ever been worked before or since, and he was rigid in his requirements of those who rode into his herds — it was years after a man started work with the JA's before he could cut a cow from Mann's roundups.

Besides being unsurpassed on the range, he was good on the trail, and when the work was done in the fall, and frost had fallen and brought immunity from Texas fever, he and his outfit were sometimes sent to help deliver the beef at Dodge. Nervous and high-strung, he was continually with the herd. He bedded his cattle on a hillside if the weather was cool;

he kept to the valley if it was warm. Those old Texas cattle responded to the changes with barometric sensitivity, and Mann knew when the sign was right and when it was wrong.

He was a fidgety Irishman, always snorting through his nose and breathing through his mouth. When Goodnight stayed with the outfit for a few days, Mann bossed him around like an ordinary waddie, and when, on his visit in 1885, Adair waked him one oppressive night, told him that his pup tent was too hot for sleeping, and asked that the boys carry water from the creek to throw on the canvas, his disgust hardly knew bounds.

'Carry water, hell,' he fumed. 'You can carry water yourself if you want it. You monkey with these boys and they'll run you off.'

When a Kansas outfit dropped into the ranch and bought fourteen hundred big steers in 1881, Goodnight, in delivering the cattle at the Mulberry Corrals, warned the Jayhawkers that they had better be careful or they would lose them. The advice was superfluous, for these Kansas boys were off the head of the creek; they were tough and wild and said they'd show these 'Goodnight haymakers' how to handle stock. In courtesy Goodnight sent Jim Burdick along to help them through the first night.

Cowboys, as a breed, will quietly and generously help any man out of a jack-pot if he but indicates a desire to be helped, but they abandon the smart, cocksure individual to his own fate as quickly as they can get rid of him. Instead of helping stand guard, Burdick rode off half a mile, staked his horse, lay down on the grass, and went to sleep. Goodnight's prediction was right. The cattle stampeded, by morning the outfit had lost every head, and some of those old steers were almost back to their original range on the Quitaque. And only a Westerner can appreciate how this pleased the JA boys.

Now old Lem Brandon, one of the most famous of the early JA boys, 'was sure aggressive, and you could get *anything* from him if you wanted it.' In keeping with the transient cowboy custom, he periodically drifted west from his home in the settlements, stayed with the JA's through the heavy work from spring till fall, and drifted back to the comfortable firesides of the farming country to remain until grass greened again in the spring.

On one trip he stopped for the night at a Milliron camp, and after supper got in a weavin' way in telling his experiences. Cowboys, sensitive to exaggerated speech, are quick to show the fact, and when Brandon got to telling them wild, his audience, one by one, simulated unusual drowsiness, and soon every man in camp was vigorously snoring away. Lem realized the joke in the midst of a mighty good tale, but he rose to the occasion and manfully told it out as though he didn't mind. Usually all hands came to life as the story was done, but at that point Lem pulled his six-shooter, and in a voice that carried no humor, roared to the sleeping beauties: 'The first son-of-a-gun that wakes up is a dead one.' And it is told that they slept peacefully until the first red streaks indicated that it was time to kick up the fire and put the 'Javy' on to boil.

After some years on the range the boys who drifted back East for short and impatient visits at home were objects of interest to those old friends who had remained behind. Bill Lampkin, after some fine frolicking on the buffalo range, went back to Illinois to see all the folks, and while there was the entire show. 'Spade' Evans tells that his friends had gathered to see him one day, and Bill, appreciative of the occasion, was doing his part to make the grass grow green.

'Mr. Lampkin,' an admiring young lady interjected, 'you say there are no trees out there?'

'Not a switch,' says Bill.

'What do you use for fuel? How do you cook?' she asked.

Nothing feazed, Bill rattled on: 'Why, we cook with grass.'

The lady exclaimed that she had always heard how hot those prairie fires got, and how rapidly they swept along.

'Yes'm,' Bill continued, without a pang of conscience. 'I remember one time when we stopped to eat dinner on the baldies; the boys throwed a saddle blanket down and we played a game of cards to see who would do the cooking. I lost. I fixed a skillet of buffalo meat, filled the coffee pot out of a dry lake, and made bread while the boys laid in the shade of the wagon and snoozed. I set the grass on fire and placed the coffee, meat, and bread in the path of the flames. There was a right smart wind a-blowing, and I kept moving the pots up to keep them in the flames, and I'll tell you it kept me pretty busy. At last the coffee had boiled, the meat was done, and the biscuits were baked to a turn. But when I looked up to call the boys to dinner, I'm the biggest liar that ever breathed if I wasn't forty miles from camp.'

Mention has been made of Old Bill Koogle, a hunter whom Goodnight is said to have outfitted for the purpose of killing buffaloes off the Palo Duro range. After the buffaloes were gone, Koogle contracted the building of many miles of JA fence, and Henry Taylor's first work on the ranch was with Koogle's fencing outfit in 1882. It was a big crew and a big job; the contract and management being shared by Koogle's partner, Albert Antrobus. The work went smoothly until, along in April, a big snowstorm struck, and fifteen of their fence-builders, swearing that 'they wouldn't work in any damned country where it snowed in the summertime,' walked off and left them.

After much work around the ranch they pulled their bull teams into headquarters, and to close out the partnership, began dividing their camp outfit. One took this yoke of oxen, the other that, one took this skillet, the other that, and so the division proceeded equitably and fairly until at the last only one sack of flour was left. Old Nigger Fox, observing the split-up, said Koogle hesitated a moment, reached up in the chuck-box, pulled out a butcher knife, and cut the sack half in two. Antrobus lit a shuck for Wichita Falls, where he deposited his money in a bank owned by a man named Israel, whereby hangs another tale, while Koogle invested his in the Sacra and Sugg Ranch on the Salt Fork.

Koogle died in Clarendon a long time ago, and Henry Taylor made the funeral arrangements, asking Old Man Buntin, the pioneer undertaker, to fix Bill up for burial and to call him over when the job was done. After a while Buntin sought Taylor with word that the corpse was ready.

WAYMAN BROWN

Taylor went over to see his old employer stretched out on a cooling board, and as he looked at him sadly, the Old Man proudly spoke up and said: 'There ain't no flies on Billie!' And that was the last of old Bill Koogle, though Koogle Jump-Off, on the JA range, perpetuates his name and memory.

Perhaps the most unusual and peculiar adventure associated with the JA range revolves around one of its most picturesque characters, Wayman Brown. A long, lank native of Arkansas, at seventeen years of age he packed his clothes in a pillow slip and pulled out for Texas to become a cowboy. In 1887 he began working for Goodnight on the JA's. Bound up within his wind-weathered frame, once as tough as old bull-hide, are

the qualities of the race that first poured over the West —
integrity, dignified reserve, loyalty, and quiet and dangerous
courage. Beneath his big black hat his keen eyes still shine
from cavernous depths, though his long, drooping white mustache and his wind-seamed face bespeak the ravages of many
seasons on a droughty range. When seen at the T Anchor
reunion, a gathering of men in mellow, reminiscent years, one
gathers from his quiet composure that he has never indulged
his confidence or invited familiarity. A rather sad figure, he
seems, yet an admirable character who still loves a twenty-
five-year-old saddle horse above all the comforts of life.

He has had a few friends whom he trusted implicitly —
Goodnight, Henry Taylor, and W. H. Patrick — and principally
from them are gathered the fragments of this story. Like
the average cowboy he carried his frontier Colts forty-five, but
besides he always toted a butcher or Bowie knife in his bootleg,
a peaceable enough sort of man whom most people knew it was
best to leave alone.

When Goodnight left the JA's, Brown continued work under
Farrington and George Case, the wagon boss. Case had given
Brown a silver-mounted Bowie knife, and one morning when
he ordered Brown to get his horses, the cowboy refused. 'Case
got pretty intimate with me,' he explained, 'and I'm ashamed
to say I cut him up with the knife he had given me.'

Wayman pulled out of the lower country, leaving his bed
at the bunkhouse. He was very clean and particular about his
hot roll, however, and soon wrote Henry Taylor, at Clarendon,
that he wanted the bed sent to him, at his hardware store.
Besides being finicky about his roll, he was unusually thrifty,
and cowboy-like, kept all his personal possessions except his
saddle, chaps, and spurs — his outfit — rolled up in his tarp
and suggans. He asked Taylor to unroll his bed and take care
of the eight hundred dollars in bills he would find therein.
Taylor followed directions, found the money, and deposited
it to Wayman's credit at the local bank.

In time Wayman drifted into Clarendon, and after a few

days around town called on Taylor for his money, saying he was going to 'loan' it to Jack Hall, of Young, Hall and Company, a mercantile firm. Shortly the firm went broke, and in the partition of the residual properties among its creditors by lawyer S. H. Madden, it is said that for some reason the cowboy's claim was overlooked. The legal merits of the case are unknown, but Wayman Brown, used to direct elemental relationships instead of moratoria, reasoned only that he had lent the results of several years' hard work, and now, in the language of the snipe-hunters, was left holding the sack.

He went to his debtors and left the impression that they might live longer if the money was paid by a certain date. Meanwhile, his moodiness grew more noticeable, both in town and in camp at the Sacra-Sugg Ranch on the Salt Fork, now owned by Johnnie Martin and Goodnight, and everyone observed that he was 'acting queer.' A tramp dropped into camp one day, got his dinner, and lay down in the doorway to enjoy a nap. Wayman, passing in and out, stepped over him a time or two before pulling his six-shooter and shattering the floor on both sides of the vagrant's head, and when last seen the guest was drifting across the sand hills at a long lope.

In the course of his brooding, Wayman decided that Goodnight was spending too much for salt and bran, and at times might be seen sowing a patch, broadcast, with the idea of growing his supply at home. One day as the cowboys were preparing dinner, he threw his saddle across the stove, jumped astride, and spurred and quirted with a will until they pulled him off. And every little while he would kick up his heels like an old gaunt cow, and run and jump in the water tank, complaining that the heel-flies were after him. It was a tragic episode, and all his friends shook their heads sadly.

'Poor old Wayman,' sympathized Goodnight and many another, 'he's brooded over his troubles until he's gone crazy.'

In town he decorated his horse with a hundred yards of ribbon, and with colors a-flying, paraded through the streets emitting cowboy yells, 'and with his long hair and mustache,' said Taylor, 'he looked wolfish, and was.' As his designated day of grace approached, he helped himself to a box of forty-five shells at Taylor's store without a word to anyone, though heretofore he had always paid in cash. Then, looking as wild as an Arab, he again marched down to see his debtors, and by report they paid him cash, and in full. Next day, without a word, he handed Taylor a dollar bill — the price of a box of six-shooter shells — and said he was on his way to Canada.

If anyone still wonders what would have happened had he not been paid, his curiosity may be settled by inquiring into the nature of the breed and the character of the man. 'And he would have come clear, too,' Henry Taylor concluded, 'as he could have got plenty of people who would have sworn he was crazy.' It seems passing strange that some folks still think so.

XXIV. LORE OF THE RANGE

As MUST be evident to those who have followed the story thus far, Goodnight loved and lived close to the soil of the earth. It is a pity that he, close observer of nature on the Great Plains of North America, did not know that sensitive man, who contemporaneously lived with and loved the fauna of the pampas at the other extremity of the Western World, W. H. Hudson. How greatly were they different! Yet how much were they alike!

It is good to imagine them sitting together in the wind, beneath the cool shade of the wide gallery at the Goodnight Ranch, both mellow with years, minds alert in age, spirits still young and zestful, and though lacking in laboratory science, each loaded with thousands of observations, impressions, and sensations, that, unfortunately, can never befall the cloistered scientist, nor, for that matter, any other inhabitant of this modern, mechanical world. And not the least interesting to themselves would have been their excursions into the border-lands of science and psychology, the psychic effects of wind and odors, the promptings of the subconscious mind, and along other speculative paths that the expert either fears or disdains to explore.

Goodnight was not a scientist, in the strict meaning of the word, and perhaps the naturalists will deny him. Though Burbank encouraged him, the general scientific world did not. Yet for nearly a century he quested with an almost incomparable zeal, and the lore that he stored up in his massive

head touched every zone of life that he had seen and experienced
throughout the years. Cattle, horses, antelope, turtles, curlews, prairie dogs, bears — he was companion to them all.

Casual visitors remember him also for his fighting goat,
his herd of elk, the Mexican deer, the cross-bred wild turkeys,
the hybrid hogs, the antelope, the seven-horned Navajo sheep,
the rejuvenated bulls, and the buffalo. Then, too, there were
his persimmon trees, transplanted from a foreign zone to
flourish on Spring Creek, his fondly nurtured arboretum in the
old ranch yard, the scattered wild-plum thickets sprung from
his own sowings up and down the Palo Duro, and his exotic
lilies, still blending their colors with those of the badlands.

Sometimes he recalled the remedies that a wild land suggested, and hardy natures endured as counter-irritants if not
as cures: coal-oil for lice, prickly-pear poultices for wounds,
salt and buffalo tallow for piles, mud for inflammation and
fevers, bachelor's button for diarrhea, buffalo meat juice as a
general tonic, and many another.

Interlarding his general conversation were pointed observations upon the growth of the land — cottonwoods, mesquite, mistletoe — with particular attention to varying forms
for latitude and altitude, humidity and aridity. In passing he
noticed that tumbleweeds, crab grass, cuckleburs, and love
vine, like the bobwhite quail, are not found in a wild country,
but belong to a civilized terrain. Yet sunflowers were found in
the wilderness, and the matured heads were sometimes gathered
by station hands on the Butterfield Mail Line as supplemental
horse feed.

Of what tremendous importance was the everlasting wind!
Hudson would have enjoyed talking with him of its psychic
effects, of its play upon the overwrought nerves of the women
of the Staked Plains, and of its influence on soil and growth.
When he was too old to work, Goodnight liked to sit on the
open gallery as the wind tore at the trees in the yard and tossed
his shock of white hair like the mop of an angry buffalo bull.
The short-grass turf then held most of the soil in place, and the

eternal wind swept the flies away from the range cattle that grazed into it, and spun the mills over this vast range to lift the underground water to its earthen tanks. When his wife complained of the wind, he voiced the sentiment of the pioneer plainsman — 'you get to where you never notice it.' In truth, he would not have felt right if the wind hadn't blown.

He casually observed the effect of the wind on the Great Plains fauna. Wild animals always range into the wind; so do wild cattle, unless in a storm. A herd driven with the wind may be nervous and ill at ease. One pointed into the breeze steps out with an assurance and a right free will not altogether due to lessened heat, dust, and flies. A stampeding herd circles into the wind to know what is ahead. In working a roundup, cattle should always be cut into the wind — they work easier that way. And a cowboy, loping into the breeze, feels an exhilaration that stirs his blood like old wine.

He observed the remarkable effects of scents in that open world: cows reassuring their eyesight by whiffing long-lost calves; the sensitive noses of bears pointed into the air, assorting the blended fragrances that floated down the cañon; and the magic, strengthening effect of the smell of water upon a famishing herd. Of all domestic animals, he said, the Texas mule could smell water farther than any other. If the wind was right he might detect water six or seven miles away, while a herd of Texas longhorns could easily smell it three and four miles off. 'You never realize what an odor the human animal has until you watch an antelope catch your scent. As soon as the wind carries it to him, you can hear him whistle: "W-h-h-e-e-w," he says, "what a stinking thing you are," and away he goes.'

He believed that newly born fawns and kid antelopes, like some birds, were almost devoid of scent, for he observed good hunting dogs pass close by their place of hiding and never smell them. He believed this was nature's protection. Fawns do not stir around much for the first few days, as the does come to suckle them, and immediately go away to lessen the danger of their discovery. He observed particularly the loss of certain wild instincts, protective and valuable, as animals were domesticated. 'The calf of a longhorn cow, with its hair still wet from the womb, will bristle up at the presence of a dog, whereas a finely bred Durham calf will smell of the dog and maybe try to suck it. In the Texas calf the instinct of self-protection is already in him, as though he were defending himself against a wolf.'

The story of Goodnight's contributions to range and trail equipment is a chapter in itself. There were his various additions to ranger traps, the first chuck-box on the trail, his 'discovery' of the bed tarp, his design of a safe side-saddle that came into general use, and his adaptations of stirrups, ropes, and gear. His friends recall also the experiments with buffalo tallow balm, with buffalo wool blankets, and with buffalo elixir.

To visit with him was to hear portrayed, in most vivid diction and sympathetic charm, the vast panorama of natural

history that had given life to the West. He saw the imprint
of a human hand in the rock at Hand Springs, south of Fort
Lyon. He saw nature's own photograph of a giant cinnamon
bear, perhaps 'taken' by an electrical display, on the mineral-
ized bluffs of the Picketwire. He saw great forests miniatured
in the agate of the Rockies. He observed closely and felt deeply.
Many who knew him superficially thought him rough and hard,
but he would have entranced a child with his sensitive dramati-
zation of birds and animals.

WILD LIFE

'All this Western country used to be full of curlews, and I
loved to hear them cry. They are all gone now. They were
more careless in nesting than the dove; they would drop their
eggs just anywhere without regard to how far away water
might be. One time out in Colorado I was riding along a trail
when a gawky, white-feathered young curlew popped up right
in front of me. Like young buzzards, young curlew are all
white, you know. The little fellow went running down the
trail ahead of me, with never a thought of turning out. He
was scared to death and kept saying at every jump: "Now
don't run over me, for I'm little! Now don't run over me, for
I'm little!" I can hear him yet.

'Out in that country was a kind of green grasshopper that
could not fly. Well, while young Master Curlew was running
and yelping at me not to ride over him, one of those fat green
grasshoppers flopped down in front of us. That curlew quit
running and squawking right now to gobble it up. I turned

my horse — a fine California mare — out of the trail and sat there looking at the curlew eat the hopper. He'd grab a mouthful and then wink his eye at me as much as to say, "You're all right!" The sight was exceedingly comical and sometimes I laugh now at the memory of it.'

Once as he drifted up the Tule Cañon by himself, he noticed that his mare winded something ahead. He got down, went on afoot, and peeping over a point, saw a black bear not twenty feet away, scratching into a cottonwood log that was full of grubworms. 'He didn't smell me, but he thought he heard something,' said Goodnight, 'for he raised his head and seemed to be looking right in my eye. Then he looked wise and said to himself: "Everything's all right; there's nobody around here." He worked away at the log until he was right against the bank, when I pulled my six-shooter and shot into the bank above him. The bullet plowed along it and must have cut a bushel of gravel down on his back. He reared up, threw his hands up in front of him — they were the biggest I ever saw — and began growling and cussing me. Then he ran, and I could hear him as he went over the hill, shaking gravel off, and cussing me as he went.'

There were stories as long as we had to visit, stories of birds and animals that still inhabit the open country — stories of others that once lived there but now are gone. Panthers? there were many, and a staple of ranger diet; panthers that carried full-grown deer without leaving a trace on their trails; panthers that fought like —— But Wes Sheek, his old partner and an inveterate hunter, has told the story best.

Sheek killed many deer in the Cross Timber country, and in converting their hides to buckskin, grained them, and pitched the hair into a little clearing near his house. A greenhorn visited the ranch, and Sheek regaled him with tales of panther fights, winding up with the heroic story of the two that met on the trail in the clearing, and engaged in mortal combat. One jumped upon the other, when like a flash the second climbed on top of the first, he in turn climbing back on top, and so climbing higher and higher, they passed into the sky and out of sight. For a week thereafter fur was still flying and hair was raining out of the blue.

'Now,' said Sheek in conclusion, directing the listener to the clearing in the woods, 'I want to show you where that fight took place.'

The visitor looked long and thoughtfully at the tawny hair that covered the ground, and then turned to his expansive host:

'I would never have believed that tale, if I hadn't seen the hair.'

Except for the buffalo, perhaps no Plains creature interested Goodnight so much as the impertinent little prairie dogs. Before the Civil War the nearest dogs were a hundred and fifty miles beyond the settlements — the Pease River country had its dog-towns. During the war the Vernon country was eaten clean by hordes of dogs, 'until not a spear of grass was left.' Then the dogs migrated southeast, Goodnight recalled, though after the grass came back the region 're-dogged.' According to his observations, these industrious little animals kept up a gradual southeasterly migration. While on the trail in Colorado, he found deserted towns, and in the seventy years he watched the prairie dogs, they extended their range one hundred and fifty miles to the southeast.

In 1869, when swimming the Platte with a herd — a wide river in icy flood — he found the stream full of prairie dogs headed for its south bank. He lifted one from the water and placed it on his horse's back, behind the saddle. It stayed on until he reached the north bank, where he put it in the chuckwagon, carried it on up the trail, and kept it until the outfit got back to the Pecos. At night the cowboys took it from the wagon and turned it out to graze, and as the animals make most interesting pets, the boss claimed the boys 'had a hell of a time playing with it.'

'There is an old myth,' he continued, 'that the prairie dog, rattlers, rabbits, and little owls live together in the same hole. Owls and rabbits do use the holes, separately, after the prairie dog has abandoned them. When the rattler enters, his intention is to swallow the dog, which he does, and my observation is that a dog will not enter his hole when there is a rattler in it, which he probably knows by scent. I have put dead rattlers in holes, and later found them thoroughly covered up by the dogs. They evidently attempt to cover the holes when there is a live snake in them, and it appears the rattler is aware of this, too. If you slowly pour dirt in on a rattler, he will make his appearance promptly.'

In Colorado the Goodnight cowboys often used antelope hides for saddle blankets. These animals could, according to Goodnight, go for weeks without water. Often he saw them fifteen miles from any supply, though at such times their resistance — and ordinarily their vitality is truly remarkable — seemed quite low. In his judgment this phantom of speed and life is just as intelligent as the Plains horse, though its insatiable curiosity has been the death of droves. It is a great hypocrite, as he put it, for when a man approaches a tiny kid, the mother 'hasn't a sound leg in her body until you are led away.' Likewise she will lure the smart coyote away by appearing helplessly crippled, and then she will leave him feeling foolish. The species sheds its horns each year, and according to Goodnight's observation, is the only hollow-horned animal that does.

And so the observations flowed on. All diurnal animals that he knew had black or brown eyes. When Hereford cattle were first introduced to the Plains, red spots around their eyes were common, and he never bought a bull without them. Breeders assiduously worked to eliminate these natural sun-shades and produced the white-faced cattle of today, a great mistake, he thought, for cancer-eye has spread widely since that time. 'No one ever saw a sore eye, or so-called cancer eye, that had a circle around it or was colored.' After seeing many bloodshot, watery, blue-eyed plainsmen who had squinted into the incessant glare of the open country for years, he thoroughly believed that dark eyes were better, stronger.

He invented a stirrup that would not turn over. 'The more weight you put in your stirrups, the easier it is on the horse. Your knees take up the spring. The man that sits in the saddle like a bag of sand is killing on a horse. His mount will always give out first. Just because a man can sit on a horse is no reason he is a horseman.

'When I was a boy the pure mustang had simmered itself down to one color — bay, with black mane and tail. Nature always does that; takes the strongest there is and makes the uniform. Bay was the strongest color characteristic.'

Great growth of horn is characteristic of a low, warm country, where hides, too, are heavier, thicker, better. Take the longhorn breed to a high, dry country and it ceases to be long-horned, and grows blockier, heavier, thinner-skinned, and lighter of horn.

He hated to see cattle de-horned when good polled breeds were available, and the sight of a ranchman feeding rock salt to his herds thoroughly disgusted him. When he saw the RO foreman loading out rock salt at Amarillo, he stopped and asked:

'Don't you have any sandstone out in that country?'

'Lots of it,' came the reply.

'Why don't you go back and make up a barrel of salt water,' he sarcastically suggested; 'put some big pieces of sandstone in it, and let them soak up the brine real well. Then put them out on the range. They'll wear off the tongues of your cattle a damned sight quicker, and won't cost you anything.'

First of all he was a cowman, saturated with the lore of cows and horses, as these pages have already indicated. Andy Adams added his testimony to that of many more, saying: 'He was the best cowman, the most practical Westerner, that I ever saw.' The impression of a cow sank deep into his memory, to be as readily recalled as the name of an old friend. Stories are still told of the almost uncanny ability of a few cowmen, like John

R. Blocker, who learned, individually, an entire herd. After a few weeks on the trail Goodnight could recognize, and cut, by flesh-marks alone, his herd of two to three thousand head.

And down the trails of the past plod those old cows that he remembered best, heading for a familiar range where grass had always been plentiful and the water good. In the late sixties he left a cow that escaped from his herd on the Pecos, and back-trailed through four hundred miles of wilderness and desert country, to die of old age on the Keechi range that she loved. But the most remarkable experience he had with the long-horned world was in the Panhandle.

Among those who followed him from Colorado to the Staked Plains were two pioneer Texans, George and W. D. Reynolds. They located a herd on the Canadian in 1877, and the next year sold it to the JA's. Goodnight took an outfit to gather the brand and trail it in. As they worked down the Canadian with the general roundup, keeping the brand in day herd, a big black Texas cow gave birth to a calf. It was left on the bed ground for the cook to haul to the next camp, but that independent individual, forgetfully or purposely, left the little fellow behind. Meanwhile, the herd moved down the river ten or twelve miles by a circuitous course, and directly after the outfit had stopped, the foreman, John Farrington, missed the calf. Being of a sympathetic nature, he struck back, straight across country to the bed grounds, threw the calf across the saddle before him, and retraced his direct course to the herd.

Though the trait is weaker in domestic stock, the Texas cows and calves always trailed back to the place where last they had sucked. The calf was expectantly waiting at the old camp, and the anxious cow was watching the sleepy day herders for a chance to escape along the back-trail. When Farrington got in with the calf, she was gone. He lifted the calf to the ground, and patiently set out to recover the cow, again striking direct for the old camp.

'En route, a mile or two from the bed grounds where the calf was born,' Goodnight continued, 'he met the cow, coming on his horse trail, which aroused his curiosity. Turning aside, he let her pass. She followed his horse tracks back to our herd and her calf. There is no question but what she was trailing the horse from the scent of the calf — the most remarkable thing in cow life that I know of.'

Yet no animal so charged his imagination like Old Blue. He would as soon that his own exploits were forgotten, but he was downright anxious that Old Blue be written up in history. His story has been told, and told well, by J. Frank Dobie and others, but it is a part of the Goodnight tradition and may bear telling again.

Old Blue was born in a sunny clime, beneath the lacy shade of the mesquite in southern Texas. With a herd of thousands of other flinty-hoofed brutes, he marched north one spring in the middle seventies. He crossed the rocky hills of the Edwards Plateau, felt the burning thirsts of the Staked Plains

drive, and then swelled his paunch to bursting with the brackish Pecos water. Each morning his long, steady stride carried
him to the lead, and his fine blue head swung in rhythm with
his tireless legs as he marched between the pointers along the
Goodnight Trail, up the desolate valley of the Pecos, 'grave-

OLD BLUE

yard of the cowman's hopes.' The wild-looking, soft-voiced
men, who handled that herd with matchless ease, fought Indians
on the way, it is said, and lost cattle by the hundreds, but Old
Blue led on until the salt grass of the valley gave way to the
black grama of the high plateaus. And he was as slick as a
grulla colt by the time he topped Trinchera Pass and felt the
cool wind in his face as he looked down on the fresh world beyond. He, too, was a trail-blazer, young and adventurous, and
when he raked off the flies in the shinnery as he headed down
the Colorado slope, he forever renounced the ties of his lazy
birthland, and pointed the way to Goodnight's ranch, on the
Arkansas.

His owner had received him from Chisum at Bosque Grande,
but when the herd went on as Indian beef, Blue, then a three-
year-old, was kept behind and broken to the yoke. Southern
Colorado was his home until he was brought to the Quitaque in

1877, after which he again fell into the hands of Goodnight, who realized right well that he was no ordinary ox, and who promised him then and there: 'Blue, you work no more. You'll be a leader of our herd.'

The beef was fat and the JA punchers, like the balance of the cattle kingdom, were pointing toward Dodge City, 'cowboy capital of the world.' Goodnight swung a brass bell around Old Blue's neck and as that bell rang off the miles in tune to his stride, Blue was the proudest animal that ever switched his tail at flies. At night a cowboy pitched his rope around Blue's neck, for he was as gentle as could be, slipped a leather strap around the clapper or crammed the bell full of grass, and the herd bedded in peace. Soon the beeves learned to follow the bell, and if, perchance, the clapper came undone at night, the herd would be on its feet, ready to trail, in no time.

Beyond the Beaver the outfit passed the only settler on the trail, and beside his sod house was a little field with pumpkins, squash, and melons. Cow-chips made good fuel, and the owner implored them to camp nearby, as he was twenty miles from wood. They trailed on to Seven Mile Hill, and at last looked down the slope to Dodge City. In the evening they camped on the south side of the river, while McAnulty and Cresswell had herds nearby. The JA boss turned his weather eye to the sky that night, and called to his boys: 'All saddle and tie up. We'll have hell before day.' About midnight it commenced sleeting and snowing, but all hands struck for the herd and managed to hold it, though the two neighboring ones were lost in the storm. At daylight the boss yelled: 'Loose the bell and take the river.' Old Blue broke the ice along the edge of the Arkansas, swam the stream in the middle, and headed straight for the railroad corrals as two thousand JA's crowded on his fetlocks. Soon he was at a run, and the frozen ground was shaking to the beat of eight thousand hoofs. Inside the gate he prudently jumped aside and rested, while the herd swarmed and milled against the far side of the corral. The cowpunchers jammed the steers up the chute and into the cars, and as the train pulled out for Kansas City, they, and the saddle horses, and Old Blue, stretched their necks over the top rail of the corral and watched them go.

With shelled corn in the wagon for him and the mounts, the outfit headed south across the cold baldies for the ranch, Blue stretching his legs, sometimes thirty miles a day, to keep up with the saddle horses. A party of Kiowas tried to get him while the outfit was camped on Wolf Creek, but by that time he was eating out of the skillets, and the JA cowboys would have fought the whole of Indian Nation or kept him. His name was made, and for eight years he pointed herds to Dodge, sometimes making two trips a year. He was a philosophical old steer that did not care for stampedes, but attended strictly to business, leaving others to slip their horns and hip themselves on such foolishness as running over corrals and stampeding at night. In stampede he habitually stepped aside to bawl, and if the boys 'had them milling,' he was often the cause of bringing the herd back into control.

When Mann drove one of the beef herds in 1880, he had Old Blue along. Club-Footed Jack looked after the steer, hobbled him out with the horses at night, and unhobbled and drove him in with the horses of a morning. Old Blue prowled around the pots and pans looking for stray pieces of meat, biscuits, and prunes, while the outfit broke camp, and Mann yelled at the hands: 'Let 'em graze.'

When they began to get dry, Club-Footed Jack unleashed the clapper and drove Old Blue directly through the herd to the point. The scattered beeves looked for him and the bell, bawled their heads off and fell in behind. This herd had been buggering and running from everything, but as they hesitated in the wings of the railroad corral, Blue stopped and lured them on by bawling while the JA hands were busy behind, and the snaky ones were soon inside.

Some cowpunchers watched the JA outfit pen the herd, remarking: 'Those steers must be from the bull-chip ranch.'

'What do you mean?' asked Frank Mitchell.

'They must have been roped in the open, branded at a bull-chip fire, and never saw a corral before.'

'You're right,' he chimed, as he broke for town.

THE JA OFFICE

Occasionally at home Old Blue had work to do, as when they necked him to an outlaw steer down in the cañon, and turned him loose. He was big and stout — weighed around fourteen hundred pounds — and as he thought of the corn in the trough at the ranch, he dragged his unwilling yoke-mate directly into the corral. Mainly, however, he lived a life of pampered ease until the boys gathered the beef in the fall.

His last days were spent in retirement on the Palo Duro, petted, honored, and admired. After twenty years of adventure such as few men and no other steer experienced, he died of age and idleness, and his cowboy friends chopped off his horns and reverently nailed them above the ranch office door. Emerson Hough's Old Alamo, marching *North of Thirty-Six*, and Andy Adams's Poker Steer, changing hands on the turn of a card, may bask in the reflected glory of the most representative animal of the cow country, king of all the longhorns — Old Blue.

A word should be dropped in passing for Old Maude, a Texas cow brought from Colorado with the original Goodnight herd. She was as faithful to her duties at home as Old Blue with the wild bunch at Dodge, for the conservative Henry Taylor swears that she had twenty-seven calves, 'by actual count.'

'She was a great hand to pry into things,' he said, 'and one day when we were gone, she horned into the commissary. When we got back she had eaten a side of bacon and half a bushel of dried apples, and couldn't get out of the door. We worked her out an inch at a time, and got her up by the spring at the Old Home Ranch, where she lay down in great misery.

'"Old Maude will be dead in the morning," I said.

Mrs. Taylor carried her a bucket of water, and next morning I went back, and Maude wasn't dead. Long after she had lost her teeth, Mrs. Taylor made mush for her to eat. She loved Mrs. Taylor, and would bawl at her as far as she could see her. When we left the ranch, Jud Campbell didn't want to go to the trouble of caring for her, and drove her off up the cañon and shot her. If it hadn't been for that, she'd be living yet. I told him: "No good will come to you, Jud, for killing Old Maude." And sure enough, he got down with a bad leg, and stayed in bed for months and months.

'"Now," I said, "he's paying for Old Maude."'

From the late fifties until he died, seventy years later, Goodnight knew and lived with the buffalo. I doubt if any man, red or white, has so loved the breed or known them better. For fifty years he raised them on his ranch, developing one of the best-known herds in America. For years he was in the 'southern herd,' which, he says, 'would probably average a hundred and twenty-five to a hundred and fifty miles long, and twenty-five miles wide. The buffaloes in it were as thick as they could conveniently graze and left not a particle of grass behind them.'

'I know there were two different herds,' he said, which 'should be termed the Northern Bison and the Southern Buffalo; while they are no doubt the same species, there is enough difference in the two for any judge of animals to observe it at once. I know that the southern herd never went as far north as the Arkansas River. I also know that the northern herd came as far south as the Wichita Mountains, and then turned and drifted back.' The animals rarely got out on the High Plains, though finally they were driven there by the hunters, and they were unknown beyond the Pecos.

It was Goodnight's firm belief that they migrated for food, for 'at the starting of grass they turned north, and never until grass did start.' Then as they turned back in the fall, they left no grass behind them. Only a few stragglers, 'too old and feeble to keep up with the herd,' dropped out as 'they kept their course from the northwest to the southeast' until they struck the edge of the timber, along the Colorado River. This belief was supported by the fact that after the large herd was killed out, small bunches located — stopped migrating.

Varied and widely scattered experiments at buffalo ranching were made in the Western country. While engaged in hunting buffaloes for Fort Bent, in 1840, venturesome Dick Wootton conceived the idea of raising the calves. In 1871 a bill was introduced in Congress proposing the preservation of the species, though Goodnight's interest was still earlier.

The spring of 1866 was late, and the growth of grass and the start of the buffalo migration correspondingly tardy. On his Elm Creek Ranch Goodnight conceived the idea of starting a domestic herd. He knew that if he pursued a bunch of cows at a moderate gait, the youngest calves would drop behind as they grew tired, and that, by cutting in between a very young calf and the fleeing cow, checking his horse until it came up, and then turning off the trail, the calf would follow his horse. All cowboys have seen newly born range calves tolled along in the same way.

'The first time I went out to get buffalo calves [he wrote], I moved them up a little until three of the calves fell behind. I cut them off and they followed me home and into the corrals. When night came I roped them and put them to their foster mothers, Texas cows. Later I went and cut out two more in the same way. I wanted six, so I went out again and found one about twenty-four hours old. I scared the cow off some distance, [and] put the calf on my horse. The cow returned and attacked me so viciously that I had to kill her to save my horse. I felt badly over it then, and the older I get [he wrote, sixty-two years later], the worse I feel about having to kill that cow.

'I moved the six calves and their foster mothers down to Parker County, [and] turned them over to a friend who agreed to care for them on shares for half [but he] got tired of the business and sold out, and never even gave me my part of the money.'

Ten years later, Goodnight located in the Panhandle while the buffalo slaughter was at its height. Dodge City was hunter headquarters, Adobe Walls was founded for the trade, and Mobeetie vied unsuccessfully with Fort Griffin, which became for Texas what Dodge City was for Kansas. Near the foot of the Plains, Tepee City and Rath City enjoyed brief but wild careers, and Fort Concho caught the trade at the southern extremity of the range. Hunting turned from a profitable adventure to a big business, and men swarmed to the range, until the buffaloes were killed out.

Mrs. Goodnight had been distressed by the slaughter. Sometime in 1878, Goodnight rode down the cañon and joined the outfit. Next morning Mann dropped him off on the circle with orders to drive out the head of Wagon Creek. He shook out his reins and on the way ran into a little bunch of buffaloes, roped a heifer calf, flanked it, and tied it down. Remounting, he followed the others out of Wagon Creek Cañon to the mesa, picked out a bull calf, and smeared a loop on him. The little fellow ran under his horse, as they always try to do, causing him to pitch all over the place. Goodnight jumped off and hazed the calf back into the cañon, taking vigorous buttings along the way. Leaving them both tied down, he proceeded with the drive until the roundup was in, when he sent the cook with the wagon to haul the calves to the ranch.

These calves were placed on Texas cows, much against the will of the cows. A visitor observed how they hated the little brown buffalo calves, and how they kept them fought off until Goodnight arrived. When he walked into the pen, the calves kept their eyes on him until he picked up a stick, then broke for the cows, and got their clabber in peace.

Leigh and Walter Dyer roped two more calves, and thus was the Goodnight buffalo herd begun. Later, the T Anchors gave him a captive, and two more were secured from Colonel B. B. Groom's ranch on the Canadian. Mitch Bell, good-hearted veteran of the Palo Duro, clearly recalls their delivery. Goodnight sent him, Lem Brandon, Sam Carter, and Old

Blue after the buffaloes — a yearling and a two. Carter drove
the wagon, carrying the camping outfit and horse feed, as
they were out three nights on the way. They tied Old Blue,
roped and dragged the buffaloes up, and necked them real
close to him. Then ——

CAPTURE OF THE FIRST CALF

'Then,' said Mitch Bell, 'we turned Old Blue loose, and he
was the maddest steer I ever saw. He jerked the little one
down, drug him a long ways, and I thought was going to kill
him, sure. But finally he got up, on the same side with the
other buffalo, and he stayed there all the way back to the
ranch. Blue hardly slowed up with them until he struck the
Canadian, two or three miles from where we turned him loose.
We had made three camps on the way up, and every time he
came to one of these spots where we had camped, several
days before, he never failed to pick the place and stop.'

The first bull was known as Old Sikes. He knew not the
meaning of barbed wire, for the general roundups sometimes
picked him up as far down the river as the Shoe Bar range.

When he took a notion to wallow in the middle of the roundup, he invariably scattered it far and wide, and his very appearance scared some cow-horses out of their wits. He came to the horse corral at the ranch at feed time, stuck his head under the gate, lifted it off the hinges, and ate his fill of corn, while the terrified mounts almost stifled themselves in getting away.

In the early spring of 1886, Goodnight sent Bell and Charlie Heissler to bring him home. They found him many miles to the east, gathered up armfuls of buffalo bones as they rode along, and by chunking one at him occasionally, drifted him into the Shoe Bar. Charlie looked at the six-foot fence, and said: 'He can't get out of here,' and then stomped over to the bunk house to auger the Shoe Bar punchers.

Next morning they went to the corral to get their horses and resume their journey, and Old Sikes wasn't in sight. They took his trail and followed him to the Salt Fork, and he had jumped every fence he came to. As they had sent the wagon back to the ranch, they gave up the chase and returned without him. The summer roundup gathered him on the RO range. Goodnight, whose patience was a little worn, cut and dehorned the old bull and threw him into the buffalo pasture, which had been built in the meantime. He got as fat as a bear, and that fall the Colonel sent Henry Taylor out to pen him. Old Sikes got on the prod and chased Taylor out of the pasture, much to the Colonel's disgust.

'Hell, you don't know how to pen a buffalo,' he fumed.

And immediately he buckled on his big Mexican spurs — those with the jingling bells, pulled down the long bull-whip he had plaited himself, saddled old Shystocker, and loped down to the flat to show the boys how buffaloes were handled. Old Sikes, still pawing the earth, grunted a warning, and charged. Shystocker whirled in his tracks, and — with Goodnight's working him down the hind leg with the coils of his bull-whip, and Sikes's horns combing the cuckleburs out of his tail at every jump — almost flew back to the ranch. The Colonel never said another word, but on Christmas Eve, 1886, an immense, fat carcass, weighing nine hundred and sixty-four pounds, was hanging beside the mess-hall, and next day all the old-timers said it was better than beef.

OLD SIKES

The herd had begun to grow, and when Goodnight left the JA's, he moved it to his ranch, to the north, where until recently it could still be seen. For years it numbered from two hundred to two hundred and fifty head. Their care cost the owner a fortune, but as he watched them grow, he gathered impressions of the species quite at variance with the popular point of view.

The buffalo is not stupid; it is smarter than the Plains horse or the antelope. It does not resort to fraud to protect its young, but will fight at once and fight anything. It can go without drinking twice as long again as a cow, and possibly can smell water eight or ten miles away 'if the wind is right.' He believed it to be the hardiest and thriftiest of the bovine world. With two more incisors than a cow, it gets more food, and out of more difficult places.

It has fourteen ribs, one more than the cow, and hence a

hardier nature and a longer hump — the choicest of meat. On the open range it rarely had disease or screw worms; never lay down with its feet up a slope, as cows sometimes do; and never got on the lift. As final evidence of hardihood, some lived to be forty to fifty years old, and some of his own cows continued to breed until they were thirty-five.

The animal has about a third larger brain than the cow, and 'uses it.' For example, Goodnight observed horses that would not move from a knit-fly, but never a cow too poor and weak to throw a wall-eyed fit and run herself to death from a heel-fly. 'But the buffalo cups his feet up under him, lies down on them, goes to chewing his cud, and tells the heel-fly to go to hell.'

Notwithstanding their intelligence, they have a peculiar propensity for jumping off bluffs, and might voluntarily go off a bank ten to fifteen feet high, and with perfect impunity, instead of going a few yards out of their way to get down.

Goodnight attracted international attention by producing the cattalo. Old Sikes had been put to sucking Texas cows, and when he grew to maturity readily served them. In 1883, the roundup caught a half-breed, a cattalo calf, near the carcass of a Texas cow, which was bound to have been its mother. It was more than a freak to Goodnight — it was a challenge to the breeder. As he watched it grow into a 'sort of a striped, brindle yearling,' his mind was busy. In 1885, O. H. Nelson made him a present of two Polled Angus heifers, and Goodnight, considering the breed the hardiest of common cattle, and the buffalo the smartest and hardiest of Plains animals, conceived the idea of crossing them to produce a beef breed that might 'stand the high altitude and severe winters as the buffalo themselves do.' It was a long, tiresome, and expensive experiment, from which certain facts are remembered.

He agreed with breeders generally that it was best to start with the male sex of the breed whose qualities he wished primarily to establish in the new breed, so he placed the buffalo bull with the muley heifers, rather than a domestic bull with his buffalo cows. He found that a cow so bred stood about one chance in four of delivering her calf. If the calf was a heifer, the cow stood a fifty-fifty chance of delivering it and living. A bull calf never came on the first cross; the cow always slunk her calf or both died in attempted delivery. Why? He never knew. The usual reason advanced by amused scientists, even by Dr. W. T. Hornaday, was that the cow could not give birth to the calf because of the hump. It was now Goodnight's time to be amused. Both cattalo and buffalo calves are smaller at birth than common calves, and he added, 'Of course the hump does not count, as they do not have any. Nature never works backwards — never does things in a bungling way as far as my knowledge extends. No humped animal has any hump when born, no more than a horned animal has horns. They grow on afterwards.'

When a half-breed cow — the cattalo — is four years of age, she can be bred to either a domestic or a buffalo bull. Goodnight bred his first back to the buffalo, and got a good percentage of three-quarter buffalo calves, both male and female, though it was ten years after he began the breeding before he got the second cross. He always suspected that a half-breed bull would have been fertile, but the three-quarter was infertile. On the other hand, the three-quarter cow was fertile, and readily bred, either to a domestic or buffalo bull. Goodnight then placed a Polled Angus bull on his half-breed cows, getting a cross of three-quarters Angus and one-quarter buffalo, which was fertile. This male was placed on the three-quarter buffaloes, and bred regularly, so that by 1917, he had 'a fairly established race of about forty head that have proved so far superior to any breed of cattle known,' he claimed.

The breed seemed immune to disease, particularly blackleg, required less feed than domestic stock while gaining flesh faster, produced a sweeter and more uniformly marbled tallow, lived and multiplied to a much greater age than other breeds, and weighed heavier — the cows from eleven hundred to sixteen hundred pounds off Panhandle grass. They did not run from flies. They rose like a horse, on their front feet first, which enabled them to get up when weak, and made them less likely to get on the lift. They did not drift in storms, were solicitous mothers, and were not bad to run and fight, but located even better than common stock.

They required less salt than common cattle, scarcely disturbed their waterings, and refused to eat loco. They had eight incisors, which enabled them to bite off the grass as low as a buffalo, and gave them the benefit of the rich seeds in the tussets of the buffalo grass. Their meat had less fiber, was tenderer, and for some reason seemed 'easier to keep or cure than beef.'

Goodnight kept them many years, and was thoroughly convinced of their value, but abortion became so prevalent, and the expense so great, that he sold them. So much for the buffalo!

If the bulls cannot be heard bawling around during breeding

season, he contended, especially of an evening, the range is
short on bulls. There must be enough in the pasture to cause
them to hunt for the cows. He liked his old buffalo bulls so
well that he refused to cut them until he discovered that the
usual balance of heifer and bull calves was disturbed in favor
of the latter sex — until finally about two-thirds of his calves
were bulls. Then he cut the old bulls, and found that the
fifty-fifty average was again established, which was largely
the basis of his belief that old bulls produce a higher percentage
of bull calves. He thought, too, that their calves were better.

There was little intrusion of outside blood into his buffalo
herd, and after years of experimentation, he concluded that
opposition to inbreeding of animals was largely prejudicial.
In writing Edmund Seymour, President of the American Bison
Society, he contended that selection was most important of all,
and urged him not to remove a bull for 'fear of in-breeding.
There is nothing in it,' he added. 'If so, Adam and Eve's
people are out of luck.'

One of his most talked-of discoveries was made on the
Goodnight Trail in 1867. When being trailed or worked, stock
cattle have a tendency to get in heat, and upon starting with
a herd of cows, Goodnight always put in a number of bulls.
The trail is doubly hard on them, and after their testicles had
been banged and bruised between their legs for several hundred
miles, they sometimes died. He lost two on the Pecos drive,
and another, a big dun bull from South Texas, had swelled
and was about to die. Goodnight roped and threw him and
got down to cut him, thinking he might recover. As he got
out his knife, and thought how he could hardly spare another
bull, an idea struck him.

He called to a hand to bring him a piece of grass rope, then
quite rare, from the wagon. He pushed the dun's seeds up
against his belly, and cut off the entire bag. He unraveled a
piece of the rope, and having no needle, took his knife, punched
holes in the skin, and sewed up the wound like an old tow
sack. Within a week, instead of being dead, that bull was in

the lead of the herd giving everything trouble, and his voice was as coarse as ever. Thereafter Goodnight practiced the operation generally upon his old bulls on the range, almost doubling, he believed, their period of use. Of course, as he said: 'It does not make a young bull of an old one, but it does enable the old one to do a great deal of work. After finding it to be a great success, I had it published, much fun was made of it, and little attention paid to it. Now, it is practiced on men. . . . I have followed it on animals for many years and it served its purpose.' Throughout the Southwestern range country this operation is known as 'Goodnighting,' and though the cow country is skeptical, the practice has some support in surgical and athletic circles.

Goodnight believed no better hands nor finer men ever ate beef out of a skillet than the pioneer cowboys of the Plains. The only code that held them to their places around a herd under any and all conditions was a sense of individual responsibility — pride in an ethic of rugged individualism. No labor union protested their lot; no welfare worker tore his shirt to better cow-camp conditions; no woman's club proposed child labor laws to keep junior cowboys from eating *frijoles* and taking the trail. Yet somehow they managed to live, and happily. 'They did not only go through all the privations and discomforts of life, and hard work, and exposure,' Goodnight explained, 'but the real hours of the cowboy in actual service, when working on the open range, were about eighteen hours. They performed this with no complaint. They not only did the work as cow-hands, but they served as soldiers and officers as well.'

After many years spent in observing the remarkable vitality of the High Plains animals, and particularly the transformation in cattle and horses that were brought from lower, lush, and humid zones, he would have agreed heartily with the ethnologic and physiographic principle, stated by Henry Fairfield Osborn, to the effect that 'intelligent progressive and self-adaptive types of mankind arise in elevated upland or semi-arid environments where the struggle for food is intense and where reliance is made on the invention and development of implements as well as weapons.'

For years before Osborn wrote these lines, this old cowman believed the Staked Plains were the choice soil of Texas. 'It produces better cattle,' he would say, 'why shouldn't it produce better men?' Half a lifetime before he had observed the effects of the high, arid zone, and though he had studied no ethnology except in Indian camps and on the Western range, and his physiography was learned while scouting with rangers and pointing herds of Texas cattle, he had observed much life and made his deductions. 'I believe the day will come,' he said, 'when the mountain and prairie states of America will produce the finest race of men and women the world has ever known.... We should bear in mind that we must meet by brains in the West the problem that is being presented by numbers in the East.'

During seventy years of his mature life he struggled with the problems of the open country, and liked it. Government subsidy for its people, and paternalistic removal to lands where life was comfortable and easy, would have galled his sensitive soul. He died in time. Of course the scientific world denied him, but we who recall our traditions in the shade of ranch corrals like to remember him as the Burbank and the philosopher of the open range.

XXV. AT THE END OF THE GOODNIGHT TRAIL

AFTER following the Goodnight Trail in its meanderings throughout the West, it is necessary, at last, to stop cutting for sign and head toward its end.

Colonel Goodnight, as he came to be called, after leaving the JA Ranch, operated the Quitaque in partnership with L. R. Moore, of Kansas City, until 1890, when he sold Moore his remaining half interest. The land was checker-boarded with school sections, subject to settlement by nesters, and Goodnight was relieved to get shed of its attendant troubles and confine his range operations to the country north of the JA's, around the Goodnight station, on the railroad.

But the worst ravages of drought, depression, illness, and advancing age could not dull his zest for life. He was as anxious to venture as ever, and, unfortunately, became interested in mining operations in Mexico. Bill McCamey, of the buffalo range, had learned of a mine at the southern tip of Chihuahua, deep in the Sierra Madres; had induced A. L. Matlock to go see it; and had interested him in its possibilities. Matlock solicited Goodnight, and together they went to El Paso, to Jimenez by rail, to Parral by wagon, then by a six-day pack trip through the mountains to Guadalupe y Calvo, across the Sierra Mohinora through the snow, and dropped down, down into the Galeana Arroyo on the west, where oranges grew about the mine.

The workings were old, especially rich in silver, and were said to have produced their millions. Matlock had already invested, and Goodnight, acting upon his advice, went into the company, along with Wasson and Daugherty, of Gainesville. They had a stamp mill especially made, so they could pack it through the mountains on the backs of mules. When it was installed, they reduced the ore at the mines, and then packed the metal out to Culiacan, far to the south.

Money flowed into the enterprise like water, until the glowing reports from McCamey began to pall on the American owners. Again Goodnight and Matlock went down to investigate, and what they learned was so maddening that only the cowman's intervention kept Matlock from killing McCamey. Other management proved little more satisfactory, and, after sinking somewhere between three and four hundred thousand dollars in the enterprise, Goodnight drew out of Mexico, along with the others, and allowed the mine to revert to the original Mexican owners.

Near Goodnight, Texas, after sale of the Quitaque, he bought a hundred and sixty sections including the Sacra-Sugg Ranch on the Salt Fork, and some school land, and Johnnie Martin took charge of the ranch soon afterward. The Goodnight-Thayer Cattle Company was incorporated, and continued its operations, with Martin as one of the later partners, until about 1900, when Colonel Goodnight further restricted his range operations to his home ranch near the railroad. Here he lived almost to the end of his days.

His interests were still those of fine cattle, buffalo, cattalo, and native game — the life of the soil. Here he built heavy corrals for handling his buffaloes, bred and sold fine bulls, experimented with crops, protected the wild life, and sought with a truly passionate zeal to improve his country. And here, as an old man, this extremely sensitive nature, contemptuous of sham, hypocrisy, and littleness, settled himself behind the mask of a brusk exterior to watch the race go by.

As population grew, the needs of educational facilities were more obvious, and, with Mrs. Goodnight, he built the Goodnight College, a co-educational institution that placed particular emphasis upon the problems of Staked Plains life. After building the plant, they tendered it to the Methodist Church, with the understanding that they should have the authority as to determination of its policies. The Church declined the offer, and the College opened in 1898 under the control of the cowman and his wife. The boys rode in from the ranches, some with suggans and clothes packed in a tarp on an extra saddle horse; others drifting a milk cow or two before them to turn into the college pasture; others with a quarter of beef to hang on the shady side of the dormitory. The school operated for several years, part of the time under the supervision of the Baptist Church, and filled a place in pioneer education upon the Plains. It was unusual, it is said, in having had in attendance the sons of more cowmen than any other school in existence. Even until today, Colonel Goodnight's benefactions to the cause of education on the Staked Plains exceed those of any other man. Once he humorously observed that though he had not been in school himself since he was nine years old, 'my school house business has been real expensive — paying for the other fellow's.' He always cherished high regard for a disciplined, well-trained mind, and few things pleased him more than to meet a rangy plainsman who said: 'Colonel, I got my schooling at the Goodnight College. Remember when —— ?'

In spite of his desire to be alone, people gravitated to the ranch from far and near, particularly the ubiquitous sightseer, scaring or shooting his game and invading the privacy of his home. His caustic reception of many of these was the basis of widespread stories, as well as of the erroneous impression of his nature held by many of his own fellow countrymen, who thought him an irritable, eccentric old man.

For forty years people came to hear his stories and write his experiences. Usually they met with rebuffs, though he who sought 'information' on cattle, Indians, buffaloes, trails, and other topics pertaining to Western life, was welcome, and if he was a skillful interviewer usually gathered, indirectly, what he wished to know about the Colonel. For years, Edmund Seymour, President of the American Bison Society, and John R. Freeman, another old friend, implored him to dictate his reminiscences, or let someone write them for him. He told Freeman he desired no biography, for he feared the writers 'would mix too much red paint in it.' He answered Seymour in greater detail:

'...all my life I have avoided publicity or newspaper notoriety. I still have a horror of such. However, I am always willing and have been always willing to put any facts in print that could do the present or future generations any good. It has been my aim through life to try to have the world a little better because I lived in it....

'I have added much to this Western World in the way of breeding animals. This of course will be judged by the community after I am gone. I would be much pleased to have the

Government to take an interest in obtaining such data as would benefit mankind hereafter, but as to my own private life, I only wish to be let alone and only ask that my country-men treat my record charitably.'

One amusing feature of his extended correspondence with Seymour was the development of a warm controversy with Buffalo Jones, widely publicized Westerner, with Seymour in the inadvertent rôle of intermediary. The expansive Jones, with his well-known tendency to stretch the blanket, was the type that thoroughly disgusted Goodnight with 'Western literature,' and put him on the prod worse than an old buffalo bull. Back in the drawing-rooms of the East, Jones was telling how he had killed the bear, and Seymour began writing Good-night the details of his 'experiments' with cattalo, his helping 'guard Billy the Kid,' and so on. At first Goodnight answered patiently, pointing out, however, his doubts as to whether Jones had ever produced a cattalo. Insistent letters flowed on, the old man's patience became worn, and he wrote, in some irritation, that 'it has only been my aim to get you to under-stand the difference between hot air and facts.' Still the cor-respondence continued, Goodnight admitting that Jones was 'quite a wonderful fellow in his way,' that he had 'no desire to pick any breeding feathers off of him,' but that after all, in regard to the cattalo, 'it is a question of who bred them on the ground and not on paper.'

'Jones has been quite a hunter, and has been over a great deal of the Northwest,' he continued. 'In that country they have great wind storms, known as "chinook winds." They are warm and harmless, but the Colonel seems to have got in one of those storms, and imbided immense quantities of hot air. It has been escaping from him ever since — mostly from the wrong end.'

As to guarding Billy the Kid at Mesilla, in 1882, Goodnight observed that it was 'quite likely' that Jones would be guarding him then, as the Kid had been killed 'a year or two before.' At Goodnight's insistence, John W. Poe, one of the posse that trailed the Kid to his death, wrote his account of the killing to keep the record straight, and thus gave to the public one of the most stirring accounts of that interesting episode.

Goodnight relentlessly drove himself at his work until the end. When he was ninety-one, I saw him swear at the sight of men lounging on the north side of a building: 'I'll be damned if I could ever find time to lie in the shade.'

And since he was busy, he was difficult to interview. A high-pressure reporter from a Kansas City paper made the long journey to the ranch and found him sweating over a pair of post-hole diggers, the dirt a-flying. He rushed up to the Colonel, thrust out a glad hand, and breezily announced: 'Colonel Goodnight, Brown is my name.'

Straightening from the task the Colonel drilled him with his eye, and roared: 'What in the hell can I do about it? I didn't name you.'

Others suffered a similar reception. When L. F. Sheffy, the retiring secretary of the Panhandle-Plains Historical Society, first called upon him, the Colonel was fixing a gate to one of the corrals. Upon announcing his name, Sheffy was greeted no less vigorously: 'I don't give a damn what your name is; what in the hell do you want?' But he and the historian became good friends.

He had no patience with shoddy work and loose methods. At the JA's, he kept a mesquite grub patch, where he tested the word of wandering cowpunchers when they said they wanted to work. If they spent the required number of days grubbing mesquite roots — a most menial task for a cowboy — he put them on horses and sent them to the outfit. Yet he set no standard that he did not meet himself. No man on the ranch could move as much dirt in road-building, or wield an axe or grubbing hoe more efficiently than he. He loved to engineer a difficult task, to mortise the corners of a log house, to shoe a mule, and to work in the shop at the anvil.

Justin McCarty, one of his hands, recalls that there was never an idle day on the Goodnight Ranch. If a rainy spell came, the Colonel would rout the boys out of the bunkhouse, lead them down to the shop, and spend the day extracting nails from scrap lumber and hammering them straight, though he could have bought more new nails for half a dollar than the entire crew salvaged in a day. His frugality puzzled the boys, who watched him give seventy-five thousand dollars to a college and spend a small fortune experimenting with buffaloes. They purposely scattered nails along the paths at the ranch to see the old fellow stop, pick them up, and carefully save them. And so it was, too, with scraps of buckskin, tallow, and the wool from the mops of his buffalo bulls. 'I believe it's a sin to waste,' he would say. Thus he carefully saved bushels of wild-plum seed, even soliciting them from his neighbors when he was a very old man, and scattering them up and down the Palo Duro Cañon, explaining that he always liked to have some around; that he was planting these to take the place of the old ones when they should die. They brought him seed while remarking that the present thickets would live longer than he.

He had no grub patch at Goodnight, Texas, but when a boy came by and applied for work, he gave him a shovel and a grubbing hoe, showed him a wild gourd vine of healthy pro-portion, and told him to dig it up, being careful to get every particle of its roots. Thinking that the job would soon send the boy on his way, he went about his own affairs until, late in the day, he happened to pass that way again and the young-ster had half the yard dug up. 'You're just the boy I've been looking for,' he said, and kept him for years.

— HDBusbee —

GOODNIGHT RANCH

He was audaciously honest, though when his cowboys helped vote the Armstrong County seat away from older Washburn to Claude, Washburn seemed to feel that he had stolen it. On the other hand, his relations with some of the county officials were hardly cordial, because he immediately blocked an attempt by some to let the jail contract to a man who bid more than double another, 'because there was no rake-off on the last.'

He hated the tracks a cow thief made. Shortly before his death, T. D. Hobart sat in his sick-room conversing softly with a friend. They were talking of another old-timer, unaware that Goodnight was hearing, and mentioned that thieves were bothering his cattle. From the sick-bed came a roar: 'They ought to steal them all, God damn him! — That's the way he got his.'

Of course, thieves both cursed and feared him, impugning his honesty, and reiterating the old charge of its being just a case of the 'big ones getting after the little ones.' When George Clutts, a witty old cowpuncher, drifted into the Quitaque and asked for work, Al Barton, the foreman, sent him to see the owner.

'George, they say you're a cow thief,' Goodnight answered.

'They say the same thing about you, Mr. Goodnight,' came the prompt reply.

'Go down and tell Barton to put you to work,' shouted the old man.

He prosecuted thieves relentlessly, and when in the trial of a known rascal at Claude, the jury was hung on the basis of insufficient evidence, he became infuriated with his fellow jurymen, declaring they ought to send the scoundrel to the pen 'on general principles.'

For years he was a close friend of Kiowa, Comanche, and Taos Indians, gathering tribal history and lore for himself and his friends, and articles of interest for various museum collections, never objecting to overcharges because he thought it was all right for the Indians to get the best of the white man for a change. He donated hides and tallow to the clans for ceremonials at Taos, urged their cause in Congress, and contributed a foundation buffalo herd to the tribe when he was poor in worldly goods himself.

He appreciated the Indian's integrity, character, and sense of humor. Once when he was entertaining a group of Comanches and Kiowas from Oklahoma, an old Indian admired one of his horses tied nearby, looked at the brand, and slyly remarked: 'We bought some of those horses once.'

'Yes,' snapped the host, with a twinkle in his eye. 'Bought them while I was asleep.'

He carried some of the Comanches to the Palo Duro, saw them look upon their old camp grounds, watched their mingled emotions, and felt his soul quake for having taken the gorge from them. He always admired Quanah Parker. He exercised as much influence over him as any man, and kept up his friendship until the Indian died. When plans were being made for his burial beside Cynthia Ann, Goodnight wrote: 'It is proper that he should be buried by his mother as he, one time, had six wives and ... could not easily be buried by the side of all.'

When he and I once visited at Taos, he was greeted by two daughters of his old friend, Chief Standing Deer. He was alone in a room on the south side of the Pueblo when one of the daughters heard of his coming, and rushed across from the other side, threw her arms about him, and broke down, crying. He told of the meeting, later.

'And what did you do?' Mrs. Goodnight asked.

'I cried too,' he said simply.

His aversion to being photographed approached ferocity, but his figure was so striking and his background so colorful that he was frequently importuned. Buck Dunton, one of the more noted Taos artists, was anxious to sketch him, and Mrs. Goodnight begged him to go to Dunton's for the purpose. He swore manfully that 'There were as many pictures of Goodnight in Texas as there were buzzards, and just about as useful,' but when she asked it as a personal favor, he consented.

In the late eighties, he brought J. C. Cowles, a student and friend of Albert Bierstadt, to the Palo Duro to paint the Old Home Ranch, the cañon, and other scenes. He had scores of pictures made of the range, cattle, hands, and outfits by an itinerant photographer, but the splendid file was destroyed by fire. He was interested in literature, and encouraged serious writers, but condemned to what he considered the appropriate place flippant, smart, and supercilious scribblers.

Women entered but slightly into his active life, but those who did were held in high regard. In spite of his explosive nature, he was deferential to others, extremely courteous to women, and considerate of the amenities of good taste.

Mrs. Goodnight died in 1926, and was buried in the village cemetery at Goodnight, from the church she and her husband had helped to build. Dry-eyed and grief-stricken he left before the ceremony was over, and, very much alone, went back to the big house and sat in front of the fireplace, an empty chair beside him. His mind turned back to the long ago. His long-barreled rifle rested in the curves of a couple of buffalo horns above the mantel, along which the worn inscription still read: '*Seek ye first the kingdom of God and his righteousness, and all these things shall be added unto you.*' On one side of the room hung the picture of Loving, his old partner; on another that of his noted buffalo, Old Sikes; while the open fire etched on the wall between them the shoulders and the massive head of a very old man, suggestive of the strength, dignity, and courage of Old Sikes himself.

The silence was broken only by a great clock against the wall, ticking the lonely hours away — a clock that he had given to her and personally inscribed:

In Honor of

Mrs. Mary Dyer Goodnight
Pioneer of the Texas Panhandle

For many months, in 1876–1877, she saw few men and no women, her nearest neighbor being seventy-five miles distant, and the nearest settlement two hundred miles. She met isolation and hardships with a cheerful heart, and danger with undaunted courage. With unfailing optimism, she took life's varied gifts, and made her home a house of joy.

He became sick as the sad years dragged. The doctor left him medicines. Always scornful of them, however, he was a poor patient, and once, after having taken some, he stormed out at solicitous friends: 'Get away from me! I'm old enough to die and I'm ready to die.' Then he got up, went to the telephone, and roundly cursed the doctor for having given him medicine that 'would kill a God damned mule.' But he didn't die.

At the age of ninety-one he married Corinne Goodnight, an earnest young woman who called to see him because of his name, found him sick, and nursed him back to health. In the meantime the ranch had been sold with a provision that he might live there the rest of his days, and fortunately, in spite of the hard times, he managed to get out with a small equity. His last summers were spent at Clarendon, and the winters at Phoenix, Arizona.

For four years I had been making notes upon his life, but he shrank from the idea of a book about himself. Even after he had finally consented, he berated himself unmercifully for doing so, and his mortification was deep and genuine until overcome by his desire to help. Once, after we had talked the long day through, and on until bedtime, I pressed him for the details of a story about the devious maneuvers of prominent frontiersmen of Texas. It was a story of shady transactions, of no interest in history, he said, and when I pressed the matter, he lost his temper, and with the accumulated feeling of ninety-three years, castigated himself with terrible violence for being so lacking in taste as to detail his intimate thoughts for biographical purposes. I was sick at heart as we parted for bed. He knew it, too, and was sorry, but unrelenting and stern.

Half undressed, he came back from his room in the best of good humor to tell me another story. Then he laughed and said:

'When you are wanting some of these things, you remind me of a little dog chasing a passenger train. I've always wondered what in the hell he'd do with it if he caught it.'

At the breakfast table he stormed out fiercely because the coffee was not poured. Then he was as gentle as a baby when it came. Cowman-like, he went to the table to eat, and for nothing else. Hardly a word passed from his lips after the meal was ready; and once the last bite was taken, the habit of a long lifetime promptly drove him away. No matter who the guests might be, it was apparently a physical impossibility for him to stay. He was always the first to finish, and if at a café, he left the table and went out and sat on the curb of the sidewalk until the others were through. He excused himself graciously, saying that he had got the habit on the range and trail, and swore that his stomach actually hurt if he did not get up immediately and leave.

Though deeply religious and reverential by nature, he was impatient with institutionalized religion. 'If I were living in hell,' he said, 'under the government of the devil, and hell were attacked, I'd defend it to the last, or I'd get out.' He built two churches and always helped to support them, though many are the amusing stories told about him and his clerical friends. They were always welcome at the Goodnight Ranch, and after services by a circuit rider one Sunday, Mrs. Goodnight had the preacher in for dinner. She was doing her best to keep the conversation going, while the master of the ranch attended strictly to business at the end of the table. Finally, Mrs. Goodnight asked the visiting minister where he was from, and when he said, 'Oklahoma,' the Colonel poised his knife-ful of black-eyed peas in mid-air, fixed the gentleman of the cloth with those unforgettable eyes, and exploded:

'Damned poor recommendation! Damned poor recommendation!'

Aunt Molly, greatly abashed, exclaimed in distress:

'Why, Charlie, you know there are many good people in Oklahoma.'

'Damned scarce, Mary,' came the rejoinder. 'Damned scarce.'

Like his ways of life, his ideas of religion were simple and straightforward. 'You say Christ has come along and converted you,' he replied to inquiring preachers. 'Well, I have never had that feeling. I can't be a hypocrite and a liar.

I've never been roped in that way, so I'll stay where I am.'
Then he explained: 'When the disciple asked Christ what he
must do to be saved, Christ answered: "You must be born
again."'

When the listener ventured a broad generalization, he took
the words out of his mouth, saying: 'Exactly. It means growth!
Evolution! If I could take the JA longhorns and breed them
into the best herd in America in eleven years, what could I
do in eleven million?'

THE WHITEFACE

At his wife's solicitation he joined the church shortly before
his death, but when someone asked him what church it was,
he answered, characteristically: 'I don't know, but it's a
damned good one.'

Someone, admiring his great shock of white hair, once observed that he must have taken good care of it. 'Yes,' he
answered significantly, as he thought of Indian days, 'taking
care of my hair was my chief concern for years.'

'You've had lots of luck in your day, Uncle Charlie,' remarked John Freeman.

'Yes, John,' he answered in measured words. 'If all the

good luck and all the bad luck I've had were put together, I reckon it'd make the biggest damned pile of luck in the world.'

He seemed to break all the dietetic rules laid down by the scientific world. He lived on little but meat, for years, and the coffee he drank would have put Red River on a rise. Once in a while he enjoyed a toddy, and for more than the ordinary lifetime, consumed tobacco like a furnace. Henry Taylor tells of seeing him smoke a box of fifty cigars in a day's drive from the JA's to the Quitaque, and his consumption of chewing tobacco is already a tradition. For months after he left his den at the Goodnight Ranch, the odor of tobacco clung to it like persistent incense.

When he was ninety-one, he quit tobacco completely, and to my inquiry, some months later as to when he had stopped, he snapped: 'Last October 10th, at nine o'clock at night.'

His recreation was simple and as old as the race. When he was tired and worried, nothing rested him so much as to drive out in the pasture among the buffalo. And though he complained, in 1887, that he was too old to look after the Palo Duro ranches, he was planning, in 1929, to go back into the cow business. 'Old age hath its honors,' he once grunted, as he struggled to get into a car, 'but it's damned inconvenient.'

Throughout the West no one could excel him in downright cussing. He could cuss in more varied ways, more eloquently, and more beautifully than any other man I've ever heard. In talking about an acquaintance, he once said, most seriously, that he was a mighty good man with but one serious fault: 'he cursed too damned much.' Before women, preachers, and all his vigorous language ripped up from the very soil of the earth, and yet so far as I know never gave offense to anyone, simply because it was not profanity after all, but a vernacular, full of the saltiness of time.

In late years his correspondence was heavy, but no one was more punctual in writing than he. He dictated reams of letters in clear, concise style, almost until the day of his death. He was tremendously affected by the death of old Bose Ikard; but, disgusted with the reports that Billy the Kid was still alive, threatened to mark his grave, 'so there will be no question about it in future years.'

In the fall of 1929 he went back to Phoenix, sold some buffalo meat to the butcher shops there, and enjoyed a buffalo roast on Thanksgiving. He was proud of that buffalo meat, from the herd he had started when he roped Old Sikes on Wagon Creek, just fifty-one years before. On December 2, he had his first heart attack. A week later he ate another good meal of buffalo meat, dictated fourteen letters, and had another attack. In the afternoon, Mrs. Goodnight raised the bedroom shades, and as the sunlight streamed in, he exclaimed, 'That's fine.' The doctor thought he was dying as he sank back on the bed. In an hour he revived.

Then he began planning a son-of-a-gun stew for Christmas dinner, and was still mad because the cook had left one of the numerous ingredients out of the last he had made. On the evening of the eleventh, he ordered some coffee, sat up in bed and drank it scalding from the cup, as he had done so many thousands of times before. Then he laid himself down upon his mattress, as hard as a cow-camp bed, with his head on the special pillow, as unyielding as the seat of a saddle, and with the hot coffee warming his body, as his fiery spirit still warmed his soul, died just at saddling-up time on the morning of December 12, 1929.

His bow-legged, gray-headed JA cowboys lowered his massive casket into the grave, and with tears streaming down their leathery, wind-carved faces, shoveled in the dirt that covered him up. And there in the graveyard at Goodnight came to rest at last this dominant, driving, restless plainsman. More appropriately, he should lie at the edge of the Palo Duro Cañon, which, splashed with the enduring colors of ages, verdant with grass that will never be plowed, carves out of the Staked Plains an everlasting memorial to the pioneering spirit of Charles Goodnight.

The Goodnight Trail has been a long one. And were he alive today to see this book, he would raise his two-hundred-pound frame upon his wide-bowed legs, steady himself upon his cane, thrust his fine head forward like a bull on charge, bore into the depths of this writer's soul with those fiery eyes, and unburden himself with the story he told at a buffalo hunt on the Goodnight Ranch.

Old Indian friends from Oklahoma as well as many neighbors from the Plains were there as his guests, and much to his disgust began attesting their high esteem of the host — the scout and ranger, blazer of the Goodnight Trails, preserver of the buffalo, father of the Panhandle, Burbank of the range. Through interpreters the Indians added their tribute, too, and finally the throng called upon him for a speech. He demurred, but they insisted, and at last he arose to say:

'This reminds me of a trip I made down the Fort Worth and Denver one time to buy some bulls. I expected to come back that night, but finding that I couldn't come, I went to the station to wire Mrs. Goodnight. I wrote out the message:

MRS. CHARLES GOODNIGHT
GOODNIGHT, TEXAS.

CANNOT GET HOME TONIGHT. GOODNIGHT.
CHARLES GOODNIGHT

'I handed it to the operator, who read it and handed it back, saying: "Too damned much Goodnight."'

My story is done. For ten years I lived with a great and ample nature. But as I think of his untended grave on the Staked Plains of Texas, with the buffalo grass gently encroaching thereon, I can hardly believe that his own country understood the depths of his nature, the sturdiness of his character, or the caliber of the man. Yet his tradition rides high on the dusts of the trail and my tribute at last is his own:

'I wish I could find words to express the trueness, the bravery, the hardihood, the sense of honor, the loyalty to their trust and to each other of the old trail hands,' he once wrote of his Texas cowboys. 'They kept their places around a herd under all circumstances, and if they had to fight they were always ready. Timid men were not among them — the life did not fit them. I wish I could convey in language the feeling of companionship we had for one another. Despite all that has been said of him, the old-time cowboy is the most misunderstood man on earth. May the flowers prosper on his grave and ever bloom, for I can only salute him — in silence.'

THE END

A Note on Bibliography

A NOTE ON BIBLIOGRAPHY

GOODNIGHT'S own recollections are the principal sources of this book. Two volumes, referred to throughout as 'Recollections,' I and II, were compiled by various officials of the Panhandle-Plains Historical Society, Canyon, Texas, and by Mrs. Goodnight. The first, of eighty-five typewritten pages, is in the Archives of that Society, along with many of my own notes. Volume II, of one hundred and forty pages, is in my own files. My personal notes, made throughout a period of three years, number several hundred pages, and supplement these reminiscent accounts.

This material has been enlarged through personal interviews with and letters from many old-timers, and I make particular acknowledgment to the following, whose stories I have written down: A. P. Anaya, Francisco De Baca, R. E. Baird, I. H. Bell, M. E. Bell, Max Bentley, Ab Blocker, Frank Bloom, W. H. Boyd, Wayman Brown, R. T. Bucy, T. S. Bugbee, Dick Bussell, Luke Cahill, Capt. R. G. Carter, W. D. Casey, J. T. Christian, Woods Coffee, S. O. Crawford, Col. M. L. Crimmins, J. M. Daugherty, Lucius Dills, James S. Duncan, James H. East, J. H. Evans, L. Gough, Mrs. Joseph K. Graham, Mose Hays, T. D. Hobart, Henry F. Hoyt, Cleo Hubbard, W. S. Ikard, Harry Ingerton, G. R. Jowell, Frank Lloyd, Maj. Royal S. Loving, Murdo MacKenzie, Justin McCarty, Dave McCormick, W. S. Mabry, John Marlin, John W. Martin, A. L. Matlock, Sam H. Milliken, J. K. Millwee, Frank Mitchell, D. W. Moore, O. H. Nelson, W. H. Patrick, Francis M. Peveler, Jack Potter, John Rumans, Mrs. Marion Russell, Fred Scott, Silas Sheek, Charles A. Siringo, D. H. Snyder, Jr., A. L. Steele, Vas Stickley, Mike Studzinski, Pablo Suezo, H. W. Taylor, Raymond Thatcher, A. W. Thompson, F. C. Varner, J. Phelps White, E. C. D. Willburn, H. C. Williams, Horace Wilson, and J. P. Wilson.

Various manuscript collections have been consulted. Several letter presses from the JA Ranch, salvaged from the fire that destroyed the ranch office soon after Goodnight left the properties, dating from 1886 to 1888, were especially useful. The J. F. Evans Letters, 1880 to 1890, in the files of the author; scattered letters gleaned from the Spur, the Matador, and the XIT Ranch files; and the Robert Moody, Ed Burleson, and James B. Barry Papers, as well as the J. A. Rickard interview with B. F. Gholson, the Willis Lang diary, 1860, the John S. Ford 'Memoirs,' and the Indian transcripts, all at the University of Texas, have been used.

The Governor's papers, 1859 to 1865 in the Texas State Library, and the Adjutant-General's archives at Austin have been indispensable for the period of the Civil War. For that immediately following, the County Records of Fremont and Pueblo Counties, Colorado, and Palo Pinto, Wheeler, and Donley Counties, Texas, have been valuable.

The records of the United States penitentiary, Cañon City, Colorado, the papers of the Court of Indian Claims, 1893 to 1903, Washington, the 'Constitution and By-Laws of the Panhandle-Stock Association,' with the Panhandle-Plains Historical Society, the Minutes of the Northwest Texas Stock Association, Fort Worth, and various theses at the University of Texas have added to the story.

An extensive file of correspondence between Edmund Seymour and M. S. Garretson, both of New York City, and Colonel Goodnight, covering the years 1917 to 1929, and letters between Goodnight and friends, 1926 to 1929, in the files of the author, have been used to the extent needed.

Judge E. B. Ritchie, of Mineral Wells, furnished me his notes upon the early history of that section, and located the J. H. Baker diary, 1858 to 1872, which was made available for consultation by Miss Elizabeth Baker, Seattle, Washington. J. Frank Dobie opened for me his notes and unpublished articles on Goodnight.

The principal newspaper files of value were the *New Mexican*, Santa Fé, 1866 to 1873; *Colorado Chieftain*, Pueblo, 1868 to 1876; *Ford County Globe*, Dodge City, Kansas, 1879 to 1884; *Globe Live Stock Journal*, Dodge City, 1884 to 1885; *Northern Standard*, Clarksville, Texas, 1855 to 1865; *Dallas Herald*, 1860 to 1885; *Fort Griffin Echo*, 1879 to 1882; *Fort Worth Gazette*, 1884 to 1887; *Galveston News*, 1882 to 1887; *Tascosa Pioneer*, 1886 to 1888; and a dozen other papers for scattered materials.

Merritt Beeson, of the Beeson Museum, Dodge City, Kansas, tendered me exceptional help with newspaper materials, while the Panhandle-Plains Historical Society not only inducted me into the field of History, but furnished me much of my material.

My gratitude, too, is due E. D. Dorchester, Freeport, Texas, who furnished me a helpful map entitled 'Trails Made and Used by the

4th U.S. Cavalry'; and Dane Coolidge, Jerome Stocking, J. T. Christian, and Wayman Brown, for pictures which served as source material for the artist, H. D. Bugbee. Various excerpts from the manuscript have appeared as special articles in the *Southwestern Historical Quarterly, Panhandle-Plains Historical Review,* and the *Southwest Review.*

CORNELIA ADAIR, *My Diary, Aug. 30—Nov. 5, 1874.* 1918.

ANONYMOUS, *The Great Elizabethtown Gold, and Copper Mining District.*

HUBERT HOWE BANCROFT, *History of Nevada, Colorado, and Wyoming.* 1882–1890.

    History of Arizona and New Mexico. 1882–1890.

EDWARD F. BATES, *History and Reminiscences of Denton County.* 1918.

FREDERICK R. BECHDOLT, *Tales of the Old-Timers.* 1924.

DON H. BIGGERS, *Shackelford County Sketches.* 1908.

Biographical Cyclopedia of the Commonwealth of Kentucky. 1896.

JOHN HENRY BROWN, *Encyclopedia of the New West, 'Texas.'* 1881.

    Indian Wars and Pioneers of Texas. (189–?).

H. F. BURTON, *History of the JA Ranch.* 1928.

LYMAN C. CHALKLEY, *Abstracts from the Records of Augusta County, Virginia.* 1912–1913.

JOHN CLAY, *My Life on the Range.* 1924.

HOWARD LOUIS CONARD, *'Uncle Dick' Wootton.* 1890.

JOHN R. COOK, *The Border and the Buffalo.* 1907.

JAMES COX, *The Cattle Industry of Texas and Adjacent Territory.* 1895.

JACOB DE CORDOVA, *Texas.* 1858.

J. T. DE SHIELDS, *Cynthia Ann Parker.* 1896.

Dictionary of American Biography. 1931.

E. T. DUMBLE, *Third Annual Report of the Geological Survey of Texas.* 1890–1893.

H. P. N. GAMMEL, *Laws of Texas.* 1898.

PAT F. GARRETT, *The Authentic Life of Billy the Kid.* 1927.

J. K. GREER, *Buck Barry, Texas Ranger.* 1932.

FRANK HALL, *History of the State of Colorado.* 1889–1895.

J. H. S. HAMERSLY, *Army Register.* 1880.

JOHN A. HART, *History of Pioneer Days in Texas and Oklahoma.*

ROBERT F. HILL, *Geography and Geology of the Black and Grand Prairies, Texas.* 1901.

F. W. HODGE, *The Handbook of American Indians.* 1907.

W. C. HOLDEN, *The Spur Ranch.* 1934.

G. A. HOLLAND, *The Double Log Cabin.* 1931.

IRVING HOWBERT, *Memories of a Lifetime in the Pike's Peak Region.* 1925.

HENRY F. HOYT, *A Frontier Doctor.* 1929.

J. M. HUNTER, *The Trail Drivers of Texas.* 1920.

HENRY INMAN, *The Old Santa Fe Trail.* 1897.

JOHN W. LOCKHART, *Sixty Years on the Brazos.* 1930.

R. B. MARCY, *Exploration of the Red River.* 1854.
Prairie Traveler. 1859.

E. S. OSGOOD, *The Day of the Cattleman.* 1929.

WM. B. PARKER, *Notes Taken in Unexplored Texas.* 1856.

H. G. PEARSON, *James S. Wadsworth of Geneseo.* 1913.

MRS. RACHEL PLUMMER, *Narration of the Perilous Adventures, etc.* (*Reprint*). 1926.

JOHN POPE, *Report of Exploration of a Route for the Pacific Rail-Road, 1854.*

Prose and Poetry of the Live Stock Industry of the United States. 1905.

Publications of the Arkansas Historical Association. 1906.

Senate Ex. Doc. No. 61, 31st Cong. 1st Session, *Reconnaissances of Routes from San Antonio to El Paso.* 1850.

R. N. RICHARDSON, *The Comanche Barrier to South Plains Settlement.* 1933.

CHARLIE SIRINGO, *Riata and Spurs.* 1927.

JEROME C. SMILEY, *History of the State of Colorado.* 1901.

H. SMYTHE, *Historical Sketch of Parker County.* 1877.

JAMES W. STEELE, *New Guide to the Pacific Coast.* 1888.

WALTER B. STEVENS, *A Series of Interesting Letters.* 1892.

H. S. THRALL, *Pictorial History of Texas.* 1879.

R. G. THWAITES, *Early Western Travels.* 1904–1907.

R. E. TWITCHELL, *Leading Facts in New Mexican History.* 1911.

W. P. WEBB, *The Great Plains.* 1931.

H. YOAKUM, *History of Texas.* 1855.

Index

INDEX

476 *Index*